Flyfisher's Guide to™
IDAHO

Fishing Titles Available from Wilderness Adventures Press, Inc.™

Flyfishers Guide to™

Flyfisher's Guide to Alaska

Flyfisher's Guide to Arizona

Flyfisher's Guide to the Big Apple

Flyfisher's Guide to California

Flyfisher's Guide to Chesapeake Bay

Flyfisher's Guide to Colorado

Flyfisher's Guide to Colorado's Lost Lakes and Secret Places

Flyfisher's Guide to Connecticut

Flyfisher's Guide to Eastern Trophy Tailwaters

Flyfisher's Guide to the Florida Keys

Flyfisher's Guide to Freshwater Florida

Flyfisher's Guide to Idaho

Flyfisher's Guide to Mexico

Flyfisher's Guide to Montana

Flyfisher's Guide to Michigan

Flyfisher's Guide to Minnesota

Flyfisher's Guide to Missouri & Arkansas

Flyfisher's Guide to Nevada

Flyfisher's Guide to the New England Coast

Flyfisher's Guide to New Mexico

Flyfisher's Guide to New York

Flyfisher's Guide to North Carolina & Georgia

Flyfisher's Guide to the Northeast Coast

Flyfisher's Guide to New England

Flyfisher's Guide to Oregon

Flyfisher's Guide to Saltwater Florida

Flyfisher's Guide to Tennessee

Flyfisher's Guide to Texas

Flyfisher's Guide to the Texas Gulf Coast

Flyfisher's Guide to Utah

Flyfisher's Guide to Virginia

Flyfisher's Guide to Washington

Flyfisher's Guide to Western Washington Lakes

Flyfisher's Guide to Wisconsin & Iowa

Flyfisher's Guide to Wyoming

Flyfisher's Guide to Yellowstone National Park

Best Fishing Waters™

California's Best Fishing Waters

Colorado's Best Fishing Waters

Idaho's Best Fishing Waters

Montana's Best Fishing Waters

Oregon's Best Fishing Waters

Washington's Best Fishing Waters

Anglers Guide to™

Complete Anglers Guide to Oregon

Angler's Guide to the West Coast

Saltwater Angler's Guide to Southern California

On the Fly Guide to™

On the Fly Guide to the Northwest

On the Fly Guide to the Northern Rockies

Field Guide to™

Field Guide to Fishing Knots

Fly Tying

Go-To Flies™

Flyfishing Adventures™

Montana

Trout Adventures™

North America

Flyfishing Northern New England's Seasons

Flyfisher's Guide to™
IDAHO

Ken Retallic and Rocky Barker

Flyfisher's Guide to™ Series

Wilderness
Adventures
Press, Inc.™

Belgrade, Montana

This book is dedicated to our families:
Laurie, Lara, Heidi, and Michelle Retallic;
Tina, David, Daniel, and Nichole Barker.

Acknowledgments

So many people aided us in our education on Idaho waters that we are certain in our thanks to leave out people who gave generously of their time. Tina Barker meticulously collected most of the information on hotels, restaurants, hospitals and the like of which we are extremely grateful. Many people in Idaho's Department of Fish and Game gave us important information, statistics, research data, and publications including Jack Trueblood, Mark Gamblin, Dexter Pitman, Herb Pollard, Steve Pettit, Bill Schoeder, Dan Schill, Tim Cochnauer, Ned Horner, Kent Ball, Dick Scully, and Rod Parker. Bart Butterfield of Fish and Game helped us compile the geographic data for the maps. Andy Brunelle, Ken Kohli, Joe Hinson, Steve Stuebner, Paul Emerson, Terry Holubetz, and Rob Thornberry all took us to their favorite spots even though they knew we were writing a book. Almost every fly shop owner and manager we talked to was extremely helpful, especially Jimmy Gabettas and Jimmy Gabettas Jr. of All Seasons Anglers in Idaho Falls, Mike Lawson, of Henry's Fork Anglers in Island Park, Bill Schiess of B.S. Flies at Henry's Lake, Spence Warner of the South Fork Lodge in Swan Valley, Roger Schwartz of Silver Creek Outfitters in Ketchum, Richard Escott of Lick Creek Fly Shop in McCall, Joe Norton of Twin River Anglers in Lewiston, Joe Roope of Castaway Anglers in Coeur d'Alene, and Greg Webster of the Bent Rod in Mackay.

Chad Colter of the Shoshone-Bannock Tribal Fishery Department showed us around the Fort Hall Bottoms and Bruce Staples taught us the fine points of fly tying and shared valuable advice.

Finally, we thank our families for giving us the space and time to write this book and for sharing in the joy, the solace, the excitement, and the renewal we get from fishing.

TABLE OF CONTENTS

Author Ken Retallic. Laurie Retallic photo.

Foreword

I heard the siren call of the Henry's Fork long before I drove over Targhee Pass in 1983 and dropped into the broad bowl of the Island Park Caldera. My first stop to peruse the legend's serpentine meanders captured me forever. As sunset dissolved into the twilight of a serene July evening, I watched enraptured as a long line of fly casters floated their flies down the sweeping curves of the river at Last Chance. I quivered with desire to join them, but couldn't stay. A mere 70 miles down the road a new job awaited.

The Henry's Fork tugged me back in short order, but it was only the first of many discoveries. The South Fork of the Snake, close enough for quick afternoon getaways and easy day trips, has been an irresistible magnet. The diversity of other streams across the state has made exploration of them almost a compulsion.

Ironically, another job I tried very hard to get in 1983 was in Alaska. Fate dispatched me to the Gem State. I have no regrets—except for Idaho's endangered chinook and sockeye salmon. If it can hold on to its dwindling steelhead runs, Idaho will continue to have it all in cold-water fly fishing. Who could ask for anything more?

Rocky Barker joined me at the Idaho Falls Post Register in 1985. Through our work at the paper and on numerous jaunts into the backcountry, we have learned much together and from others about the phenomenon called Idaho. It is truly one of the last best places, with a wild heart unique in the Lower 48.

We hope you will cherish it, too.

Ken Retallic
Idaho Falls, Idaho

IDAHO

Major Roads and Rivers

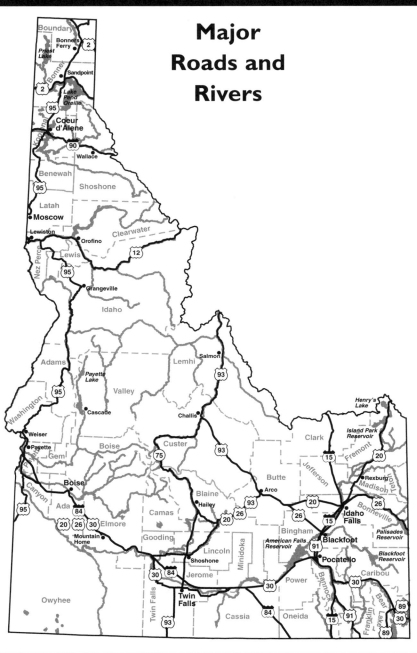

© Wilderness Adventures Press, Inc.

INTRODUCTION

How to Use This Guide

The Gem State's spectacular wilderness and backcountry playgrounds are the largest outside of Alaska. Idahoans escape the rat race by taking advantage of countless opportunities to fish, canoe, float boat, whitewater raft, hike, climb, horseback ride, hunt, and camp in the state's majestic alpine forests and picturesque sagebrush deserts.

For fly fishers there are an amazing variety of streams available to test their mettle against blue-ribbon trout. At first daunting in its magnitude, the pursuit often becomes a life-long avocation.

The streams' sources flow like vines off the Continental Divide, the backbone of the Northern Rocky Mountains. From these snow-capped crags, a legion of classic mountain streams collect forces to produce hallowed names in flyfishing annals—Henry's Fork, Henry's Lake, Silver Creek, South Fork of the Snake, South Fork of the Boise, Salmon, Clearwater, Kelly Creek, Lochsa, Selway, and St. Joe. Emerald green lakes and tarns scattered like handfuls of pearls beckon from the secluded reaches of the central wilderness.

This guide shows you how to fish Idaho's fabled waters. They have drawn international praise and their feisty wild trout make the pilgrimages worthy adventures. Consider the prodigious cutthroat and trophy brown trout of the the South Fork of the Snake:

"I know of no other river that combines these species of wild trout in such numbers and sizes of fish.... The South Fork is a continental crown jewel," says John Randolph, editor of *Fly Fisherman* magazine.

But the intent of this guide is not to hot-spot fishing opportunities. There is plenty of elbow room on Idaho's rivers and lakes. Many suggestions are provided on how to get away from the madding crowds. Follow them and your reward will be the experiences of a lifetime. Even on popular streams with good road access, solitude is just around a bend or a short hike upstream from a bridge. True adventurers pack into the backcountry to see what's on the other side of a hill ... and the next.

Idaho is a big state. Its major highways circle a wild, roadless primitive area larger than New England. Most of its counties are bigger than some Eastern states. To get from one side of Idaho to the other requires a long drive around the wilderness. To get from eastern Idaho to northern Idaho, the better route is to drive through western Montana and back into Idaho. Some Snake River access sites in Hell's Canyon can be reached only from Oregon or Washington.

On a first trip to Idaho, it is best to dip into its aquatic treasures by setting your sights on selected streams or drainages, or on specific types of fishing. Idaho has a game fish package to suit all tastes—vibrant cutthroat trout, trophy rainbows and browns, sea-running steelhead, and warmwater bass and panfish.

To aid in planning trips to the best fly fishing waters, this guide is divided into five sections. The informational focus of each is on that region's predominant drainages, its fish, and the service hubs that cater to fly fishers. The best bets for each region are discussed in detail. Suggestions for rewarding side trips are offered.

Maps to get you headed in the right direction are provided for all the top fly fishing streams and key lakes. They pinpoint public access sites, boat ramps, and campgrounds. Inexperienced boaters are advised to exercise caution on the larger rivers. The Teton canyon, Payette, Salmon and the Snake in Hell's Canyon shouldn't be floated without first going with a guide or a friend who knows the waters well.

Tips on fly patterns and major hatches, where recorded, also are given. They are the product of personal experience and the advice of a host of experts who have dedicated their lives to Idaho's alluring fly fishing waters.

Most of the latter are professional outfitters, guides and fly tackle shop owners who stand ready to help you have the best possible experience on streams or lakes. Call or write for assistance in trip planning and reservations, or stop in and chat about current fishing conditions. More than a thousand phone numbers and addresses are listed.

The chapter on Idaho's game fish details the life histories of the fish and offers additional tips on how to tackle each species. The chapter on aquatic insect prey of trout lists most of the major hatches in Idaho and the Northern Rockies and provides tips on fly patterns and presentations.

Useful information at the back of the guide includes current fishing license fees. These are updated periodically. Changes in fishing regulations, however, are established and published on a two-year cycle.

An equipment checklist includes additional tips on trip planning and hiring a guide. The ultimate goal of the guide is tight lines for all who use it. Good luck.

BOAT PERMIT REQUIRED TO LAUNCH

Well, the powers that be finally found a way (in 2009) to charge a fee for non-motorized boaters to launch their vessels on Idaho waters. Actually, the new permit requirement applies to all boats, foreign and domestic.

But it's for a good cause: funds will be used in attempts to halt the pervasive spread of exotic, foreign species in the state's waterways.

Beware, out-of-state boaters. You may be stopped at key border crossing locations equipped with wash stations and be required to clean your boats before proceeding to use in Idaho waters.

Under the new permit requirement, an owner of any boat that is registered in Idaho or another state and an owner of any non-motorized vessel is required to purchase and display an Idaho Invasive Species Fund (IISF) sticker on the vessel in order to legally launch and operate in Idaho.

The Idaho Fish and Game, Idaho Department of Parks and Recreation and Idaho Department of Agriculture web sites have links to provide boaters with a list of vendors and their locations where IISF stickers may be obtained. Sales of the permits will primarily be run through the Fish and Game vendors system, and the permits will no longer be available at state parks offices.

Also, in a break with the two-year tradition, the Idaho Fish and Game Commission adopted a three-year fishing seasons and rules brochure for 2013 that extends through 2015. The rules book includes several significant regional changes but it is always wise to check current regulations for wherever you plan to fish.

Additionally, diehard anglers and hunters have the option of purchasing a three-year hunting or fishing license. The cost of the license is three times the cost of an annual pass. There is no real savings, except people pay one vendor service fee, which saves them $3.50 compared to the cost of buying a pass every year.

Inflatable, non-motorized vessels must be less than 10 feet in length to be exempted from this requirement.

IDAHO

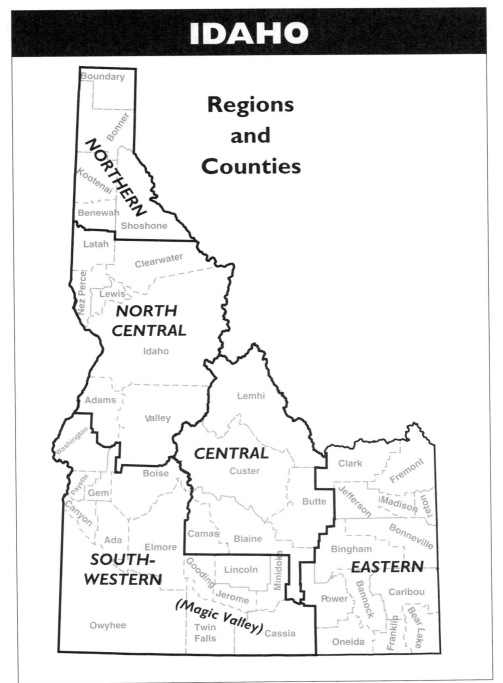

Regions and Counties

Boundary

Bonner

NORTHERN

Kootenai

Benewah

Shoshone

Latah

Clearwater

Nez Perce

Lewis

NORTH CENTRAL

Idaho

Adams

Lemhi

Valley

Washington

CENTRAL

Clark

Fremont

Payette

Gem

Boise

Custer

Butte

Jefferson

Madison

Teton

Canyon

Bonneville

Ada

Elmore

Camas

Blaine

Bingham

SOUTH-WESTERN

Gooding

Lincoln

Minidoka

EASTERN

Jerome

Power

Bannock

Caribou

Owyhee

(Magic Valley)

Twin Falls

Cassia

Oneida

Franklin

Bear Lake

© Wilderness Adventures Press, Inc.

Eastern Region

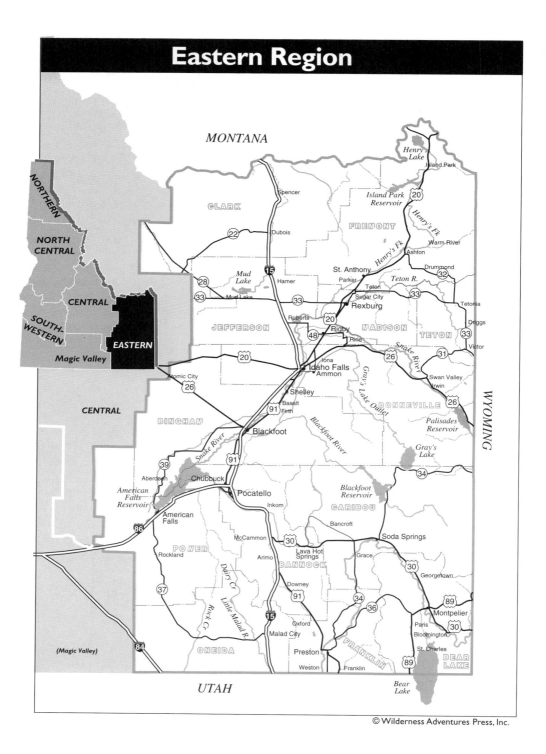

© Wilderness Adventures Press, Inc.

EASTERN IDAHO

B lessed with an abundance of premiere trout streams and a renowned trophy trout lake, eastern Idaho is a fly fisher's paradise. Mecca for the most dedicated is the Henry's Fork. Its Last Chance-Railroad Ranch stretch in Island Park creates legends passed on from generation to generation. The tales about its scholarly rainbows and the international clientele who test their skills against them make the pages of every major fly fishing magazine in the world. Expert fly fishing authors devote a chapter to the Henry's Fork in each book they write. The tales are true as far as fly fishers can tell the truth. But it is not even half the story.

There is a lot more to tell about the Henry's Fork than the hallowed waters of the Railroad Ranch and Box Canyon. It is not a long river, but it packs a lot of wallop downstream, too. The trout, including browns, are less picky.

Next on the upper Snake River drainage hit parade is Henry's Lake. Even fly fishing beginners cut their teeth on trophy cutthroat, rainbow-cutthroat hybrids, and brook trout in its pristine waters.

Basking in their shadows of fame are the South Fork of the Snake, most recently among the discovered dry fly fishing wonders of North America, and the often overlooked but exceptional Fall, Teton, and upper Blackfoot rivers. Yellowstone and finespotted Snake River cutthroat are the foremost quarry of these praiseworthy streams. The South Fork also is the Idaho record-setting waters for brown trout.

The lower Snake holds trophy fish little exploited by non-resident fishers. The southeast corner of the state has prime lakes holding trophy trout and bass.

What more could you ask for? How about virtually unlimited elbow room and public access to forest and meadow streams?

Almost 70 percent of Idaho is preserved as wilderness, national forest or public range land. Two national forests, the Targhee and Caribou, and the largest Bureau of Land Management district in the state are the largest landholders in eastern Idaho.

You may come here with a destination in mind but you will soon fall prey to its open spaces. Solitude is just around the bend of every mountain stream. Bushwhacking to see what is around the next bend draws you on and on.

For those with only a limited time to explore, all the major rivers and Henry's Lake are serviced by expert outfitters and guides. They will open doors for later explorations on your own, or you will return year after year to experience the best of the best under their tutelage.

The principal service hub of the region is Idaho Falls, the state's fourth largest city. Pocatello, the third largest, is just down the road on Interstate 15. Out-of-state hubs that take advantage of eastern Idaho's excellent trout fishing are Jackson in western Wyoming and West Yellowstone in southwestern Montana.

The two resort communities of the region are Island Park on the upper Henry's Fork and Swan Valley/Irwin on the South Fork of the Snake.

Enjoy.

The Teton Mountain Range is a stunning backdrop to a day on the lower Henry's Fork.

Your fly fishing credentials aren't complete until you've caught a big rainbow on (the Railroad Ranch) part of the Henry's Fork. Its always been one of the most challenging trout-fishing experiences on earth.

Mike Lawson, outfitter and former owner
Henry's Fork Angler in Island Park

Henry's Fork of the Snake River

Graduate School Fishing for Ph.D. Trout

The venerable reputation of the Henry's Fork of the Snake River as a dry fly stream is a siren call that seduces an international class of fly fishers to test its sophisticated rainbows. A lot of first-time visitors to the West's premiere trout streams are surprised at the size of the fish and sometimes unprepared for the tussle, especially on the Henry's Fork.

On its most challenging spring creek fishery, it can be a humbling river during an angler's first exploratory ventures into its gently flowing crystal-clear waters. Attempting to catch one of the Railroad Ranch's well-educated trout can lead to one of the purest lessons in frustration possible. On days when you connect, the Henry's Fork delivers one of life's most exhilarating experiences.

Elsewhere this multi-faceted river is much more forgiving. You still have to do your homework, but if you learn to catch trout here, you can catch fish anywhere. It is the epitome of what fly fishing is all about.

The river's most compelling attraction is its complex carpet hatches of mayflies and caddis that feed fast-growing wild trout. The region's geological history has ensured a plentiful food supply. Mineral-rich waters produce abundant growth of plankton, algae, and aquatic vegetation. Aquatic insects and small trout gorge on the bounty. Large trout at the top of the food chain have the best of all worlds.

Studies by state biologists show the average length of a four-year-old Henry's Fork rainbow in Island Park is 17.4 inches. The average for six-year-old rainbows is 21.3 inches. Four-year-old fish on Idaho's other better rainbow streams average much smaller: 15.5 inches on the Snake River; 14.8 on the Spokane River; 14.3 on Silver Creek, Big Wood River, and South Fork of the Boise; and 14 on the Big Lost River.

The majority of fly fishers flock to the upper river. On key dates—Opening Day, the salmonfly hatch, the season opener on Railroad Ranch, the Western green drake hatch—Island Park revels in the crowds and festivities of a college reunion. Friends make annual pilgrimages and take refresher courses from scholarly rainbows. Families dedicate their entire vacations to the Henry's Fork.

Its magnetism was summed up by former *Morning Tribune* outdoors editor Bill Loftus. "Green drakes. Those two words are enough to put marriages in peril as fly fishers scramble to the shores of this famous stream, abandoning families and careers in the process. Expect to find crowds and fish when the fishing gets hot and hectic."

If these scenes sound too hurly-burly for your tastes, don't despair. Those who cherish more serene or secluded inspirations from fly fishing can find them here. Just bide your time or go round the bend or up the road to your own special place.

Public access is virtually unlimited in a national forest, alpine playground of spectacular beauty inhabited by a host of wildlife and waterfowl. The river's gentle meadow-stream flows permit easy, comfortable wading. Its high-walled, fast-water canyons challenge the strength and skills of experts and neophytes.

A complicated set of fishing seasons and regulations protect its versatility. To be safe, always check the latest Idaho Fish and Game regulations pamphlet. Most of these regulation changes were initiated in the 1990s during a period when the river was experiencing decline. Some feared its actual demise, particularly in the Last Chance-Harriman stretch. The Henry's Fork Foundation and Henry's Fork Watershed Council were formed out of concerns for better management of the river and its resources.

The quality of the Henry's Fork was suffering because too many trumpeter swans and other waterfowl were eating the aquatic vegetation, and a string of low-water years led to winter flows too low for the health of the birds and the fishery.

By 1995, more than 1,000 swans had been captured at Harriman State Park and Red Rock Lakes National Wildlife Refuge in southwestern Montana and transplanted in southern Idaho and surrounding states. Hazing the swans also has reduced winter use at Harriman. Continuation of the program has allowed significant increase of aquatic plants and improved habitat for waterfowl and fish. While some agreements have been reached, efforts continue to obtain better minimum winter flows.

Debates continue over another threat—siltation. When Island Park Reservoir was drained in 1992 at the height of the drought, 50,000 to 100,000 tons of sediment were unintentionally dumped into the river. Although much of it was flushed downstream the following year by high spring releases, a lot remains. While foundation scientists say it will have long-term effects on small fish survival because it is clogging the rock crevices where they hide in winter, Fish and Game biologists say the increased sediment will induce badly needed aquatic plant growth that will raise water levels and provide protection for the fish in the rock cobble along shore.

Meanwhile, a series of heavy water years granted a reprieve to resident fish. There was increased survival of young trout and the wily old rainbows were returning. By 1995, many anglers felt the wild rainbows were back in force, just the way they prefer it, and the trend continued into the new century. Many feel the river is fishing as well or better than its legendary heyday in the 1970s.

Part of the river's apparent rebirth in 1993 was due to the huge numbers of large rainbows flushed downstream when the Island Park Reservoir was drained the previous autumn.

"It is clear the reservoir has played a major role in the quality of the Henry's Fork," says Mark Gamblin, regional fisheries manager. "The hydropower penstock (and a lip on the spillway) will cut down movement of fish out of the reservoir. We plan to study and determine a management plan for both the river and reservoir."

A total watershed management approach to protect the river is the ultimate goal of the Foundation and Council.

Float fishing offers an opportunity to cover more water.

Over the ensuing decade, many of these issues and others have been addressed or are being worked on. The pendulum has swung in the Henry's Fork's favor again, and even protracted drought conditions have failed to knock it down and out.

The combined efforts of many – including new management strategies of Fish and Game, research and restoration projects by Henry's Fork Foundation and water management cooperation from irrigators – have preserved its ranking as one of the "Great Rivers of the West."

Evidence of increased fishing opportunities in the upper river are revealed in the following fish counts:

Cutthroat returned to upper river: Fish and Game periodically surveys trout populations in the upper most reach of the Henry's Fork, from the confluence of Henry's Lake Outlet downstream to Mack's Inn. Degraded habitat and the lack of dissolved nutrients in the water keep this reach from being as productive as those below Island Park Dam, but it has improved in recent years.

In 2002, Fish and Game began stocking Yellowstone cutthroat trout in this reach to improve the fishery. Historically, a large proportion of the rainbow trout found in this section during the spring were fish moving into the upper river from Island Park Reservoir to spawn in March and April. Because the spawning run was largely over by the opening of fishing season, these fish contributed little to the upper river fishery. Cutthroat trout, however, generally spawn in June and July and have the potential to establish a migration of spawning fish that will benefit the upper river fishery.

A Teton Valley Lodge guide helps land a trout on the Henry's Fork.

Density estimates from 2002-2004 averaged about 238 trout per mile. The estimated density in 2007 was 619 fish per mile. Yellowstone cutthroat trout comprised 50 percent of the electro-fishing catch compared to less than 5 percent in 2002.

The increase in trout abundance and the percentage of cutthroat trout in the sample indicate the program is working.

Winter flows benefit Box Canyon: In 2007, for the first time since 2002, Fish and Game exceeded its long-term average fish density goal of 3,000 trout per mile in the Box Canyon. Population estimates in 2007 showed over 3,700 trout per mile, which is more than double the estimates from 2003.

Although some of this increase can be attributed to better winter snowpack, much has to do with improved winter flow releases from Island Park Dam since 2005. Winter flows are widely recognized as the driving force behind trout populations in the Box Canyon.

Rainbow trout size structure was encouraging, with a healthy balance of juvenile fish and older age-classes, which is also being reflected in improved fishing downstream through Last Chance and Harriman State Park.

Back to back wet winters in 2008 and 2009 continued the trend with many old-timers experiencing some of the best fishing they've seen in more than a decade.

The Henry's Fork and Henry's Lake are the heart and soul of Island Park, a 33-mile string of hamlets, resorts, and small housing developments located along Highway 20, which runs through the Targhee National Forest.

This summer and winter playground begins 75 miles north of Idaho Falls. Just over the Continental Divide is the West Entrance to Yellowstone National Park, the birthplace of six first-class trout streams, the Madison, Firehole, Gallatin, Yellowstone, Lamar, and Snake rivers.

On its southwesterly course, the Henry's Fork bisects the Island Park Caldera, one of the planet's largest collapsed volcanoes. Island Park's eastern rim overlaps the Yellowstone caldera, a mammoth tea kettle still percolating over a hot spot on the North American tectonic plate. Upper and Lower Mesa Falls plunge over the cap rock of one of three catastrophic volcanic explosions that blasted out the Island Park and Yellowstone calderas. The first was 1.8 million years ago, the second and third in 600,000-year intervals. They are the top links in the chain of explosions that erupted 14 million years ago and slowly carved the Snake River Plain in a sweeping arc across southern Idaho.

Flowing 120 miles from its source, the Henry's Fork joins the South Fork at Menan Buttes to form the 1,040-mile Snake River, the largest tributary of the Columbia River. It descends from about 6,400 feet in elevation at Big Springs to 4,750 feet at its confluence.

Melted winter snows snared by the Continental Divide give birth to the Henry's Fork as a full river at Big Springs. Gushing forth at 480,000 gallons a day, the flows of this gargantuan fountain are joined 1.5 miles downstream at The Bathtub by the outlet releases from Henry's Lake, 12 miles upstream.

A gentle meadow stream of long runs, pools, and riffles, the river glides about 20 miles to Coffee Pot Rapids, where it cascades 1.5 miles through a deep canyon into the backwaters channel of the Island Park Reservoir. The tailwater flows out of the dam are supplemented a mile downstream by the Buffalo River. This is the head of Box Canyon, homewaters of the river's largest rainbows. The boulder-churned flows of the canyon trot three miles down to its mouth and spill out into the broad expanses of Last Chance and Harriman State Park.

Here the river returns to the graceful beauty typical of a spring creek fishery. Its wide, gentle flows curve in a broad S-turn for two miles through Last Chance and meander five miles through the world-famous Railroad Ranch, once the summer home of the Harriman and Guggenheim families. Several islands and three minor rapids are encountered on the river's full nine-mile course through the park, donated to the state in 1977. Still a working ranch, its cattle are kept off the river by solar-powered electric fences.

As the Henry's Fork exits the park, it picks up speed again. Four miles downstream, just below Riverside Campground, it enters its deepest, most scenic gorge, Cardiac Canyon. The river offers seven miles of challenging pocket water fishing before it swirls through the Sheep Falls chute and races to its 114-foot plunge over Upper Mesa Falls. Immediately downstream is the 65-foot Lower Mesa Falls.

Below the falls, the river's more moderate descent continues another rocky 12 miles to its confluence with the Warm River. Here the canyon abruptly widens and turns west. The next 12 miles of galloping riffles, minor rapids, and wide, deep pools are stilled by the the Ashton Reservoir.

Joining the rainbows below the falls are large brown trout and a remnant population of native Yellowstone cutthroat and cutthroat-rainbow hybrids.

The seven miles between Ashton Dam and Chester Reservoir is another premiere tailwater fishery fed by the cool flows of the dam's hydropower operation. Unheralded and lightly fished until recently, the mix of deep riffles, long shallow glides, and moderate rapids contains one of the largest populations of big fish on the river. It is doubly rewarding because the Henry's Fork is open to fishing year-round from Vernon Bridge to its mouth.

Moderate flows and good fishing continue with convenient access sites for about five miles downstream. The five miles above St. Anthony and the river's remaining 30-mile run across the upper Snake River Plain is flanked by farmland. Public access is limited, but big fish lurk here for those willing to continue their exploration.

The run-of-the-river Chester Reservoir marks the confluence of the Fall River. Ten miles below St. Anthony, the first of the Teton River's two forks enters the Henry's Fork. Both tributaries are blue-ribbon prospects in the golden circle of trout streams surrounding Yellowstone.

Flows through Island Park average 400 to 1,200 cubic feet per second (cfs), with the higher flows recorded during the July and August irrigation season. Below the falls, the spring-fed flows of Warm River and Robinson Creek pick up the pace to Ashton Reservoir. The Ashton Dam tailwaters average 500 cfs in winter to more than 1,000 cfs in summer. Spring floods on the lower river are largely a product of runoff from the unchecked Warm, Fall, and Teton rivers.

The seasonal attractions of the Henry's Fork are its prolific fly hatches. Stone- flies incite the most gluttonous attacks by trout and fly fishers in spring. Traditionally called salmonflies because of their distinctive orange markings, these "Big Macs" of the aquatic insect world open the season with a bang. The hatch can erupt as early as mid-May below Ashton. It usually works its way upstream about five miles a day through the fast-water stretches marked by Warm River, Mesa Falls, Sheep Falls, Box Canyon, and Coffee Pot Rapids. On parts of the upper river, the stonefly hatch can linger through June into early-July.

A string of mild winters and warm springs prior to 1995 brought the hatch off early, often coinciding with the Opening Day hordes on the upper river. Idaho Fish and Game biologists and Henry's Fork Foundation watchdogs hope colder flows from Island Park Dam, under new hydropower management practices, will slow the hatch's progression. This will reduce the vulnerability of the fish to first day crowds, while prolonging prime fishing opportunities.

The same goes for the river's stirring Western green drake hatch. Again, the show opens first below Ashton, often in mid-June. It is hoped colder tailwater flows will restore the Last Chance-Harriman hatch to its traditional late-June occurrence, or at least until the Railroad Ranch opens June 15.

Following the stonefly hatch is a productive emergence of golden stones that keeps the action rolling into July. Also contributing to the trout's evening feeding frenzies, June through August, are a host of caddisfly species and small golden stones, commonly called willowflies or yellow Sallies. Below Ashton, phenomenal caddis hatches in late-March and April provide fast, hard-hitting action for early season fly fishers.

Stonefly patterns, both wet and dry, work best in sizes No. 4 and 6. Golden stones are No. 8 and 10. Nymphs of both species are effective year-round, along with black rubber-legged patterns and woolly buggers in similar sizes.

Bruce Staples, renowned eastern Idaho author and fly tier, routinely catches large rainbows.

Caddis, stimulator, and attractor patterns, like humpies and Wulffs, work best in the fast-water sections in sizes No. 12 to 16.

Always a good second option during summer doldrums are terrestrial insect patterns for grasshoppers, ants, flying ants, and beetles. These can be very effective on blustery days when high winds blow them onto the water. Grasshopper patterns work in sizes No. 6 to 10. Try sizes No. 18 or 20 for ants or beetles.

No other river in the West has such a multitude of mayfly species. The blizzard swarms of overlapping hatches make fly choice very intense as large trout key in on their selected prey. July through October is when Henry's Fork dry fly fishers begin speaking Latin.

Actually, the mayfly list starts with the Western green drake, *Drunella grandis*, in late June. Its cousin, the small Western drake or flav, *D. flavilinea*, appears in July. Then there are two species of pale morning duns, *Ephemerella infrequens* in June, and *E. inermis* in July and August. The brown drake, *Ephemera simulans*, comes off in late-June on the upper river. Mid-July to mid-August, look for speckled duns, *Callibaetis coloradensis*, followed in August through September by speckled spinners, *C. nigritus*.

Throughout the summer, a batch of very minute flies comes off, including blue duns or blue quills, *Baetis parvus*; blue-winged olives, *Pseudocloeon edmundsi*; and white-winged black tricos, *Tricorythodes minutus*.

The large gray drake, *Siphlonurus occidentalis*, appears on the upper river in mid-August and below Ashton in September. Late-August and September's bonus is the mahogany dun, *Paraleptophlebia bicornuta*.

Ashton Man Lands Record Brown Trout

Wes Case knew there were some big brown trout in Ashton Reservoir on the Henry's Fork of the Snake River, but he wasn't thinking "state record" big when he went fishing on Nov. 6, 2007.

Yet, when he landed the 37-inch behemoth, he knew it had to be one of the biggest brown trout ever caught in Idaho.

It was.

A certified scale and a verified identification by Dan Garren, regional fishery manager, confirmed the 27.3-pound fish is the state record brown trout. The previous record was a 26.5-pound fish caught from the South Fork of the Snake River in 1981.

Case, an Ashton resident, has fished Ashton Reservoir for years, but previously an 8-pound brown trout was the biggest he'd ever caught.

Landing the fish was no easy feat, given that Case was only using 8-pound-test line.

"It took me about an hour to land it" he said. "It headed out to deep water and just laid there, so I just kept the pressure on it."

But fighting the fish was only half the battle. Case, who was fishing from the shore, was by himself and didn't have a landing net.

"I had to scramble down the rocks and through the brush to land it. When I finally got it up on the bank, I just sat on the shore and stared at it for about 10 minutes" he said. "It was totally amazing".

According to Garren, who examined the fish after it had been skinned by a taxidermist, the stomach con-tained two partially digested hatchery rainbow trout about 10 to 12 inches, and scales from a very large sucker. Based on the otoliths, or ear-stones, which are used to estimate ages of fish, Garren said the fish was at least 10 and maybe 11 years old.

"I'm guessing that fish had eaten a lot of rainbow trout and suckers in its years."

When summer crowds are long gone, another tiny blue-winged olive, *Baetis tricau-datus*, often guarantees the most success in October and November. Below Ashton, car-pet hatches of this prolific fly can dominate early season action when it returns in March and April. Also on the lower river, midges in late fall and winter, and again in early spring, continue the dry fly action.

With the exception of the drakes, small mayfly patterns are the rule on the Last Chance-Harriman stretch and other spring creeks. Check with local fly tackle shops or outfitters to find what works best on their individual streams.

Dry fly styles range from the basic high-winged pattern to parachute, no-hackle, par-adrake, and spinner patterns. Ultimately, size and form—surface-floating emerger, adult flying insect, or spent-wing spinner—are more important than color. Classic standby pat-terns when you can't match the hatch are Adams and Cahill patterns in appropriate sizes.

Most drake patterns are No. 10 and 12; some go from No. 12 to 16. *Callibaetis* duns and spinners are No. 14 or 16. Early season PMDs are No. 16 or 18, and No 18 or 20 in mid-summer. Spring and fall *Baetis*, or BWOs, are No. 16 or 18, and in mid-summer, No. 20 to 24. Tricos are No. 20 or 22; mahogany dun, No. 16 and 18.

Emerger and nymph patterns come in similar sizes. Standard patterns, like hare's ear, prince, pheasant, and bead head nymphs, can be good producers all season in sizes No. 12 and 14.

A Labrador retriever checks out his master's trophy rainbow caught at Last Chance on the Henry's Fork.

The solution to the spring creek puzzle of the Henry's Fork is to determine the stage of a hatch or which one of many species in a multiple "masking" hatch the trout are taking—and then to figure out what fly or stage is coming next.

The Last Chance-Railroad Ranch stretch has very little visible structure and aquatic weed beds are important hiding places for the fish. This makes reading the water difficult.

You have to look for the trout and cast to feeding fish. Ignore splashy rises—they are either small trout or whitefish. A big rainbow rarely comes out of the water, except when chasing an emerger. Often you only see its nose or a slight bulge in the stream surface. Sometimes adding to the formula for a big fish is the brief appearance of a broad, square tail as it goes down.

Don't telegraph your presence. Wade slowly and carefully to get close enough for a short, accurate cast. Avoid "lining" the fish by casting down and across stream, or directly downstream. For bank feeders, stay low and far back on the bank, or cast from mid-stream to the shore.

Be patient. Pick a trout and stay with it. Try to match its feeding rhythm with a drag-free drift directly down its feeding lane. It won't move to intercept your fly. Have confidence in your pattern selection. Give it a good test before switching to another fly. At the same time, don't get hung up on the big fly-big fish syndrome. Drakes may seem the obvious choice when they are coming off, but a very cautious rainbow may stick to its staple diet, like PMDs or BWOs.

Twilight on the Henry's Fork in autumn.

The stonefly hatch on the Henry's Fork marks the start of the general fishing season.

Don't be just a fair-weather fly fisher. Some of the best hatches come off on cloudy, rain-spitting days.

If catching big Railroad Ranch rainbows is your main goal, go for it. Elsewhere, the Henry's Fork can be less tight-fisted. It offers a variety of marvelous opportunities.

The tailwater fishery from Ashton Dam to just above St. Anthony has caught the attention of a lot more anglers. When it is hot, the lower river provides the best spring fishing in a three-state area. Just as often, the trout can be as demanding and exacting as on the more fabled Last Chance-Harriman stretches. Its aquatic insect hatches are equally robust and complex.

The primary lure is the opportunity to wet a line months before the general season opens at the end of May. The traditional year-round section of the Henry's Fork starts below the Vernon Bridge, the second one downstream from Ashton Dam. A second year-round section—from Warm River to the Ashton Reservoir—was added in 2000 to give anglers more winter and early spring options.

On the lower Henry's Fork, between the Vernon Bridge and the Chester Dam backwaters, a 2007 survey found a rainbow trout population very comparable to what was seen in 2005 and 2006, at about 800 fish per mile. Although densities were comparable to past surveys, there was a much greater percentage of juvenile fish in 2007, which reflected much-needed recruitment.

There was a notable increase in the abundance of brown trout relative to earlier estimates. Brown trout comprised about 5 percent of the population in 2005 and 2006, but were 17 percent of the population in 2007.

Interestingly, this is a pattern fisheries biologists are seeing in other parts of the region.

In the reach from Chester Dam downstream to the Fun Farm backwaters, total trout abundance increased from 503 trout per mile in 2003 to 893 trout per mile in 2007.

As in the Vernon reach, brown trout increased from about 9 percent of the electro-fishing catch in 2003 to 24 percent.

It is comfortable wading until spring runoff erupts or irrigation releases begin. The slow-moving waters of Chester Reservoir are popular with waders, canoe anglers, and a few float-boaters. The boat put-in is at Chester Dam on the east bank. As water levels rise, boaters are the ones who get the best shots at the big guys rising in mid-stream. Floaters also do well drifting from the bridge down to the reservoir.

Most years, action picks up in March as rainbow and cutthroat come out of their winter doldrums. Most effective at this time, when the banks are still encased in snow, are small bead head nymphs or San Juan worms. By late-April or early-May, cutthroat up to 18 inches and rainbows and hybrids over 20 inches are revving up for their spring spawning runs. This is when the river's remarkable dry fly action also kicks off.

Its BWO hatches are its most consistent producers, but the true beauty of the lower Henry's Fork is its early caddis hatches. Its stonefly hatch always precedes Opening Day of the general season by a week or more. For those in the know, it announces the real beginning of the new season. The good folks of St. Anthony officially open the season with their Free Fisherman's Breakfast. Thousands turn out for the annual event on the Friday before Opening Day.

After Opening Day, the stretches below Ashton Dam and downstream from Warm River are popular floats because stoneflies can bring brown trout over 20 inches to the surface, along with hefty rainbows. Both stretches offer limited opportunities to wade, although it is more difficult than below Vernon Bridge.

Perhaps the most popular float on the river is through Box Canyon, where large stonefly nymphs, woolly buggers, rubber-legs, and streamers bring the most action. Dry fly choices include stoneflies and caddis, and fast-water attractor patterns like humpies, stimulators, and Wulffs. This stretch is short enough that it can be floated more than once in a day by the ambitious. Or you can continue on down through Last Chance and the park. Box Canyon can be waded by the stout-hearted, but its roily waters make it difficult to see the many boulders and slippery cobblestones underfoot. A wader must use extreme caution. Still, there are numerous foot-worn trails down into the 100-foot canyon. Several of the best follow the east cliff from Box Canyon Campground. The reward is giant rainbows in the 24-inch class.

Cardiac Canyon is also rough wading, and its 100- to 700-foot cliffs are more vertical, with fewer trails down to the river. One of the better ones is on the west bank down to Sheep Falls. Access also is available at Riverside Campground. Numerous, winding forest roads lead to the upper canyon's east rim for the adventurous. A Targhee Forest map is useful. Reports of 24-inch rainbows netted in the canyon are becoming more common.

Cardiac Canyon is a rougher float than the Box, with boulder-strewn rapids and surging pocket waters. Floaters have to take care to not go past the Hatchery Ford boat ramp on the east bank. The road to the ramp is reached from Scenic Mesa Falls Highway 47. It has a very steep grade down to the river.

A pleasant, scenic float, one that no one should pass up, is from the Big Springs boat launch downstream to Mack's Inn or Lower Coffee Pot Campground. The ramp is on the south bank, a quarter of a mile down from the springs at an old railroad trestle. The Big Springs flows above it are off-limits to fishing and boats.

You can rent canoes at Mack's Inn or arrange shuttle service. If you float in your own boat, raft, or canoe, don't go past the campground. Coffee Pot Rapids is 1.5 miles downstream.

This float is an excellent family outing. It is a great place for youngsters and beginning fly fishers to hone their skills. It is stocked with eight- to 12-inch hatchery rainbows, and there are some wild rainbows, 15 inches and larger. A few brook trout come out of Moose Creek and other tributaries. Good-sized cutthroat occasionally make their way down from Henry's Lake.

The best wading access is at the boat ramp, Mack's Inn, and downstream to the rapids. Hatches are good and fishing is advantageous for those who prefer less demanding waters.

Kokanee salmon are running out of the reservoir again, which bodes well for late-summer fishing at Coffee Pot Rapids. In the past, large rainbows and cutthroat have followed the salmon out of the reservoir on their spawning runs. The rapids are tough fishing, but can be profitable most of the season. The easiest way into the canyon is to hike downstream from the campground.

The free fisherman's breakfast at St. Anthony is an annual rite to launch the fishing season.

Bent rods are a guarantee when fishing the productive waters of the lower Henry's Fork.

Mike Lawson guides former Senator James McClure and his wife, Louise, on the Henry's Fork of the Snake River. Rocky Barker photo.

The Idaho Nature Conservancy is attempting to improve conditions on Henry's Lake Outlet. It has an option to purchase a 1,450-acre ranch on Henry's Lake Flats. Four miles of the outlet flow through the Flat Ranch, and the Conservancy is negotiating with irrigators to get higher winter flows out of the lake.

There is public access to the upper end of the Henry's Lake Outlet where it crosses under U.S. Highway 20. It can hold some very large cutthroat, especially in wet years when they sometimes come over the lake's dam in great numbers. The first 400 yards of the outlet is closed to fishing.

Another beautiful little stream that fly fishers of all ages and skills can enjoy is Buffalo River. Its gentle, spring-fed flows glide past Island Park's largest campground on its north bank. It is stocked with hatchery rainbows and has a good population of small wild brook trout. Idaho offers a six-fish bag limit for hatchery fish and permits a 25-fish bonus on brookies. No harvest of cutthroat.

The importance of this short tributary of the Henry's Fork cannot be exaggerated. Its average flows of 200 cubic feet per second keep the river below Box Canyon alive when Island Park Dam is shut off.

In addition to the many national forest campgrounds, there are a number of private campgrounds, RV parks, lodges, and resorts in Island Park. Accommodations also are available at Ashton or St. Anthony, and in West Yellowstone, Montana.

Due to increased use and the difficulty in accessing the river below St. Anthony, two new public access and boat ramps were installed on the Henry's Fork in 2009.

The Bureau of Land Management installed a boat ramp about five miles downstream of St. Anthony at the Red Road Bridge, on the Parker-Salem Highway. The boat ramp and parking area are located on the north side of the river, across from the Fort Henry historic site.

The next new public river access on the river with a new developed ramp is 9.5 miles downriver from Red Road Bridge. It's is located at Fish and Game's Warm Slough Wildlife Management Area, 2 miles west of the Hibbard Road Bridge and 5 miles east of Plano.

For the latest information on water conditions and hatches, check with Mike Lawson at Henry's Fork Anglers or Renee Harrop at Trouthunters, both in Island Park. Fly tackle shops in Idaho Falls that closely track conditions year-round are Jimmy's All Seasons Angler and Hyde Fly Shop which has expanded its services to Island Park at Hyde's Last Chance Lodge Outfitters.

Talking to the experts can help you crack the secrets of the Henry's Fork, but always budget more time than first planned. Whatever your choice of waters, you will find it hard to tear yourself away.

HARRIMAN STATE PARK

Harriman State Park lies within an 11,000-acre wildlife refuge in the Greater Yellowstone Ecosystem in the center of Island Park, eastern Idaho's premier outdoors recreation community, north of Ashton.

Moose, elk, and sandhill cranes are common, as well as numerous waterfowl species and North Ameri-ca's largest waterfowl, the trumpeter swan.

Known as one of the best fly-fishing streams in the nation, the Henry's Fork meanders for eight miles through Harriman.

Over 20 miles of trails are available for hiking, biking, horseback riding, and cross county skiing. Horses are available for daily rental and guided horseback tours to experience bugling elk are offered in autumn.

Camping is not permitted.

Overnight Facilities

Harriman has significantly expanded its availability of rental accommodations for overnight stays by anglers and others. The park facilities are open for reservations year round.

For detailed description of each rental facilities, visit the park's web site at http://parksandrecreation.idaho.gov/parks/harriman.aspx.

Online reservations must be made at http://idahostateparks.reserveamerica.com for the following:

Yurts: Harriman's two yurts have a maximum capacity of six people; fireplace and camp stove.

Ranch Manager's House: Four-bedroom fully furnished log home with modern kitchen.

Cattle Foreman's House: Furnished three-bedroom cabin with complete kitchen.

Railroad Ranch Dormitory and Dining Hall: Groups of 15 to 40 can reserve the rustic log dormitory and original Railroad Ranch Cookhouse.

Bunkhouse and Cookhouse: Bunkhouse accommodates up to 9 people. The Cookhouse located next to the Bunkhouse has a fully equipped kitchen.

Conference Center: The Laura Clarke Scovel Education Center is a group facility with 10 cabins and a conference center, including a catering kitchen, surrounding a courtyard.

To reserve this facility call Harriman State Park at 208-558-7368

The lower Henry's Fork is one of the region's premiere winter fishing waters.

Henry's Fork of the Snake

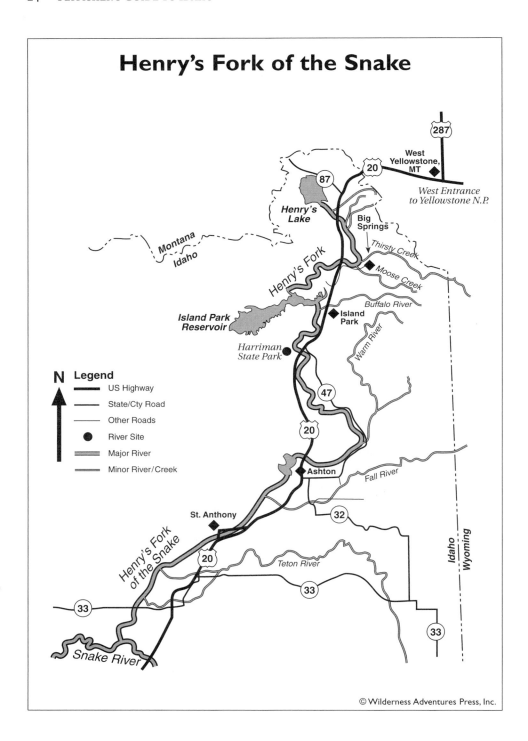

© Wilderness Adventures Press, Inc.

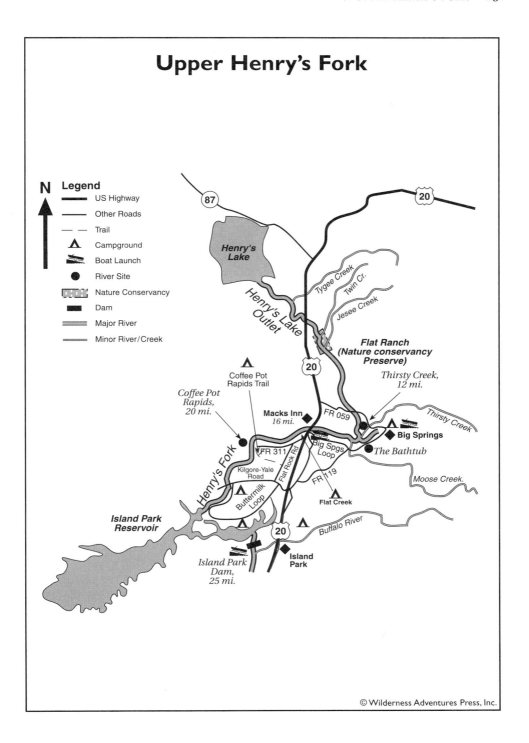

Upper Henry's Fork

Upper Henry's Fork

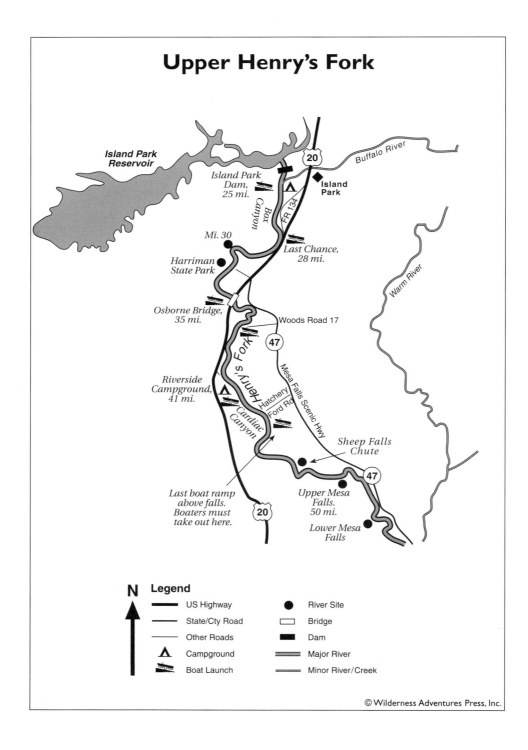

Island Park Reservoir

Island Park Dam, 25 mi.

Box Canyon

FR 134

20

Buffalo River

Island Park

Warm River

Mi. 30

Last Chance, 28 mi.

Harriman State Park

Osborne Bridge, 35 mi.

Woods Road 17

47

Henry's Fork

Mesa Falls Scenic Hwy

Riverside Campground, 41 mi.

Hatchery Ford Rd

Cardiac Canyon

Sheep Falls Chute

47

Last boat ramp above falls. Boaters must take out here.

20

Upper Mesa Falls. 50 mi.

Lower Mesa Falls

Legend

N

▬▬▬	US Highway	●	River Site
───	State/Cty Road	▭	Bridge
───	Other Roads	▬	Dam
▲	Campground	▬▬▬	Major River
⚓	Boat Launch	───	Minor River/Creek

© Wilderness Adventures Press, Inc.

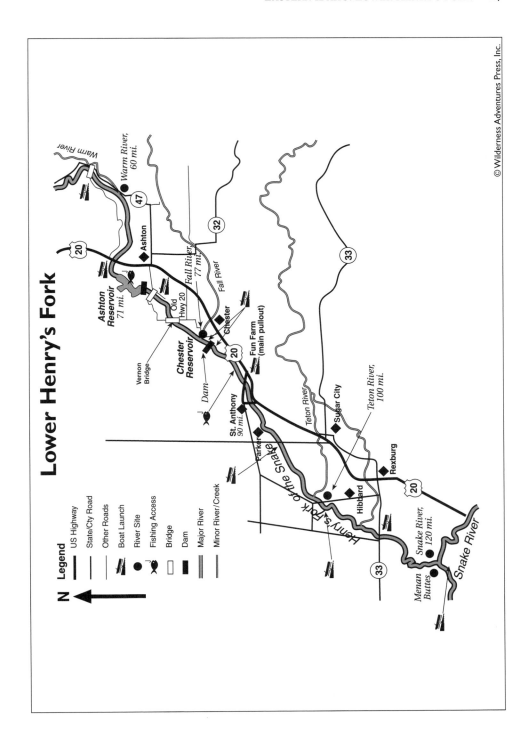

Lower Henry's Fork

Legend

N

US Highway	
State/Cty Road	
Other Roads	
Boat Launch	
River Site	
Fishing Access	
Bridge	
Dam	
Major River	
Minor River/Creek	

Warm River

Warm River, 60 mi.

Ashton

Ashton Reservoir 71 mi.

Old Hwy 20

Fall River, 77 mi.

Fall River

Chester

Fun Farm (main pullout)

Vernon Bridge

Chester Reservoir

Dam

St. Anthony 90 mi.

Parker

Teton River

Sugar City

Teton River, 100 mi.

Rexburg

Hibbard

Henry's Fork of the Snake

Snake River, 120 mi.

Menan Buttes

Snake River

Stream Facts: Henry's Fork of the Snake

SEASONS

- From mouth at Menan Buttes upstream to Vernon Bridge, open to fishing all year
- From Vernon Bridge to Ashton Dam, closed to fishing Dec. 1 through Friday before Memorial Day weekend
- From U.S. 20 bridge, north of Ashton, upstream to posted boundary north of Riverside Campground, open to fishing all year
- From posted boundary north of Riverside Campground to Harriman State Park, closed to fishing Dec. 1 through Friday before Memorial Day weekend
- Harriman State Park, closed to fishing Dec.1 through June 14
- From north boundary of Harriman State Park upstream to Island Park Dam, open to fishing all year
- From McCrea Bridge upstream to Henry's Lake Outlet and including Henry's Lake Outlet below the dam, open to fishing all year

SPECIAL REGULATIONS

- From mouth to St. Anthony, 6-trout limit, no cutthroat
- From Del Rio Bridge at St. Anthony upstream to the posted boundary north of Riverside Campground, 2-trout limit, none under 16 inches, no cutthroat
- From the posted boundary north of Riverside Campground upstream to Island Park Dam, trout limit is 0, catch-and-release, no bait, barbless hooks required; also, Harriman State Park is fly fishing only
- From McCrea Bridge upstream to Henry's Lake Outlet and including Henry's Lake Outlet below the dam, winter fishery is catch-and-release only; from Memorial Day weekend through Nov. 30, trout limit is 6, only 2 may be cutthroat over 16 inches

TROUT

- Upper river, rainbows, some over 25"; a few cutthroat and brook trout.
- Below Mesa Falls, rainbows and cutthroat-rainbow hybrids, both sometimes exceed 22"; growing number of brown trout, some over 25"

RIVER FLOWS

- Average flows are 400 cfs to 1,500 cfs, with higher flows in mid-July and August
- Dams curb spring runoff

RIVER CHARACTERISTICS

- Gentle meadow stream from Big Springs to Coffee Pot Rapids. Box Canyon strewn with boulders, large cobblestones. Last Chance to Riverside has broad, flat meandering glides, few riffles; spring creek fishery. Riverside to Warm River, river plunges through Cardiac Canyon, heavy pocket waters, three waterfalls. Below Warm River, long, deep glides, riffles and pocket waters. Ashton Dam to St. Anthony, long, wide glides, pocket waters and riffles; tailwater fishery.

FISHING ACCESS

- Mostly public land on upper river in Targhee National Forest
- Highway signs mark access sites north of St. Anthony
- Numerous boat ramps for float boats and canoes, no motors permitted
- Three waterfalls make middle of Cardiac Canyon inaccessible

MAPS

- Henry's Fork 11x17 flyfishing map by Wilderness Adventures Press; http://store.wildadvpress.com

UPPER HENRY'S FORK RIVER MAJOR HATCHES

Insect	J	F	M	A	M	J	J	A	S	O	N	D	Flies
Giant stonefly (salmonfly)				█	█								Sofa Pillow #4–6; Bird's Stone #4–6; Black Rubberlegged Nymphs #4–6
Golden stone						█							Golden Stone #4–6; Stimulator #4–6; Dark Rubberlegged Nymphs #4–6
Small golden stone						█	█						Stimulator #12–16; Yellow Humpy #12–16; Golden Stonefly Nymph #12–16
Caddis						█	█	█	█				Emergent Sparkle Pupa #14–16; Elk Hair Caddis #14–18
Pale Morning Dun						█	█	█	█				Yellow Sparkle Dun #16–20; PMD Cripple #16–20
Western green drake						█	█						Parachute Adams #10–16; Olive Sparkle Dun #10–16
Brown drake						█	█						Hare's Ear Nymph #10–16; Brown Sparkle Dun #10–16
Small western drake (flav)						█	█						No Hackle #14–16; Paradrake #14–16; Spinner #14–16
Tiny blue-winged olive, tiny brown dun, blue quill, white-winged black tricos							█	█	█				Parachute Adams #18–24; CDC Trico #18–22
Speckle-winged duns, Spinners (callibaetis)						█	█	█	█				Sparkle Dun #16–18; Spinners #16–18
Gray drake							█	█					Parachute Adams #10–12; Sparkle Dun #10–12
Mahogany dun								█	█				Sparkle Dun #16–18; Pheasant Tail Nymph #16–18
Blue-winged olive									█	█	█		Parachute Adams #16–24; CDC Baetis #16–24; Pheasant Tail Nymph #16–24

LOWER HENRY'S FORK RIVER MAJOR HATCHES

Insect	J	F	M	A	M	J	J	A	S	O	N	D	Flies
Midges (snowfly)	■											■	Griffith's Gnat #18–22; Palomino Midge #16–22
Blue-winged olive			■	■	■	■				■	■		Olive Sparkle Dun #16–24; Parachute Adams #16–24; Pheasant Tail Nymph #16–24
Caddis					■	■	■	■					Hemingway Caddis #14–16; Emergent Sparkle Pupa #14–16; Elk Hair Caddis #14–16
Giant stonefly (salmonfly)					■								Sofa Pillow/Stimulator #4–6
Brown drake					■								Brown Sparkle Dun #10–14; Hare's Ear Nymph #10–14
Golden stone						■							Stimulator #4–6; Kaufmann's Stone #4–6
Small golden stone (willowfly)							■						Stimulator #8–12
Western green drake							■						Olive Hare's Ear #10–14; Olive Sparkle Dun #10–16
Tiny blue-winged olive								■	■				Parachute Adams #18–24
Pale morning dun							■	■	■				Yellow No Hackle #16–20; Yellow Sparkle Dun #16–20
Gray drake									■				Parachute Adams #10–12; Gray Sparkle Dun #10–12
Mahogany dun								■	■				Mahogany Sparkle Dun #16–18; Pheasant Tail Nymph #16–18

Henry's Lake nestles in a bowl of the Centennial Mountains on the Continental Divide.

Compared to other lakes, it grows fish much faster. Of course, we all know that. That's why we like to fish here.

Dan Schill, Idaho Fish and Game
Fisheries Research Biologist

Henry's Lake

Crown Jewel in Golden Circle of Trout

Henry's Lake is Idaho's jewel in the crown of precious trout waters encircling Yellowstone National Park.

The lake's quiet promise is often overlooked by fly fishers focused on the Henry's Fork of the Snake just downstream, or the Madison, Firehole, and Yellowstone rivers in the park. For float-tubing trophy trout hunters, it is a world-class fishing destination.

As Idaho's premiere Yellowstone cutthroat trout factory, Henry's Lake is unparalleled. Add the fatherly contributions from Kamloops rainbow to the mix and the definition of hybrid vigor earns sensational significance. Include large East Coast brook trout and the lake's dynamite trophy fishery gets even more exciting.

Its best fishing is from the end of May to August, and again in early-fall until the season closes on October 31. Wading access is very limited, except in fall along portions of the north shore. The best way to fish the lake is from a boat or float-tube.

Trout growth rates in its fertile waters are matched by no other lake in the Northern Rockies. Four-year-old Henry's Lake cutthroat average 16 inches, compared to 14.3 inches in southeastern Idaho's Bear Lake and 12.5 inches in Yellowstone Lake. Four-year-old cutthroat-rainbow hybrids in Henry's Lake average 18.8 inches and brook trout average 16 inches. When it comes to trophy trout, cutthroat-rainbow hybrids can exceed 40 inches. Cutthroat can reach 30 inches, and brook trout, 25 inches or more.

Hybrids have been present in the lake since the 1930s. The rainbows that first interbred with cutthroat are believed to have escaped from the old Sawtell Ranch's fish-rearing ponds. The lake's first brook trout also are believed to have been escapees.

Because of their popularity with anglers, Idaho Fish and Game began stocking hatchery hybrids in the 1950s. It has been managing the lake as a trophy trout water since 1976 Size goals are 20 percent of hybrids over 20 inches, 10 percent of cutthroat over 20 inches and five percent of brook trout over 18 inches.

Brook trout devotees prowl the lake all season, but particularly during the fall spawning interval. By western standards, the lake grows very large brookies. Idaho's record— seven pounds, one ounce, 23.5 inches—was caught by DeVere Stratton of Idaho Falls on August 6, 1978. A week later he netted a six-pound eight-ounce brook trout that also would have broken the previous record.

The mainstay of the lake's fishery is its native Yellowstone cutthroat. They represent the majority of the catch. Good populations ensure future productivity. Collection of pure strain cutthroat eggs is paramount to hatchery operations that maintain the lake's cutthroat population and produce cutthroat-rainbow hy-brids.

For decades, the Henry's Lake Hatchery's annual goal was to take approximately 2.3 million green Yellowstone cutthroat eggs and approximately 800,000 green hybrid eggs to yield 1.1 million Yellowstone cutthroat eyed eggs (after about 30 days, eggs develop "eyes") and 350,000 eyed hybrid eggs for shipment to the Mackay Hatchery rearing facility.

Using Henry's Lake cutthroat females and fertilizing the eggs with kamloops rainbow milt from the Hayspur Hatchery produces the hybrid eggs. The newly fertilized hybrid eggs are then heat shocked to pro-duce sterile fish to prevent genetic dilution of the Yellowstone cutthroat genetics.

In the fall, the Mackay facility traditionally returned 1 million Yellowstone cutthroat fingerlings and 200,000 hybrid fingerlings back into Henry's Lake. Virtually all the production of the lake's facility is returned back to Henry's Lake. Occasionally a small number of eggs are used for projects such as reestablishing a Yellow-stone cutthroat fishery at Golden Lake in Harriman State Park.

Anglers lucky enough to fish Henry's Lake in 2008 and 2009 were treated to some of the best fishing the lake has seen in close to a decade. Although Fish and Game did not collect specific information on catch rates with a creel survey, many anglers reported great fishing. Some anglers even stated it was the best fish-ing they had seen in the past 25 years.

Henry's Lake can get busy when the bite is on. (Photo by Joshua Bergan)

"By most accounts, Henry's Lake is back and, if not better than ever, it's awfully close," declared Jim Fredericks, former regional fisheries manager.

"After suffering the effects of drought from 2001-2004, the fishery was much improved in 2005 and 2006 was even better. As reflected in (2008) gill net catches the cutthroat population was slightly above average and the number of large hybrids has never been better," Fredericks said. "Anglers caught numerous hybrid trout over 10 pounds, with a few reaching the 14- to 15-pound mark.

"The brook trout fishery continued to improve — a direct result of the reimplementation of the stocking program in 2002–and several 5-pound fish were caught," Fredericks added.

Like the hybrid trout at Henry's Lake, Fish and Game plants sterile brook trout in the lake to control their population and prevent the possibility of displacing native species by overpopulation.

Thanks to Mother Nature, a combination of key events in 2008 resulted in good fishing for anglers: a late spring ice breakup was followed by a long, cool summer, and the tributaries had good flows as a result of the better snowpack in the surrounding mountains.

Fredericks noted that the catch rates experienced in 2008 were correlated with higher gill-net catch rates in Fish and Game's population monitoring. Each year in May, gill nets are set throughout the lake to capture trout and provide an index of how robust the trout population is. Gill-net trend surveys are one way that Fish and Game monitors trout populations. The catch in 2008 was well above the lake's average catch of 11.5 trout per net, and explains in part the increased catch rates anglers experienced.

"Another interesting thing to look at is the high gill-net catch rate found in 2007, which was the highest we have documented since we began using gill nets in 1991," Fredericks said. "Based solely on this infor-mation, we would have expected to see very high (angler) catch rates (in 2007). However, environmental conditions were drastically different (in 2007) compared to (2008).

"During 2007, we experienced an early spring followed by a hot and relatively dry summer — neither condition is conducive to good angling on Henry's Lake. As a result, anglers did not catch the number of fish they did in 2008. This is a good example of how environmental conditions can impact a fishery regard-less of how many fish are actually swimming in the water."

Meanwhile, new rules for Henrys Lake in 2006 did away with an antiquated restric-tion that limited fishing to the hours between 5:00a.m. and 9:00p.m. Anglers can now fish 24 hours a day. Also, the lake's fishing season was extended a month to the end of November.

"The changes raised concern with some anglers about (possible) excessive harvest at night and in November," Fredericks said. "Enforcement and fisheries staff increased patrols and conducted night-time surveillance throughout the season. Though a few anglers tried night fishing early in the season, it seemed that catch rates were no bet-ter than during daylight hours and effort was almost non-existent. No violations were detected."

Float-tubers setting out on Henry's Lake need to keep an eye out for high winds.

"The November 30 season extension resulted in very little open-water fishing effort. Though catch rates were good, the cold, windy weather and ice around the shoreline kept most anglers away," Fredericks said. "The last five days of November, however, brought enough ice to support an ice fishery. Catch rates were exceptional, and the word of the fishery quickly spread. We counted 124 anglers during the brief ice fishery, most of them on the final two days of the season.

"Though most anglers harvested at least one fish, there were no instances of over limits, and the majority of fish were released. By the time it closed, the total harvest was less than 250 fish, which will have no im-pact on the overall fish population.

"We did, however, see potential for conflicts related to trespass and parking in the Staley Springs area, and we will be developing alternatives with landowners and anglers to minimize potential problems."

Still, some anglers continued to raise concerns about the effects of a longer ice-fishery if the lake freezes early.

Fredericks cautiously agreed. "The number of fish harvested in November (2006) was insignificant in the big picture. During a typical year anglers harvest around 20,000 trout, so 250 more certainly aren't going to break it."

Therefore, to accommodate the popularity of the newfound ice-fishing season, the Idaho Fish and Game Commission extended the fishing season in 2011 from Memorial Day weekend to January 1. A valid fishing license is required to fish on January 1 of the succeeding year.

Biological surveys conducted on the fishery had concluded that an ice-fishing harvest would have a minimal effect and that Henry's Lake could sustain a lot more use than it had previously been experiencing.

Anglers spent 18,338 hours ice fishing the lake between mid-November and January 1, the first full year of the new ice-fishing extension. By comparison, anglers spent 18,792 hours fishing on just the three-day opening weekend in 2009, the last year a creel study had been conducted. Preliminary estimates of spending suggest the ice fishery added $500,000 to the southeastern Idaho economy in its first year.

The average catch rate for the 2011 ice-fishing season was 0.74 fish/hour, or about one fish every hour and 20 minutes. This was higher than the summer catch rate in 2009, which was 0.63 fish/hour. Ice fishermen released 80 percent of the fish captured, which was similar to the release rate found in the 2009 summer fishery.

Biologists report ice fishermen harvested a total of 2,708 fish during the 2011 ice-fishing season, which is similar though slightly less than the number of fish harvested on opening weekend in 2009. The catch rate was highest for Yellowstone cutthroat trout followed by brook trout. Hybrids had the lowest catch rate.

IDFG staff stated they found very little illegal activity occurring during the ice fishery. Creel clerks and enforcement staff were present a minimum of four days a week throughout the ice-fishing season. The only citation written during the first season was for a fisherman who didn't have his fishing license on him.

Overall, Fish and Game creel surveys indicate that harvest rates in Henrys Lake are less than 15 percent, which is very low for such a productive, fast growing population.

"Over 85 percent of the fish in the lake die of old age or other natural causes, so we'd have to see a lot more effort and harvest than in 2006 to be concerned about the population," Fredericks said.

"We're looking at the data, keeping open minds, and looking at various options for maintaining ice-fishing opportunity without compromising the quality of the fishery or creating access problems."

Moreover, a new look at maintaining trout size in this renowned trophy fishery was made through adjustments in fish stocking numbers in 2012.

Biologists believe natural spawning in tributary creeks that benefited remarkably from several stream access improvement projects has over-populated the lake, and might have contributed to a perceived decrease in size of the fish in the lake, Bill Schiess, the premier fly-fishing guide and outfitter on the lake, stated in a 2012 opening day report in the Rexburg Standard Journal.

"This year we will cut the stocking from 1.3 million fingerlings to 750,000," Dan Garren, regional fishery manager, told Schiess. "Hopefully that will help the size increase as it has been getting smaller."

About half of the fish caught over the 2012 opening weekend were cutthroat between 16 and 18 inches. The others were larger cutthroat, cutthroat-rainbow hybrids and brook trout, Schiess stated. His focus, and that of other longtime devotees of the lake, is on ensuring the trophy size and numbers of cutthroat-rainbow hybrids.

"We saw and heard of a lot of nice brook trout taken over the (2012) weekend," said Jessica Buelow, the new manager of the Henry's Lake Hatchery. "We will keep the brook stocking at the same numbers, but will also stock sterile males and not just females. We also believe there is natural spawning taking place with the brooks (in the lake's tributaries) that help the numbers of them."

Members of the Henry's Lake Foundation jealously guard and protect the lake. In cooperation with local landowners and Fish and Game, they have worked hard to preserve its future.

Riparian improvement projects like willow planting and cattle fencing along tributary creeks are bearing fruit. Preliminary studies show a two-to-one ratio of wild trout to hatchery fish going into the creel.

The two biggest threats to the lake are nutrient overloading from increased local housing developments and drought. Low water reduces natural spawning, particularly by brook trout. Combined with plant growth, it can be deadly. An algae bloom in 1991 caused massive winter kill. Giant aerators are now placed on the lake's ice in winter to increase the dissolved oxygen content of the water. The North Fork Canal Company retains the lake's fall water levels as high as it possibly can.

Discovery of chubs in the lake in 1993 is another problem that requires close monitoring.

"Even with its problems, Henry's is still chugging along with arguably the best lake fishing in the world. I can't think of any better," says Mark Gamblin, former regional fisheries manager.

While there is a two-fish limit on the lake and its tributaries, most anglers voluntarily practice catch-and-release. Harvest rates in 1994 were only 42 percent for cutthroat and 12 percent for hybrids. Fish and Game biologists are surprised by the light harvest, but pleased.

Henry's Lake

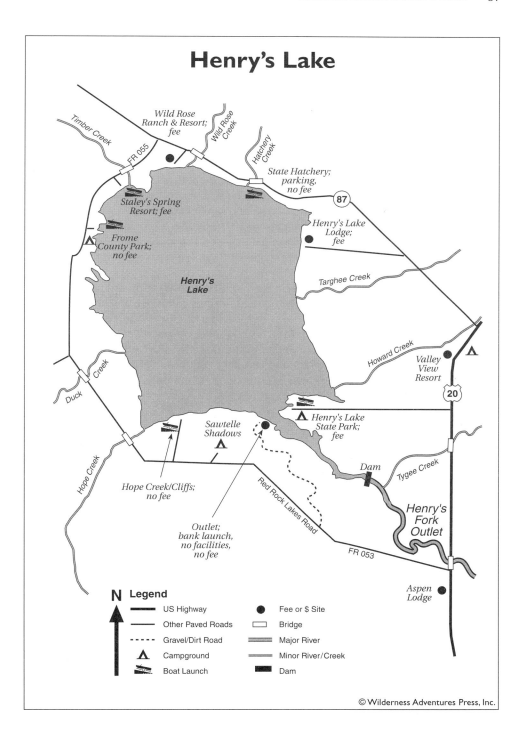

Timber Creek

Wild Rose
Ranch & Resort;
fee

Wild Rose Creek

Hatchery Creek

FR 055

State Hatchery;
parking,
no fee

87

Staley's Spring
Resort; fee

Frome
County Park;
no fee

Henry's Lake
Lodge;
fee

Henry's
Lake

Targhee Creek

Howard Creek

Valley
View
Resort

20

Duck Creek

Sawtelle
Shadows

Henry's Lake
State Park;
fee

Hope Creek

Dam

Tygee Creek

Hope Creek/Cliffs;
no fee

Red Rock Lakes Road

Outlet;
bank launch,
no facilities,
no fee

Henry's
Fork
Outlet

FR 053

Aspen
Lodge

N Legend

▬▬ US Highway		●	Fee or $ Site
— Other Paved Roads		▭	Bridge
- - - - Gravel/Dirt Road		▬▬	Major River
⛺ Campground		▬▬	Minor River/Creek
🚤 Boat Launch		▬▬	Dam

© Wilderness Adventures Press, Inc.

"Exploitation of 20 to 30 percent is more common on most lakes, but catch-and-release is common with a premiere fishery, which leads to the quality of the fishery," says Gamblin.

Henry's Lake and the Henry's Fork are named for Andrew Henry, a partner in the Missouri Fur Company. He led the first party of trappers into Idaho in 1810 after several deadly confrontations with the Blackfeet Indians in the Three Forks area on the upper Missouri River. The mountain men came up the Madison River and crossed the Centennial Mountains at Raynolds Pass, just to the north of Henry's Lake. They spent a hard winter in a camp near St. Anthony.

Surrounded on three sides by the Continental Divide traversing Yellowstone, the lake was smaller and shallower in those days. Its average depth was only five feet. Pioneer tales often mention its strange floating islands. These boggy masses of aquatic vegetation with grass growing on them mysteriously rose and sank in the lake.

Modern anglers, whose hooks become mired in the thick growth of aquatic plants by late-summer, appreciate the legend, even if they don't always believe it. A dam placed across the outlet in 1923 increased the average depth to 12 feet and its size to 6,500 acres. At its deepest point, its depth is about 25 feet.

Henry's Lake is shaped like a giant catcher's mitt, four miles wide and five miles long, and captures the flows of seven major tributaries. Springs in the lake and along its shores help moderate water temperatures year-round. The outlet's flows from its southeast corner join the Big Spring flows of the Henry's Fork 12 miles downstream.

There is public access to the upper end of the Henry's Lake Outlet where it crosses under U.S. Highway 20. It can hold some very large cutthroat, especially in wet years when they sometimes come over the lake's dam in great numbers. The first 400 yards of the outlet is closed to fishing.

When the dam increased the lake's size, it bolstered its productivity by creating shallow rearing areas for aquatic insects and fish. The lake's food chain is loaded with freshwater shrimp (also called scuds), leeches, damselfly and dragonfly nymphs, and a host of plankton, water fleas, mayflies, caddis, and midges. The latter are minor players in fishing strategies for the lake. It is possible to take fish on dry flies, but virtually all the action is with wet flies.

The most popular patterns are scuds, damselfly nymphs, leeches, woolly buggers, crystal buggers, and the Henry's Lake renegade, which has a red rib around the peacock herl. Streamer patterns for dace and sculpin, and even long slender ones for leeches, work as well, especially in fall when brookies are most active.

Generally, wet fly sizes for Henry's Lake are a little bigger than stream patterns because they are tied on long-shanked hooks. Leeches in brown, light olive, or Canadian red perform best in No. 4 and 6 Green scuds and damsel nymphs are No. 8 to 12 woolly buggers, crystal buggers, and streamers are No. 8 to 10.

Woolly buggers and crystal buggers come in red, Canadian red, black, purple, orange, olive, and brown, as well as the Halloween series of variegated colors perfected by Schiess. Ultimately, the prime colors may be greens and olives because the principal food sources are leeches, damselfly nymphs, and scuds. The damselfly hatch, the only real one on the lake, is in late-June to mid-July. Scuds and leeches are in the lake year-round.

Full sinking lines or sinking tips work best. Schiess prefers the old Wet Cell series of sinking lines. He says the belly of a Wet Cell III line sinks first and outperforms uniform sink lines six to one. He uses it in water eight to 15 feet deep. In water under eight feet, he uses Wet Cell II. For water over 15 feet, he uses Wet Cell IV.

The key to catching lake fish is to keep the fly down where they are. Keep leaders as short and as strong as conditions permit. An effective method of fly retrieval is to follow a strip, strip, pause rhythm. Keep the rod tip low or in the water. Set the hook by snapping the line in by hand, instead of raising the rod overhead. Otherwise, if it is a miss, the line has to settle to the right depth again.

When aquatic plant growth is high, cast into the channels between the weeds, or work areas where there are still two or three feet of water above the weeds. Schiess and other outfitters have extensively mapped the lake, pinpointing the major holding areas for big fish throughout the season. Many of these areas are found near underwater springs.

Henry's Lake is subject to sudden storms or strong winds. These can kick up high waves because of its shallow depths. Float-tubers should exercise caution and not over-extend themselves. Winds can force you to drift far across the lake and make it difficult to get back. A graphite rod can act as a conductor for electricity. Wait out storms from shore.

U.S. Highway 20 skirts the lake on the east and U.S. Highway 87 on the north. Forest roads circle the west and south shores.

There are eight fishing access sites on the lake, and a boat can be launched from all but one. Half are on public land. The other four, including Henry's Lake State Park and the Staley's Spring "Glory Hole," charge a fee to launch a boat or float-tube.

Six outfitters offer power boat or float-tube guiding services on the lake. Three are based in Island Park, one in Ashton, and two in West Yellowstone, Montana.

Public camping is available at Henry's Lake State Park on the southeast bank and Frome County Park on the west bank. There are a number of resorts, lodges, RV parks, and private campgrounds on the lake.

Further accommodations and services are available at Valley View, just to the east of the lake. It is the top village in the 33-mile Island Park complex along Highway 20. There are numerous campgrounds in this area. Ten miles to the northeast, over Targhee Pass, is West Yellowstone. Idaho Falls is about 95 miles to the south.

No matter where you choose to roost, the lake will beckon long after its daily 9 p.m.closing. Catching one of its brawny trout is a truly religious experience in one of nature's most exhilarating cathedrals.

Henry's Lake State Park

Just 15 miles west of Yellowstone National Park, Henry's Lake State Park is located on the southeast corner of the lake, a mile west of U.S. 20.

The park opens the Thursday before Memorial Day and closes October 31, or as weather conditions warrant. After September 15 it is wise to call ahead to see which services are available.

A boat ramp and docks are available in the park.

The park offers 45 campsites of which 26 sites have water and electricity and the remaining sites have central water. Twenty seven sites are reservable from spring opening through Labor Day.

For camping reservations call 558-7532.

Lake Facts: Henry's Lake

SEASONS
- Henry's Lake: from Saturday of Memorial Day weekend through Jan. 1 of next year
- Tributary Creeks: April 1 through June 30, closed to fishing; Hatchery Creek closed to fishing year-round
- Henry's Lake Outlet below the dam, open to fishing year-round

SPECIAL REGULATIONS
- Henry's Lake: Trout limit is 2, brook trout must be counted in trout limit
- Tributary Creeks: July 1 through March 31, no harvest of cutthroat; brook trout limit is 25, only 2 over 16 inches
- Henry's Lake Outlet below the dam, winter fishery is catch-and-release only; from Memorial Day weekend through Nov. 30, trout limit is 6, only 2 may be cutthroat over 16 inches

TROUT
- Yellowstone cutthroat, cutthroat-rainbow hybrids, and brook trout. Average mean size for hybrids is 19" and 16" for cutthroat and brook trout. Potential for trophy fish with all three species

LAKE SIZE
- 6,500 acres, 4 miles wide and 5 miles long
- Average depth of 12 feet, deepest point about 25 feet

LAKE CHARACTER
- Sits at 6,470 feet of elevation in bowl at base of Centennial Mountains on the Continental Divide. Can experience violent storms and high winds, which cause heavy wave action on shallow waters.

SIDE ROADS
- Gravel Forest Road, No. 055, skirts west shore
- Red Rock Lakes Road, Forest Road No. 053, skirts south shore

MAPS
- Targhee National Forest map for Island Park District

Island Park Reservoir

An irrigation impoundment on the Henry's Fork, Island Park Reservoir has had a checkered history as a trout producer.

Due to widely fluctuating water levels, it has a mean surface area of 8,400 acres. But at the height of the drought in 1992, the reservoir was drawn down to the original stream bed. This was the first time it was drained since it flooded Shotgun Valley in 1939.

Idaho Fish and Game took advantage of the drawdown to poison the latest infestation of nongame fish like chubs and suckers. The reservoir was restocked with rainbows, rainbow-cutthroat hybrids, Lahontan cutthroats, and kokanee salmon, but it only recently began to make a comeback.

The slowness of its recovery was partially due to continued flushing of trout through the dam during high irrigation releases. But that problem should be reduced since the dam has been modified for hydropower generation. The penstock to the generator is screened and a collar was put on the dam to limit spillover.

The dam blocks the head of Box Canyon, the most important rainbow trout factory on the Henry's Fork, and concerns have been raised about the effects of fish flushing on the river's fishery.

Mark Gamblin, former Region 6 fisheries manager, remains optimistic about the reservoir's future if good water years continue. "Island Park Reservoir is not much different than Henry's Lake in terms of nutrition. Given a chance, it can grow fish very well and very fast," he said.

"There are 2- to 5-pound rainbows and 2- to 3-pound kokanee in there, but you have to know where to look for them. And big whitefish. A 22.5-inch whitefish was caught in the reservoir in 1997, a new Idaho and world record. It weighed 5 pounds, 14.4 ounces."

Fish and Game completed a new management plan for the reservoir in 2006. The plan calls for increased rainbow trout fingerling stocking from just under 300,000 to 750,000. Unfortunately, severe reservoir drawdowns will still hinder the fishery, but Fish and Game biologists expect the increase in fingerlings will result in much better fishing during those years when more water is kept in the reservoir through the winter.

To evaluate the current fishery, including catch rates, harvest, and total effort, Fish and Game bi-ologists conducted a year-long creel survey in 2007. They were pleased to see the fishing has improved significantly since the last survey in 1994, and was much better than what anglers have reported in recent years. This is not entirely unexpected given the reservoir was over half full going into the winter of 2006-07.

The 2007 creel survey showed overall catch rates were 0.5 fish per hour (one fish per 2 rod-hours of effort). This is just shy of the goal for the reservoir (0.6 fish/hour), but is still considered good fishing on most stillwaters and is, in fact, the highest we've seen since 1980.

Additionally, 16 percent of the rainbows exceeded 20 inches, indicating an excellent fishery for large fish. Rainbows up to 10 pounds were caught in 2007, and 5- to 6-pound fish were not uncommon. Approximately 15,000 fish were harvested on Island Park in 2007 and another 7,000 fish were caught and released. Fishing effort was estimated at approximately 45,000 hours.

Trollers and bait anglers did well most of the year and fly angling was good from early summer on. The west end of the reservoir had most of the angling effort throughout the year.

The one downside noted in 2007 was with kokanee. Although the average size was 17 inches, total harvest was estimated at less than 250. This is the unfortunate result of severe drawdown and low fry plants (due to availability) from 2003 to 2005. Fry plants those three years averaged 160,000.

The good news is that kokanee plants in 2006 and 2007 averaged over a half million per year. With favorable water conditions, kokanee catch rates continued to rebound in the 2008 and 2009 high water years.

The inconsistency of Island Park Reservoir has caused it to be overlooked by some anglers. The 2007 season shows that it still has the potential to grow big trout and a lot of them. With the increase in stocking rates and better winter carryover in 2008 and 2009, anglers would do well to keep an eye on this productive fishery.

The reservoir is difficult to fish when it is high because the trout and salmon are so spread out. Its best fishing is usually in fall when water levels are down and the fish are more concentrated and actively feeding in preparation for winter.

Float-tubers and shoreline fly casters favor the coves and points that line the Grizzly Springs and Fingers areas of the reservoir near the West End Campground. It can be reached by taking Green Canyon Road, which skirts the southwestern boundary of Harriman State Park. It also ties in with the Old Kilgore Road in Shotgun Valley.

The upper backwaters of the reservoir above the McCrea Bridge on the Yale-Kilgore Road is another area popular with fly fishers, particularly when the kokanee begin their late-summer spawning run up through Coffee Pot Rapids to Moose Creek. Large rainbows and cutthroat follow the salmon out of the reservoir to their staging area in the rapids.

In 2002, regulations for Island Park Reservoir and many other stillwaters in Idaho came under the new classification of "family fishing waters." Fish and Game states: "These are designed to be easy to use (regulations), and waters were selected which provide settings for a great fishing trip for families, kids and first-time anglers."

Regulations for designated "family fishing waters" are:
- Year-round season
- General six-fish limit for trout, kokanee salmon, bass, walleye, and pike
- No bag limits on other species
- No length limits
- Standard fishing gear

Effective patterns for Island Park Reservoir

There is a damselfly hatch in late-June and early July. Green damsel nymphs and woolly buggers can be effective at this time as well as later in the season by working the shoreline weed beds. Other wet flies can include scuds, small nymphs, leeches, and streamers. Dry fly action is often sporadic and can be covered with a basic selection of elk hair caddis and stimulators and generic mayfly patterns like the Adams and Cahills.

Island Park Reservoir

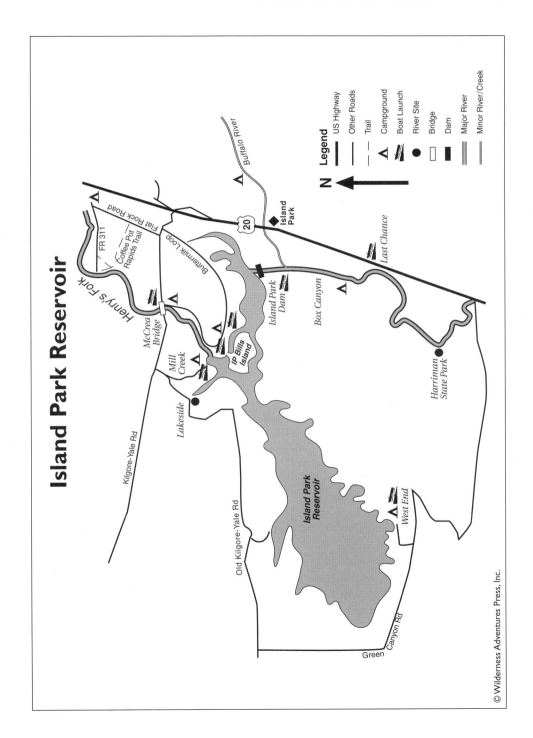

Legend

N

	US Highway
	Other Roads
	Trail
▲	Campground
	Boat Launch
●	River Site
□	Bridge
■	Dam
	Major River
	Minor River/Creek

Buffalo River

Island Park

Last Chance

Box Canyon

Island Park Dam

IP Bills Island

McCrea Bridge

Mill Creek

Lakeside

Coffee Pot Rapids Trail

Flat Rock Road

FR 311

Henry's Fork

Buttermilk Loop

20

Kilgore-Yale Rd

Old Kilgore-Yale Rd

Island Park Reservoir

Harriman State Park

West End

Green

Canyon Rd

© Wilderness Adventures Press, Inc.

Two Fish Vie for Idaho Record Book

Two cold water fish species caught in eastern Idaho waters were candidates for the Idaho Record Book in 1997.

One made it. The other was excluded because of concerns that attempts to break a record would hinder efforts to protect and recover a threatened species.

The new Idaho record mountain whitefish caught in Island Park Reservoir also is a world record. The other large fish, a bull trout/brook trout hybrid caught in the Little Lost River Drainage, would have required a new classification in the *Idaho Record Book*.

Robert K. Hall, of Glenns Ferry, caught his five-pound, 14.4-ounce mountain whitefish at Island Park Reservoir in August. The whitefish measured 22.5 inches long with a girth of 14 inches. Hall took the huge whitefish on a caddis nymph, using an eight-pound tippet and casting with a graphite fly rod.

A call from Fish and Game headquarters to the Freshwater Fishing Hall of Fame in the Midwest confirmed this mountain whitefish is the current world record. In fact, the old Idaho record whitefish may also have been a world record.

Idaho's old record was five pounds, four ounces for a fish taken in 1941 from the South Fork of the Payette River. The angler was not recorded in that catch.

Hall said his world-record whitefish is a testament to fisheries management, particularly at Island Park Reservoir.

The impoundment on the Henry's Fork of the Snake River has had a checkered career in big fish catches, but Fish and Game managers persistently maintain it produces as well or better than its famous sister, Henry's Lake. They caution, however, that Island Park Reservoir requires a more dedicated angler to solve its mysteries.

"I think the fishing is wonderful in Island Park," Hall told the *Post Register*. He noted he also caught a 10.5-pound cutthroat-rainbow hybrid from the reservoir the same summer.

"The fishing is very good and there are a lot less people than Henry's Lake," said Hall, a former president of the Henry's Lake Foundation.

Idaho's previous record whitefish was not documented as a world record, too, because the North American Freshwater Fishing Hall of Fame does not scan state records, said Mark Gamblin, former Region 6 fisheries manager.

"That also reflects a disdain that people have for whitefish," Bill Horton, resident fisheries manager, told the *Post Register*. "And that is unfortunate because they are a very good fighting fish for a very short time."

Hall agreed. He said he thought his record catch was anything but a whitefish even after he landed it.

"It was so large, I thought it had to be something else."

Meanwhile, the bull trout/brook trout hybrid record catch came from a beaver pond in north-central Custer County, west of Howe. Bull trout and brook trout are species in the char family, *Salvelinus*, which includes lake trout, Dolly Varden and Arctic char.

Boyd Burnett, of Moore, caught the eight-pound, 8.8-ounce brook trout-bull trout hybrid in a high mountain beaver pond, also in August. The hybrid fish was 24.5 inches long with a 16.5-inch girth. It was caught on a spinner lure.

It was at first thought to be a pure brook trout but later DNA testing showed it was a combination of species.

One of the problems in protecting the native bull trout, which is listed as a threatened species under the Endangered Species Act, is that it can inter-breed with brook trout that were introduced from the East by white settlers. But such interbreeding has been rarely documented in the wild.

Brook trout also interbreed with lake trout, another member of the char family not native to Idaho. Hatchery production of this hybrid, called splake, is done to introduce a fast-growing fish to put-and-take lakes. Only a few Idaho lakes have been stocked with splake.

Burnett's bull trout/brook trout hybrid was not listed as a record fish in Fish and Game's fishing regulations pamphlet because of concerns about possible effects on bull trout populations. Anglers are reminded that har-vest of bull trout is prohibited and the fish must be released immediately. Attempting to top Burnett's feat requires extreme caution and careful identi-fication of fish. When in doubt, let it go.

The department's fishing rules booklet contains color pictures of game fish to aid anglers in identification. A list of all record fish caught in Idaho also is included.

For example, attempts to break the brook trout record are still possible in eastern Idaho.

Idaho's largest brook trout was produced by Henry's Lake, due north of Island Park Reservoir. DeVere Stratton, of Idaho Falls, scored the state's brook trout record (seven pounds, 1 ounce, 23.5 inches) in 1978. Ironically, he could have broken the previous record twice in the same month. He caught a slightly smaller brook trout in Henry's Lake the previous week but failed to have it recorded.

Idaho's record bull trout (formerly listed as Dolly Varden) was 32 pounds. It was caught in Pend Oreille Lake by Nelson Higgins in 1949.

The beauty of the hike into the Bechler River, a tributary of the Fall River in Yellowstone National Park, is why Rob Thornberry is grinning. The rainbow is a bonus. Rob Thornberry photo.

There are things that are really special about fishing remote water—willing trout, beautiful country, and solitude.

Jimmy Gabettas: owner,
All Seasons Angler, Idaho Falls

Off the Beaten Track

Headwater tributaries hold pleasant surprises

A well-kept secret of Yellowstone National Park is the feisty rainbow and cutthroat trout of Bechler Meadows.

En route to Bechler Meadows and the scenic Cave Falls in the little-known southwest corner of Yellowstone, are three of Idaho's finest small-stream fishing experiences. A bonus is an isolated crystal clear lake with a rare population of grayling.

Bechler River flows into Fall River just above Cave Falls in the park, 25 miles east of Ashton. The Fall River, a tributary of the Henry's Fork, joins its famous stepsister at Chester Reservoir, 10 miles upstream from St. Anthony. Over a couple of ridges from Fall River is the Warm River, which joins the Henry's Fork downstream from Mesa Falls, 10 miles west of Ashton. In between, feeding into the Warm River, is Robinson Creek.

Horseshoe Lake, the other jaunt off the beaten track on this escape trip, abuts the park boundary, seven miles north of Cave Falls Road.

Fishing these waters is a fairly straightforward proposition. Backcountry trout are often less wary than those pounded unmercifully on better known streams. While public access is excellent, some of the better, solitary fishing requires rock scrambling or cross-country bushwhacking. This is also grizzly bear country. It is best to travel in parties of three or more and keep a clean camp.

At the end of the rainbow are wild trout, mostly in the 9- to 15-inch range, in spectacular alpine country. Views of the Teton Mountains pop up in the east as you come out of a canyon or crest a rise in the trail.

Effective patterns for the Fall, Warm, and Bechler rivers and Robinson Creek

Hit these waters at the right time and you will enjoy virtually undisturbed stonefly fishing. Elk hair caddis, stimulators, humpies, and other fast-water attractor patterns continue to work through the season, along with stonefly nymphs, woolly buggers, and standard nymphs like hare's ears and caddis emergers.

Mayfly hatches are not well documented, but you can look for them on slow-water stretches. Carry a selection of pale morning duns and blue-winged olive as well as back-ups like Adams, Cahills, small Wullfs, and renegades. Don't forget grasshoppers, ants, and beetles.

The only nitty-gritty, match-the-hatch situation you may encounter is in the Bechler Meadows. Elsewhere, if you aren't hitting, move on to better waters. If it still isn't happening, move on again. Remember, this is get-away-from-it-all country. Explore. Have fun.

BECHLER RIVER

The Bechler River descends for about 20 miles through the southwestern corner of Yellowstone. Its tumbling upper reach holds small rainbows and cutthroat. The three-mile, slow-water meadow stretch harbors fair numbers of rainbows in the 16- to 18-inch class and fair-sized cutthroat. Below the meadows, the river gallops down a rocky incline into the Fall River.

Overall, the fishery is continuing to improve as the Bechler and other streams benefit from the park's catch-and-release regulations for both cutthroat and rainbows.

It is mostly bank fishing in Bechler Meadows because the clear waters of its branching channels are deceptively deep. Grassy, overhanging banks and deep pools on the cutbank sides of the stream are prime holding areas for large trout. It is a spring creek fishery that requires fine leader tippets and refined presentations. Try to work to rising fish, early and late in the day. Prospecting in late-summer with grasshoppers can be fruitful.

You can fish it any time during the park's short season from late-May to October. In heavy snowpack years, the meadows can be wet and more difficult to hike. Mosquitoes and deer flies can be a problem as late as August.

The five-mile trail to the meadows starts from the Bechler Ranger Station. The park now charges a fee for its fishing permit, which is available at visitor centers or local fishing tackle shops.

A backcountry permit is required to camp overnight at designated campgrounds. For day hikes into the meadows, you can set up a base camp at a Targhee National Forest campground at Cave Falls. It fills fast in mid-summer, so get there early. In spring and fall, it is largely deserted.

To reach the Bechler Ranger Station, turn east off U.S. 20 onto State Highway 47 at Ashton. Turn east onto Cave Falls Road at the sign about six miles east of town.

FALL RIVER

Headwaters of the Fall River rise at an altitude of 8,500 feet on the south slopes of the Pitchstone Plateau in Yellowstone.

On its 50-mile southwesterly course to the Henry's Fork, it descends to an elevation of 5,030 feet at its mouth. The average rate of descent is more than 50 feet per mile. Its canyon is often deep and picturesque.

Flows average 730 cubic feet per second after spring runoff, which can be very high and muddy. Irrigation diversions can almost dry up the lower river in drought years.

The first 18 miles of the river flows through the park, where it plunges over Cave Falls. The next few miles dip into a corner of Wyoming before crossing into Idaho, two miles upstream from Sheep Falls.

The lower Fall River is an excellent fishery, overshadowed by its famous sisters in eastern Idaho. Michelle Retallic photo.

While it is listed on most maps as the Falls River, its name was officially changed to Fall River by the U.S. Geological Service in the mid-1980s to agree with the name local residents use for the river.

The many waterfalls along its course are the source of the original name of the river. For anglers, the name reflects the chance that you might take a tumble in its refreshing waters. It is tough wading—more difficult even than Box Canyon on the Henry's Fork. Felt-bottomed boots are necessary to negotiate its slick basalt lava streambed carpeted with slippery cobblestones. The lower section is shallower, with fewer rapids and pocket waters.

The upper river holds mostly cutthroat and its lower reaches hold rainbows and a few cutthroat-rainbow hybrids. Most are in the 9- to 15-inch range, with a few exceeding 20 inches. The lower river can offer up some surprisingly big fish from the plunge holes in the heavily eroded lava chutes above and below the U.S. 20 Bridge. Watch your step and be prepared for a line-sizzling tussle, especially if a hybrid takes the fly.

Idaho Fish and Game estimates there are 2,500 fish per mile below the Targhee National Forest boundary. It has been managing the river as a wild trout fishery, with a two-fish bag limit, since 1988. At that time it closed the river's popular winter fishing season.

Hatches on the river haven't been dated very well, but it has them all. Stock your fishing vest pockets with PMDs, BWOs, Adams, Cahills, elk hair caddis, stimulators, and other attractor patterns. Its excellent stonefly hatch in late-June draws the most attention from local anglers. Many return in late-summer for the grasshopper season, or fish it in fall with streamers. There is a good BWO, or Baetis, hatch in the fall that can bring up 18-inch rainbows.

Dark stonefly and golden stone nymphs work throughout the season, along with rubber-legs and woolly buggers. The Fall River Flasher, in green or brown, is a popular variation on the woolly bugger theme. It has a chenille body and rainbow crystal strands tied along the sides of its marabou tail. The matching-color saddle hackle is wrapped only on the head of the fly. It is also a good pattern on other fast-water streams.

There are no guided fishing services on the Fall River. The lower river can be floated easily below the State Highway 32 Bridge. The pull-out is Chester Dam on the Henry's Fork. Water flows can be low during the summer irrigation season. There is a low-head diversion dam about five miles downstream from the put-in. The most turbulent stretch is the string of lava chutes just above and below the U.S. 20 Bridge. Wading access is available at all three of these locations.

The mouth of the canyon can be reached from a county road that skirts the south bank. Turn east at the Fall River General Store on U.S. 20. At a bridge about four miles upstream, stick to the gravel road that follows the south bank. The upper end of this road climbs out of the canyon and winds through farmland to State Highway 32.

Trying to float the upper river is not a good idea. It is popular with whitewater kayakers during spring runoff.

Fishing in Yellowstone below Cave Falls requires a park permit. In Idaho, forest roads that turn south off Cave Falls Road lead to the north rim of the upper canyon. There are no developed trails down to the river, but you can bushwhack into it from several locations.

A turn-off to the south on Cave Falls Road, a mile east of the forest boundary, leads to a bridge and the Reclamation Road. This is a primitive road that goes from Ashton to Flagg Ranch, Grand Teton National Park, and the South Entrance to Yellowstone. There are a few jeep trails to the upper canyon from Reclamation Road.

If you turn west at this intersection, a high bridge crosses the river about five miles downstream. The canyon is very deep here, but you can scramble down from the bridge to reach the river. It is easier to wade downstream from the bridge. Upstream is a small hydropower plant on the north bank that takes water from the river through a diversion canal and penstock. A construction accident in 1992 dumped huge amounts of sediment into the river, but it seems to have been flushed out by the river's high spring flows.

This bridge can be reached from the west by turning south from State Highway 47 at the hamlet of Marysville, two miles east of Ashton.

A mile west of this bridge, a county road turns south off Reclamation Road to the river and a low bridge crossing it.

The Fall River is a joy to fish. Anywhere else in the world, without so many better-known waters nearby, it would be a destination stream in its own right. It should continue to improve with wild trout management.

From Dec. 1 through Friday before Memorial Day weekend, trout limit is zero, catch and release only. From Memorial Day weekend through Nov. 30, the trout limit is 2; none may be cutthroat.

Ken Retallic on the Fall River. Michelle Retallic photo.

HORSESHOE LAKE

The main drawing card of Horseshoe Lake is the graylings found in its deep, cool waters.

Rare in Idaho waters, these are hatchery plants that are doing fairly well in the pristine lake on the west border of Yellowstone. Sizes run in the 10- to 12-inch range. A beautiful silvery fish whose colors seem to change with the light, the grayling can be distinguished from whitefish by its large, sail-like dorsal fin. It puts up a scrappy but short-lived fight. The grayling has a small, delicate mouth, so small flies work best. When it takes a dry fly, it will rocket straight out of the water and snatch it on the way down.

The lake also has a good population of rainbows, renewed each year by hatchery plants. The largest never seem to get much bigger than 15 inches.

Horseshoe Lake is an excellent side trip or family outing. Only about five acres in size, it is perfect for canoers and float-tubers. Wading is difficult because it drops off quickly. Its more shallow south end is often choked with pond lilies and fallen lodgepole pine. Best bet is to float out and cast to the lilies, or use sinking lines to probe its depths.

There are a few mayfly hatches and its caddis hatch can be strong at times, but small wet flies for lake insects and invertebrates, fished deep, usually work best.

Access to the lake is from the Cave Falls Road. Watch for the sign about five miles after you pass the Targhee National Forest boundary line. There is a small, primitive campground on the west shore. Launch your canoes or float-tubes there. There is an Idaho Youth Training Camp on the east shore, but you can enter the lake south of it.

ROBINSON CREEK

Robinson Creek is a prototypical mountain stream, perfect for anglers who like to fish small waters in solitude. Its headwaters rise in Yellowstone and it flows into Idaho just north of Horseshoe Lake. Its mouth is at the end of a deep canyon, where it flows into the Warm River a half-mile upstream from the Henry's Fork.

After the spring runoff drops and the creek clears, usually by mid-June, the fish are fairly easy to catch. Later in the season, the larger rainbows and brown trout become more selective and the fishing becomes more challenging.

It is possible to take cutthroat, rainbow, brown or brook trout, and whitefish in a single day on the creek. Most are pan size, but a few exceptional trout proffer pleasant surprises.

Fly fishers do well on mayfly, caddis, and attractor dry flies, and small nymphs. There is a good population of stoneflies, although nymphs are more effective throughout the season. Streamers work for browns in the deeper holes.

While the stream is comfortable to wade, it is not always easy to get down the steep slopes of its heavily wooded canyon. A trail above Horseshoe Lake is one way to get into the upper canyon. There are a number of forest roads that lead to the creek, but most have gates on them and you have to hike in.

Fall, Warm, Bechler Rivers & Robinson Creek

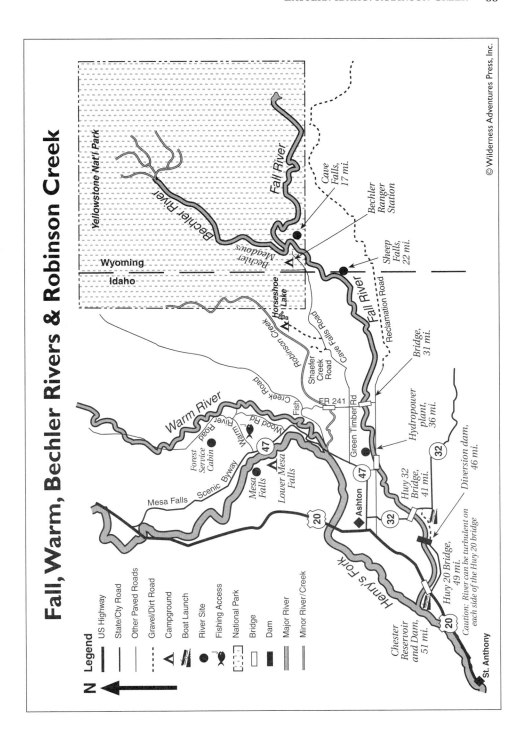

Legend

US Highway	
State/Cty Road	
Other Paved Roads	
Gravel/Dirt Road	
Campground	
Boat Launch	
River Site	
Fishing Access	
National Park	
Bridge	
Dam	
Major River	
Minor River/Creek	

N

Yellowstone Nat'l Park

Bechler River

Wyoming
Idaho

Bechler Meadows

Horseshoe Lake

Fall River

Cave Falls, 17 mi.

Bechler Ranger Station

Sheep Falls, 22 mi.

Reclamation Road

Robinson Creek

Cave Falls Road

Shaefer Creek Road

Fall River

Bridge, 31 mi.

Warm River

Fish Creek Road

FR 241

Forest Service Cabin

Warm River Road

Wood Rd

47

Mesa Falls

Scenic Byway

Mesa Falls

Lower Mesa Falls

Green Timber Rd

Hydropower plant, 36 mi.

32

Ashton

47

20

32

Huy 32 Bridge, 41 mi.

Diversion dam, 46 mi.

20

Henry's Fork

Huy 20 Bridge, 49 mi.

Caution: River can be turbulent on each side of the Huy 20 bridge

Chester Reservoir and Dam, 51 mi.

St. Anthony

A county road a mile east of the forest boundary turns north to the only bridge crossing the creek. There are long, meandering glides and pools upstream from the bridge. Below it, the river enters a deep, high-walled canyon. Its banks can be negotiated, although you have to cope with thick willows and other brush in places. This road continues to Fish Creek Road, which turns west to Warm River or back to State Highway 47.

WARM RIVER

The Warm River is a charming, spring-fed stream that tumbles almost due south through a scenic canyon for about 20 miles before it turns abruptly west and joins the Henry's Fork.

It is the perfect place to learn fly fishing. The lower river is stocked with hatchery rainbows and is very popular with families. Small, juvenile brown trout also can be found in the lower river.

Above Warm River Springs it has mostly small brook trout.

A campground two miles above its mouth is one of the prettiest in the West. Parking for anglers and picnic tables are available at the campground. It can be reached by taking the Scenic Mesa Falls Highway 47 east from Ashton or south from Island Park.

To get away from the crowds fishing at the campground, hike or bike up an abandoned railroad grade. You can scramble down to the river anywhere along this trail, or continue north, passing through a tunnel, to reach the river's upper canyon.

Another way into the top of the canyon is to take the Warm Springs Road east off Highway 47 and park at the old hatchery site. A cabin by the huge spring gushing out of the canyon wall can be rented from the Forest Service. It is an idyllic setting with good opportunities to see wildlife. Moose are common.

Hike down from the spring's parking lot for the best fishing on the river for 12- to 15-inch rainbows. The river drops 200 feet in 1.5 miles midway through the canyon, but you can still probe its pools and pocket waters from the bank.

Small mayfly, caddis, and attractor patterns, and small nymphs, like soft-hackle caddis emergers and hare's ears, work well. The river gets good PMD and BWO hatches on its lower waters, which are more fun to fish after summer crowds depart.

From Dec. 1 through Friday before Memorial Day weekend, trout limit is zero, catch and release only. From Memorial Day weekend through Nov. 30, the trout limit is 6; none may be cutthroat.

In the Teton Canyon, big fish on big flies says it all.

Rob Thornberry, Editor
Intermountain Hunting and Fishing

Teton River

Undiscovered in the Shadow of Fame

With the majestic Teton Mountains looming against the valley's eastern horizon, the Teton River is the most scenic trout stream in North America.

Its trout match the picture-postcard memories of a day on this remarkable, little-known river. Trophy-sized Yellowstone cutthroat and rainbow trout lurk in the meandering meadow stream of the upper basin and the raging pocket waters of the narrow, high-walled canyon. A few holdover brook trout from a long ago stocking program can be found in the upper valley.

Halfway between the South Fork and Henry's Fork of the Snake River, the Teton is a Cinderella stream often ignored by anglers intent on testing its more famous step-sisters. They are missing the boat. If there was ever a side trip made in heaven, this is it. On a

With the west face of the Teton Mountains in the background, the Teton River's upper valley is the most scenic fishing experience in the West.

good day, the Teton can outshine either of its stellar sisters with surprisingly exceptional fish in both the valley and the canyon. Like a lot of western rivers the Teton's character changes with the terrain, and the previous winter's snowpack plays a major role in how soon you can work the river. Heavy spring runoff in an exceptionally wet year can create high flows well into July, but in normal water years, flows stabilize by late-June.

The river's best season runs from July to October. Some like to end the season in the valley with a cast-and-blast outing, hunting for waterfowl or grouse in the morning and fishing in the afternoon.

The long glides of the meadow stream, with still pools, over-hanging banks, and occasional riffles, end just below State Highway 33, where the river enters its steep, narrow canyon. This is called Harrop's Bridge. End a valley float here. Waders can go a short way downstream during low flows and get back. Leave the rest between Harrop's Bridge and Felt Dam to the locals. In the canyon below Felt Dam, a float trip is not advised unless you go with someone knowledgeable at the helm.

Foot access routes into the canyon are limited. Wading is difficult and fishing its white-capped waters requires some rock scrambling. The reward is big fish on big flies, both dries and wets.

There is good public access for boaters and waders on the basin's slow-flowing waters. The number of big fish in the valley is increasing annually. Catching them requires more finesse with a more delicate selection of flies.

The Teton flows northwest about 75 miles from its headwater tributaries in the foot-hills of the Teton Mountain Range and Palisades Mountains to its confluence with the Henry's Fork of the Snake River. It descends from about 6,000 feet in the upper valley to 4,860 feet at the Henry's Fork. From where Trail and Pine Creeks join, just west of Victor, the Teton is a classic spring creek fishery flowing through a broad bowl. Sixty tributaries flowing off the Teton foothills and the Big Hole Mountains, on the west, feed the river and its small side channels. Lined in places by thick ranks of willows, the river meanders 30 miles in a northwesterly course through the valley from State Highway 31 to the State Highway 33 crossing.

Known as Pierre's Hole in fur trapper days, the valley was the scene of several annual trading fairs for mountain men and their Indian allies. The 1832 rendezvous ended in a pitched battle with the Blackfeet Indians.

Below Harrop's Bridge, the Teton turns west and plunges between 1,000-foot cliffs on its descent to the Henry's Fork. Its 25-mile gallop through the canyon is churned by huge boulders and plunge holes. The upper string of rumbled pocket waters and deep pools moderate about three-fourths of the way downstream, where the canyon widens and the river is cutting new meanders through deposited silt. In this quieter section there are longer glides and riffles, some minor rapids and braided channels.

The shaded south wall of the canyon is heavily forested on its upper end. Downstream, the north wall's sun-baked volcanic outcrops are eroded into sentinel towers and pock-marked domes more common to the deserts of the Southwest. Adding to the canyon's Old West dimensions is a healthy population of rattlesnakes. This may be unsettling to some, but generally they slink off long before you ever see them. On hot days, though, avoid shaded areas like rock shadows and thick bushes where snakes may be holed up to escape the heat.

Below the canyon mouth, the river flows a few miles though the broad Upper Snake River Plain before it splits into two forks. Both are essentially irrigation canals that flow about 10 miles to their junctures with the Henry's Fork.

The river's blue-ribbon trout fishing—of days past and once again—is overshadowed by its other claim to fame. The Teton's dubious distinction in history is that it is the only river the U.S. Bureau of Reclamation tried to dam and failed. The dam on the lower end of the canyon blew out June 5, 1976, as it was filling for the first time, three years after construction began. Its collapse was blamed on internal erosion of the core material.

All that is left is a huge, truncated pyramid of packed earth and gravel near the canyon mouth. It is a bizarre memorial to the 11 lives lost in the flood that swept across the plain and rampaged through the communities dotting the lower Teton, Henry's Fork and upper Snake River. The damage to fishery and wildlife habitat was immeasurable, especially to local residents who treasured the canyon as their own private hunting and fishing preserve.

For the most part, the canyon fishery has come back on its own, above and below the dam.

An angler fishes the lower canyon of the Teton River below the sheer walls of its remote canyon.

The lower Teton harbors the biggest cutthroat trout in Idaho. Electro-shocking surveys have brought up 25- and 26-inch fish. The mean length of cutthroat in the South Fork of the Teton is 14 inches, 13 inches in the canyon and nine inches in the valley. A unique strain of the Yellowstone cutthroat, the fish rear in the lower Henry's Fork and move up into the Teton. Idaho Fish and Game is looking for ways to protect this valuable resource. Part of the problem is that portions of the river are managed as irrigation canals. The other threat is hybridization with rainbows. An increasing number of cutthroat-rainbow hybrids 20 inches and larger provide exciting action for those who tackle the canyon.

There are two existing dams in the canyon. Felt Dam, a small hydropower operation that diverts a section of the river through a pipe, is four miles downstream from Harrop's Bridge. Linderman Dam, an irrigation diversion, is another 10 miles downstream. Both add to the complications of floating the canyon, which is not a good idea for newcomers anyway.

There are two public boat ramps on the canyon. Both were originally intended to serve the Teton Dam reservoir. The bottoms of both ramps are a bit rough because they were not intended to go all the way down to the stream channel. In wet weather, four-wheel-drive may be needed.

A popular access site on the south bank before the dam failed is no longer usable. The bottom of the Linderman Road was washed out in 1976.

Spring Hollow, the upstream ramp, is on the north bank about seven miles below Felt Dam. To reach it, turn west off State Highway 32, about 15.5 miles north of its intersection with State Highway 33 The turnoff to the gravel county road is just north of a railroad grain elevator. Keep bearing almost due west, sticking to the gravel at farm road forks. The pull-out is just above the failed Teton Dam, about 15 miles downstream.

The downstream ramp is on the south bank just above the breached dam. It can be reached by turning north off State Highway 33, about three miles east of Newdale at the sign for the dam overlook. To reach the ramp, turn east just before the parking lot onto a rough dirt road. It is about a mile to the first left into the canyon.

Out of five Teton River outfitters, only the Teton Valley Lodge based in Driggs, and Hyde Outfitters out of Idaho Falls, float the "Narrows" at the top of the canyon.

Its top run, starting below the mouth of Bitch Creek, requires a Herculean effort. Guides slide the float boats down the steep cliff, while their passengers scramble down the rocky, slippery slope. Teton Valley Lodge head guide Tom Fenger says only aluminum float boats provide enough friction to make the feat possible, although there is always a risk of the boat running away from them. The lodge wears out a boat a season to give eager fly fishers a shot at the upper Narrows. Its two other runs are relatively docile to reach because the lodge puts in at Spring Hollow and a private access site.

Adventurous floaters should not be foolhardy and attempt the Bitch Creek descent on their own. The better option is to hike down and explore the upper canyon on foot.

The Bitch Creek canyon is very difficult to wade downstream from State Highway 32, although it has good fishing for 15-inch trout. Upstream of the highway, it is a great little mountain stream and easier to handle. Get to it from roads in Targhee National Forest. You will need a Wyoming license if you cross the state line.

The Teton River's upper canyon is as remote as you'll find in eastern Idaho.

Another unmarked trail into the top of Teton Canyon is about a hundred yards below the gate on Powerline Road to the Felt Dam parking lot. Hard to find, it bears to the right and descends steeply down switchbacks to the mouth of Badger Creek. The walk down to the hydro dam is not worth the effort. River levels can change radically during dam operations.

To reach the Felt Dam parking lot, turn west off State Highway 32 at Felt onto Powerline Road, about three miles north of the State Highway 33 intersection. A turnoff on this road, six miles northwest of Felt, also provides public access to fish lower Badger Creek.

Serious fly fishers after big fish in the lower canyon should ignore the turn off to the old boat ramp and continue another 100 yards to a steep, rocky road that descends into the canyon to an irrigation pump. This road requires a four-wheel-drive vehicle with high clearance. If you don't have one, hike down. When you reach the bottom, walk crosscountry as far upstream as time allows. It is a tough walk, sometimes through thick, head-high stands of grass. The best fish are found where the canyon narrows and the river becomes more turbulent.

You can walk down from the gate on a gravel road just east of the overlook parking lot to fish below Teton Dam, although the view is exceptionally disappointing. The landscape is a barren waste of flood-washed debris, boulders, cobble stone and gravel cut by the new channel of the river. Just above the unused spillway arcing down the north canyon wall is a boulder-strewn hole that harbors monster fish. But the curved concrete ramp is an ironic testament to dams in the West. Spray-painted with graffiti, it is used by high school and college students as a used-tire roller derby. Quixotically, irrigators still routinely call for replacement of the dam in the same location.

The canyon's big fish reputation comes from its stonefly and grasshopper seasons. Savage hits on the stonefly hatch begin about the third week of June in the lower canyon and extend into July with an overlapping, prolific golden stone hatch. Depending on the weather, the grasshopper action runs from around late-July until September. Small hopper patterns can be very effective when the so-called Mormon cricket is present.

Caddis, humpy, stimulator, pale morning dun and Adams patterns also work on the canyon's quieter waters. Stonefly nymphs and variations on the theme, like woolly buggers and rubber-legs, are always good options as well as muddlers and streamers.

The Teton River Canyon offers one of the best early summer stonefly hatches in the West.

The bigger fish are found around the boulders and rocks of the fast-water stretches, under over-hanging banks and in the plunge holes eroded into the lava rock stream bed along the north cliff.

Fishing the basin's meadow stream is less adventurous but the payoff is just as rewarding. Some fear the valley's pastoral tranquility is destined for over-development. Its population is skyrocketing as people seek a less expensive place to live or play. Many are spilling over the Tetons from the western Wyoming resort town of Jackson.

Still, the upper Teton's serene beauty offers pleasant family oriented fishing opportunities. At the same time, it provides dry fly purists numerous challenges to take trophy trout feeding on tiny flies. It is a relatively shallow river, easy to float or wade after its spring rampage ends.

Wildlife and waterfowl are abundant along the river's banks and in the surrounding marshes.

The fish have displayed a series of comebacks since 1988, even at the height of a prolonged drought. That is when Idaho Fish and Game put to work a $1.7 million settlement it received from the federal government for fish and wildlife losses incurred by the Teton Dam failure. Most of it has been pumped into agreements with Teton Basin farmers and ranchers to fence stream banks against cattle intrusions, plant willows and obtain angler and hunter access. The U.S Soil and Conservation Service has been a major player in the upper Teton's restoration, although silt buildup is still a problem in portions of the stream.

The upper river was receiving hatchery plants of eight- to 12-inch rainbows as late as 1995, but Fish and Game has since switched this program to local ponds. No problem. The real action comes from wild populations of Yellowstone cutthroat and previously introduced rainbows.

Although, the upper Teton River Yellowstone cutthroat trout population has been depressed for a decade or more, it may be showing signs of improvement.

Catch and release fishing rules apply to cutthroat trout in the Teton River and its tributaries. All cutthroat trout caught must be immediately released unharmed.

The trout population in the upper Teton River is regularly monitored by electrofishing. Two reaches near Driggs have been surveyed periodically since 1987.

The 2005 combined survey results were a mix of good news and bad news. Fish and Game estimated 44 cutthroat trout per mile. Though this is only about a fourth of the 19-year average of 191 per mile, it was a four-fold increase from the record low 2003 estimate of 10 per mile.

The increase was the result of some much needed juvenile recruitment, which has suffered from years of drought.

The rainbow and hybrid population also improved to an estimated 517 fish per mile. This is the second highest number on record and double the long-term average of 264 per mile. Fish and Game esti-mated there were 242 brook trout per mile, which is the highest on record and 35 percent more than the long-term average of 179 per mile.

However, many see the burgeoning brook trout populations as yet another threat to the health of cutthroat populations in the drainage.

Fly hatches are rich and varied, typical of a spring creek fishery. An early season bonus is an extension of the stonefly hatch up into the lower basin.

The upper valley action begins most years with the Western green drake hatch in late-June. Small mayflies — pale morning dun, *Baetis*, *Callibaetis* and tricos — come off July through October. Caddis hatches are varied and should be fished when timely. Grasshopper and ant options are best in late-July until autumn frost. Another bonus in late-August to September is the gray drake hatch.

Dry fly patterns and nymphs should match these selections. Except for the drakes, big flies are not always a good option, and sizes become smaller as the season progresses and river flows dwindle. Best action is on dry flies cast to rising fish along willow-lined channels, deeper pools and at the mouths of feeder streams. Since cutthroat are part of the mix, the fish are a little more forgiving than on other spring creeks. But only a little. Good presentation is still the name of the game. You may get only one chance at a fish. Takes can be very subtle, so keep your eye on the fly.

It is easier and more productive to fish the upper end of the valley from a flat-bottomed boat or canoe because of heavy silt in places and thick aquatic vegetation. On the lower half, the river has a gravel bottom and is comfortable to wade. Average depth of the river is about three feet. Although the river is flanked on both banks by century-old farms and ranches, public access is excellent. Prominent signs on State Highway 33 direct anglers and hunters to county roads crossing or ending at the river. Most of the same access sites can be reached from county roads that parallel the west side of the river, although some are not as well marked. The rule of thumb is to head for the bridges.

Four of the seven access sites have boat ramps. The largest site, which offers the most opportunities to wade both sides of the river, is Rainey, northwest of Driggs.

An angler fishes the lower canyon of the Teton River during its prime mid-summer grasshopper season.

Elk hair caddis and other attractor patterns often are all that are needed on the canyon stretch of the Teton River.

Primitive campgrounds are available at Rainey and both Fox Creek sites. One of the most popular nearby national forest campgrounds is at the head of Teton Canyon, east of Driggs. Teton Creek is closed to fishing until July 1. If you cross the state line, a Wyoming fishing license is required.

Motel and restaurant accommodations are excellent and relatively inexpensive in Driggs, Victor, and Tetonia, and at the Grand Targhee Ski and Summer Resort, along with several RV trailer parks and private campgrounds. The closest major city is Idaho Falls, 90 miles to the west.

There are two outfitters based in the valley. Three others make runs from Ashton, Idaho Falls, and Jackson. Several new fly shops and outdoor equipment stores in Driggs and Victor can help with flies and information on the river. Most fly shops in Idaho Falls, Swan Valley, and Island Park keep track of Teton River conditions and fly hatches.

Effective patterns for the Teton River

Stoneflies, golden stones, stimulators, humpies, No. 6-10; grasshoppers, No. 8-12; green and gray drakes, No. 10; small mayflies, No. 16-22; caddis and stimulators, No. 12-16; golden stone nymphs, rubber-legs, woolly buggers, No. 8-14; caddis and mayfly nymphs, No. 14-20.

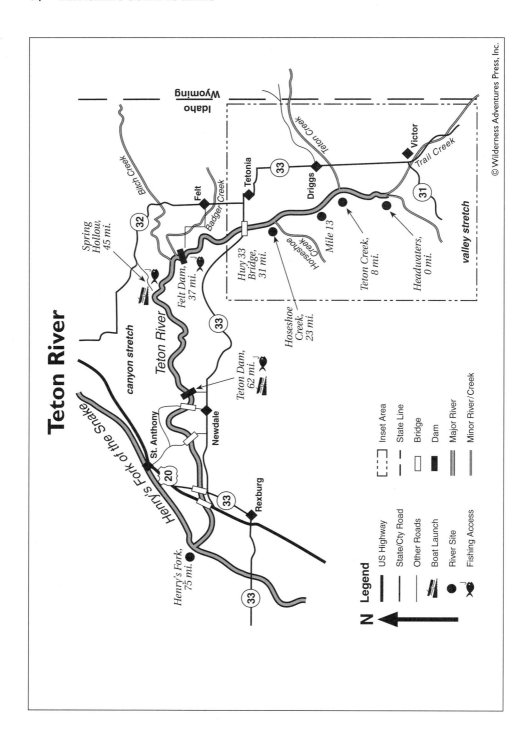

Teton River

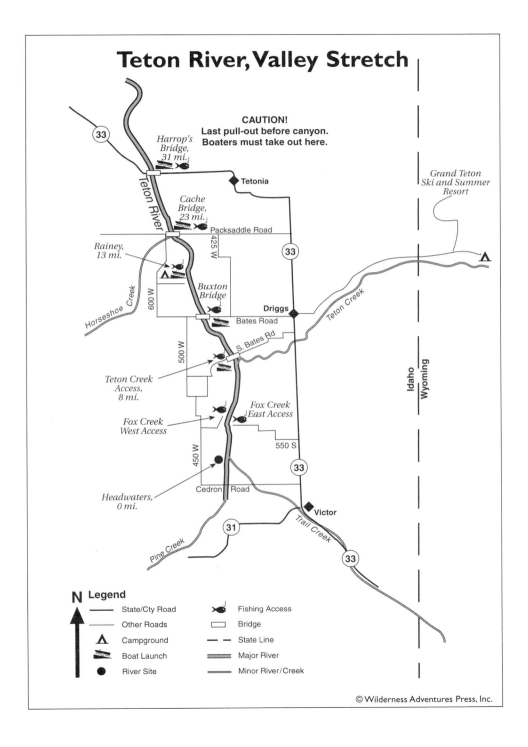

Teton River, Valley Stretch

CAUTION!
Last pull-out before canyon.
Boaters must take out here.

33

Harrop's Bridge, 31 mi.

Grand Teton Ski and Summer Resort

◆ Tetonia

Teton River

Cache Bridge, 23 mi.

Packsaddle Road

425 W

33

Rainey, 13 mi.

Buxton Bridge

600 W

Horseshoe Creek

Teton Creek

◆ Driggs

Bates Road

S. Bates Rd

500 W

Teton Creek Access, 8 mi.

Idaho | Wyoming

Fox Creek East Access

Fox Creek West Access

550 S

450 W

33

Cedron Road

Headwaters, 0 mi.

◆ Victor

Trail Creek

31

33

Pine Creek

Legend

N

—— State/Cty Road	Fishing Access
—— Other Roads	Bridge
Campground	– – State Line
Boat Launch	Major River
River Site	Minor River/Creek

© Wilderness Adventures Press, Inc.

South Fork Teton River

When most people think of the Teton River fishery, they think of the Teton Valley or the canyon.

Certainly, the valley sees more angling pressure than the river below Rexburg. However, portions of the lower river, which splits into the North Fork and the South Fork, hold a respectable trout population. It remains important habitat for the population of Yellowstone cutthroat trout that moves between the lower Henry's Fork and the Teton River.

In 2006, Fish and Game sampled the South Fork of the Teton below U.S. Highway 20 to assess the fishery and trout population trends.

The surveys showed the population has increased from previous surveys. Fish and Game found 220 trout per mile, with a species composition of 68 percent cutthroat trout, 22 percent rainbow trout, and 10 percent brown trout. Although trout densities aren't high compared with some of the other regional streams such as the Henry's Fork, surprisingly, cutthroat densities are seven times higher than found recently in the Teton Valley.

Particularly noteworthy was the size of the fish. Fish and Game collected cutthroat trout up to 23 inches and brown trout up to 22 inches.

If you happen to explore the South Fork, remember that the rules were changed in 2006 to prohibit harvest of cutthroat trout in the Teton River and its tributaries.

Also, most adjacent land is privately owned, so ask first.

Another option would be to fish the South Fork in a canoe and take out on the Henry's Fork at Beaver Dick Park boat ramp below the State Highway 32 bridge.

Stream Facts: Teton River

SEASONS AND SPECIAL REGULATIONS
- Teton River: From Dec. 1 through Friday before Memorial Day weekend, trout limit is 0, catch and release. From Memorial Day weekend through Nov. 30, the trout limit is 6; none may be cutthroat.
- Tributary Creeks: April 1 through June 30, closed to fishing; July 1 through March 31, the trout limit is 6; none may be cutthroat.

TROUT
- Yellowstone cutthroat in 10" to 15" class; growing number over 18", a few exceeding 20"
- Wild cutthroat-rainbow hybrids and rainbows up to 25"

RIVER MILES
- About 75 miles from where Trail and Pine Creeks join to form the Teton to its confluence with the Henry's Fork of the Snake River. It descends from about 6,000 feet in the upper valley to 4,860 feet at the Henry's Fork

RIVER FLOWS

- Spring runoff usually over by late-June most years; can continue to mid-July in wet year
- Summer and fall flows moderate to sometimes very low, depending on irrigation needs

RIVER CHARACTERISTICS

- For its first 30 miles, the Teton is a smooth, meandering meadow stream flowing through a broad basin. Its wide, slow flows and glassy glides are fed by numerous tributaries and surrounding marshy riparian areas. Below State Highway 33, the river enters a deep, picturesque canyon and plunges downstream for about 25 miles through pocket waters rumbled by huge volcanic rocks. A few miles below failed Teton Dam, river splits into two forks and continues 10 miles to Henry's Fork

BOAT RAMPS

Seven public access sites in upper valley, four have usable boat ramps.

- Bates Bridge, 5 miles southwest of Driggs, west bank
- Buxton Bridge, 4 miles west of Driggs
- Cache Bridge, 10 miles northwest of Driggs, west bank
- Harrop's Bridge, 10 miles west of Tetonia, east bank
- Other access sites are Fox Creek East, 5 miles northwest of Victor, east bank; Fox Creek West, 7 miles northwest of Victor, west bank; Rainey, 8 miles northwest of Driggs, both banks

SIDE ROADS

- At town of Felt on State Highway 32, Powerline Road leads to Felt Dam parking lot and unmarked, steep trail down 1,000-foot cliff to mouth of Badger Creek.
- Spring Hollow boat ramp on north canyon bank is at end of gravel county road that goes west from State Highway 32, about 15.5 miles north of its intersection with State Highway 33. The turnoff is just north of a railroad grain elevator. Keep bearing almost due west, sticking to the gravel at farm road forks.
- On canyon's lower end, take turnoff 3 miles east of Newdale on State Highway 33 to failed Teton Dam overlook, turn right on dirt road at parking lot. First left a mile east okay for most cars; next left into canyon requires four-wheel-drive, high clearance.

MAP

- Targhee National Forest map for Driggs Ranger District
- *Idaho's Best Fishing Waters* map book, by Wilderness Adventures Press

TETON RIVER MAJOR HATCHES

Insect	J	F	M	A	M	J	J	A	S	O	N	D	Flies
Giant stonefly (salmonfly)						X							Bird's Stonefly #4–8; Bitch Creek Nymph #4–8
Golden stone						X	X						Stimulator #6–10; Kaufmann's Stone #6–10
Grasshopper								X	X				Jay/Dave's Hopper #8–12; Parahopper #8–12
Pale morning dun							X	X	X				Yellow Sparkle Dun #16–20; PMD Cripple #16–20; Poxyback PMD #16–20
Caddis								X	X	X			Emergent Sparkle Pupa #14–18; Elk Hair Caddis #14–18; X-caddis #14–18

TETON RIVER (VALLEY STRETCH) MAJOR HATCHES

Insect	J	F	M	A	M	J	J	A	S	O	N	D	Flies
Western green drake						X							Olive Sparkle Dun #12–16; Quigley Cripple #12–16; Olive Hare's Ear Nymph #12–16
Pale morning dun						X	X	X					Sparkle Dun #16–20; PMD Cripple #16–20; Pheasant Tail Nymph #16–20
Tricos								X	X				CDC Trico #18–22; Polywing Trico #18–22
Callibaetis								X	X				Sparkle Dun #18–20; Grey Nymph #18–20
Grasshoppers								X	X	X			Jay/Dave's Hopper #8–12; Henry's Fork Hopper #8–12
Ants								X	X	X			CDC Ant #14–18
Gray drake									X	X			Gray Sparkle Dun #10–12; Parachute Adams #10–12

If there were but one river to fish the rest of your life, this would be the choice of many fly fishers. The South Fork offers everything a trout stream can offer.

John Pehrson, outfitter and co-owner
Teton Valley Lodge, Driggs, ID

South Fork of the Snake River

Queen of the Dry Fly

When campfire tales turn to cutthroat trout, fly casters wax poetic about the South Fork of the Snake River. It's impossible to think of one without daydreaming about the other.

Rated as the top cutthroat stream in the West, the South Fork's phenomenal fly fishing is the product of more than a decade of special efforts by Idaho Fish and Game. Its comeback as a first-class fishery is proof of the effectiveness of special regulations to protect this beautiful, native trout of the Northern Rockies.

The South Fork is a tailwater fishery that flows out of Palisades Dam. In western Wyoming, the river is called the Snake, but in Idaho it is called The South Fork. Idaho maps show the Snake beginning at the confluence of the South Fork and the Henry's Fork.

The South Fork's best season is from July to October. Dry fly enthusiasts love it. Old timers, who have fished the river for more than 25 years, proclaim that it is fishing better than ever. Outfitters advertise that it is the best dry fly stream in the country, maybe the world. For those who make their living on it, this spectacular fishery is a treasure passed on from father to son. Spence Warner, resident dean of local outfitters and former owner of South Fork Lodge, shakes his head in amazement at the river's growth in popularity. Seasons that brought in a mere 20 float trips in the 1970s have burgeoned today to 750 bookings a year.

That's not to say the river is perfect. Idaho Fish and Game biologists and Trout Unlimited watchdogs have several concerns. Most pressing are the threat of cutthroat hybridization from a growing population of rainbow trout and the need for guaranteed sustained winter flows to protect recruitment by young fish.

Many fishers, who once thought they had the river's bounty to themselves, grumble about the dramatic increases in fishing pressure and boat traffic. The South Fork has been discovered, big time. There are eight licensed outfitters who provide services on the river, but officials say they represent only 10 to 12 percent of the boat traffic.

Officials and scientists are confident the health of the fishery and size of the river enable it to absorb a lot more action than it is already receiving.

"What I can tell you is the South Fork is one of the finest fisheries in the country. We are very, very fortunate to have rivers like the South Fork and the Henry's Fork," says Mark Gamblin, former regional fisheries manager.

Fishing the West narrator Larry Schoenborn (left) plays a Yellowstone cutthroat trout on the South Fork, accompanied by Spence Warner, former South Fork Lodge owner (center) and broadcaster Curt Gowdy.

Still, for nearly two decades Fish and Game has been waging a continually escalating battle to preserve the genetic purity of Yellowstone cutthroat in the river and its tributaries and maintain the South Fork's status as one of the last strongholds of this hallmark native species of the West.

A variety of restricted regulations strategies were tried but resulted in limited success. Weirs were placed on key spawning tributaries to keep rainbows out and let only cutthroat in during spring, but kinks still have to be worked out. Special flushing flows in spring from Palisades Dam are a continuing attempt to limit the success of rainbow spawning in the main river. And the winter fishing ban on the upper river, above Heise, was dropped. The entire South Fork is now open to fishing year round.

But the real all-out-war against rainbows was initiated when harvest limits were dropped for both rainbows and rainbow-cutthroat hybrids, also known as "cuttbows". Take every rainbow caught home – or donate it to charity kitchens – is the current philosophy. Eat a rainbow, save a cutthroat.

Fish and Game and Trout Unlimited have even resorted to bribery to encourage anglers to take home all the rainbows they net. In 2010, there were 575 rainbows swimming in the upper river with reward tags in their snouts, promising lucky anglers payoffs ranging from $50 to $1,000.

Meanwhile, cutthroat are now protected by a no harvest, catch-and-release rule for the South Fork and its tributaries. Also, Rainey, Palisades, Pine and Burns creeks are closed to fishing from April 1 through June 30. From July 1 through March 31, no cutthroat harvest is permitted; the brown trout limit is 2, none under 16 inches; and there is no limit on harvest of rainbow trout and cutthroat-rainbow hybrids.

The other key species in the river, brown trout, are protected by a two-fish limit on harvest, none under 16 inches.

A fish count on the river in the fall of 2012 found more than 5,692 fish per mile in the Conant stretch of Swan Valley, the highest number recorded since the mid-1980s. It also was the second consecutive year with fish numbers exceeding 5,000 per mile.

However, the bad news is that rainbow numbers were higher than cutthroat total, reported Brett High, regional fisheries biologist. There were 1,931 rainbow per mile and 1,707 cutthroat per mile, reversing a three-year trend in increasing cutthroat numbers.

A continued increase in brown trout also helped to boost the overall numbers, which High perceived as perhaps another worrisome trend. It's estimated there are 1,438 brown trout per mile. That's almost double the count in 2010 and the 10-year average for the river.

The sudden increase is disconcerting because of concerns that browns might muscle cutthroat out of the river, High told the Post Register:

"Other states have had issues with brown trout out-competing and displacing cutthroat," High said, citing Utah's Logan River as a specific example.

"It is a concern they could do the same on the South Fork. The brown trout population is doing something new and it has us worried."

The annual survey in Swan Valley also recorded 11,522 whitefish per mile.

On the lower river, in the Lorenzo stretch, brown trout numbers dominated the fishery as expected. Biologist estimated 1,262 browns per mile, which is close to the 10-year average.

Cutthroat numbers were estimated at 517 per mile; rainbow at 23 per mile; and whitefish at 5,212 per mile.

Another factor affecting rainbow trout abundance in the South Fork is harvest.

"Since 2004, anglers have annually harvested approximately 20 percent of the rainbow trout population," Garren said. "However, recent studies have shown that anglers are releasing approximately half of the rainbow trout they catch each year. If anglers would keep these captured fish, we could make a greater impact on the rainbow trout, and hold them to a lower abundance."

So, in 2010, Fish and Game initiated a "fishing lottery" that challenges anglers to find 575 rainbows in the river with rewards on their heads. Participants in the "angler incentive program" will have to harvest rainbows and turn in the heads for examination in order to win rewards as high as $1,000.

"The challenge is the aquatic equivalent of finding a needle in a haystack," said Greg Losinski, regional Fish and Game spokesman. "In this case, 575 rainbow trout of varying sizes have had tiny wire 'tags' implanted in their snouts. These tiny wires are etched with microscopic markings to indicate their value. No state dollars are being used for this program; only money from federal sources."

The reward breakdown is: 300 of the tags are worth $50 each; 200 are worth $100; 50 are worth $200; 20 worth $500; and 5 are worth $1,000 each. The tagged rainbows may be anywhere in the river between Palisades Dam and Heise.

"Modeling conducted by Idaho State University scientists suggests exploitation rates in excess of 30 percent are required to reduce rainbow trout populations in combination with other management activities, such as spring freshets and reserving spawning tributaries for cutthroat trout," explained Brett High, fisheries biologist. But, if the reward program works, harvest rates may "increase to as much as 80 percent or more of captured fish harvested, which should increase exploitation rates to more meaningful levels."

However, people won't just be able to bring in a fish and get a check. The whole process will take about a month, High said.

Once a month, biologists will use an ultra-sensitive metal detector to determine if each fish head has a winning tag. Once tags are located and removed they will need to be examined under a microscope to read the code indicating the reward amount.

Fish can be dropped off during business hours at the Fish and Game regional office, 4279 Commerce Circle in the St. Leon Business Park in Idaho Falls. Or in spring and summer, they can be donated to charity by placing them in freezers provided at the Conant and Byington boat ramps. Also, anglers who keep their fish can leave just the heads in the same freezers. Instructions and angler receipts are provided at the drop-off sites.

Wild populations of native Yellowstone cutthroat and Snake River finespotted cutthroat provide scrappy dry fly action year-round. Most of the action is with fish ranging from 12 to 15 inches, but there are good numbers of cutthroat over 18 inches. A few trophy fish exceed 20 inches.

On a good day, a float boat's fly fishers can catch and release more than 50 fish. Waders have to work a bit harder, but netting 20 to 25 fish a day is possible. Most often these kinds of opportunities occur in early July at the peak of the salmonfly hatch or when there is a blizzard of willow or caddisflies. Casting into a caddis or pale morning dun feeding frenzy at the lip of a riffle—with fish stacked up like boxcars in a switching yard—offers an experience replayed on the camera of the mind's eye for years to come. Grasshopper season is another real kick. It often extends well past the first frost.

A Yellowstone cutthroat rises to a fly.

The cutthroat's reputation for gullibility is basically deserved, but it becomes more challenging to catch after being stung a few times by hooks and as hatches overlap. South Fork cutthroat can be very selective during a multiple hatch. They may key on a "no-see-um" while fly casters continue to flail the water with patterns for flies too big or too few in between. But the river always offers a window of opportunity. If there is no hatch in progress, a light-colored elk hair caddis, orange or yellow stimulator, parachute Adams or light Cahill may bring a surprising wallop to the hook. The real challenge to matching the hatch comes in fall, the best season on the South Fork. The standard fly then is often a tiny blue-winged olive or parachute Adams.

Big is sometimes better when it comes to cutthroat and nymph patterns, if only to keep from catching the plenitude of whitefish that reside in the river. Best bets for good-sized cutthroat on nymphs are stonefly, woolly bugger, super renegade and Madame-X patterns. They work on brown trout and rainbows, too.

The South Fork is a trophy brown trout stream. Its strong population of browns provides most of its action in the 15- to 25-inch range. The river harbors excellent opportunities to score on trophy fish with big nymphs or streamers.

A state record fish may be just a fly cast away, since the South Forks' 26-year claim to Idaho's brown trout record fell in 2007.

Wes Case of Ashton reeled in the largest brown trout on record in Idaho in November 2007. Case caught the 27.3-pound hog in Ashton Reservoir on bait with 8-pound test line on a spinning reel. It was 37 inches long and 24 inches around.

The previous Idaho record was a 26.4-pounder, 36.5 inches long and 24.75 inches around caught by Farrell Oswald of Idaho Falls in the South Fork in April 1981.

Catching South Fork browns on dry flies is another rush for the fly fisher on this premiere stream. Stonefly and grasshopper seasons are the obvious times, but the river's prolonged golden stone and willow fly hatches provide consistent action for both browns and cutthroat. Some of these greedy, bank-hugging monsters rocket to the surface to take a stonefly nymph or super renegade before it has a chance to sink.

The dramatic growth in rainbow trout population in the South Fork fishery is a mixed blessing. From 12 to 24 inches, they'll make a reel sing a dazzling tune. The down side to these moments of excitement is a disconcerting number of rainbow-cutthroat hybrids.

Fish and Game is disturbed by the growing number of the non-native fish in the upper river. The source is uncertain, since the department stopped stocking the river in 1982 and key cutthroat spawning tributaries two years later. It is suspected that some misguided anglers are illegally dumping rainbows into the river. There are no rainbows in Palisades Reservoir.

Despite their popularity to some anglers, biologists continue to seek ways to eradicate rainbows from the South Fork.

Numerous whitefish in the river are often viewed as a nuisance by trout anglers. They are indicative of a healthy stream, however. They're also tasty when properly prepared. If you are going to take home fish for supper, take a stringer of whitefish. The harvest limit is very liberal.

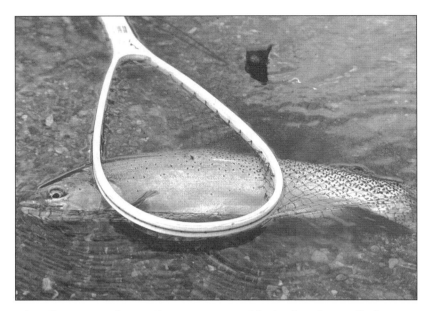

The Yellowstone cutthroat is the premiere trout of the South Fork, one of its last strongholds.

The Snake River finespotted cutthroat also occurs in the South Fork, but is more commonly found in Jackson Hole, Wyoming.

After its flows are slowed by the Palisades Reservoir on the Idaho-Wyoming border, the river flows 64 miles from the dam to its confluence with the Henry's Fork near the Menan Buttes. It descends from 5,280 feet at Palisades to 4,750 feet at its confluence.

On its northwesterly course, it runs through a narrow channel for the first nine miles. It then widens and flows around several island complexes below a towering cliff on the south bank and continues through broad, braided channels past the Swan Valley Bridge to the Conant Valley boat ramp, 15 miles below the dam.

At this point, the river leaves U.S. 26 and enters a deep, picturesque canyon. The 25-mile canyon run is dotted by a series of islands once considered for wilderness protection. The south side of the canyon's high volcanic cliffs fades away a few miles above the Heise Bridge, 43 miles below the dam. The river veers away from the north cliff just above Twin Bridges, north of Ririe. From here, the river passes through a broad floodplain. Farmland flanks the river, and public access is very limited.

The towering cliffs and surrounding mountains are carpeted with lush stands of lodgepole pine and Douglas fir. Throughout its floodplain, the South Fork is sheltered by a thick cottonwood forest. This is the largest, remaining stand of riparian cottonwoods in Idaho. It provides crucial habitat for birds and wildlife, including bald eagle, osprey, peregrine falcon, great blue heron, and a host of migrant songbirds. Sightings of elk, deer, moose, coyote, otter, and beaver are always possible. Geese, ducks, and mergansers are common, and trumpeter swans again are making the river a winter stopover.

The South Fork is a big, rowdy river. At times it can be very unforgiving with strong currents, standing waves and powerful eddies even at low flows. Waders should stick to smaller side channels and riffles, or hug the banks of the main channel. The rule of thumb practiced by most waders who grew up on the river is not to go in over your knees.

Float boaters and rafters should be wary of side channels blocked by debris and of the many diversions for irrigation canals on the lower half of the river. There are two that are extremely dangerous. The diversion for the Great Feeder Canal across from Heise has claimed many lives over the years and a number of heart-stopping near misses. It is on the south bank 1.5 miles below the Byington boat ramp. The other is the Reid Canal, three miles below Twin Bridges on the north bank.

The channels between Twin Bridges, north of Ririe, and the U.S. 20 Bridge at Lorenzo, north of Rigby, contain numerous snags that occasionally claim a boat or two, especially during high-water years. Debris blocked one of these channels in the high-water year of 1995 and made it impassable.

That year's protracted cold, wet spring forced officials to make a major adjustment in flood control releases from Palisades. Flows exceeded 18,000 cubic feet per second on Opening Day weekend, and continued above 14,000 cfs through June. In July, releases were bumped to 22,000 cfs when Palisades threatened to overflow.

By contrast, after a very dry winter, Opening Day flows in 1991 were only 4,000 cfs as irrigators took advantage of another cold, wet spring to preserve water in the unfilled reservoir.

Most years, spring runoff affects the river into early-July, but flows remain high throughout summer due to irrigation releases up to 14,000 cfs. In a good water year for irrigators, flows may be dropped to 8,000 cfs by September. The river is lower and more accessible to waders in fall after irrigation releases end, usually by October 1 when flows begin to drop below 4,000 cfs.

In recent years, biologists and anglers have been successful in gaining better fish-sustaining winter flows of 1,200 cfs out of Palisades. Low-water winter fishing on the downstream stretch dispels cabin fever for resident anglers in winter and early spring.

Anyway you look at it, this is big water. The river continually reroutes itself as it cuts new channels and shifts gravel bars. With the opening of each season, anglers always find new avenues to discover and explore.

Its size and volume demand respect from both boaters and waders. It has claimed less than a half-dozen lives the past decade, but many are the tales of close calls, lost boats or equipment. Small boats and canoes are not recommended during spring or summer flows.

Fishing access is excellent. Eleven public boat ramps are available from Palisades Dam downstream to the confluence with the Henry's Fork. Boating traffic can be very heavy on holidays and during the stonefly hatch. These giants of the aquatic insect world first appear in late-June below Twin Bridges and the hatch works its way up through the canyon to Swan Valley by mid-July.

As the boating pressure continues to grow on the river, it is likely some form of stricter regulation will become necessary. Already, registration forms must be filled out to camp in 15 designated camping areas in the canyon stretch accessible only to boaters between Conant Valley and Lufkin Bottom. Campers in this area must carry portable toilets.

To protect nesting bald eagles, peregrine falcons and great blue herons, a number of areas are posted against foot traffic until July 31. Study the maps at boat launch sites.

National forests border the north and south banks for major stretches and provide the best access for wading and bank fishing. Forest roads follow the river on the north bank from the Twin Bridges, north of Ririe, east past Heise to road's end at Black Canyon. On the south bank, a gravel river road extends from the Swan Valley/U.S. 26 Bridge to Palisades Dam.

Summer fishing on the South Fork is better and more comfortable from a boat. The easiest one-day floats are on the upper stretches, with the last pull-out before the canyon at Conant Valley. Runs through the canyon can be made as long one-day floats or over-nighters. Most anglers float this stretch all the way from Conant Valley to Byington. Shorter trips can be done by pulling out at Cottonwood or Wolf Flat. The latter two are good put-ins for short floats through the lower canyon. They are particularly effective during the early stages of the stonefly hatch.

A popular late fall or early-spring float is from Byington to Twin Bridges. However, any float between Twin Bridges and Lorenzo at the U.S. 20 Bridge should only be done with boaters familiar with that stretch.

The South Fork produced Idaho's previous state record for brown trout. Setting a new record is just a fly cast away.

The river can be fished on foot in summer. It just takes more work to avoid crowds concentrated at key locations like bridges and boat ramps. Along the river roads, longer walks, sometimes through thick brush and willows, put you on productive side channels and riffles. Waders who explore are advised to avoid swift water or unstable gravel.

After September, the river becomes the realm of the wader. Anglers who love this type of fly fishing are able to spread out across broad expanses of water previously inaccessible. It is a lot easier to get around because you can walk major portions of the river channel now above water. The crowds of summer are gone, the weather pleasant and cottonwoods ablaze in gold. This is the time for some the best dry fly fishing in the West.

Fishing styles and techniques on the South Fork vary with the season. In late spring and early summer, it is a straightforward proposition. You don't have to be leader-shy at this time. In fact, boat anglers should tie on strong leader tippets to avoid losing too many flies that are snagged while casting to the banks.

Like most big-water streams of the West, boat anglers do very well casting repeatedly to the banks, stream structures and shear lines between fast and slow water as they float past. Big buggy patterns, both dry and wet, work best early in the season. Size and presentation of flies become more demanding as the season progresses. The key is to keep the fly on or in the water as long as possible.

Gravel bars and riffles are worked heavily by both boaters and waders, especially when caddis, willowflies, and mayflies are hatching. The same goes for quieter bank side holding areas that contain prime feeding lanes.

In fall, after irrigation flows are cut off, the fishing requires more finesse. Shallower waters transform the many channels of the South Fork into classic dry fly adventures more commonly associated with smaller rivers. The fishing is much more intricate and

A guided flyfishing float trip down the South Fork offers a summer excursion with extra amenities.

delicate. Fly sizes become diminutive and leader size critical. Presentation again is a big part of the successful fly fisher's repertoire.

Fall is the time trophy brown hunters are most on the prowl. For these guys, being delicate is no consideration. Big, bad, and ugly nymphs and streamers dragging the bottom is the name of the game. Egg patterns work on or below fall spawning redds, and also attract hovering cutthroat and rainbows. Hard-core trophy hunters, cast from the same mold as steelheaders, hammer the tailrace waters below Palisades Dam for the river's largest browns right up to the end of the season, Nov. 30.

A number of anglers are concerned about the vulnerability of browns during spawning. Fish and Game is being pressured to either post known redds or to make the spawning beds catch and release.

Whatever your approach, the South Fork is not a one-day, love it and leave it proposition. True appreciation comes with quality time spent on its waters and in its environs.

Base camps can be set up at numerous excellent National Forest campgrounds conveniently located up and down the river and along Palisades Reservoir. RV and trailer parks are available in Swan Valley and Irwin, Heise, and Idaho Falls, the nearest major city with the most motel and restaurant accommodations. Several lodges and guest ranches are located in Swan Valley, Conant Valley and Irwin.

Outfitting and guide services are concentrated in the Swan Valley-Irwin area, but also are available from operations based in Idaho Falls, Ashton, and Driggs, as well as Jackson, Wyoming.

Shuttle service for boat trailers is available in Swan Valley-Irwin and in Heise-Poplar.

In Idaho Falls, fly tackle shops with the most current reports on river conditions and fly hatches are Jimmy's All Seasons Angler and Hyde Float Boats and Fly Shop. Take the time to chat with Jimmy Gabettas at All Seasons or the folks at Hyde Float Boats. In the Swan Valley-Irwin area, visit with the folks at the Sandy Mite Cafe & Fly Shop and the fly shops of the outfitters at the South Fork Lodge and The Lodge at Palisades Creek. They will all tell you the same thing. Within the South Fork's waters dwell the memories of a lifetime.

Effective patterns for the South Fork of the Snake

Stonefly dries like sofa pillow and double-humpies, 4-6; hoppers, 12-8; yellow Sallies, elk hair caddis, stimulators, and humpies, 12-16; light Cahill, PMD, BWO, renegade, and Adams, 4 and 16 in mid-season and down to 18-22 in fall. Dark stonefly nymphs 4 and 6 work all season, along with Madame-X, super renegades, and woolly buggers ranging from 8-14. Caddis and mayfly patterns for nymphs and emergers in 14 -16 work on riffles all season. New bead-head patterns very effective. For big browns, use large nymphs, woolly buggers, muddlers, and streamers to pound brush-covered banks during spring high-water and fall cold-water periods; egg patterns and weighted nymphs produce well during fall spawning.

ADDED ADVENTURES ALONG THE SOUTH FORK

Palisades Reservoir flooded the Grand Valley of the South Fork in 1959. When full, its backwaters extend upstream into western Wyoming. Water levels drop drastically due to irrigation releases. Palisades is basically a deep-water fishery and gets little attention from fly fishers. It contains good-sized finespotted Snake River cutthroat, brown, and lake trout, as well as kokanee salmon.

Several of its tributaries are attractive alternatives to fly fishers who like to fish small mountain streams. Most popular are Big Elk, McCoy and Bear creeks for excellent cutthroat fishing. The Salt River, a Wyoming tributary, also draws fly fishers in late fall when heavy drawdown of the reservoir exposes the river channel on the Idaho side of the state line. Their goal is to intercept brown trout running upstream to spawn.

Downstream from the dam, excellent South Fork tributaries include Rainey and Pine creeks. An alpine side trip can be made to the Upper Palisades Lakes on the headwaters of Palisades Creek.

For a day trip or an overnighter, try one of these Palisades Reservoir or South Fork tributaries:

Salt River

To get to it, go east on U.S. Highway 26 to Alpine, Wyoming, and turn south on U.S. Highway 89. About 5 miles south of town, turn west on the McCoy Creek Road to cross back over the Idaho state line. Watch for pullovers and scramble down the exposed reservoir bank to reach the river.

Because of heavy erosion, it isn't pretty and the exposed flats can be muddy. But if you time it right, the brown fishing can be excellent. Large streamers, nymphs, and woolly buggers work best. Egg patterns are not an option.

There's a large campground at the mouth of McCoy Creek that also attracts elk and deer hunters in fall.

McCoy Creek

In addition to the Alpine route, upper McCoy Creek can be reached via the Bone Road east of Idaho Falls. Take Lincoln Road east and turn south at the intersection. Follow the signs to Gray's Lake National Wildlife Refuge, but a mile before the refuge boundary turn north on the McCoy Creek Road and cross over the Caribou Mountain foothills into the creek's drainage.

This is a 60-mile drive on dusty gravel roads with no services after you pass the Bone general store. The brilliant colors of fall make it a worthwhile trip, although spring and summer draw the most fly fishers. Above Bone, you also will pass through the Willow Creek drainage that has excellent fishing in good water years.

McCoy Creek, which is closed to fishing until July 1, has cutthroat and brown trout. Most of the cutthroat are in the 8- to 14-inch range but the creek can hold some surprises up to three pounds. In 1996, new regulations placed the creek in wild trout management, with a two-fish limit, none under 16 inches, and a July 1 - November 30 fishing season.

Fish the slower water stretches and pools, and along overhangs and undercut banks with standard dry and wet fly patterns. The same goes for the other creeks.

The lower South Fork offers some of the best winter fishing in eastern Idaho, often on surprisingly warm days.

The Swan Valley section of the upper South Fork offers many braided channels to explore.

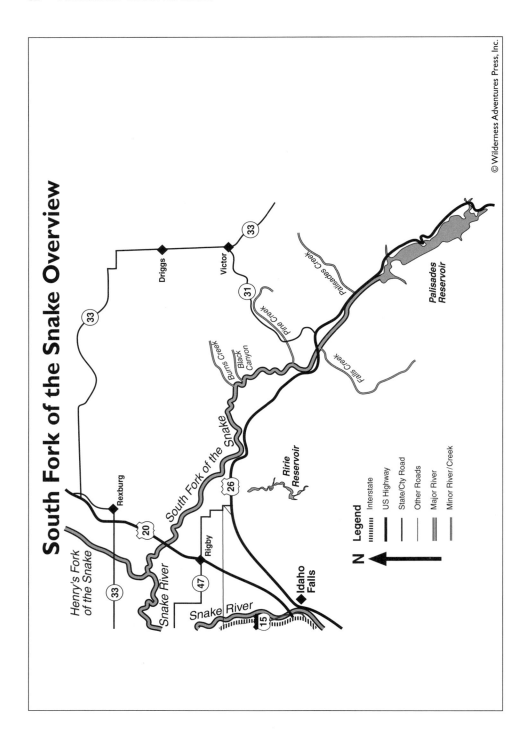

Upper South Fork of the Snake

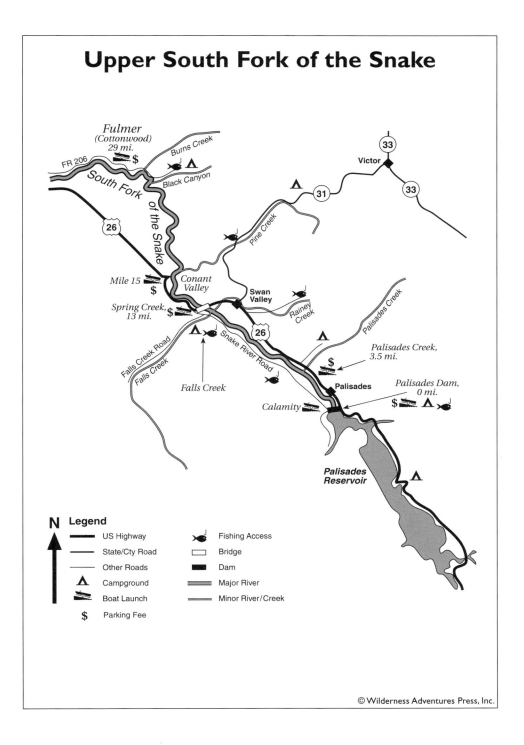

Fulmer
(Cottonwood)
29 mi.

Burns Creek

Black Canyon

FR 206

South Fork

of the Snake

26

Victor

33

33

31

Pine Creek

Mile 15

Conant
Valley

Swan
Valley

Rainey
Creek

Palisades Creek

Spring Creek,
13 mi.

Falls Creek Road

Falls Creek

Snake River Road

Falls Creek

26

Palisades Creek,
3.5 mi.

Palisades

Palisades Dam,
0 mi.

Calamity

Palisades
Reservoir

N **Legend**

	US Highway		Fishing Access
	State/Cty Road		Bridge
	Other Roads		Dam
▲	Campground		Major River
	Boat Launch		Minor River/Creek
$	Parking Fee		

© Wilderness Adventures Press, Inc.

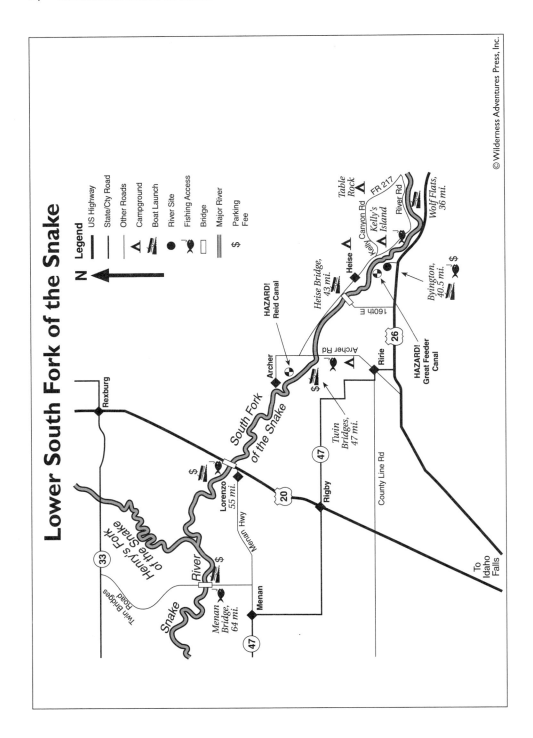

Lower South Fork of the Snake

Bear Creek

Also rising in the Caribou Mountains on the south flank of the reservoir, Bear Creek is reached by crossing Palisades Dam and following the road to Bear Creek Campground. The view is spectacular en route to the stream.

Ignore the waters near the campground and hike upstream two or three miles where you start to get into serious fishing. This a prime spawning stream. Some large cutthroat linger into late summer or early fall. There is a 6-fish limit, no cutthroat.

Big Elk Creek

Flowing out of the Palisades Mountains, the mouth of Big Elk Creek and a small campground are about three miles east of Palisades Dam on U.S. 26.

Like its sister streams, it has excellent cutthroat fishing. Spawning kokanee also run upstream in late-summer, although they are sometimes difficult to catch. There is a 6-fish limit, no cutthroat.

Upper and Lower Palisades Lakes

The trailhead is at a small campground on Palisades Creek in Irwin, north of U.S. 26 a few miles west of Palisades Dam. Watch for the sign. Another landmark is the Lodge at Palisades Creek, which has an excellent fly tackle shop.

An eastern Idaho flyfisher plays with his new toys the day after Christmas.

The easy hike to the lower lake is 4 miles with an elevation gain of about 530 feet. The 25-mile hike to the upper lake climbs another 500 feet in elevation. The trail attracts heavy use from hikers and horseback riders in summer.

Unlike most other lakes in the region, Upper and Lower Palisades are open to fishing only during the general fishing season. Fish them as you would any other alpine lake with standard dry and wet fly patterns. Concentrating on the feeder stream on the upper end of Lower Palisades is one of your better options.

Camping is permitted at the lakes. There is a 2-trout limit.

Rainey Creek

This is one of the prettiest mountain streams in the region. Most of the lower end flows though private land in Swan Valley and is little fished. To get to its upper, tumbling waters and braided channels, turn north off U.S. 26 at the Rainey Creek Road about a mile east of the Swan Valley Commissary. The other landmark for the turn is a large church. The Targhee National Forest boundary is about three miles up the road and a primitive campground another 2 miles.

This is classic mountain stream fishing for mostly small cutthroat. It gets surprisingly little pressure.

Closed to fishing from April 1 through June 30. From July 1 through March 31, no cutthroat harvest is permitted; the brown trout limit is 2, none under 16 inches; and there is no limit on harvest of rainbow trout and cutthroat-rainbow hybrids.

Pine Creek

This is the largest tributary of the South Fork. A principal cutthroat spawning stream, its season doesn't open until July 1. In the years before stricter regulations to protect the native trout, that often meant it had to be fished the first week of July or risk being skunked. Now, it's a favorite side trip through the summer. Its gentle upper valley flows are a joy to fish. Its true challenge is the deep canyon it plunges through to enter the South Fork.

Pine Creek is closed to fishing from April 1 through June 30. From July 1 through March 31, no cutthroat harvest is permitted; the brown trout limit is 2, none under 16 inches; and there is no limit on harvest of rainbow trout and cutthroat-rainbow hybrids.

To get to it, turn north off U.S. 26 onto State Highway 31 at the Swan Valley Commissary intersection. You will catch a glimpse of the creek at the bridge crossing the canyon about 5 miles up the road. One option to get into the canyon is to turn back and take a gravel road to the west, a hundred yards south of the bridge. The landmark to look for is a large sign for the Pine Creek Ranch. Continuing northeast from the bridge, there are several pullouts at which to park and scramble down to the creek. A mile upstream, the highway parallels the creek through the valley before it begins to climb to Pine Creek Pass.

Stream Facts: South Fork of Snake River

SEASONS
- South Fork: Open to fishing all year
- Tributary Creeks: Closed to fishing from April 1 through June 30

SPECIAL REGULATIONS
- South Fork: No harvest of cutthroat trout; brown trout limit is 2, none under 16 inches; no limit on harvest of rainbow trout and rainbow-cutthroat hybrids.
- Tributary Creeks: From July 1 through March 31, no cutthroat harvest is permitted; the brown trout limit is 2, none under 16 inches; and there is no limit on harvest of rainbow trout and cutthroat-rainbow hybrids.

TROUT
- Yellowstone and Snake River finespotted cutthroat in 12" to 18" class and a few 20" to 22"
- Brown trout in 15" to 25" class; trophy fish exceed 30", including Idaho's former record brown (26 lbs. 6 oz., 36.5")
- Fish and Game attempting to reduce as much as possible growing population of rainbow and cutthroat-rainbow hybrids. Major concern is possible listing of Yellowstone cutthroat as a threatened or endangered species
- Numerous whitefish, 6" to 20"

RIVER MILES
- 64 miles from Palisades Dam tailwaters to confluence with Henry's Fork. It descends from 5,280 feet at Palisades to 4,750 feet at its confluence.

RIVER FLOWS
- Spring runoff can exceed 20,000 cfs and affect river through July
- Summer flows high due to irrigation releases up to 14,000 cfs
- Fall flows reduced after October 1 to 5,000 cfs or less
- Winter flows are 800 to 1,200 cfs

RIVER CHARACTERISTICS
- The South Fork is a big, pushy river with strong currents even at low flows. There are no rapids or waterfalls, but watch for debris in side channels. Boaters should avoid dangerous canal diversions. Canoes are not recommended during high spring flows.

BOAT RAMPS
- Mile 0—Palisades Dam, north bank, concrete
- Mile 35—Irwin, north bank, concrete
- Mile 13—Spring Creek (U.S. 26 Bridge), south bank, concrete
- Mile 15—Conant Valley, south bank, concrete
- Mile 29—Cottonwood, north bank, concrete
- Mile 36—Wolf Flats, north bank, dirt

SOUTH FORK OF THE SNAKE RIVER MAJOR HATCHES

Insect	J	F	M	A	M	J	J	A	S	O	N	D	Flies
Midges (snowfly)													Griffith's Gnat #18–22; Parachute Adams #18–22; Palomino Midge #16–22; chironomid larvae #18–22; brassie #16-20
Baetis													Olive Sparkle Dun #16–22; Pheasant Tail Nymph #16–22; Parachute Adams #16–22
Giant stonefly (salmonfly)													Sofa Pillow #4–6; Bird's Stone #4–6; Kaufmann's Stone Fly Nymph #4–6
Golden stone													Stimulators #6–10; Golden Stonefly Nymph #6–10; yellow Salley #12-16; yellow humpy #10-16
Pale morning dun													Yellow Sparkle Dun #16–20; PMD Cripple #16–20; Poxyback PMD #16–20
Pink Albert													Pink Albert, pink lady, pink Cahill, red quill, light Cahill, cream dun #16-14
Grasshopper													Parahopper #8–12; Henry's Fork Hopper #8–12; Jay/ Dave's Hopper #8–12
Mahogany dun													Mahogany Sparkle Dun #16–18; Pheasant Tail Nymph #16–18
Caddis													Emergent Sparkle Pupa #14–16; Elk Hair Caddis #14–16; Hemingway Caddis #14–16; yellow Salley #12-16; yellow humpy #10-16

- Mile 40.5—Byington, south bank, concrete
- Mile 43—Heise Bridge, south bank, dirt
- Mile 47—Twin Bridges, south bank, concrete
- Mile 55—Lorenzo (U.S. 20 Bridge), north bank, dirt
- Mile 64—Menan Bridge, south bank, concrete

SIDE ROADS
- In Swan Valley, a gravel road through Caribou National Forest follows south bank and provides best access to wade channels and bank fish.
- Upstream from Twin Bridges and continuing past Heise, a gravel road through Targhee National Forest hugs north bank into lower canyon past Burns Creek.

MAPS
- South Fork Snake River 11x17 flyfishing river map, by Wilderness Adventures Press
- *Idaho's Best Fishing Waters* map book, by Wilderness Adventures Press

A guide and one of his clients savor a South Fork experience, while a companion appreciates the moment.

Pay to Park and Play

South Fork boaters, anglers and recreationists who use the facilities or park at improved boat launch sites on the river are required to pay a parking fee during the river's four-month heavy use period. The fee season runs from May 23 through Sept. 30.

Parking passes are required at the following boat launch sites: Palisades Dam, Palisades Creek (Huskey station), Spring Creek, Conant, Fulmer (Cottonwood), Byington, Twin Bridges, Lorenzo Bridge (U.S. 20), Menan Buttes, and Mike Walker (between Menan and Roberts on the Snake River).

The daily fee is $3 per vehicle per day. Season pass options include one pass for $30 or two passes for $45. Passes are transferable between vehicles, but the pass is good only for the vehicle in which it is displayed.

Season passes are available at:

- Eastern Idaho Visitor Information Center (523-1012)
- Palisades Ranger District Office (523-1412)
- BLM's Idaho Falls Office (524-7500)
- Byington Boat Access (the host is off Tuesday and Wednesday)
- Conant Boat Access (the recreation technician is off Monday, Tuesday, and Wednesday and will usually be working at other sites after noon on the other four days).

An automated fee machine is available at the Conant Boat Access. Day and season passes are available 24 hours a day. Passes may be purchased by cash or credit card.

If you purchase a season pass, the machine will provide you with a receipt that functions as a temporary pass (valid for 10 days). If you bought the two passes for $45 option, just tear off the bottom of the receipt for your second pass.

Save the temporary pass for verification and contact the technician at Conant (if available) or call the Eastern Idaho Visitor Information Center at 523-1012 to receive your permanent Season Pass.

Here are some rules to remember at use fee sites:

- If you park one vehicle at Conant and leave another one at Byington, you must pay the fee for both vehicles. (Suggestion: buy the two-for-$45 season pass package).
- If you launch (or park) at Byington and go downriver, you are still required to pay the daily fee.
- If you launch from an informal or private site where fees are not charged

and someone shuttles your vehicle to a site where fees are charged, you are still required to pay the daily fee and display a permit receipt or season pass in that vehicle. If one of the two are not displayed when your vehicle arrives or is parked, you may receive a warning or a violation notice.

- When you pay for a vehicle at one site, your pass is good, for that day, at the other five sites.

- Many boaters use multiple vehicles to complete their shuttle. Some users park temporarily at Byington while they shuttle another vehicle to Conant. For those anglers there is a designated "FREE" two-hour parking area at Byington to accommodate the temporary user. The designated area is for shuttle driver vehicles only.

- The bottom line: If any of your vehicles are in any fee site parking area, they must have a visible, dated permit stub or season pass. If they do not, chances are good you will receive a warning or violation notice.

Note: Payette River season passes also are valid at fee sites on the South Fork of the Snake, and South Fork season passes are valid at Payette fee sites in western Idaho.

A guide catches a Kodak moment on the South Fork.

Minimum Impact Boating and Camping

Due to the pristine nature of the South Fork Snake River canyon, camping is permitted only in 11 designated camp areas between Conant Boat Access and Lufkin Bottom. You may choose a campsite anywhere within a camp area, but it is best to select an existing site that has an existing tent ring.

A free self-issue permit is required and is available at the boat access areas. The trip leader must have this permit in possession during the overnight river visit and display it to BLM or Forest Service personnel upon their request.

(Note: Additional information, campsite permits and river maps are also available at BLM Idaho's website at www.blm.gov/id/st/en.html)

Camping is prohibited within a Bald Eagle Habitat area.

Water is not available at the camp areas. If necessary to use water from the river boil, filter, or chemically treat all drinking, cooking and dish washing water.

Waste Disposal: Portable toilets are required for overnight camping. Overnight campers from Conant Boat Access to Lufkin Bottom must carry out all solid human waste using an approved carryout system. (Day-use boaters also are now required to carry portable toilets.) At a canyon camp, set up your toilet fa-cilities in a location screened from view and at least 100 feet from the water.

Trash: River users are responsible for packing out all garbage and trash, including food scraps. Never sink cans or bottles in the river. Before leaving camp, make a final check for small trash such as cigarette butts and twist ties. Do not burn trash in campfires.

Fires: Do not build fires in old fire rings. Use a fire pan or gas stove. Do not cut living trees for firewood. Burn "dead and down" wood instead of cutting dead tree limbs. Many more overnight campers use the canyon nowadays and much of the firewood is being gathered and used. Bring your own firewood.

Additional regulations were established in 2009 to extend efforts to protect the unique natural resources along the entire river corridor. These changes will also assist managing agencies in properly maintaining the river corridor in an age of shrinking budgets coupled with increased visitor use. Some of the new regulations that pertain to all users of the river corridor include:

Fire Pan Required: In order to prevent additional vegetative and soil distur-bances, fire pans are now required. Fire pans should be elevated off the ground to prevent scorching and should be at least 12-inches wide, with a 1.5-inch lip around its outer edge to sufficiently catch fire remains. All ash needs to be packed out with visitors before leaving their campsite.

Portable Toilets and Certified Waste Disposal Bags (i.e., WAG° Bags or RESTOP°): The human waste problem is getting worse on the rivers due to increased use and the fact that people are not properly disposing of human waste.

All overnight and day use boaters are required to carry out human waste property (i.e., portable toilet or certified waste disposal bags). Portable toilets must be reusable, washable, water tight, and SCAT Machine or RV dump compatible. Portable toilets with snap-on lids (ammo can or plastic buckets) are required to have a rubber gasket in the lid. Plastic bag liners are not acceptable unless they are the Environmental Protection Agency (EPA) approved WAG bag or RESTOP systems.

Dump Stations: Three dumping stations are available for disposal of waste: Palisades Dam (located in campground); Byington Boat Access; Beeches Corner (junction of U.S. Highway 26 and Ammon Road on the eastern edge of Idaho Falls).

The Bureau of Land Management has also established designated "campsites" within previously established camp areas on the lower river.

Lufkin Bottom now has seven designated "campsites," where previously visitors were allowed to camp anywhere on the Lufkin Bottom bench. New management direction requires visitors to camp only in the designated campsites, marked with brown signs, rather than anywhere they choose.

Establishing these designated campsites will help decrease vegetation loss within the camp area, minimize wildlife disturbances, and will help focus use to the designated campsites. Most of the designated campsites were already an established site but were not labeled as such.

There are five new designated camp areas with multiple designated campsites in each. These new areas are downstream from Lufkin Bottom, with the furthest designated campsite located across the river from Wolf Flats Boat Ramp. The new sites are named Black Canyon, Warm Springs, Rattlesnake Point, Mud Creek, and Clark Hill.

The BLM and US Forest Service planned to designate additional campsites in 2010 on the upper stretches of the South Fork from Palisades Dam to Conant Boat Ramp. Currently, there are no plans to designate campsites downriver from Heise Bridge due to the constantly changing river characteristics and limited overnight use.

Call the Eastern Idaho Visitor Center at 205-523-1012 or the BLM at 208-524-7500 if you have any questions or for more information concerning where to purchase required equipment.

UPPER SNAKE RESERVOIRS

Two popular summer recreation sites near Idaho Falls are Palisades Reservoir, 50 miles to the east on the South Fork of the Snake, and Ririe Reservoir, 5 miles east of town in the Willow Creek drainage.

Palisades Reservoir

Palisades Reservoir, on the South Fork of the Snake River, is a 16,100-acre reservoir designed as an irrigation storage, power generation, and flood control impoundment. It is located in some of the state's most scenic country, near the Idaho-Wyoming border.

Access to the reservoir, for both shore and boat anglers, is best on the northwest side, along U.S. 26. Camping is available at Elk Creek, Alpine and Hoffman Campgrounds, and there are additional boat launch pads along the north shore. A boat launch at Calamity Campground on the south shore and the road back into the popular Bear Creek area are reached by driving across the dam. To get to McCoy Creek on the upper end of the lake, anglers have to drive to Alpine, Wyoming, and drive 3 miles south to the access road.

Fluctuating water levels in Palisades has resulted in an inconsistent fishery. Though most of the angler pressure occurs during the summer months, spring and fall actually provide the best fishing opportunities. Catch rates typically drop off dramatically in mid- to late June, then pick up quickly when cooler temperatures arrive in September. During these cooler months, there is good fishing for both boat and shore anglers. Shore anglers may, however, find some difficulty reaching the undeveloped shoreline due to the steep slopes in some areas.

The predominant game fish of Palisades Reservoir is Snake River finespotted cutthroat trout, both wild and stocked. Second in angler popularity is the brown trout. Though not as abundant, the browns provide a good trophy fishery with an average length of nearly 17 inches. Also in the lake are kokanee salmon and lake trout. The lake trout are relatively few in number, but can be found in deep water.

Boat anglers troll the deep waters of Palisades. But flyfishers occasionally find good bank fishing just after ice-out while brown trout are still cruising the shore and cutthroat begin entering tributaries for their spring spawning runs.

Through the summer and fall flyfishers can work flooded shallows before the reservoir is drawn down by irrigation releases, or concentrate on coves and the mouths and outlet arms of the lake's tributaries.

Popular streams emptying into Palisades are Big Elk and Indian creeks on the north shore, and Bear and McCoy creeks on the south shore. Morning and evening hatches supply occasional excellent surface action in summer in the arms. When temperatures drop in late fall brown trout begin to stage in these areas for their migrations upstream to spawn.

Another excellent autumn brown fishery is the mouth of Wyoming's Salt River. It can be fished in heavy drawdown years with an Idaho license by crossing mud flats west of the Wyoming state line.

Fishing for kokanee can be challenging on Palisades. Trolling deep during summer is the usual tactic, but the landlocked salmon are accessible to flyfishers in late summer and early fall when they move up into tributaries, like Big Elk Creek, to spawn.

Palisades Reservoir is a "family fishing water," open year-round with a six-fish limit for trout, no size limit. No bag limit on kokanee; standard fishing gear for all species.

Palisades Reservoir

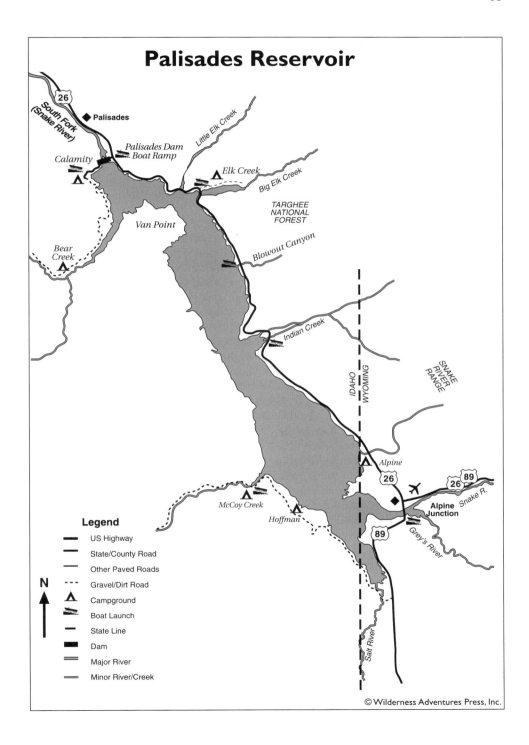

Legend

— US Highway
— State/County Road
— Other Paved Roads
- - - Gravel/Dirt Road
▲ Campground
Boat Launch
— State Line
■ Dam
Major River
Minor River/Creek

N

© Wilderness Adventures Press, Inc.

Ririe Reservoir

Ririe Reservoir, located on Willow Creek east of Idaho Falls, is a popular playground for local residents.

A campground and boat launch above the dam is reached by driving 12 miles east on U.S. 26 to the sign for the Ririe Recreation Area and turning south to the reservoir. The Blacktail Recreation Area on the southwest corner of the lake is reached by driving straight east about five miles on Lincoln Road. This site has a launch pad and picnic facilities.

Since irrigation drawdowns are not reducing summer pool levels, as in many other Idaho reservoirs, the result is a stable fishery with easy access throughout the fishing season. Whether you are interested in a casual afternoon of bank fishing, or a full day of boat fishing, Ririe offers a variety of fishing opportunities.

The fishing season on Ririe is somewhat different than other lakes and reservoirs in Idaho. Ice fishing is restricted to the area from the dam to the posted boundary about 1 mile upstream. This is done to reduce impact to the several thousand elk that use the adjacent Tex Creek Wildlife Management Area as their winter range. Without such a closure, disturbances to the elk would likely push them toward adjacent agricultural lands.

Six different species of game fish are available to anglers in the reservoir. The most abundant species are rainbow trout, smallmouth bass, kokanee salmon, and yellow perch, in that order. Brown trout and cutthroat trout are also present in smaller numbers. Rainbow trout and smallmouth bass have been the most popular fish with anglers in recent years. However, kokanee salmon and yellow perch can also provide some good fishing for those who take the time to seek them out.

Ririe's rainbow can be caught by shore and boat anglers alike, but since most of the reservoir's banks are steep cliffs, trolling from boats is a popular method of fishing. Flyfishers can get away from motor boat traffic by taking a canoe or small boat up into the outlet arms of Willow and Meadow creeks.

Since kokanee prefer cool, open water, those fishing from boats will have the most success. Kokanee in Ririe can be found most commonly in the lower two miles of the reservoir, towards the dam, by deep-trolling anglers.

Unlike the kokanee, the smallmouth bass do not like open water and will be found where cover from brushy areas, rocky shorelines or rock outcroppings occur. These popular game fish are aggressive fish eaters so streamers and popping bugs are effective flies. The secret to success is to fish around structures or rocky areas and keep moving around to new shoreline until you find them.

Fish slip through the dam's outlet and fishing is occasionally good just downstream from the dam.

Bank anglers should keep an eye out for rattlesnakes throughout the reservoir's shoreline and its tributaries.

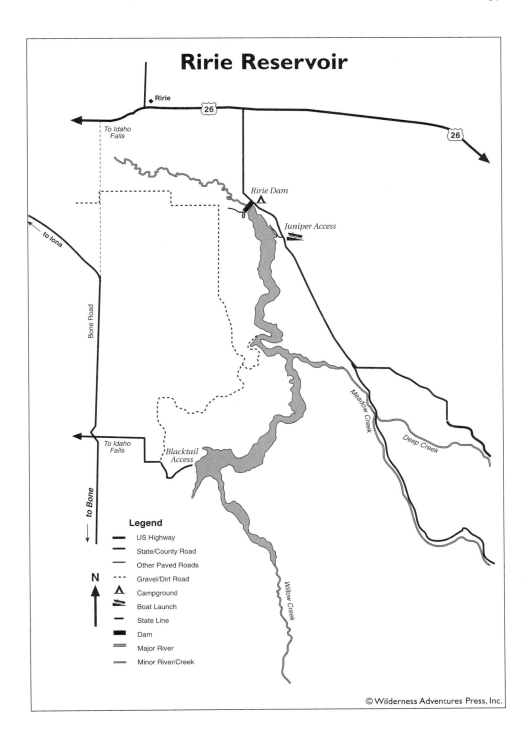

Ririe Reservoir

Ririe

26

To Idaho
Falls

to Iona

Ririe Dam

Juniper Access

Bone Road

Meadow Creek

Deep Creek

To Idaho
Falls

Blacktail
Access

to Bone

Willow Creek

Legend

N

— US Highway
— State/County Road
— Other Paved Roads
--- Gravel/Dirt Road
△ Campground
⤇ Boat Launch
— State Line
▬ Dam
═ Major River
— Minor River/Creek

© Wilderness Adventures Press, Inc.

Large browns—over 20 inches—are fairly common especially between Gem Dam and Shelley and Blackfoot and Tilden Bridge.

Jimmy Gabettas, owner,
All Seasons Angler, Idaho Falls

Snake River and Southeast Lakes

The forgotten river

The character of the Snake River changes dramatically once the Henry's Fork and the South Fork combine north of Idaho Falls.

A series of dams to produce electric power for Idaho Falls has tamed this magnificent river. A series of reservoirs and deep runs make the 41-mile stretch between the confluence and Gem State Dam a place for bait and spin fishermen rather than fly fishers. Idaho Falls plants thousands of rainbow and there are a few places, such as the tailwater below the actual Idaho Falls along the greenbelt, where a fly caster can hook nice fish when conditions are right.

This has become a working river. It has traded its Orvis khakis for work shirts and flannels. Irrigation diversions take millions of gallons of water out of the river along the 37-mile stretch between Gem State and Tilden Bridge, southwest of Blackfoot. In 1993, a 10-mile stretch was drained dry by mistake in the spring, leaving thousands of fish flopping on dry land. Moreover, access is limited because most of the land along the river is either in farms, subdivisions, or industrial use. The Idaho Department of Fish and Game acknowledges that the unstable flows, the siltation from farm practices, and lack of interest limits its ability to improve what should be prime trout waters. However, there are areas south of Idaho Falls that offer good fishing opportunities. For a first venture into these waters, it helps to go with someone who knows the river.

The best stretch is below Gem State. Drift-boat fishers are learning that the Snake south of Shelley and Firth has many of the same desirable characteristics that the South Fork has, even if it is not as wild. It has wide riffles and deep pools that hold rainbows from 12 to 18 inches. There also are cutthroats and cutthroat hybrids, though they are very few in number. The stockings in the reservoir above and in the river keep rainbows in the cover along the banks just like cutthroat hang on the South Fork. However, it is brown trout, sometimes over five pounds, that attract fly fishers away from the region's blue ribbon streams.

Floaters have 30 miles of river to work. The two most popular floats are from Gem State to Firth—a 20-mile trip—and from Blackfoot to Tilden Bridge—a 15-mile trip. The bridge is east of Rockford on State Highway 39.

Waders have limited opportunities near the boat landings, at the North Bingham County Recreation area at Shelley, at the Rose Bridge eight miles north of Blackfoot, and in low water in other areas near roads. Some other places open up if you get permission from landowners.

Perhaps the best time of the year for waders is in late October and November when the browns are spawning. The area below Gem State Dam becomes hot this time of the year and fly fishers can benefit as much as spin and bait fishers. Since this stretch of river is open all year it offers early-season opportunities on rainbows and cutthroat running upstream to spawn.

The 20 miles of river below Tilden Bridge is a Class I trout stream that gets little pressure because of limited access. The Shoshone-Bannock Tribes own the southern bank, and the northern banks are in farmland. This area has perhaps the best potential for improvement in the next few years. The pull-out is a bank ramp at the McTucker Island public access site southeast of Springfield.

Below American Falls there are six miles of Class I trout waters running to Eagle Rock. Even though this is a put-and-take fishery, some lunkers live in this area. Trophy rainbow from five to ten pounds are not uncommon. This stretch gets a lot of pressure—Fish and Game estimates about 58,000 angling hours annually—but it also gets many fish that migrate out of American Falls Reservoir because of warm temperatures. Unfortunately, the warm water and low oxygen from the reservoir make this area less than ideal for wild trout production. The flows are cut way down in the winter, adding to trout problems.

Below Eagle Rock the river opens up into big water that flows through a large canyon. Motorboats are needed here and it is not noted as prime fly fishing water.

The Snake River River below American Falls offers opportunities for large trout in lightly fished waters.

Effective patterns for the Snake River

Caddisflies make the up the bulk of the hatches in these stretches of the Snake. However, blue-winged olives come off both in the spring and in the fall and are important for fishers. There are weak hatches of the other traditional bugs, giant stoneflies, green and brown drakes, *Callibaetis*, golden stones and pale morning duns—but the fishers sporting caddis imitations can't go wrong in the riffles. However, the big fish in the Snake eat a lot more minnows than they do most everywhere else so Muddlers, Mickey Finns, Zonkers and other streamer patterns are the best.

Idaho Fish and Game dropped the cutthroat trout slot-limit on Region 5 streams in 1996.

On the Snake River, from Eagle Rock upstream to American Falls Dam, the limit is 0, catch-and-release for all game fish species from Oct. 16 through Friday before Memorial Day weekend. No bait allowed, barbless hooks required. From Saturday of Memorial Day weekend through Oct. 15, the limit is 2 bass, any size; trout limit is 6, only 2 may be cutthroat and only 2 trout over 16 inches.

From American Falls Reservoir upstream to the confluence of the South Fork and Henry's Fork at Menan Buttes, the trout limit is 6, only 2 may be cutthroat.

AMERICAN FALLS RESERVOIR

The Snake River flows into American Falls Reservoir about 15 miles west of Blackfoot and northwest of Fort Hall Indian Reservation.

At full pool, the 56,000-acre reservoir is the second largest impoundment in Idaho. Primarily built as a water storage reservoir for irrigation, it also provides electric power, and flood control protection.

Historically, American Falls Reservoir has been one of the best fisheries in Idaho. But the fishery is dependent upon the availability of water to maintain the minimum pool necessary to carry over fish from year to year. In drought years it experiences extensive drawdown.

The dam is located near the city of American Falls, adjacent to Interstate 86, west of Pocatello. Numerous access sites, complete with ramps and docks, make it easy to use for boaters as well as shore anglers.

The Sportsman Park access on the north side of the dam is particularly popular, and American Falls provides a large city park with facilities east of town.

Also on the north side below the dam and power plant, a public boat ramp and dock area provide fishing access to the Snake River. Idaho Power Co. also maintains American Falls Park, a day-use area near the power plant village on the south side of the dam.

The other main route to American Falls Reservoir is to take State Highway 39 west from Blackfoot. The highway offers good access to the lower Snake River bottoms and the backwaters of the reservoir in the Springfield area. There also is good shore access at the Springfield Wildlife Management Area south of town.

Rainbow trout are the most popular fish in American Falls Reservoir. Fish from 5 to 6 pounds are not uncommon. Cutthroat and brown trout are also found.

The Snake River finespotted cutthroat occurs in tributary creeks of the Salt River rising in southeastern Idaho.

Shoreline fishing can be good early in the year. As water temperatures climb in the summer, fish move to deeper water near the dam where boat anglers have better success trolling. As waters cool in the fall, reservoir-wide fishing again picks up.

Flyfishers often do best at the mouth of the Snake River or by working up into other arms of the reservoir, or exploring the shallows along the city park east of American Falls.

Anglers who gain access to American Falls Reservoir through the Fort Hall Indian Reservation need a Shoshone-Bannock tribal permit. Check with the tribal office for further information.

Record Trout Caught In American Falls Reservoir

Michelle V. Larsen-Williams of Pingree broke a 61-year-old record when she caught a new state record rainbow trout on the Snake River just above American Falls Reservoir in July 2009. The fish weighed just over 20 pounds. It was 34.25 inches long with a girth of 22.25 inches. She caught it with a worm on 14-pound test line and a 12-pound leader.

It was the third rainbow trout weighing more than 18 pounds that had been caught in the American Falls Reservoir -- above it and below the dam -- that summer.

The previous Idaho rainbow trout record was a 19-pounder caught by R.M. Williams in 1947 in Hayden Lake in northern Idaho.

SPRINGFIELD RESERVOIR

Located near Aberdeen, 15 miles west of Blackfoot on State Highway 39, Springfield Reservoir is managed as a trophy trout lake.

Its popularity has grown considerably since stricter regulations were put in place. Also, since it is spring fed it is one of the few local options for open water and dependable fishing in winter.

"It's been around a long time, but just in the past couple of years was recognized by Idaho Fish and Game regulations as a trophy lake," says Mel Moore, an Idaho Falls fan of Springfield Lake. "They plant it with larger fish, instead of those of smaller size.

Before then, "birds of the area were fishing all the small fish out before we could get to most of them. So the decision was made to make Springfield a trophy lake and discontinue planting of smaller fish," Moore explained.

"It has been a nice turn-around for this lake. Winter and early spring fishing seems to be the best. Again in the late fall and following winter. There's some nice sized fish here and they like to take you for a ride."

Angler reports indicate a fast catch rate and occasional fish in the 8- to 10-pound range.

There is a 2-trout limit at the lake, none under 20 inches. Special regulations also require barbless flies and lures.

The Bonneville cutthroat occurs only in the Bear River drainage of southeastern Idaho.

OTHER SOUTHEAST IDAHO TROUT FISHERIES

Southeastern Idaho has several other areas of at least seasonal interest to fly fishers. The Portneuf River is an irrigation ditch with a great past. There are efforts to improve its water quality and to change the flow to benefit fishing. It is not going to happen quickly. One of the few bright spots is the stretch below Lava Hot Springs, where a few wild rainbows survive and the fall brown trout fishing can be decent.

The Chesterfield and Twenty-Four Mile reservoirs on the Portneuf are among the most popular fly fishing spots in the area, however the lack of good spawning and lake-level management only for irrigation needs prevents them from producing wild fish. Fish and Game routinely plants rainbows. Five-pounders have been taken by float-tubers in Chesterfield.

The Black Canyon of the Bear River above Grace offers reasonably good rainbow fishing and a few of the Bear Lake strain of cutthroat. Many of the tributaries of the Bear River still have good wild trout fisheries, including strains of rare Bonneville cutthroat. Among them are the Thomas Fork, St. Charles Creek, the Malad, and Cub rivers, Bloomington, Paris, Montpelier, Georgetown, Eight Mile, Williams, and Cottonwood creeks.

Bonneville cutthroat are catch-and-release on the Thomas Fork, Dry, Giraffe, Preuss, and St. Charles creeks, and their seasons are July 1 to November 30.

Generally the meadows in the upper and middle stretches of these tributaries are the best places to fish. The lower stretches suffer from siltation and warmer water temperatures.

Impoundments in this corner of the state are deep, but the shallows can be fished effectively with floating lines and long leaders for cruising trout. Small nymphs, scuds, damselfly nymphs and the Sheep Creek Special, a *Callibaetis* pattern, are good options. Dry fly choices include midges, speckle-wing *Callibaetis* and damselflies. Two of the reservoirs are managed as trophy trout fisheries:

Daniel's Reservoir

This 375-acre impoundment on the Little Malad River is very popular with float-tubers. It also fishes well from a canoe or by wading the shallows in search of cruisers. Concentrate on sight casting to feeding trout. It is about 14 miles north of Malad City. Turn west on West Daniel's Road.

There is a two-fish limit, none under 20 inches, for cutthroat, rainbows and cutthroat-rainbow hybrids. Barbless flies or lures only, no bait. One line only when ice fishing.

Twenty-Four Mile Reservoir

Located near the tiny, pioneer community of Chesterfield, north of U.S. Highway 30, this 45-acre reservoir is popular with float-tubers and shoreline stalkers who like relative solitude.

Follow sportsmen access signs from town. It has a two-trout limit, none under 20 inches, for rainbows and cutthroat-rainbow hybrids. Brook trout must be counted in two-fish limit. Barbless flies or lures only, no bait. One line only when ice fishing.

Chesterfield Reservoir

Chesterfield Reservoir on the Portneuf River is an easy access family fishery and one of the most popular lakes in the region with float-tubers.

It is located near the historic town of Chesterfield, east of Pocatello. To reach it take U.S. 30 to Lava Hot Springs and watch for signs for the road leading north to the town and the reservoir.

The 1,600-acre reservoir has good shoreline and boat fishing facilities. Unimproved campsites are also available.

Chesterfield has long been a popular place to catch good-sized hatchery rainbow trout. Idaho Fish and Game stocks both catchable and fingerling rainbow trout in the spring and fall. Fish exhibit good growth rates and catch rates are some of the best in southeast Idaho. Brown trout have been stocked which is expected to soon provide a trophy fishery.

However, in drought years the reservoir has experienced serious problems.

Shoreline access is readily available and bank fishing is often quite good in the early summer and fall. Boat anglers can expect good success throughout the summer trolling a variety of lures.

Float-tubing is also popular on Chesterfield Reservoir. For flyfishers, matching the hatch is the key. Early season you will want to use leeches on a sinking line. As summer progresses, damsels, chironomids and mayfly hatches come on. Check with All Seasons Anglers in Pocatello or Idaho Falls to see "what's hot."

There is a 2-fish trout limit on Chesterfield Reservoir.

Non-tribal members fishing on the extreme upper end of the reservoir, within the Fort Hall Indian Reservation, need a Shoshone-Bannock Tribal fishing permit. Consult tribal regulations for details.

WARMWATER FISHERIES

Trout aren't the only game fish residing in eastern Idaho's waters. Good warmwater fishing for largemouth bass and pan fish is found in the southeast corner of the state south of Pocatello.

Float-tubers who work the region's ponds and reservoirs have learned that a 20-inch largemouth bass is just as hard to catch as a trophy trout. Plenty of action on 10- to 12-inch bass and a growing number exceeding 16 inches keep the pursuit interesting. Excellent table fare, feisty bluegills spice up the fly fishing options.

In spring use a sinking line or sinking tip with woolly worms, woolly buggers, leeches, Stayner ducktail, and other stillwater patterns you already have in your vest pockets. When the water warms up surface activity increases. Switch to a floating line and use floating spider flies and deer hair popping bugs to work the weed lines.

For advice on which ponds are working best, check with Chuck Collins at Jimmy's All Seasons Angler in Pocatello.

Two of the region's ponds are managed as trophy largemouth bass fisheries:

Condie Reservoir

This 115-acre reservoir is just off State Highway 34 about eight miles north of Preston. It has a two-bass limit, none under 20 inches. Also has bluegills and receives hatchery plants of rainbows.

Glendale Reservoir

A 230-acre reservoir, it is two miles north and four miles east of Preston. Watch for sportsmen access sign on Highway 34 It has a two-bass limit, none under 16 inches. Strong population with highest catch rate in region. Also has one-pound bluegills and receives hatchery plants of rainbows.

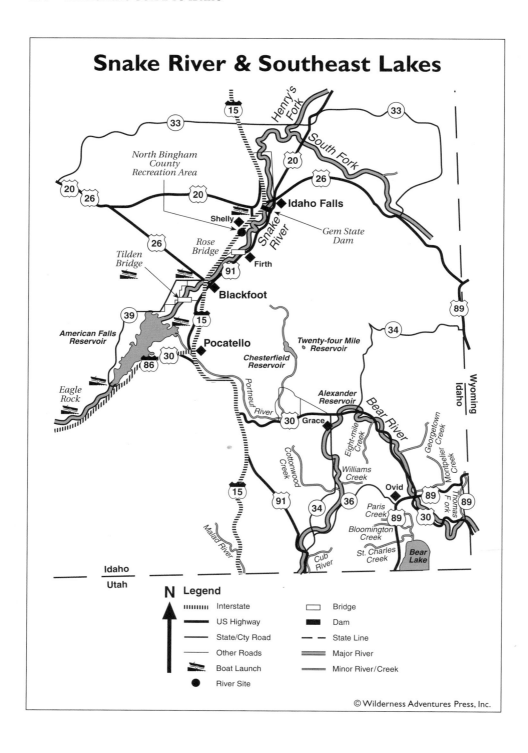

Snake River & Southeast Lakes

North Bingham County Recreation Area

Idaho Falls

Shelly

Gem State Dam

Rose Bridge

Tilden Bridge

Firth

Blackfoot

American Falls Reservoir

Pocatello

Twenty-four Mile Reservoir

Chesterfield Reservoir

Eagle Rock

Alexander Reservoir

Grace

Eight-mile Creek

Cottonwood Creek

Williams Creek

Ovid

Paris Creek

Bloomington Creek

St. Charles Creek

Bear Lake

Georgetown Creek

Montpelier Creek

Thomas Fork

Cub River

Malad River

Portneuf River

Snake River

Henry's Fork

South Fork

Bear River

Idaho

Utah

Wyoming

Idaho

N

Legend

Interstate		Bridge	
US Highway		Dam	
State/Cty Road		State Line	
Other Roads		Major River	
Boat Launch		Minor River/Creek	
River Site			

© Wilderness Adventures Press, Inc.

Stream Facts: Snake River, Gem State Dam to American Falls Reservoir

SEASONS AND SPECIAL REGULATIONS
- From Eagle Rock upstream to American Falls Dam, the limit is 0, catch-and-release for all game fish species from Oct. 16 through Friday before Memorial Day weekend. No bait allowed, barbless hooks required. From Saturday of Memorial Day weekend through Oct. 15, the limit is 2 bass, any size; trout limit is 6, only 2 may be cutthroat and only 2 trout over 16 inches.
- From American Falls Reservoir upstream to the confluence of the South Fork and Henry's Fork at Menan Buttes, open to fishing all year. Trout limit is 6, only 2 may be cutthroat.

FISH
- Rainbows over 20"
- Browns over 25"
- Cutthroat and cutthroat hybrids up to 20"

RIVER MILES
- 50 miles of river total
- Mile 0, Gem State
- Mile 15, Firth
- Mile 25, Blackfoot
- Mile 35, Tilden Bridge
- Mile 50, McTucker Island

RIVER CHARACTERISTICS
- Riffles and deep pools, some large rapids that are tricky
- Good cover along the shoreline where big fish hold but little access for waders

FLOWS
- Winter flows range from 1,000 to 1,500 cubic feet per second
- Summer flows range from 3,000 to 4,000 regulated by dams and irrigation diversions

BOAT RAMPS
- Gem State
- Firth
- Blackfoot
- Tilden Bridge
- McTucker Island

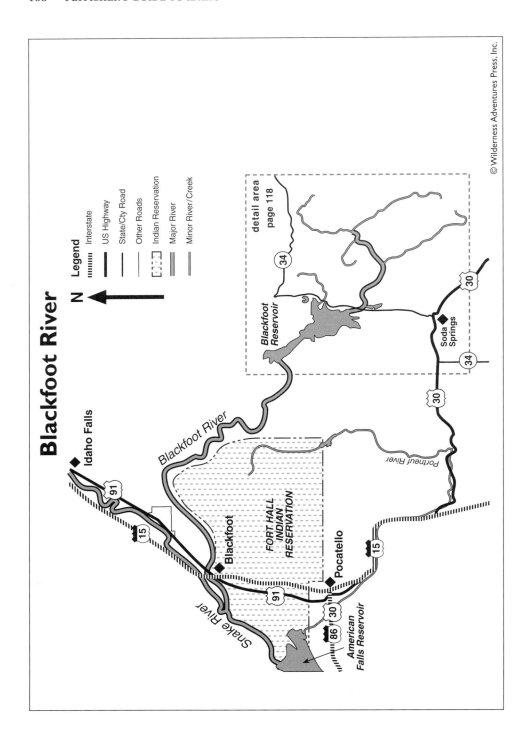

Blackfoot River

N

Legend
||||||| Interstate
——— US Highway
——— State/Cty Road
——— Other Roads
[::::] Indian Reservation
——— Major River
——— Minor River/Creek

detail area
page 118

Blackfoot Reservoir

Soda Springs

30

34

34

30

Blackfoot River

Portneuf River

Idaho Falls

91

15

Blackfoot

FORT HALL INDIAN RESERVATION

Pocatello

91

15

30

86

Snake River

American Falls Reservoir

The Blackfoot has some of the largest stoneflies I've seen anywhere.
Bruce Staples, *Snake River Country: Flies and Waters*

Blackfoot River

Returning to glory

Until recently, the Blackfoot River was a fishing destination with a rich history and little else. It was one of Idaho's best native Yellowstone cutthroat fisheries from the 1950s through the 1970s with fish up to 15 pounds caught out of the Blackfoot Reservoir downstream from the high country headwaters. Its thick populations of giant stoneflies, fed by the river's rich nutrient base, helped its trout grow large quickly. The Upper Blackfoot river system—including the reservoir—was a natural fish factory.

Unfortunately, it didn't last. The fishery collapsed in the early 1980s due to overharvest of fish by reservoir fishers, siltation, and streamside habitat destruction due to poor ranching practices, and poor water conditions caused by drought and dewatering by irrigation farmers.

In 1995, the river with a past was given a future. The Idaho Department of Fish and Game purchased the 1,720-acre Stocking Ranch on the Blackfoot immediately downstream from the confluence of the tributaries of Lanes and Diamond Creeks. The key piece of real estate includes 75 miles of the river and the lower end of an important cutthroat spawning tributary, Angus Creek. The purchase of the ranch along with already implemented harvest limits on Blackfoot Reservoir make the Blackfoot River a place fly fishers should watch closely.

The immediate effect of the ranch purchase on the health of the entire river was to remove cattle from the banks of this pivotal river stretch. Fish and Game rested the entire meadow in 1995 and again in 1996. It manages grazing primarily on the uplands as an exchange area with other ranchers in the upper drainage to allow its streamside areas to heal through reduced siltation and water temperatures. Downriver, a deal between ranchers and Fish and Game will return a channelized section to its original streambed.

Nearly as important is the necessary river access this ranch provides to anglers on a river that had precious little before. With little access, the constituency for improving the fishery was relatively small. Now that too will change. Fish and Game has already constructed two parking areas and plans to build boat landings above and below the ranch. More facilities are planned at this relatively isolated meadow surrounded by the Caribou National Forest. As fly fishers discover the Stocking Ranch, it has the potential of equaling the Harriman Railroad Ranch or the Silver Creek Nature Conservancy Preserve as a required stop on the fly fishing trunk line.

The Blackfoot River flows from its 7,000-foot-high headwaters in the surrounding Caribou National Forest to the Snake River five miles south of the city of Blackfoot at a 4,400 foot elevation. Along with its tributaries, it flows a total of 346 miles—about 105 miles for the main river. It takes a winding, westerly course, flowing through timbered lands and open meadows, though an open valley into a lava canyon and down on to the Snake River Plain. The Blackfoot Reservoir that captures the upper 45 miles of flows for irrigation was built in 1909 and reconstructed in 1987, which raised its level and altered the channel below.

The river's best fly fishing waters are 20 miles north of Soda Springs, above where it crosses Idaho Highway 34. The Stocking Ranch can be reached by turning east on the Blackfoot River Road, which turns into Forest Road 095, and eventually becomes the Lanes Creek Road. Parking is located a mile past the junction with Forest Road 121 and also on the Diamond Creek Road 1.5 miles east of the first parking area. It is easiest reached by driving northeast from Pocatello, but is also close enough to Idaho Falls and Jackson Hole for day trips. The fastest route from these two towns is to take the Grays Lake Road west from Freedom, Wyoming to Henry on State Highway 34.

Many of the great fly fishing rivers of Idaho are tailwater fisheries like the Henry's Fork and the South Fork of the Snake River. Dams above the river stretch regulate the flows, allowing the fish to fatten in relatively stable conditions. The Blackfoot has a tailrace fishery below the reservoir, but it is poor for the opposite reasons. Low winter flows in the drought years of the early nineties have eliminated most of the river's fish population. Improvements to the dam even limited the number of fish that escaped downriver. Unless irrigators and streamside landowners completely change the way they look at the 60 miles of river below the dam, it is doomed to mediocrity just like the Portneuf River to the south.

Blackfoot Reservoir plays a very different but equally important role in the quality of the headwaters fishery. Cutthroat live most of the year in the 19,000-acre reservoir. In late May, they leave the reservoir and head up the Blackfoot River to spawn in headwater creeks like Angus, Diamond, Slug and Lanes. This migration adds fish in the 16- to 24-inch category to the smaller fish in the resident cutthroat population. Moreover, it replenishes the brood stock and when healthy retains a supply of fish to fill good river habitat. In late June and July the spawners return to the reservoir and give fly fishers a window of phenomenal action. Even as late as September anglers report a few stragglers in the river. Anglers can harvest six trout from the reservoir, but none can be cutthroat.

Fishing season on the river above the reservoir doesn't begin until July 1 to protect these spawners. From July 1 through November 30, the trout limit is 6, no cutthroat may be kept, no bait allowed and barbless hooks required. The stream is closed to fishing from December 1 through June 30.

In the drought years there were times when no spawners entered the Blackfoot. It takes three good years to fill the reservoir, and in 1995 it was on the upward swing. Fish and Game biologists recorded 2,000 spawners headed up river that year. That's far less than the hundreds of thousands that would run as far as 60 miles up its tributaries in its heyday, but better than the zero spawners that returned in the late 1980s.

The best time to hit the Blackfoot is in early July, not only because of the presence of the spawners, but also because of the salmonfly hatch. This spring-fed jewel is thick with three-inch-long chocolate-colored stonefly nymphs. They turn into dive-bomber-sized salmonflies in late June, about the same time as their cousins on the South Fork of the Snake.

Early season fly fishers can find success on the reservoir with float-tubes or boats. Rainbows were planted in the reservoir in the 1960s, about the time fishing pressure increased. They provide the bulk of the big-water action, especially near the dam where evening float tubing can be especially effective in early June. Damselflies, large emergers, prince nymphs, bucktails, streamers, and leech patterns are most effective.

River anglers will find the river character changes as they move from the Upper Valley down to the reservoir. They should start at the Stocking Ranch. The river meanders through the meadow, forming cutbanks and a series of pools and riffles that offer good opportunities for waders. Boaters can use drift-boats through this section but the river is narrow in some points and shallow, especially in the upper reaches. A take-out is provided on the southwest side of the ranch on the Blackfoot River Road—Forest Road 095—south of the old guard station. At the bottom of the meadow, the Fish and Game property ends and the river runs into the Caribou National Forest for three miles through a small canyon known as the Upper Narrows stretch. The gradient is steeper through the narrows and the river runs faster through a straighter series of pools and riffles to just below the Slug Creek Bridge, another access point. Then the river drops into a large meadow known as the Lower Valley. Most of the area is private land and access is difficult even with permission. Bruce Staples, one of Idaho Falls best known fly tiers and author of the book, *Snake River Country*, says fishing in the Lower Valley is best avoided in July when carp as large as 20 pounds swim up into the river. He says they drive the trout out by clouding the water when they spawn in the muddy bottom of this lower stretch.

At the bottom of the meadow, the river turns into a deep run into the reservoir. Fishing here is limited by thick willows. Fish and Game and Caribou County have a campground just off Highway 34 on the Blackfoot River Road. Another campground lies seven miles north on the reservoir in the hamlet of Henry.

Fish and Game also has been stocking a separate strain of Bear Lake cutthroat in the Little Blackfoot River, which enters the reservoir at Henry. This experimental effort has suffered from the same low water conditions and overharvest in the reservoir that have hurt the Blackfoot's Yellowstone cutthroat. But it also could benefit from the conditions that are driving the larger river's comeback.

The large stoneflies make popular patterns like the sofa pillow, Mormon girl, or large stonefly nymphs effective early on the Blackfoot. Pale morning duns come off from June through July. A small green drake hatch also comes off in June but is usually over when the season opens. It also has good hatches of golden stones, small and medium caddis and mayflies throughout the season. Elk hair caddis, Adams, blue-winged olives, and Yellow Sallies are a few of the dry patterns that work. Muddlers and streamers are also very good on the Blackfoot, as are grasshopper patterns in August and September. Longtime Blackfoot River anglers say early morning and evening fishing are best. Sunny afternoons are the slowest time.

Blackfoot River: Detail

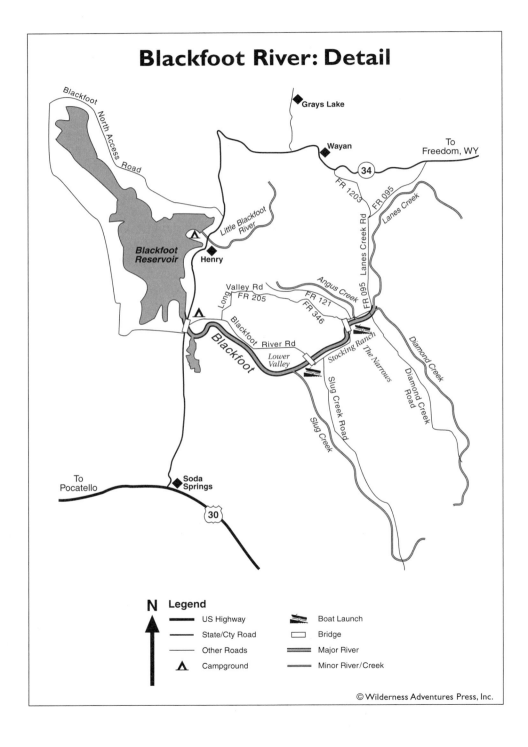

Blackfoot North Access Road

Grays Lake

Wayan

To Freedom, WY

34

FR 1203

FR 095

Lanes Creek

Little Blackfoot River

Lanes Creek Rd

Blackfoot Reservoir

Henry

Valley Rd

Long

FR 205

Angus Creek

FR 121

FR 346

FR 095

Blackfoot River Rd

Blackfoot

Lower Valley

Stocking Ranch

The Narrows

Diamond Creek

Diamond Creek Road

Slug Creek Road

Slug Creek

To Pocatello

Soda Springs

30

N

Legend

— US Highway

— State/Cty Road

— Other Roads

▲ Campground

Boat Launch

☐ Bridge

Major River

Minor River/Creek

© Wilderness Adventures Press, Inc.

Even as the Blackfoot returns to its glory, its isolated location—80 to 100 miles away from airport hubs like Idaho Falls, Pocatello and Jackson—will keep the fishing pressure comparatively low. The scenery is breathtaking with the Caribou Mountains in the background and only ranches in the vicinity. The Blackfoot offers the fly fisher a chance to step back in time to another world without walking into a wilderness.

Effective patterns for the Blackfoot River

Stoneflies like sofa pillows or Bird's stone work best in 4 and 6; golden stonefly are 8-12; PMDs vary from 14-18 as do other mayfly patterns. Grasshopper and ant patterns are deadly in August and September. Standard nymphs like the hare's ear, prince, and March brown, and stonefly imitations such as Bitch Creek work well. Muddlers from 4-14 are very effective here. Streamers, leeches, and sculpins are also popular.

Stream Facts: Blackfoot River

SEASONS AND SPECIAL REGULATIONS

- Upper Blackfoot River: From July 1 through Nov. 30, the trout limit is 6, no cutthroat may be kept, no bait allowed and barbless hooks required. The stream is closed to fishing from Dec. 1 through June 30.
- Diamond and Lane Creeks, and tributaries: From July 1 through Nov. 30, the trout limit is 6, no cutthroat may be kept, no bait allowed and barbless hooks required. The stream is closed to fishing from Dec. 1 through June 30.

FISH

- Yellowstone cutthroat and rainbows in the reservoir and below
- Yellowstone cutthroat and brook trout in the upper river

FLOWS

- Average flows are 168 cfs

RIVER CHARACTERISTICS

Gentle meadow stream for the first eight miles, then faster waters through the narrows as the gradient increases. Slower meandering runs through the Lower Valley, then flat, deep runs into the reservoir. Below the reservoir, unstable river level controlled for irrigation.

FISHING AND BOATING ACCESS

- Mostly private property through the upper river
- Boat landing on the Stocking Ranch, Mile .5, then 7.5 miles of Fish and Game land and a boat landing at Mile 8, followed by Caribou National Forest land through the Narrows
- Access at the Slug Creek Bridge at Mile 12 and at Caribou County campground at Mile 30
- The final public access before the reservoir is at the Highway 34 Bridge at Mile 31
- Boat landing all around the reservoir off Government Dam Road on the southwest and the Blackfoot North Access Road on the northeast and at Henry

MAPS

- Caribou National Forest map for Soda Springs Ranger District

BLACKFOOT RIVER MAJOR HATCHES

Insect	J	F	M	A	M	J	J	A	S	O	N	D	Flies
Green drake						█							Olive Sparkle Dun #10–12; Quigley Cripple #10–12; Olive Hare's Ear Nymph #10–12
Giant stonefly (salmonfly)						█							Bird's Stone #4–6; Sofa Pillow #4–6; Bitch Creek Nymph #4–6
Golden stone						█	█						Stimulator #6–10; Kaufmann's stonefly Nymph #6–10
Pale morning dun						█	█	█	█				Yellow Sparkle Dun #14–20; Parachute PMD #14–20; PMD Cripple #14–20
Blue-winged olive						█					█		Olive Sparkle Dun #16–20; Pheasant Tail Nymph #16–20; CDC Baetis #16–20
Caddis										█			Hemingway Caddis #14–16; Goddard Caddis #14–16; Emergent Sparkle Pupa #14–16

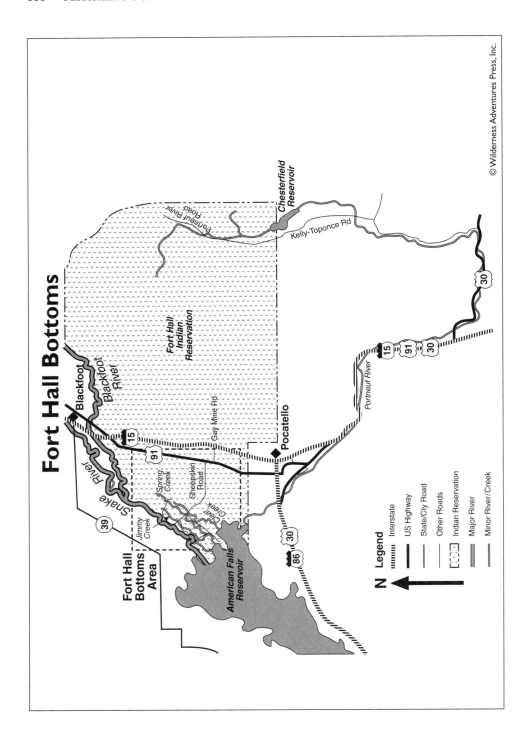

© Wilderness Adventures Press, Inc.

My grandfather was a medicine man. One day he showed me a spring out here. He talked to the water and said, "your soul and that water's soul can communicate."

Arnold Appenay, quoted in *The Snake River* by Tim Palmer

Fort Hall Bottoms

Water and soul

If you consider fishing a religious experience, you can appreciate the Indians of the Fort Hall Indian Reservation.

The connection between the Shoshone and Bannock Indians and the rivers and fish of southern Idaho goes beyond subsistence and recreation. For centuries, their ancestors migrated around Idaho, Wyoming, and Montana, following the salmon runs and the buffalo, celebrating the spiritual link between man, fish, water, animal, and land.

When they were exiled to the nearly two-million-acre reservation in 1868, they continued to follow fish and game through the seasons. Eventually the bison disappeared and the salmon runs declined. Today, 3,500 tribal members live on the remaining 544,000 acres of the reservation. They still hunt and fish throughout the region under treaty rights, but they increasingly depend on the reservation fishery for both religious and subsistence fishing.

Luckily for them and for modern-day flyfishers, the mostly sagebrush desert uplands of the reservation harbor a lush 36,000-acre wetland known as the Fort Hall Bottoms. Springs bubble from beneath the Snake River Plain producing more than 650 billion gallons of water annually — enough to fill the adjacent American Falls Reservoir. These springs flow to the Snake River through several classic spring creeks that the tribes have opened to non-members.

These trout-laden waters were once the secret haunts of only a few knowledgeable eastern Idaho flyfishers, but no longer. The reputation of Fort Hall Bottoms' spring creeks has grown to rival those of storied streams like the Henry's Fork and South Fork of the Snake.

Fees and regulations may change annually. Rates in 2010 ranged from $175 for an annual pass (only 175 available) to $35 per day or $50 for two-days (6-rod daily limit). The annual pass goes on sale the first week of April and often sells out the first day. Permits are sold only during business hours, 8:00a.m. to 4:00p.m., at the Fish and Game Department office at the Fort Hall town site. However, daily permits will be post-dated for next day or the weekend.

For more information, call the Fort Hall Fish and Game Department at 208-478-3956.

For general Fort Hall Indian Reservation information, call 238-3700.

Trophy fishing regulations, improved stream husbandry, and clear, cool spring water make the spring creeks of Fort Hall Bottoms one of Idaho's premiere hidden fisheries. Native Yellowstone cutthroats, rainbows, cuttbow hybrids, and brown trout grow fat and heavy, especially in the deeper waters of lower Spring Creek and Jimmy Creek.

The season runs from mid-April, depending on conditions, through October 31: Catch-and-release for cutthroat and rainbow trout. Three-fish limit on brown trout, none over 12 inches. Artificial lures only.

Spring and Clear creeks are the two best known of the Bottoms streams. Clear Creek runs for seven miles below Sheepskin Road, the boundary for non-Indian anglers. Spring Creek has about 12 miles of fishable waters below Sheepskin when the American Falls Reservoir level is down. Tribal members are allowed to fish the entire creek but most of their own pressure comes during the spawning seasons in the stream stretches north of Sheepskin.

Chad Colter, the coordinator of the tribe's resident fisheries program and a fisheries biologist and tribal member, has headed a successful program to improve stream habitat on both creeks by erecting fences, installing wing dams, and planting willows to shore up the banks. These valuable streams were becoming shallow and wide due to overgrazing along their banks and fluctuating water levels from American Falls Reservoir.

A fly fisherman himself, he has seen remarkable improvement, especially in the smaller Clear Creek. It used to be an angler would have to walk a hundred yards before passing a fish on Clear and area fly fishers rightfully avoided it. Today, anglers pass a fish every six steps and interest is rising.

Spring Creek has always been the favored water of Bottoms fly fishers. It averages about 3,000 trout per mile, Colter said. Spring Creek Road, also called Sheepskin Road on some maps, turns south just before the Spring Creek Bridge. In the spring, a four-wheel-drive with high clearance is a must. Regular cars are used in the summer, but call ahead to the fisheries office before taking a car far down Spring Creek Road any time of the year. From Sheepskin south, waders have good access for the next four miles until just before the Cable Bridge. Just below Cable Bridge is a boat landing for fishing the deeper sections of Spring and Jimmy creeks. Boating is not allowed above the boat landing, but float-tubers might want to try the area just above the landing. The largest fish are found in this lower section of the creek. Colter has seen 8- and 12-pound hybrids taken in the boat landing hole and in the area around Cable Bridge.

The best time to fish Spring Creek is from 11 a.m. to 3 p.m. and then again from 5 p.m. until dark.

Most non-Indian anglers in the Bottoms are fly fishers and kill few fish. Cutthroats are protected and only two other trout can be legally kept with only one under 15 inches allowed. Creel census results show fishers release 90 percent of what they catch.

Effective patterns for the Fort Hall Bottoms spring creeks

Caddis patterns, light Cahills, leeches, woolly buggers, and streamer patterns are good all year. A gray drake hatch comes off about the time the season opens and continues into June. Pale morning duns start in June then come off the rest of the season. Like Silver Creek, Spring and Clear Creeks boast a nice trico hatch in August and September.

The Portneuf River starts on the eastern side of the reservation more than 30 miles away and enters the Chesterfield Reservoir northwest of Soda Springs. A tribal permit allows fishing on the portion of the three-mile-long reservoir within the reservation boundary. For most of its length the Portneuf is a disappointing, sediment-filled natural canal for irrigators. However, in the lower three-and-a-half miles near the Pocatello Airport that lies within the boundaries of the reservation, the river takes on a new character as it is bathed with cold spring water. Brown trout up to 16 pounds have been taken in these waters passed up by even savvy area fly fishers. The flow stays above 200 cubic feet per second year-round.

Most of the year the fishing pressure on the reservation is light, especially when compared with nearby comparable fisheries like the Henry's Fork and Silver Creek. Only during the first month of fishing, which starts April 22, can the Bottoms be considered busy, attracting up to 50 anglers a day. That's because Idaho's general season doesn't open until the end of May. High water conditions elsewhere kept numbers unusually high in 1995 and tribal leaders, concerned about the number of non-Indians using tribal lands, placed a moratorium on new permit sales in June.

Colter and others in the tribe hope to expand fishing opportunities for non-members as a way to increase tourism and create more jobs. Developing Indian outfitting service in the Bottoms and along the 15 miles of Snake River that flows along the reservation boundary could make the Fort Hall fishery a major destination for fly fishers.

Already anglers from 22 states have discovered this clearwater gem in the heart of Indian Country only minutes away from Pocatello and its airport services. But because of tribal politics, it's important that anglers planning a trip to the Bottoms check ahead with the tribal fisheries office to ensure that permits are available.

The tribes also offer excellent pheasant and waterfowl hunting in the fall. An extensive stocking program keeps the Bottoms filled with pheasants, and goose hunting along the American Falls Reservoir is as good as anywhere in the country. The opportunity to mix a wing-shooting trip with fly fishing in October makes Fort Hall even more appealing.

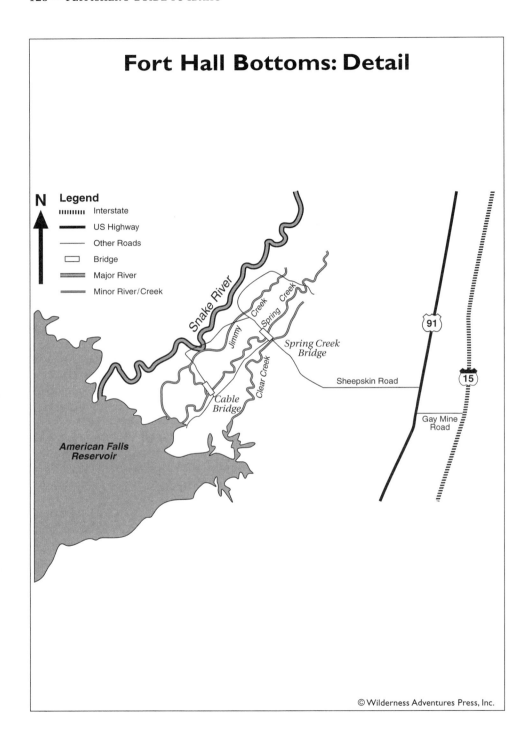

Fort Hall Bottoms: Detail

N

Legend
- ⊞⊞⊞ Interstate
- ▬ US Highway
- — Other Roads
- ▭ Bridge
- ▬ Major River
- — Minor River/Creek

Snake River

Jimmy Creek

Spring Creek

Spring Creek Bridge

Clear Creek

Cable Bridge

American Falls Reservoir

91

15

Sheepskin Road

Gay Mine Road

Stream Facts: Fort Hall Bottoms Spring Creeks

SEASON
- Mid-April to October 31. Call tribal fish & game at 208-478-3864.

PERMITS AND LICENSES
The Shoshone-Bannock Tribes of the Fort Hall Indian Reservation issue permits to hunt and fish on their lands, south of the Blackfoot and Snake rivers, west of Blackfoot and north of Pocatello. Hunting permits issued by the Shoshone-Bannock tribes include waterfowl and ring-necked pheasant. The tribes also require a refundable deposit against possible damages during hunting season. Fees and regulations change annually. For more information, call the Fort Hall Hunting and Fishing Department at 478-3956. For general Fort Hall Indian Reservation information, call 238-3700. Tribal hunting and fishing permits include information on where non-residents are permitted on the reservation. Study it carefully to avoid trespass.

SPECIAL REGULATIONS
- All cutthroat and rainbow trout must be released immediately
- Three-fish limit on brown trout, none over 12 inches.
- Barbless hooks only

RIVER MILES
- Spring Creek, 12 miles
- Clear Creek, 7 miles
- Snake River, 15 miles
- Portneuf, 35 miles

RIVER FLOWS
- Spring Creek: 300 cfs base flow
- Clear Creek: 150 cfs

CHARACTERISTICS
- Spring, Clear, Jimmy, and the lower Portneuf are classic spring creek waters with good wadable stretches in the upper reaches and deeper boat and float-tube runs in the lower ends

BOAT RAMP
Cable Bridge boat landing at Mile 4 on Spring Creek—access to Spring and Jimmy creeks

Central Region

HUB CITIES
- Ketchum/Sun Valley
- MacKay
- Stanley
- Challis
- Salmon

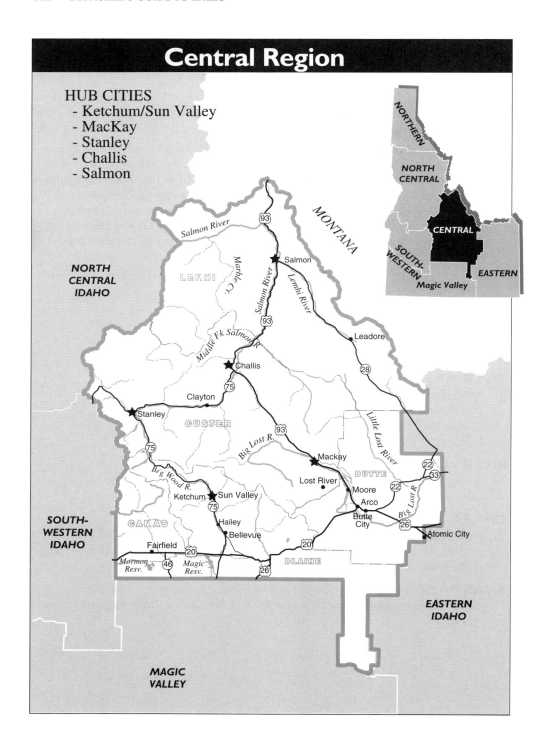

CENTRAL IDAHO

Few fly fishing destinations offer a better range of accommodations, family diversions, and most important, variety of quality fishing opportunities than central Idaho. Ketchum-Sun Valley is one of America's most beloved destination resort areas even without fly fishing. So the fly fisherman who doesn't want to desert his family or make them suffer through his own personal quest has a special opportunity.

"This is the one place I know where you can bring your family fly fishing and not have them complain the whole time," said Roger Schwartz, a long-time fishing guide in Ketchum.

Wilderness hiking, horseback riding, miles of paved paths for rollerblading, swimming, summer ice skating, golf, tennis, celebrity-watching, art galleries, nightlife, excellent cuisine, and a downtown retail area that could challenge the most experienced shopper make the Wood River Valley a family vacation dream.

However, anglers who want to avoid the glitz have several other choices as well. Salmon and Challis maintain the character of Old West ranching and mining towns with good visitor amenities. Stanley lies in the middle of some of the most breath-taking scenery in America. Most of central Idaho remains roadless, wild and untamed, reachable only by whitewater raft, horseback, airplane, or a good set of legs.

Silver Creek stands as one of the best fly fishing waters in the world. Its highly educated and often large rainbow trout draw thousands of anglers a year to test their mettle. Big Wood River, running out of the Sawtooth National Recreation Area right through the middle of Ketchum and Hailey, has turned into a phenomenal fishery in its own right. Over the hill, the Big Lost River adds a tailrace fishery and miles of pocket stream action to the mix.

The Middle Fork of the Salmon River runs a hundred miles through the wildest country in the Lower 48 filled with cutthroat trout. Cutthroat also swim in hundreds of alpine lakes in central Idaho's high mountain wilderness waiting for the hardy anglers who want to see the country from more than just a canyon bottom.

Steelhead fishing in the main Salmon from Corn Creek to Stanley adds a reel-burning, rod-bending jolt to central Idaho's cornucopia of options for fly fishers.

Best of all he loved the fall
The leaves yellow on the cottonwoods
Leaves floating on the trout streams
And above the hills, the high, blue, windless skies

Ernest Hemingway,
Sun Valley, Idaho, 1939

Big Wood Magic

Western Stream With Eastern Flavor

The sun also rises on the Big Wood River.

Long overshadowed in fly fishing sagas by the enchanted Silver Creek, the Big Wood's trout rise to a fly as captivatingly today as they did in those bygone days when Ernest Hemingway fished on its tranquil autumn waters. Hemingway completed his classic novel, *For Whom the Bells Tolls*, in a room of the Sun Valley Lodge in 1940. Photographs on the famous ski resort's hallways preserve memories of the era's preeminent outdoorsman and many other celebrities who played in the Big Wood Valley. Its fly fishing, upland bird hunting, and skiing drew him back often. In his retirement years, Hemingway settled in Ketchum and lived there until he committed suicide in 1961. His grave is an unadorned slab of black granite in the Ketchum cemetery.

The upper Big Wood is responding well to management strategies to produce trophy rainbows, although the tougher regulations were bitterly opposed by non-fly fishers in the late-1980s.

"This river is coming alive," says Roger Schwartz, longtime fly fishing guide in Ketchum. "Even in the keeper sections, people are returning big fish."

Fish and Game studies show the average length of four-year-old rainbows in the Big Wood is 14.3 inches, the same length recorded on Silver Creek and the South Fork of the Boise River.

Big Wood anglers can expect to catch rainbows mostly in the 12- to 14-inch range. Rainbows 16 inches and larger are becoming more common, and the river occasionally delivers a fish exceeding 20 inches. It also contains a few brook and brown trout.

The browns usually are found below Bellevue, although the lower river has been hit hard during the past decade's drought. Twice, irrigation diversions dried up the river from Bellevue downstream to Glendale. This is the lower end of the wild trout management stretch, with a two-trout limit, none between 12 and 16 inches. It extends upstream to the State Highway 75 Bridge at Greenhorn Gulch, downstream from the East Fork.

The upper river fared much better, including the catch-and-release stretch from the Ketchum Bridge upstream to the North Fork of the Big Wood. It provided sufficient water to sustain good fish populations because it is above the irrigation diversions and the streambed has less leakage.

Unfortunately, there are even greater threats to the Big Wood: development in the upper flood plain and the apparent presence of whirling disease. The discovery of whirling disease, a bacteria that attacks the spine and nervous system of fish, at the Hayspur Fish Hatchery in 1995 required the eradication of thousands of trout fry in one rearing pond. So far, the crippling disease has not caused the extensive population losses that have occurred on the Madison River in Montana.

In recent years, the upper Big Wood's popular winter whitefish season essentially became a defacto catch-and-release winter trout season. It was made official in 1996. A no-harvest winter trout season on the Big Wood extends from the North Fork downstream to Magic Reservoir from November 30 to March 31. The no-harvest restriction permits barbed hooks, according to Fred Partridge of the Fish and Game's Jerome office.

"That means it is now legal to fish for trout. They don't have to lie and say they're fishing for whitefish," Partridge said.

However, the winter whitefish season was closed on all streams in the Magic Valley region, except for the Upper South Fork of the Boise above Anderson Ranch Reservoir. The closure was put in place to protect trout in Silver Creek, the lower Malad River, and Billingsley Creek in the Thousand Springs area.

Above the North Fork, the Big Wood receives hatchery plants of rainbows, along with its two most popular tributaries, Trail and Warm Springs Creeks, that join the river in downtown Ketchum.

Rising at 8,500 feet, the source of the Big Wood is the snowmelt off the southern slopes of the Boulder Mountains east of Galena Summit in the Sawtooth National Forest. The Big Wood flows southwesterly 95 miles to the Snake River, falling to an elevation of 2,730 feet at its mouth. A portion of the upper river, tumbling down steep, heavily forested slopes, is in the Sawtooth National Recreation Area. Below the North Fork, it meanders through a broad valley, passing through Ketchum, Hailey, and Bellevue, and flows onto the sagebrush desert of the Snake River Plain.

The Big Wood River between Ketchum and Hailey is a year-round fishery of remarkable opportunity.

Its lower flows are stilled by Magic Reservoir and diverted by numerous irrigation canals. The canyon and Richfield Canal below Magic Dam have a reputation for growing large fish even though both can be quite depleted of water in dry years.

Fly fishers concentrate on the 20-mile stretch from below Bellevue upstream to the North Fork. You can fish in downtown Ketchum or Hailey or seek out more secluded spots upriver and down along its many braided, tree-lined channels.

The favorite stretch for flyfishers is the catch-and-release waters that extend from the Greenhorn Gulch/Highway 75 Bridge, 5 miles north of Hailey, upstream to the confluence of the North Fork of the Big Wood, 8 miles north of Ketchum.

A 2006 follow-up survey reinforced observations of remarkable increases in trout populations over the 20 years since surveys started, said Rob Ryan, regional fisheries biologist. The river's popularity grew in tandem with population growth but "a fishing pressure impact was not recorded."

Ryan said fish 5 inches and larger were recorded in transects at three sites on the river to observe effec-tiveness of management strategies.

In the two-fish limit section, 2,891 fish per kilometer were recorded in downtown Hailey. In the catch-and-release section, 2,394 fish per kilometer were recorded in mid-valley, about 3 miles south of Ketchum. In the general-season, six-fish limit waters above North Fork only 295 fish per kilometer were recorded.

By comparison, similar surveys in 1986 found only 500 fish at Hailey, 800 in mid-valley and 200 above North Fork.

Mean length for age 4 rainbows was 14 inches throughout the river, but Ryan kept hinting that larger rainbows are frequently recorded in mid-valley. They also live longer: 39 percent of the population in mid-valley is 5 years or older, compared to 19 percent in Hailey.

Some of the easiest public access sites are at the Highway 75 and county road bridges crossing the river. Under Idaho law, if you stay within the high water mark when fishing or walking the shoreline, you won't be trespassing.

But trespass is rarely an issue on the Big Wood between Hailey and Ketchum and on Trail Creek in Sun Valley. These are resort communities and they welcome visitors. A bike path parallels most of the river and numerous trailhead parking lots are scattered up and down the valley. Many waterfront landowners also have granted 10-foot public access easements that permit anglers and hikers to roam comfortably along the river banks.

Pick up a copy of "Fishing in the Wood River Valley: Map and Guide" at local fly shops before heading out. It's published by the Blaine County Recreation District, and includes public access sites for Silver Creek.

Above the North Fork at the Sawtooth National Recreation Area headquarters 8 miles north of Ketchum, Highway 75 parallels much of the river, which flows down through federal lands from its headwaters in the Boulder Mountains.

The best fishing begins in July after spring runoff subsides and stays good through summer. Fall weather is often moderate, and fishing can be spectacular and less crowded. The new no-harvest winter trout season runs from January through March. Occasional mild, sunny days offer relatively pleasant fishing for those who have mastered midge hatch techniques. Black-and-white trico patterns work, too.

Winter fishing on the Big Wood often produces more whitefish than trout, but hey—you're fishing.

One of the Big Wood's strongest attractions for fly fishers who may be uncomfortable on the West's larger rivers is that it is a fun stream to fish. It is mostly easy wading and offers classic opportunities to read the waters and catch decent-sized trout from its long runs and deeper pools. The trout aren't always as big as Silver Creek's, but you'll net more fish if you play your cards right.

Fishing the Big Wood is prototypical mountain stream trout hunting. Use the same techniques you would on the tumbling waters of a freestone stream in New Hampshire, Colorado, or northern Spain—just like Hemingway did. When in doubt about a mayfly or caddis hatch, ask the local experts. Chances are you already have most of the basic flies in your vest pockets.

Effective patterns for the Big Wood River

Royal Wulffs, renegades, Adams, blue-winged olives, pale morning duns, light Cahills, elk hair caddis, humpies, and stimulators, 10-16 Some mayflies and midges work better in 18 to 22 in late fall or winter.

Early July: golden stoneflies, 8; western green drake, 10-12; small yellow stones or willowflies; Caddis predominate throughout the season in a variety of sizes and colors from 14-18. Grasshoppers and other terrestrials, August through fall; giant western red quills, 10-12, rusty spinners, 16-18, in late-August; mahogany duns, 10-12, in September.

Nymphs (tied with or without beadheads): hare's ear and prince, 10-16; Zug bugs, 10-14; stoneflies and woolly buggers, 8-12 muddler minnows, streamers, and sculpin patterns also are effective.

Stream Facts: Big Wood River

SEASON
- General season on upper river, Saturday of Memorial Day weekend through Nov. 30
- No-harvest winter trout season, from the North Fork downstream to Magic Reservoir, Nov. 30 to March 31

SPECIAL REGULATIONS
- Glendale Diversion (three miles below Bellevue) upstream to Greehorn Gulch Highway 75 Bridge, two-trout limit, none between 12 and 16"
- Highway 75 Bridge up to North Fork, catch-and-release
- North Fork to headwaters, six-trout limit
- One barbless hook per fly or lure permitted in catch-and-release section only during winter
  no-harvest season

FISH
- Rainbows average 12 to 14", increasing in number above 16" and a few in 20" class
- Some brook trout, and a few browns, mostly below Bellevue

RIVER MILES
- 95 miles from headwaters to Snake River confluence
- Approximately 20 miles, North Fork to Glendale Diversion
- Another 25 miles to Magic Reservoir

RIVER CHARACTERISTICS
- Small, narrow tumbling mountain stream from headwaters to North Fork. River widens and continues down wooded, braided channels through Ketchum, Hailey, and Bellevue, as it bounces off the west cliff face of the Smoky Mountains and enters a broad plain on its braided run to Magic Reservoir. Easily wadable most of course; numerous long, shallow riffles, cascading runs, pools, and cutbanks. Irrigation diversions below Bellevue can drastically lower water levels.

FLOWS
- Spring runoff generally peaks in May or June, falls rapidly and stabilizes by August
- Upper river very vulnerable to drought or incessant dry spells

BOAT RAMPS: N/A

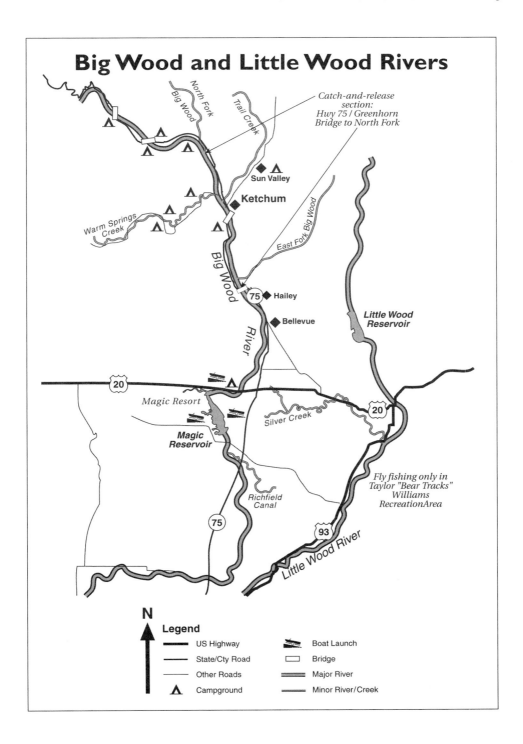

Big Wood and Little Wood Rivers

North Fork Big Wood

Trail Creek

Catch-and-release
section:
Hwy 75 / Greenhorn
Bridge to North Fork

Sun Valley

Ketchum

East Fork Big Wood

Warm Springs
Creek

Big Wood

75 Hailey

Bellevue

River

Little Wood
Reservoir

20

Magic Resort

Silver Creek

20

Magic
Reservoir

Fly fishing only in
Taylor "Bear Tracks"
Williams
RecreationArea

Richfield
Canal

75

93

Little Wood River

N

Legend

▬▬	US Highway	Boat Launch
—	State/Cty Road	▭ Bridge
—	Other Roads	Major River
▲	Campground	Minor River/Creek

Little Wood River

Bear Tracks

An almost unknown treasure in the lava rock and sagebrush desert south of Carey are the Little Wood River's trophy brown trout in the Taylor "Bear Tracks" Williams Recreation Area. Lunkers in the six-pound class lurk here. Rainbows of 16 inches or better also reside in the four miles of fly-fishing-only, catch-and-release waters virtually out of sight of passing motorists on U.S. Highway 93. Good fishing continues about 15 miles downstream to Richfield.

These are the source of the browns that have become established in lower Silver Creek, which in dry years supplies the only flows for the Little Wood. Irrigation diversions often dry up major portions of the river above the creek's mouth upstream to the Little Wood Reservoir. Above the reservoir, the Pioneer Mountains stretch of the river is managed for wild trout, with a two-trout limit.

In the desert, the river cuts its winding channel through rolling sandy hills and plunges through a number of narrow lava chutes that empty into deep pools with swirling eddies. The banks are thickly lined in places by willows and deeply undercut by peak flows.

An added attraction on the lower Little Wood is its year-round fishing season. Since spring awakens earlier in the desert, resident fly fishers often tap its pleasures before the Memorial Day weekend opener on most other rivers. There are often numerous mild days in March or April to work its quiet waters before spring runoff from the mountains takes over the river in May.

Its best seasons are late June and July and late September when trophy brown trout hunters begin their search for autumn spawners. Most years, the water gets too low and warm in late summer, although in a good water year, it is worth exploring with a grasshopper pattern.

Depending on conditions and hatches, you can expect action from the standard dry fly patterns in your vest. Most trophy hunters ply the river with big nymphs and woolly buggers and No. 2 and 4 muddler, zonker, Matuka, and other streamer patterns.

To get to the Bear Tracks and lower Little Wood take State Highway 75 south from Ketchum and turn east on U.S. Highway 20. At Carey, turn south on U.S. Highway 93 and watch for public access signs below the Silver Creek crossing. If you are coming from Idaho Falls on U.S. 20, turn south at Arco and continue south through Carey on U.S. 93.

There are excellent accommodations, restaurants, and services at the resorts and towns in the Big Wood Valley. Some lodges and motels offer special off-season rates in late-spring and early-fall. There are a number of private campgrounds and RV parks, and the Sawtooth National Forest has numerous campgrounds north of Ketchum.

Stream Facts: Little Wood River

SEASON
- Open to fishing all year.

SPECIAL REGULATIONS
- Above Little Wood Reservoir, Baugh Creek to headwaters, two-trout limit.
- Taylor "Bear Tracks" Williams Recreation Area (between Richfield and Silver Creek mouth) catch-and-release, fly fishing only, single barbless hook
- Below Little Wood Reservoir to mouth, except Taylor "Bear Tracks" Williams Recreation Area, general 6-trout limit

FISH
- Small, wild rainbows and a few brook trout above reservoir.
- Strong population of brown trout in the 14" to 16" class, some exceeding 24" between Silver Creek and Richfield; also rainbows up to 16"

RIVER MILES
- 40 miles from headwaters to confluence with Big Wood
- Area of prime interest is the 12 miles from Silver Creek to Richfield
- Fly fishing only waters in the Bear Tracks preserve run about four miles

RIVER CHARACTERISTICS
- High-desert stream that meanders through rolling, sandy hills bisected by basalt ridges. Moderate early-spring and late fall flows cascade down lava rock chutes and spill into a series of long serpentine glides, cutbank pools, and occasional shallow, rocky riffles. Late summer flows are often too warm to fish.

FLOWS
- Spring runoff usually peaks in late-May or June
- Summer irrigation diversions virtually dry up river above Silver Creek, which often sets the flow rate through the Bear Tracks at 400 cubic feet per second or less

BOAT RAMPS: N/A

MAGIC RESERVOIR

Rainbow trout and perch are the primary fish in Magic Reservoir. During good water years, large shallow areas along the southwest side of the reservoir produce huge quantities of small aquatic insects which are available for both to eat. During these years, trout and perch grow rapidly and provide anglers with great fishing.

The trout fishery in Magic Reservoir depends on spring stocking of hatchery rainbow trout. Trout remaining in the reservoir for two years or more easily reach 4 and 5 pounds.

A growing number of brown trout also attract trophy fish hunters.

An impoundment on the Big Wood River, Magic Reservoir is located south of U.S.20 about midway between Ketchum and Twin Falls, a few miles east of Fairview.

"For fly anglers, the best fishing occurs in the spring after ice-out, and in the fall when the browns are preparing to spawn in the lower sections of the Big Wood River," said a spokesman for the Idaho Angler, a Boise fly shop and outfitter.

"There is some good near-surface action with perch minnow imitations when the fish are in shallower water. They will go to great lengths to chase and catch a well-tied imitation."

At full pool the reservoir has an area of 3,700 acres, is 5 miles long and 1.5 miles wide, and has a maximum depth of 120 feet. Boat ramps in the East and West Magic resort areas are usable throughout the summer. Ramps accessible from U.S. 20 are only usable at high water levels. Arms of the reservoir back up into the Big Wood River and Camas Creek in good water years. The Big Wood outlet below the dam also can be productive for anglers. Magic Reservoir has ample opportunities for bank anglers. Access is easy along the southwest side from Lava Point past West Magic resort to the dam. Anglers can also reach the reservoir at East Magic resort, Hot Springs and Moonstone areas. Camping is allowed at Lava Point and along the shoreline.

Boat anglers do well trolling throughout the reservoir, however, areas along the east side and in the narrows may be best. The use of boats also allow anglers to reach a few isolated areas in the narrows or in the inlet bays that are difficult for bank anglers to approach.

A third method of fishing that is popular at Magic Reservoir is float-tubing. Anglers fishing from tubes primarily fly fish using either small dry flies or sinking wet flies. When using dry flies, anglers normally try to match the hatch which is most often midges. When using wet flies, leaches and small midge larvae imitations are good.

Brown trout are found in low numbers throughout the reservoir, but tend to concentrate more along the rocky eastern shore. Some anglers drift along the shore casting flies into the rocky areas similar to fishing for bass.

Recommended flies include conehead perch minnow and other streamer patterns, large black and blood leeches, Stayner ducktails, woolly buggers and Carey buggers.

Magic Reservoir

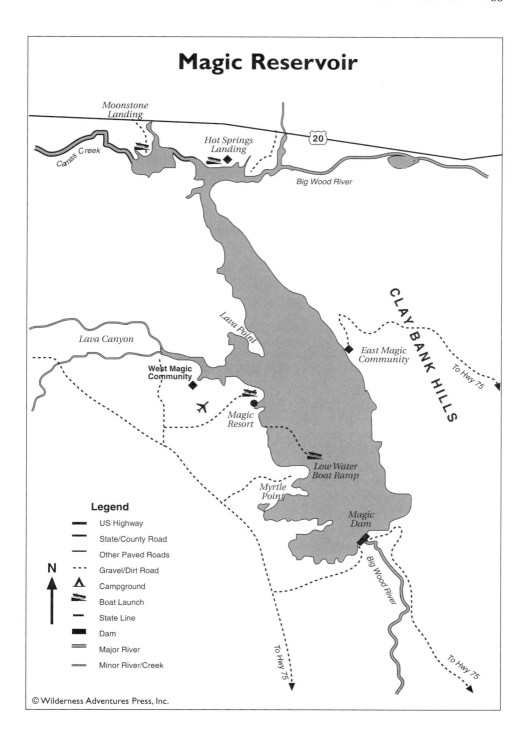

Moonstone Landing

Hot Springs Landing

20

Camas Creek

Big Wood River

CLAY BANK HILLS

Lava Canyon

Lava Point

East Magic Community

To Hwy 75

West Magic Community

Magic Resort

Low Water Boat Ramp

Myrtle Point

Magic Dam

Big Wood River

Legend

━━ US Highway
━━ State/County Road
━━ Other Paved Roads
--- Gravel/Dirt Road
△ Campground
Boat Launch
━ State Line
■ Dam
━ Major River
━ Minor River/Creek

N

To Hwy 75

To Hwy 75

© Wilderness Adventures Press, Inc.

Magic Reservoir was designated as a "family fishing water" in 2002. Regulations for these waters are:

- Year-round season
- General six-fish limit for trout, bass, walleye and pike
- No bag limits on other species
- No length limits
- Standard fishing gear

Other "family fishing waters" in Central Idaho include:

- Little Camas Reservoir, west of Fairfield
- Little Wood Reservoir, north of Carey
- Fish Creek Reservoir, east of Carey
- Camas Ponds, 1 and 2, northeast of Fairfield
- Featherville Ponds, Featherville
- Gavers Lagoon, west of Picabo

Twilight on Silver Creek is the epitome of flyfishing at its best.

We call Silver Creek the graduate school of flyfishing. There's not a fish in that system that hasn't been stuck at least once.

Roger Schwartz, Ketchum fishing guide

SILVER CREEK

Idaho's river of dreams

There comes a time in the life journey of a fly fisher when the soul needs testing as much as the mind.

The skills of casting, reading water, fly selection, and presentation have been honed to fine edges. Countless giants have been caught and released. The motivation that carries an angler from river to stream no longer involves mere numbers or goals.

Place becomes as important as pounds. The combination of immaculate stream with fabled fish, awe-inspiring scenery and classic hatches commands the angler's quest. Ultimately it brings him to Silver Creek, Idaho's quintessential river of dreams.

Loving Creek's restoration is another example of Idaho's fishers commitment to preservation of its fisheries.

Silver Creek is the definition of spring creek. It begins in cold aquifers below the place where Idaho's high desert turns into craggy, snow covered peaks. Its waters bubble from watercress lined springs into boggy, weed laden tributaries—Stalker, Grove, and Loving Creeks—into the main channel. It flows through working cattle ranches, and meanders past fields of alfalfa, barley, and potatoes before carving its way through desert sagebrush into the Little Wood River. Despite great changes in weather and land use, Silver Creek's water temperature and nutrient rich clarity remain constant. Such conditions are nearly perfect for growing large trout and Silver Creek lives up to its potential.

It hasn't always been that way. The Smokey and Pioneer Mountains to the north serve as a backdrop for the creek Field and Stream once called the finest dry fly stream in America. It built a reputation in the shadows of the Sun Valley Ski Resort 30 miles to the north near Ketchum. Union Pacific Chairman Averell Harriman had chosen these mountains to build the West's first major destination ski resort. The resort needed attractions for the summer season and the region's hunting and fishing was a good fit. Harriman's public relations people invited Ernest Hemingway and a host of Hollywood stars to sample the area's natural wonders. Silver Creek's giant rainbows were a press agent's dream and the small Idaho stream quickly gained a worldwide reputation. Affluent anglers from all over the country made pilgrimages to Silver Creek, which became one of the most important fly fishing addresses in the world in the 1940s and 50s.

Alas, such a fishing nirvana could not be sustained for long under the dual stress of fishing pressure and agricultural development. From opening day through the end of the season, Idahoans and visitors alike fished the river hard, following the traditions of the day and keeping most of their catch. Fewer and fewer rainbow, reputed to come from a genetic stock of giant rainbow known as the McCloud stock, survived to spawning size.

Meanwhile, as the stream was building its reputation, farmers were draining many of the marshes upstream and replacing them with fields of barley for making Coors beer. Ranchers were ranging their cattle along the creek, destroying the banks and the streamside vegetation that kept the water temperatures down in the hot summer afternoons. Feeder streams widened because of erosion and siltation caused by the detrimental agricultural practices.

In the face of these problems, Silver Creek's fishery declined and its reputation waned. In the 1970s, as the popularity of fly fishing was growing dramatically, the Henry's Fork of the Snake surpassed Silver Creek in both fishing quality and notoriety.

Ernest Hemingway was not much of a fly fisherman by the time he settled in Idaho. Luckily for Silver Creek and us, his son Jack was. In 1975, the Sun Valley Corporation put 479 acres along the creek's finest stretch up for sale, presenting the ominous possibility that a third threat to the river, second-home development, would arise. Jack Hemingway led a group of local sportsmen on a search for a buyer to save their cherished creek. They went to the Nature Conservancy, a national environmental organization that buys and protects ecologically significant land, and convinced them to purchase the parcel. Hemingway brought Ernest Schweibert, the noted fly fisherman and author, into the fund raising campaign and the Silver Creek Preserve was born.

Hemingway, as a member of the Idaho Fish and Game Commission, led the fight to make the preserve open to fly fishing only and to establish catch and release regulations. The Nature Conservancy restored the banks and river conditions on the preserve under the care of Guy Bonnivier and others. But they didn't stop there.

Leading by example, the Conservancy was able to convince many of its ranching and farming neighbors to place their lands into conservation easements that prevented development and improved the quality of Silver Creek. Today more than 30 miles of Silver Creek and its tributaries and 9,195 acres of habitat are protected. A cooperative fencing program has prompted landowners to fence off ten miles of the river. Ranchers continue to improve grazing practices and water quality is getting even better.

With special regulations along most of its length, the stream has responded remarkably. Once again, Silver Creek is the home of rainbows and brown trout up to 28 inches. It also sports brook trout and a few mountain whitefish. Studies have shown fish densities as high as 3,000 trout per mile. The winter whitefish season on Silver Creek was closed in 1996 to give added protection to trout.

The Silver Creek Preserve of the Nature Conservancy ranks among the most renowned spring creeks in the world.

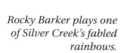

Rocky Barker plays one of Silver Creek's fabled rainbows.

Silver Creek starts on the southwest side of the Wood River Valley in southcentral Idaho, five miles east of the junction of State Highway 75 and U.S. 20 within the Silver Creek Preserve. It can be reached by turning south off Highway 20 on the road just east of Mud Creek five miles from Highway 75. A clear sign for the preserve is also located at the turnoff four miles west of Picabo on Highway 20, on the Kilpatrick Bridge Road.

Stalker Creek, Silver Creek's first tributary, is lined with willows and is only 20 to 40 feet wide. The silt bottomed stream is not a great fishery, but it has access on the west side of the preserve and a place to put in a canoe. It runs east for a mile, then joins larger Grove Creek, which becomes Silver Creek. From here Silver Creek meanders east and then turns south another mile downstream, where it joins with Sullivan Lake inside the preserve. This stretch is the finest on the entire river for large rainbows and browns. It circumvents several islands and is a great place to wade. However, wading etiquette on Silver is different than many other rivers, especially in the preserve. Fishing pressure is high and trudging downstream casting in every hole is considered impolite at best. It kicks up mud and disturbs the fish. Most fly fishers along this stretch find a spot and work it. Like all spring creeks, Silver's banks are marshy and often there is no easy way to get in and out as on the gravel-bottomed rivers Westerners usually fish.

The creek flows for three-quarters of a mile through excellent fishing water just in front of the Preserve cabin. From its deck you can survey the bends and channels that snake through the marshy bottom. During the peak season, the smart fly fishers come early and grab their spot, guarding it jealously until the famous Silver Creek trico hatch begins mid-morning. Loving Creek comes in from the north here and the water gets deeper.

The toughest wading in the preserve comes in the area below Loving Creek known as the S-Turns. This short deepwater stretch has its share of large fish but they are hard to reach in anything like a convenient casting position. Below the S-Turns, the river widens into a flat pond where float tubing is permitted and is the only effective method of fishing. Most float-tubers park at Kilpatrick Bridge, on the eastern boundary of the preserve and hike back toward the cabin along the road about a half-mile, then walk the lower slough trail to reach the water. Signs on the water inform the tuber his restrictions to moving upstream from here.

Below the Kilpatrick Bridge, Silver runs into the Purdy Ranch, a private section that requires coveted fishing access rights, owned by about 300 people. Float tubers or fly fishers in canoes can float through, but cannot go above the high water mark, which in this spring creek is basically the river. This huge pond is filled with large, hard-to-catch rainbows and browns. At the bottom lies a falls that is not navigable so floaters must return the way they came.

The next good access point lies at Highway 20. From this point onward the river is shared with bait and spin fishers. But don't be a snob and pass up the area north of Highway 20. In its waters hide more large browns and rainbows than are found in many trophy stretches of other rivers. A slot limit of two fish, with all trout between 12 and 16 inches protected, keeps this section of Silver Creek top drawer.

Fish and Game owns a large area known locally as Point of Rocks that can be reached from the road that turns north at Picabo, or the road just west of where Silver Creek crosses Highway 20 west of Picabo. Access is also located north of Picabo below Point of Rocks. The rest of the area is private property and access is limited.

Silver Creek crosses Highway 20 again east of Picabo, which has a handy store with flies, sandwiches, drinks, and gas. The road south of Picabo off of Highway 20 goes to the only other public access point, four-and-a-half miles south, known as Priest Rapids.

One other area shouldn't be missed by spring creek aficionados. On Loving Creek, the Idaho Department of Fish and Game has diverted the stream that has fed the Hayspur Hatchery into its historic channel below the brood pond. This marshy spring area has been restored and has fantastic fishing. Like the S-Turns, it is not easy to reach the best spots. You can keep what you catch if it is larger than 20 inches.

Between 9,000 and 10,000 people signed the visitors' log at the Silver Creek Preserve in 1995, and the overwhelming majority were anglers. Between July 1 and mid-August, the preserve's stretches are packed. Silver Creek's big rainbows have had to adjust to the presence of people. Roger Schwartz, a long-time Ketchum guide, explains how the fish manage to grow so big in the face of the crowds of anglers working flies through their habitat. "These fish have learned to feed with fishing pressure," he says.

The sight of noses breaking the surface to take natural flies all around a fisher's presentation occurs with frustrating frequency on Silver Creek. This is the place where every little detail matters.

Leaders as long as 15 feet with tippets ranging from 5X to 8X are a must. When using the relatively large 5X guides recommend mudding the tippet to reduce glare or using low visibility tippets now available. The size and pattern match for flies must be precise at Silver Creek.

The standard method of presenting the fly to Silver Creek's lunkers is a downstream cast with a sweeping mend. Downstream presentation may be illegal on the chalk streams of England, but it is a necessity on Silver Creek. Fishermen who choose to ignore this basic rule will have a long, perplexing day.

Just as walking down the river is considered bad form here, so is flailing the water optimistically, hoping to coax a fish to feed. This is a place where fishers hunt out their spot, watch and wait for a feeding fish, then carefully set up their cast to present the fly without leader glare and drag. That's not to say nymph fishing is out. In fact, it can be a very effective tactic at the right time. But again, the match and presentation in Silver Creek's crystal clear water is important.

That said, the fisher's trip to Silver Creek should start in the fly shops of Ketchum and Sun Valley. They stock the specialized patterns that can make the difference between a big day and merely a lovely day in the sun. Beginners and veterans will benefit from fishing Silver with a guide.

Pale morning duns come off from May through August in sizes from 16 and 18 early down to 20 in the late summer. The Baetis or blue-winged olive is another hatch that comes off sporadically through the season starting in June. Smaller versions, 18 to 22, usually are the match.

The big hatch here is the brown drake in June. These large mayflies, tied in No. 10, are found in their thickest numbers north of Highway 20 in the Point of Rocks area. When they come off in the first weeks of June, many Silver Creek Preserve regulars move up north. However, there are drakes in the preserve as well. Emergers are often more likely to fool the larger fish than dries.

Callibaetis mayflies begin to hatch in late June and are important through much of July. They run in sizes 18 and 20, and the classic pattern is the parachute Adams.

In late July, the tiny trico hatch begins, and the fish seem to concentrate on them when it happens. All of the good trico patterns are tied in size 22, so it takes fine tippets and telescopic eyes to fish them.

Caddis patterns are most effective in June and in October. Grasshoppers and crickets are big in August, and beetles and ants work well in the early season. A mahogany dun hatch comes off late September and early October.

For those who can't get enough of pursuing brawny trout with teeny flies, a winter no-harvest trout season was granted by popular demand in 2000. Downstream from the Highway 20 Bridge, the creek is open to fishing from December 1 to February 28.

Effective patterns for Silver Creek

Sculpins, leeches, and streamers are effective for the large browns. Woolly buggers are also popular, especially when working the ponds. Nymph patterns follow the hatches and subsequently are rather small. Pheasant tails, Zug bugs, and poxy back, wing case nymphs are popular, as well as nymphs tied to match the blue-winged olive hatches.

There is camping at Hayspur, Point of Rocks, and Priest Rapids, but the best accommodations are in Ketchum, Sun Valley 35 miles north on Highway 75), and Hailey (25 miles north). Friedman Memorial Airport in Hailey has commercial air service.

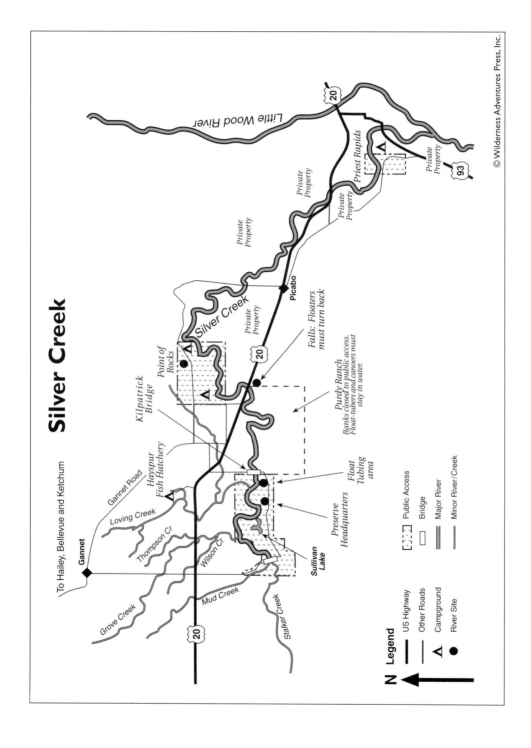

Silver Creek

Stream Facts: Silver Creek

SEASONS
- Downstream from Highway 93, open year-round
- Above 93, Memorial Day weekend through Nov. 30
- Downstream from Highway 20, below Purdy Ranch, no-harvest winter trout season, Dec. 1 to Feb. 28; no bait

SPECIAL REGULATIONS
- No motors
- From the county road bridge north of Picabo upstream to the bridge at milepost 1872 on Highway 20 west of Picabo, two-trout limit with none between 12" and 16"
- From the bridge at milepost 1872 to Kilpatrick Bridge, catch-and-release, no fishing from boat; float-tubes permissible
- From Kilpatrick Bridge west, fly fishing only, catch-and-release. No fishing from rafts or boats; float-tubes permissible below S-bends

FISH
- Rainbows, some over 27"
- Browns, some over 27"
- Brook trout

RIVER MILES
- Mile 0, Stalker Creek access
- Mile .5, Silver Creek access
- Mile 1, Silver Creek Preserve Cabin
- Mile 2, Kilpatrick Bridge-
- Mile 4, Highway 20 access
- Mile 4.5, Silver Creek West access
- Mile 5.5, Point of Rocks
- Mile 6, Old Larkin Ranch
- Mile 7.5, Picabo access
- Mile 14, Priest Rapids Campground

FLOW
- Average flows are 103 cfs with a low flow of 59 cfs and a high flow of 104 cfs

RIVER CHARACTERISTICS
- Spring creek running through marsh for most of its length with several large pond areas too deep to wade. Few beaches or easy wading entry points. Silt bottom in some areas, especially in Stalker Creek and in the lower river north of Highway 20.

FISHING ACCESS
- The best is at the Silver Creek Preserve. Other good spots are the Hayspur Hatchery on Loving Creek, Point of Rocks on the Picabo Road, and Priest Rapids just north of Highway 93 on the Picabo Road.

MAPS
- Silver Creek Preserve map available at the cabin
- Silver Creek 11x17 flyfishing map, by Wilderness Adventures Press

SILVER CREEK MAJOR HATCHES

Insect	J	F	M	A	M	J	J	A	S	O	N	D	Flies
Midges					█	█	█	█	█				Griffith's gnat #18-22; Parachute adams #18-22; Palomino midge #16-22; chironomid larvae #18-22; brassie #16-20
Pale morning dun						█							Yellow Sparkle Dun #16–20; PMD Cripple #16–20; Poxyback PMD #16-20
Blue-winged olive					█				█				Parachute Adams #18–20; Olive Sparkle Dun #18–20; Pheasant Tail Nymph #1820
Brown drake						█	█						Lawson's Brown Drake #10; Brown Sparkle Dun #10; Hare's Ear Nymph #10
Mayfly							█						Parachute Adams #18–20
Trico						█	█	█	█				CDC Trico #20–22; Polywing Trico #20–22
Caddis							█	█					Emergent Sparkle Pupa #14–16; Spent Wing Caddis #14–16; Hemingway Caddis #14-16
Grasshopper; cricket								█	█				Henry's Fork Hopper #8–12; Meadow Hopper #8–12
Mahogany dun								█					Mahogany Sparkle Dun #16–18; Pheasant Tail Nymph #16-18
Callibaetis						█		█	█				Parachute Adams #14; Speckle Win #14-16; callibaetis spinner #16-18
Flavinella							█		█				BWO #14, parachute olive hare's ear #14, olive sparkle dun #14=16

Float tubing on Silver Creek's lower waters is a popular option for an extended day of fishing.

Trophy rainbow are Silver Creek's premiere calling card.

Every day is OK in Copper Basin. You are at the very top of the world and there are miles and miles of valley around you. My dad (Ted Trueblood) and Pete Barrett camped there for years and years. They had already been around the world to catch big fish. What excited them in Copper Basin was catching fresh wild trout and cooking it in the skillet for breakfast.

Jack Trueblood,
Idaho Fish and Game

The Big Lost River

Out from the shadows

The Big Lost River had lived up to it name as far as fly fishers were concerned— until recently.

Located over Trail Creek Pass from the Wood River Valley center of fly fishing in Idaho, its attributes were lost in the shadows of Silver Creek and the Big Wood River. As fly fishing grew in the late 1980s and early 1990s a growing stream of anglers began finding their way over the hill into an entirely different fishery than either of the two better-known rivers.

In tributaries like Summit and Wildhorse Creeks and the East, West and North Forks of the river, they found small streams with few people, a far cry from the crowds of the glitzy valley. Further down, below the Mackay Dam, an excellent tailwater fishery offered the chance for big rainbows beneath Idaho's highest peaks.

Friends of the Big Lost have a special place in their hearts for its mountain whitefish. Many consider it to be a unique subspecies because it's evolved in the closed basin after being separated from the Snake River drainage at the end of the last Ice Age.

Although mountain whitefish were once prolific in the river, by 2005 their populations in the river and tributaries had declined to only about 2 percent of historic levels.

Consequently, the Big Lost may be the only stream in the West with a catch-and-release ban on harvesting whitefish.

Meanwhile, since whitefish can't jump, Trout Unlimited has been leading a cooperative effort with landowners, water users, and state and federal agencies to provide critical fish passage over migration barriers.

In 2007, a rock ramp fish ladder was constructed over the Darlington Diversion. Prior to the ladder, fish were prevented from moving upstream over the diversion during much of the year.

The newly created channel permits easy upstream movement for both juvenile and adult whitefish. Moreover, the benefits of these facilities are not limited to mountain whitefish. Rainbow trout, brook trout and the native non-game species in the Big Lost River now are able to move freely over the diversion.

The project was primarily funded by the Natural Resources Conservation Service and was installed with labor and equipment donated by the Big Lost River Irrigation District. This effort, combined with additional projects in 2008 and 2009 insure that mountain whitefish and all other fish in the Big Lost River once again are able to move freely up and down the main-stem from below the Blaine Diversion to Mackay Dam.

These efforts resulted in dramatic improvements in total fish populations almost immediately Fish and Game biologists reported.

In 2007, biologists found an overall increase in whitefish numbers, both above and below Mackay Reservoir. Particularly encouraging was the large number of 2-year-old whitefish, indicating good reproduction and juvenile survival in 2005. Total estimated abundance in the drainage above the reservoir was 11,663, compared with 2,116 in 2003. Below the reservoir, total abundance was recorded at 1,832, compared with 627 in 2002.

Though this shouldn't be regarded as evidence that the population is out of the woods, it does show the population is resilient and can rebound given habitat improvements and favorable precipitation conditions, biologists reported

"Not only did we see an increase in abundance, but we saw an expansion in distribution as well. Streams such as Fall Creek and Wildhorse Creek, where we found no mountain whitefish in 2003 had, in some cases, numerous whitefish in 2007," fisheries biologists reported. "This is in part due to translocation efforts conducted from 2004-2006.

"During those years, over 3,000 juvenile mountain whitefish salvaged from dewatered reaches of the main-stem Big Lost River were transported and released in portions of the drainage where mountain whitefish were historically abundant but were not found in 2003. It is particularly encouraging to see the translocated fish still residing in the upper reaches of the drainage one to two years after their release, indicating the habitat is suitable to mountain whitefish."

Not surprisingly, the conditions that led to an increase in the mountain whitefish population also seem to have benefited the trout populations. Densities of age 1 and older rainbow trout in the river below Mackay Reservoir were over 3,500 fish per mile in 2007, which is the highest estimated density that's been seen since 1987. Trout densities in the section below Mackay Dam are comparable to trout densities in the South Fork and Henry's Fork of the Snake, which is truly impressive considering the relative sizes of the three rivers.

As with whitefish, the size structure of the trout population was indicative of good recruitment in 2005, with an abundance of 2- to 3-year-old fish. Eighty-three percent of the captured fish were over 12 inches, and 10 percent were over 16 inches. By comparison, in 1987, 53 percent of the population was over 12 inches, and 13 percent was over 16 inches.

The Big Lost River gets it name because it does in fact get lost. It is the largest of eastern Idaho's "sink" streams that run out into the Arco Desert and drain through underground sinks into the Snake River Plain Aquifer. It shows itself again in the Hagerman area on the Snake River as Thousand Springs.

It begins in the Pioneer, Boulder, and Big Lost River Ranges. The Pioneers have peaks exceeding 11,000 feet. The Big Lost Range rises above 12,000. The high peaks make for striking scenery throughout the valley, which is one of the least populated in Idaho and the West in general.

It is filled with sagebrush yet along the river, especially above and below Mackay, giant cottonwoods turn the streamside area into a lush oasis. Below the reservoir, the Lost River goes to work filling irrigation ditches that water potatoes and grain. For the past decade, drought and the fact that more and more water is diverted, it has drained the river annually only a few miles south of Mackay. This is not just a case of seasonal low water. The river ended in early summer and often never returned until the next spring around Arco.

Anglers can bet there won't be much water past the Moore Diversion Ditch about 25 miles downriver. Even when there is, the poor water quality and low temperatures preclude much chance for trout.

However, the area immediately below the dam is excellent and growing in popularity. Mackay Reservoir, a 4,600-acre impoundment, is heavily stocked, and many of those fish end up going over the dam. It hurts the fishery of the reservoir but makes the area below it excellent. Idaho Department of Fish and Game biologists say many 2- to 4-pound fish are found in the stretch and fish up to 8 pounds are sometimes reported.

Persistent anglers who favor the lower river report that rainbows are found in good numbers from 16 to 23 inches long. But make no mistake these fish are hard to catch.

The river here is crystal clear, and light tippets of the kind needed to fish Silver Creek are regular equipment. The river is not wide—as little as 20 feet in places—and it's hard to get a good cast along the bushy shoreline. Below the surface, it has its share of logs and snags. Finally, much of the river even below the dam is private land, so access is limited.

Big Lost River above Mackay Reservoir is remote fishing in lightly fished waters.

Big Lost River

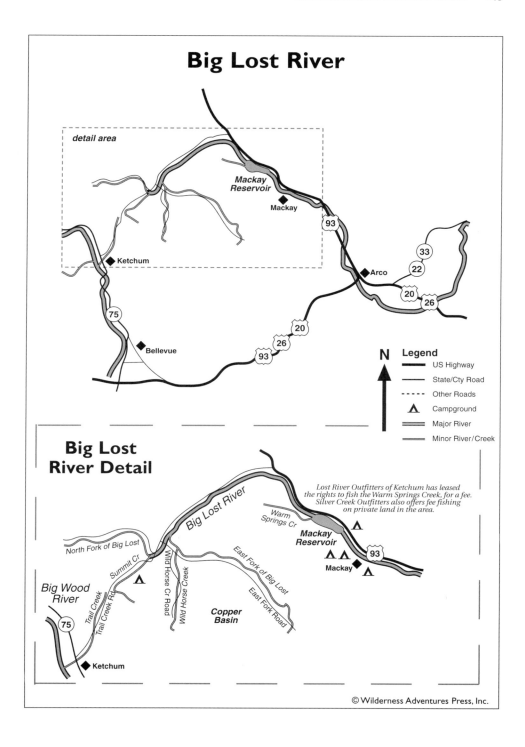

detail area

Mackay Reservoir

Mackay

93

33

22

Arco

20

26

20

75

20

26

Bellevue

93

N

Legend
— US Highway
— State/Cty Road
- - - Other Roads
Λ Campground
▬ Major River
▭ Minor River/Creek

Big Lost River Detail

Big Lost River

Lost River Outfitters of Ketchum has leased the rights to fish the Warm Springs Creek, for a fee. Silver Creek Outfitters also offers fee fishing on private land in the area.

Warm Springs Cr

Mackay Reservoir

93

North Fork of Big Lost

Summit Cr

Wild Horse Cr Road

Wild Horse Creek

East Fork of Big Lost

East Fork Road

Mackay

Big Wood River

Trail Creek

Trail Creek Rd

Copper Basin

75

Ketchum

© Wilderness Adventures Press, Inc.

The two primary accesses are off Highway 93, at the base of the dam, and two miles downstream just south of the Trout Haven Campground. Fishermen can hike downstream along the river below the high water mark. However, you need to be a strong wader to do this since the water is usually high during the irrigation season that runs from May through September.

The area above the reservoir is private land for about 30 miles. It is full of springs and presents a spring creek fishery that compares to Silver Creek. Of special note is Warm Springs Creek, which runs into the reservoir west of the Big Lost. These fisheries are open on a lease fee basis only. The ranchers have leased their ground to Ketchum outfitters in the past so check with them first.

Trail Creek Road, which runs past the Sun Valley Resort east out of Ketchum, goes over Trail Creek Pass and into the Summit Creek drainage. Along the road, anglers have good access to the river and its tributaries for about 30 miles. Summit has a healthy population of brook trout and some rainbows. Fifteen miles from the top of the pass, it runs into the North Fork of the Big Lost, which runs southeast out of the Boulders and follows the Trail Creek road east. This stretch only a few years ago was pretty good but has gone downhill. The East Fork comes out of Copper Basin five miles downriver. Most of Copper Basin is public land with good camp sites, and great access to the West Fork and East Fork. Below the East Fork Road, Trail Creek Road follows the river downstream another 10 miles through public land before beginning to enter private land. All of the area is desolate with no services until Mackay.

Baetis (blue-winged olive) mayflies and caddisflies begin the season as is the case on most of the rivers of the region. When the regular season opens Memorial Day weekend pale morning duns begin to come off and continue through the summer. The river has few large stoneflies but does have a intermittent golden stonefly hatch from early July into August. Mahogany duns come off in the fall, leading into another Baetis hatch.

When the season really begins depends mostly on how releases are done from the dam. Also, heavy snowpack years keep the river running high into July.

Effective patterns for the Big Lost River system

(Most are effective from mid-August on. After September go small.)

Green drake, 10-12; little yellow may, grizzly Wulff, light Cahill, ginger Bivisible, Quill Gordon, 14-16; blue-winged olive, 16,18; chocolate dun, 16-18; parachute Adams, 10-14; CDC rusty spinner, 16-18; gray Wulff, royal Wulff, trude, 10-16; golden stone, 8; small yellow stone, 12; caddis, 12-20; sparkle dun, 14-18; stimulators: olive/orange, 12-16, yellow/orange, 6-14; humpy (red and yellow).

Nymphs: hare's ear, 8-18; Prince nymph, 8-14; Zug bug, 12-16; pheasant tail, 8-18; golden stone, 8; muskrat nymph, 12-16; shrimp, 12-16; sow bug, 12-16; little yellow may; partridge and yellow soft-hackle, 14-16; brown flashback, 12-16; midge patterns (ie, brassies, pupa), 16-22.

Streamers: silver muddler minnow, spruce fly, Mackay Special.

Stream Facts: Big Lost River

SEASONS AND SPECIAL REGULATIONS
- Dec. 1 through Friday before Memorial Day weekend, the trout limit is 0, catch-and-release; whitefish limit is 0, catch-and-release
- Saturday of Memorial Day weekend through Nov. 30, the trout limit is 6; whitefish limit is 0, catch-and-release

FISH
- Rainbows over 20"
- Brook trout, cutthroat, and cutthroat hybrids in the upper section

RIVER MILES
- Mile 0, Trail Creek Pass
- Mile 15, North Fork
- Mile 20, East Fork
- Mile 60, Mackay Dam
- Mile 62, Trout Haven access
- Mile 85, Moore Diversion

RIVER CHARACTERISTICS
- Pool and pocket water in the upper stretches changes with sagebrush banks transforming to spring creek above the reservoir and into tailrace fishery below the dam where wading is tough and access limited.

FLOWS
- Flows above 2000 cubic feet per second below the dam in the summer make wading difficult

BOAT RAMPS
- On Mackay Reservoir

Other Sink Streams

There are several other streams that sink into the desert between Mackay and eastern Idaho that fly fishers should consider if they are camping and traveling through the area. They aren't classic fly streams but do offer the opportunity to catch and keep fish. Just northeast of the Big Lost River Valley is the Little Lost River Valley, where Sawmill Creek flows out of the Lemhi Mountain Range and boasts a one-fish-per-hour catch rate for rainbows and brook trout. It is reached by taking Highway 93 south from Mackay to Arco, going straight on Highway 20 to Highway 22 and turning left or north. Go to Howe and turn north on the Little Lost River Road. Drive 40 miles and turn right on the Sawmill Canyon Road and drive up into the forest another 15 miles to the Timber Creek Campground. The creek is not easy to reach but the fishing is good on caddis and mayflies.

In the next valley, Birch Creek offers some fine small creek fishing. From Howe take Highway 22 to Highway 28 and turn north. Go 20 miles and you start seeing river access and camping on the left. The stocked river offers good camping and fishing opportunities. Three other creeks, Beaver, Medicine Lodge and Camas also begin in the mountains and end in the desert. They are located east of the Birch Creek Valley near Dubois. Again, they are small, stocked creeks with campgrounds that offer anglers traveling between central Idaho and eastern Idaho a change from the larger rivers.

*Brook trout provide some fine small creek fishing in Idaho's
sink streams. Art Today photo.*

Steve Hyde of Idaho Falls poses with a steelhead taken on the Upper Salmon River.
Photo by LaMoyne Hyde.

... in the late 1800s, large wooden flatboats called 'scows' were able to navigate the river, but only one way ... down! Hence, the name, "River of No Return."
Salmon Valley Chamber of Commerce

Upper Salmon River

River of No Return harbors robust steelhead

The Salmon River defines the splendor and indomitable spirit of Idaho's wild heart, its majestic snow-capped mountains, pristine free-flowing streams, and courageous seafaring salmon and trout.

The longest unfettered river in the state, it rises from the scalloped crags of the Sawtooth and Smoky Mountains. Sparkling rivulets trickle off the melting snowpack to merge into icy rills cascading down the rocky, pine and fir carpeted foothills. The newborn river flows onto the upper floor of the Stanley Basin into a series of spring-fed channels that gather into a frothing run through a short canyon below Redfish Lake. It is the first of many whitewater canyon runs on its 408-mile northwesterly lope to the Snake River.

Most renowned for its steelhead fishery, the river's upper reaches offer respectable fishing for resident trout and hatchery "catchables" in the 10- to 12-inch range.

The Salmon's pace quickens and broadens through the lower valley as it collects the frigid spillover of alpine lakes dotting the Sawtooth and White Cloud mountains. Below Stanley, it exits the basin and enters another narrow canyon on its 7,100-foot descent from its source to its mouth.

The Yankee Fork, East Fork, and a legion of mountain creeks feed its plunge between sheer, rocky cliffs and heavily forested slopes. Above Challis, the canyon widens into a broad mountain valley and at the town of Salmon the river picks up the flows of the Lemhi River.

Below the North Fork it enters the second deepest river gorge in North America. The famed Middle Fork spews from its canyon and doubles the Salmon's flows, and a few miles downstream at Corn Creek it says goodbye to roads and civilization.

This is the canyon where it became known as the "River of No Return." Its raging rapids challenge river runners of all skills. In 1805, it turned back the Lewis and Clark Expedition at Pine Creek Rapids and forced the explorers to find another route to the Pacific Ocean. Today, the Salmon and Middle Fork bisect Idaho's most renowned wild-and-free playground.

The lower Salmon collects the South Fork on its wilderness run and briefly reenters civilization at Riggins before plunging into a narrow, treeless, semi-arid canyon. Slicing the east cliffs of Hell's Canyon, it joins the Snake in the deepest river gorge in North America.

Unchecked by dams, the Salmon is the longest river in the Lower 48 that rises and flows entirely within the boundaries of one state. Its 125-mile stretch in the Frank Church-River of No Return Wilderness is protected as a Wild and Scenic River.

The Salmon and its tributaries were for centuries the spawning and rearing waters of teeming hordes of anadromous chinook and sockeye salmon and steelhead trout. Their 980-mile migration from the Pacific to Stanley Basin headwaters is the longest in the Lower 48 and southwestern Canada, and second only to the upstream run of the Yukon River's king salmon.

Once upon past times, salmon returned to spawn in the Stanley Basin in such great numbers that horses were spooked from the river when pressed to cross it. Writhing fish choked the channels so full that men could walk across their backs to the other side. Today, the Salmon's sea runners are fading shadows in the mists of history. Listed as endangered species, Idaho's chinook and sockeye are off-limits to anglers.

The wilderness run of the Salmon River holds major white water stretches.

Wild steelhead also must be released immediately. But in good return years, the river has a viable fishery for hatchery-bred A-run steelhead. These are the smaller of Idaho's two steelhead strains and average four to eight pounds. The B-run steelhead, which average 12 to 16 pounds, and can exceed 20 pounds, primarily run up the Clearwater drainage. Wild B-run steelhead also return to the Middle Fork of the Salmon. An attempt to establish a B-run migration to the East Fork of the Salmon was discontinued.

Steelhead are still the Upper Salmon's claim to fame, but water flows and temperatures play major roles in how far upstream a run extends in fall. When nature cooperates with cool weather, the fish often pass Corn Creek by October and continue up the canyon. Some race as high as the North Fork or higher before laying up for the winter when water temperatures drop below 40 degrees, usually in late November.

The primary steelhead time on the Upper Salmon is in early spring when the run erupts in earnest again. Anglers can start looking for ice break-up around February. March though April, from the Middle Fork upstream into Stanley Basin, it often becomes an upstream race for both fish and fly fishers. The spring run accelerates when water temperatures get above 44 degrees. This may occur in stages as the river warms and cools with the weather.

The 175 miles of the Salmon from Stanley Basin to North Fork is paralleled by State Highway 75 and U.S. 93. A rough gravel and dirt road follows the river another 40 miles from North Fork to the edge of the wilderness at the Corn Creek boat ramp.

Principal resort towns with outfitting and guide services, accommodations, restaurants, and supplies, are Stanley, Challis, and Salmon. Limited services are available at Clayton, North Fork, and Shoup, and a few resorts in the canyon above the Middle Fork.

Except for numerous stretches of private land between Clayton and North Fork, public access to the river is excellent. Forest Service and Bureau of Land Management campgrounds with primitive facilities can be found all along the river. Redfish Lake has the largest full-service campground in the watershed.

No permits are required to run the river during the fall and spring steelhead seasons. Both float boats and jet boats are permitted in the wilderness stretch, although float boaters have to go all the way to pullouts above Riggins. But given the Salmon's huge number of rapids, newcomers and inexperienced boaters are advised to make their first runs with guides or friends who know it well.

The majority of anglers fish the upper river from the banks or gravel bars. This can require some serious rock scrambling in the narrow canyon down from North Fork. Below Corn Creek, the canyon opens up some along an excellent trail following the river.

On the highway sections, spin-casters and bait fishers tend to concentrate on the deep holes. Fly casters who scout the river can find decent uncrowded stretches to wade between North Fork and Salmon, just below Challis in the Penal Gulch area, above the East Fork and below Sunbeam. Above the blown-out dam at Sunbeam, the river becomes progressively shallower and more accommodating to waders.

A trio of flyfishers cast to promising waters for steelhead in early spring on the upper Salmon River.

Whenever you go into the water, it is a good idea to take a wading staff. If you think it would be safer with a life vest, don't go in.

Also watch out for the busy traffic on the narrow canyon's highways. The Salmon's steelhead draw devotees from throughout the state and around the world.

It is a classic steelhead stream that rises in stairstep fashion with string after string of rapids, rocky riffles, and pools. Cast to resting steelhead at the lower end of a pool just above a riffle or rapids. They rest in the flowing tail outs, along the lower sides of pools, and around boulders before continuing upstream.

As the run progresses through the river's shallow upper reaches and riffles, stalk the banks for moving fish taking advantage of quieter flows or pausing for short rests. The thinner waters of the lower Stanley Basin stretch are popular with late-spring fly fishers who like to cast to visible steelhead.

A 9-foot, 7- or 8-weight graphite rod and a reel with a disc drag and 150 to 200 yards of backing are basic steelhead tackle. Attach a floating or weight-forward line and carry sinking tips. Use tapered leaders under nine feet and 2X or 1X.

Steelhead fly patterns are a personal choice, although most anglers use bright flies on sunny days and dark flies in shadowed waters or on overcast days. Popular western steelhead flies, No. 6 to 2, include the green butt skunk, purple peril, Skykomish sunrise, polar shrimp, and muddler patterns. Egg patterns are effective when spawning is occurring.

Most outfitters have tackle shops and can offer advice. Three who specialize in fly fishing for steelhead are Bill Bernt of Aggipah River Trips and Terry Meyers of Silver Cloud Expeditions, both in Salmon, and Bill Mason of Snug Outfitters in Sun Valley.

Permits are required to run the Wild and Scenic stretch of the Salmon from June 20 to September 7. They are issued through a winter lottery conducted by the North Fork Ranger District. Commercial float trips also are available. This is basically a whitewater thrills excursion. The middle section of the Salmon is not known for its summer fishing.

The best summer fly fishing on the Upper Salmon is above the East Fork.

Idaho Fish and Game regularly stocks hatchery rainbows throughout the Stanley Basin, which has relatively easy wading. Steelhead smolts, larger rainbows that survive a winter or two, and a few cutthroat and bull trout add to the mix of opportunities.

Although small, the smolts can be spunky fighters. The bull trout can get to 20 inches, but are a protected species and must be released. Cutthroat also are catch-and-release. Restrictions placed on rainbows limit harvest to only hatchery rainbows with missing adipose fins.

The Salmon River below North Fork has attractive steelhead water.

Floater Guide Salmon River

All reservations and fee payments to float the Wild and Scenic Main Salmon River must be made online. Make all pre-, post-, and controlled season arrangements with http://www.recreation.gov or call 1-877-550-6777

Lottery applications will be accepted only online, beginning December 1 and ending January 31.

For complete details on floating Salmon River through the wilderness, visit the Four Rivers Lot-tery web site: www.fs.fed.us/r4/sc/

For additional information, contact: North Fork Ranger District, PO Box 180, North Fork, ID 83466; (208) 865-2700; Fax: (208) 865-2738

For shuttle and flight services, equipment rentals, and other businesses, contact Chambers of Commerce at Challis 208-879-2771; www.challischamber.com; Stanley Chamber 800-878-7950; www.stanleycc.org; or Salmon Chamber 208-756-2100; www.salmonchamber.com

Fee Payment

The permit holder is responsible for submitting complete and final payment of all recreation fees for the entire group Three (3) days prior to launching. Fees must be submitted to www.recreation.gov.

Please read the Recreation Fee section for more details regarding payment requirements and re-fund policy.

Invasive Species Boat Sticker

Idaho State Boating Law requires that all vessels (motorized and non-motor-ized) display the Idaho Invasive Species Fund sticker to legally launch and operate on Idaho waters. Inflatable, non-motorized vessels less than 10 feet long are exempt. Go to http://parksandrecreation.idaho.gov or call 1-800-247-6332 for more information and purchase options.

Trip Duration

During the Reserved Control Season, (June 20-September 7) group size determines trip length for non-commercial parties:

Groups 21-30, maximum trip length of 6 days, 5 nights; groups 11-20, maximum trip length of 7 days, 6 nights; groups 1-10, maximum trip length of 8 days, 7 nights.

During Pre- and Post- Season the maximum group size is 30 and the maximum trip length is 10 days.

Passenger List

A formal, complete passenger list will be required on the day of the launch. At that time. each per-son will be required to sign a document certifying that the float is a private trip.

Recreation Fee Guidelines

A $6.00 non-refundable Lottery Application fee is required for each lottery application submis-sion.

If a permit is purchased outside of the lottery a $6.00 non-refundable reserva-tion fee is required for each reserved permit.

All persons floating the Wild Section of the Main Salmon River must pay a Recreation Fee in the amount of $4.00 per person per day (or any part of a day) or be a valid Middle Fork/Main Salmon Rivers Season Pass holder. A fee reduction of 50% is available to Senior or Access Pass holders (formerly Golden Age or Golden Access Passports). Season pass holders and persons using a Senior or Access Pass for a fee discount must present their pass, along with their photo ID, to the launch personnel issuing the permit.

Permit holders will be responsible for payment of fees for their entire group. Payment will be made to www.recreation.gov. Final payment must be made three (3) days prior to the actual launch date. Please read the refund policy carefully before submitting payment.

The permit holder must acknowledge any pass holders (Season, Senior or Access) at the time of final payment for the group. Refunds will not be made if the permit holder overpays for pass holders.

Season Passes are available for purchase from the Middle Fork and North Fork offices for $40.00. An order form is posted at www.fs.fed.us/r4/sc/

Purchases of maps and season passes need to be made ahead of time from the North Fork Ranger District. (Also see order forms posted at www.fs.fed.us/r4/sc/) The launch site will still supply the permit holder with one free map.

Campground fees will be accepted in the fee tube at the campground.

The America the Beautiful Interagency Annual Pass is not accepted on the Middle Fork or the Wild Main Salmon rivers.

Refund Policy

Payments can be adjusted until three (3) days prior to the launch date. Refunds will be credited back to the credit card within a few days. No shows will not receive refunds of prepaid fees.

Cancellation Policy

A reservation is not transferable (exceptions may be made on a case-by-case basis for medical or special circumstances; call the North Fork District Office if you have questions about your situation).

If you cannot make the trip, you must always provide a cancellation to the res-ervation system; no exceptions. Cancellations should be entered at the recreation. gov as soon as possible, but have to be received no later than 21 days prior to your launch date.

There will be no exceptions to the 21-day cancellation requirements during normal water flows. The time requirements may be waived, but a cancellation must

The Sunbeam Dam site on the Upper Salmon River no longer hinders steelhead and salmon runs.

always be submitted. When submitting your cancellation, please go to your existing reservation with recreation.gov and follow the instructions.

Failure to provide timely cancellation will trigger a no-show penalty. No-show status restricts you from holding a permit on this river for three years.

Trip Requirements

Permit holder must be 18 years old by the launch date.

Confirmation now required. You must confirm your lottery reservation and pay a portion of your recreation fees no later than March 15. Unconfirmed reservations will be automatically cancelled and re-leased on March 16. All reservations made after this date will be required to pay a portion of their recreation fees at the time the reservation is made to confirm their reservation.

Upper Salmon River

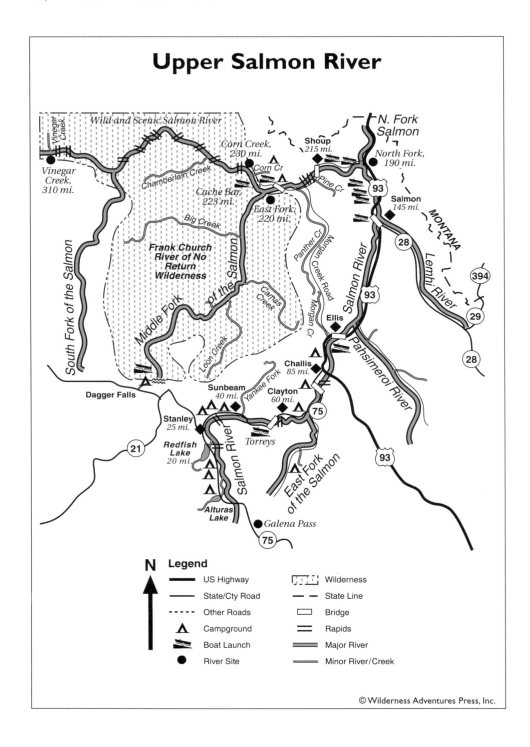

N

Legend

——— US Highway

——— State/Cty Road

- - - - Other Roads

Λ Campground

Boat Launch

● River Site

Wilderness

— — State Line

▭ Bridge

= Rapids

Major River

Minor River/Creek

© Wilderness Adventures Press, Inc.

All boaters floating the Main Salmon are required to obtain a trip permit before launching at any time of the year.

Boaters floating the South Fork and exiting onto the Main Salmon must obtain a permit from the Krassel Ranger District, 208-634-0600. South Fork floaters who exit the Main Salmon the same day they enter the river corridor do not need a Main Salmon River permit.

There are eight launches per day allowed on the Main Salmon from Corn Creek during the con-trolled season -- June 20 through September 7 -- and these are assigned through the 4 Rivers Lottery System at www.recreation.gov. River camp sites will still be assigned at the launch site.

Pre- and post-season launches should also be obtained through www.recreation.gov; there is no limit to the number of launches from Sept. 8 through June 19.

The successful applicant (or reservation holder) becomes the permit holder; he/she must accompa-ny their group at all times while on the river. Permits are not transferable.

Conditions of Float Permit

The permit holder will sign a permit affirming that they have read and under-stood the definition of a private float trip. The permit holder is then authorized to enter onto the Wild Section of the Main Salmon. Permit holder signs the permit and accepts responsibility for the group; the permit holder must accompany the group at all times while on the river.

Carry a porta-potty with sufficient carrying capacity for the number of persons in your group (a person generates approximately 1 lb. of waste per day). If you have a pet, you must transport out all pet feces. A biodegradable plastic bag system will be allowed if it meets EPA Group II waste standards and its waste bags can be disposed of in landfills. A hard-shell waterproof container is required for the used waste bags. This system is suggested for emergency day use only and not recommended for large amounts of waste accumulation.

Use a firepan or ash container to carry out all campfire ashes and charcoal. Ashes and charcoal are to be carried out. Build fires only in safe locations within a fire pan. Tend them with extreme care and completely extinguish prior to retiring for the night or leaving the area. Do not build fire rings.

Pick up all garbage including foil, plastic bottles, cans, cigarette butts, and pop tops, and carry them out of the river area to a provided dump site and recycling sta-tion.

Do not use soap, not even biodegradable soap, in any stream, river, lake or hot springs.

Carry a mesh strainer fine enough to filter coffee grounds. This should be used to strain food par-ticles and other materials from your dish- and gray-water.

Carry a bucket and a shovel for fire fighting.

Effective patterns for the Upper Salmon

There is a sporadic stonefly hatch in late-June, but depend more on nymph patterns. Wet and dry caddis fly patterns are good options through the season. A few grasshopper flies, standard mayfly patterns like the Adams or blue-winged olive, and attractor patterns like the royal Wulff, renegade, humpy, and stimulator can fill out your vest pockets. By fall, the upper river can get quite low. Fly presentation needs to be more delicate and precise.

The Indian Riffles below Sunbeam are closed in late-summer to float boats, rafts, and anglers to protect a drastically diminishing number of spawning salmon.

Stream Facts: Upper Salmon River

SEASON
- Open all year for trout, except posted area between Redfish Creek and Sawtooth Hatchery weir; see regulations

SPECIAL REGULATIONS
- Rainbow over 20" considered steelhead; see regulations for seasons
- Hatchery steelhead open to harvest, special permit required
- Cutthroat catch-and-release on Main Salmon and principal tributaries
- From mouth to headwaters, rainbow harvest permitted only for hatchery fish with clipped adipose fin. Wild rainbow must be released.
- All bull trout in all waters, catch-and-release

FISH
- A-run steelhead, average 4 to 8 lbs.
- A few cutthroat, wild rainbow, and bull trout
- Most action on hatchery rainbows
- Steelhead smolts present year-round

RIVER MILES
- 230 miles from headwaters to Corn Creek, road's end above wilderness
- Mile 20, Redfish Creek
- Mile 25, Stanley
- Mile 40, Sunbeam
- Mile 60, Clayton
- Mile 85, Challis
- Mile 145, Salmon
- Mile 190, North Fork
- Mile 215, Shoup
- Mile 220, Middle Fork
- Mile 230, Corn Creek

RIVER CHARACTERISTICS
- Headwaters to Redfish Creek, the Salmon is a shallow, mountain meadow stream, with braided channels, long glides, riffles and cutbanks. River widens and pace quickens through lower Stanley Basin before it enters first of many deep canyons with whitewater runs, boulder-choked chutes, intermittent pools, and shallow, rocky runs. Returns to a valley environment above Challis that continues past Salmon before it plunges into scenic River of No Return Canyon below North Fork. Frequency of rapids builds through canyon and river enters Wild and Scenic stretch above the Middle Fork. Wilderness run from road's end at Corn Creek is 79 miles to Vinegar Creek, 25 miles above Riggins.

FLOWS
- Spring runoff usually peaks between 20,000 and 15,000 cubic feet per second at Corn Creek in May or June, falls rapidly through July to 5,000 cfs or less in August, and stabilizes through fall.
- Winter and early spring flows well below 2,400 cfs, especially in dry years

BOAT RAMPS
- Stanley
- Indian Riffles
- Torrey's
- Shoup Bridge (south of Salmon)
- Island Park (Salmon)
- Morgan Bar
- Tower Rock
- Red Rock
- Fourth of July Creek
- North Fork
- Deadwater
- Cache Bar
- Corn Creek

The lower Salmon River drops more than one foot per mile in elevation.

Chinook Season Returns to Upper Salmon

In the summer of 2009, the Idaho Fish and Game Commission opened 130 miles of the Salmon River from Island Park in the city of Salmon upstream to the Sawtooth Fish Hatchery above Stanley for chinook salmon fishing for hatchery fish.

This was the first time in more than 30 years that salmon fishing had been opened on this much of the Salmon River. The season was open from June 20 through July 26.

Initially fishing was quite difficult, mainly because of river conditions. Salmon River flows on opening day were 7,030 cubic feet per second, which is 40 percent greater than the 10-year average on that date, and made fishing challenging.

The first recorded chinook kept was on June 28 near Sunbeam Dam. Throughout the season, a total of 3,519 chinook were harvested, of which 2,918 were adults (fish remaining in the ocean at least two years) and 601 were jacks (fish remaining in the ocean for only one year).

The peak of fishing success from the city of Salmon to the Pahsimeroi River occurred during the weekend of July 18 and 19. The peak of the fishery above the Pahsimeroi River occurred during the Fourth of July weekend.

By the second week of July, salmon were entering hatchery traps in greater numbers than required for daily brood-stock collections. Most of the excess fish were recycled back into the river. The Sawtooth Hatchery released hatchery salmon at Torrey's Hole, above Clayton, and the Watts Bridge, downstream of Challis. The Pahsimeroi Hatchery released salmon into the river at the city of Salmon.

Anglers fished for more than 60,000 hours and averaged a salmon caught for every 12 hours of fishing.

Salmon fishing devotees hope this wasn't a flash-in-the-pan event. And, so far, prospects for a continued season on the upper river look promising.

A pre-season forecast for the 2010 run of Snake River spring and summer chinook salmon returning to Idaho indicated that fishing in 2010 would be every bit as good as it was in 2009 for Pahsimeroi Hatchery stocks. However, adult returns to Sawtooth Hatchery near Stanley were not expected to be adequate to provide a fishery above Ellis.

So, stay tuned for future years. Fish and Game biologists will monitor the runs closely and plan fishing seasons based on actual count numbers.

Salmon Memories
Ghost fish in River of No Return haunt elderly angler
By Vicki Runnoe

The face is weathered, the hands gnarled by time and service. The body is a bit stooped from years of both hard work and hard play. But the eyes are alive with the experiences of time and the remembrances of long ago. And when salmon or steelhead are mentioned, they shine with the joyous wonder of the child inside the man.

Leonard Bruderer, approaching his eighth decade, has been hunting and fishing in Idaho since 1937. A native of Brigham City, Utah, he remembers the days of the big fish when catching a 30- to 50-pound salmon was not unusual.

At 16, Leonard got his first taste of fishing for chinook at the Boat Hole on the upper Salmon River near Ellis. Using an old cane pole with a Sears reel, Irish linen line, big treble hooks, and nuts or bolts for weights, Leonard would strip out some line, give it a heave into the river, hang on, and hope. "If you caught one, you wanted to drag it out ASAP—don't let them get into the current." Fishermen who could not land their salmon in time were forced to jump right in and "surf with the salmon" until the next opportunity to land the big fish came along. Floating with a hooked salmon from Deadman Hole to Tunnel Rock was popular especially on a hot July day. Once while fishing the Yankee Fork, Leonard's brother, Delbert, hooked a salmon and jumped in the water with the fish. Leonard grins at the remembrance: "That fish went one way around a big rock and my brother went the other. He lost the fish and his pole, glasses, and hat. We had a blast, I tell you."

Back in those days, camp was usually made right on the beach where boats landed and put in. Stretched out under the stars, Leonard and his family would listen to the sounds of fish migrating through the darkness; a river full of splashing fish. "At night we would lay on the beach and hear splashing. Think 'beaver,' but our flashlight showed tails of fish as they swam by." After a week or two around Ellis, camp might be broken and moved to Meyers Cove up Camas Creek.

Fishing sometimes took a serious turn as it did one day at the Sunbeam Dam. A drowned man floated past the dam from Sunbeam to Torrey's Hole. Leonard and other fishermen tried desperately to retrieve the man's body, but the water carried it too swiftly out of reach. They never heard whether that man's body was ever recovered from the river.

In 1942, Leonard was married and, now accompanied by his wife, Donna, continued the annual fishing trips. It was in the late 1960s that the couple began noticing that the big chinook were not as common as before. Their numbers seemed to be declining with each passing year. Worse yet was the condition of many of the chinook the Bruderers caught. Some were in "pretty tough shape with sores on their heads and strips of skin hanging off." Some were also blind.

Rumors circulated among the fishermen that high nitrogen levels caused the health problems fishermen were seeing in the chinook. The salmon fishery continued to decline. In 1974, Leonard saw Idaho's last statewide salmon fishing season. He quietly remembers (in 1999), "We were told that the runs could come back in a few years. That was 25 years ago."

With the salmon fishing at an end, many fishermen including the Bruderer family turned to the challenge of steelhead fishing. Leonard's first encounter with steelhead, "the original wild yellow-bellied steelhead" came in the 1940s when he fished with a "solid glass Hornel rod christened 'Old Red.'" Scanning the water at Black Hole one day, Leonard spotted tails rippling the water's surface. Instantly recognizing steelhead, he put on his waders and "waltzed into the hole." Putting on a spinglow, Leonard tossed it out and "didn't catch anything. I could see them and feel them swimming around me. I finally threw out ahead of the fish and we hit! Upstream, downstream, across the river! There's nothing comparing those fish to these steelhead today."

In their pursuit of steelhead, Leonard and Donna ventured farther downriver. Fishing "right at the transition of winter and spring—right at ice breakup" required some ingenuity for staying comfortable through the unpredictable weather steelhead fishermen sometimes endure. Leonard's first camper was of his own design and was built in the back of a truck. His "brother like to froze to death riding in this" on one memorable trip. Equipped with only a gas lantern for heat and a steel bed, it did not have any of the modern conveniences of the comfortable home-away-from-home he now tows behind his truck. "We went for basic preservation back then" he said. "Today we have all sorts of equipment. Back then we didn't."

The downriver steelhead trips brought the Bruderers into new country, allowing them to see "all sorts of things." One day at Betty's Hole, a favorite spot, Leonard remembers becoming the object of great curiosity for a family of four river otters.

As he fished, the otters carefully inspected all his equipment before slipping back into the river. "Of course I didn't have a camera," he says.

These downriver steelhead trips began to be shared with more and more fishermen as time went by. Time not fishing was often spent cleaning up other peoples' litter as Leonard and Donna strolled along the roads. The fishing changed too. The stamina and fight of the fish is just not the same as the wild steelhead of years ago. The "original wild fish jump when hooked. These hatchery fish sulk; they get hooked and settle down. The 'B' fish are better, but it's a different kind of fishing. Not to say they're bad, just different."

Different or not, Leonard cherishes having the chance to catch them and returns to Idaho each year to try his luck. Besides the lure of steelhead, there is the chance to renew old acquaintances, swap fish stories, and revisit the past.

Still, Leonard worries about the future of steelhead fishing. He sees more and more people mishandle fish. "Nothing disturbs me more than people who waste! When we fish, we catch it, land it, kill it, take it home and eat it. Too many people carelessly handle fish." He wonders if he will ever have another chance to catch one of the big chinook. For the first time since his marriage, Leonard made the 1999 fishing trip alone. His wife's health did not allow her to accompany him and he misses her company. His eyes mist over as he says huskily "We made memories. Now all we have is memories left."

But oh, what memories!

(Vicki Runnoe, an Idaho Fish and Game employee, is a regional conservation educator in the department's Salmon Regional Office.)

LISTING WON'T STOP STEELHEAD FISHING

To date, steelhead fishing has not been affected by the 1997 listing of wild Idaho steelhead as a threatened species.

The National Marine Fisheries Service included Idaho's Snake River steelhead in its listing of many Pacific Northwest steelhead runs under the Endangered Species Act. The move had long been anticipated and opposed by the Idaho Fish and Game Commission and the department.

"We do not expect any adverse effects on steelhead fishing opportunity in the short term. If there are negative effects, they will most likely come (later) as restrictions to our ability to produce and stock hatchery steelhead in the numbers and places we need to stock them to optimize returns to the sport fishery," former Fisheries Chief Steve Huffaker said. "We feel we have taken sufficient measures to protect wild steelhead, and will continue those efforts. We will work cooperatively to correct any legitimate concerns over harvest of juvenile steelhead in trout fisheries, but will very strongly resist any unnecessary restrictions," he added.

Idaho outlawed harvest of wild steelhead after the 1984 fishing season. Where wild steelhead might be caught, barbless hooks are required and wild fish must be returned to the water immediately and unharmed.

Idaho fisheries managers and other state officials often have pointed out that listing Idaho chinook under the Endangered Species Act has not helped the salmon recover and, because the causes of the steelhead decline are the same as for salmon, they do not expect listing to help wild steelhead numbers. Improved migration of juveniles downstream in the spring to the Pacific Ocean is seen as the most vital factor in recovering steelhead as well as salmon.

"The same limiting factor that is causing chinook to decline needs to be addressed to fix wild steelhead," Huffaker said. "We wish they hadn't listed them because that will just mean more paperwork, more lawsuits, more politics among federal agencies and very little meaningful help for the fish.

"In their listing notice, NMFS referred to hatcheries, harvest, and habitat as the causes for their decline. They left out hydro (hydropower-generating dams), which is a huge factor in Snake River fish. They also stated there was no commercial harvest on steelhead. Treaty tribes under US v. Oregon can harvest and sell 32 percent of the wild B-run (the predominant steelhead of the Clearwater drainage) and 16 percent of the wild A-run (most common steelhead in the Salmon drainage) in commercial gill net fisheries. What planet is NMFS on?"

Steelhead fishing is the name of the game on the Salmon River, but often a pleasant surprise is a bull trout—a threatened species that must be released unharmed. Michael Retallick photo.

These mountains around here are high, rugged and craggy. It's a real alpine experience. Most of the lakes have smaller fish but some of them have fish up to five and six pounds.

Greg Webster, The Bent Rod, Mackay

Central Alpine Lakes

Rocky Mountain high in wilderness playground

Stanley Basin, a subalpine valley in the shadows of the Smoky, Sawtooth, White Cloud, and Salmon River mountains, awards the traveler with one of Idaho's most glorious panoramic vistas.

Many visitors to this wilderness playground view it for the first time from a scenic turnout on State Highway 75 below 8,700-foot Galena Pass, north of Ketchum. Most summer fly fishers topping the pass are headed into the largest wilderness area outside Alaska. Of prime interest are the more than 300 alpine lakes dotting the pine and fir-covered slopes.

Resort towns serving the central wilderness are Stanley on Highway 75, and further downstream on the Salmon River, Challis and Salmon on U.S. 93 Forest Service campgrounds are scattered throughout the region. The ones at Redfish Lake are the largest and most developed, and include a resort. They fill up early in the day at the peak of the season in July and August.

Among the most popular alpine lakes are those in the Sawtooth Wilderness, which is a part of the Sawtooth National Recreation Area. Maps and additional information can be obtained at its headquarters just north of Ketchum. A district ranger's office is between Redfish Lake and Stanley.

The craggy linear peaks that give the range its toothy appearance and name shelter dozens of lakes on a well-maintained trail system. Thousands of hikers a year climb into these 10,000-foot mountains and many are wise enough to carry a pack rod and a box of flies. For some tips on fly patterns, see the section of this guide on alpine lakes above McCall.

Redfish Lake in the Stanley Basin is the starting point of many explorations in the Sawtooth National Recreation Area.

The Sawtooth National Recreation Area is a popular backcountry wonderland.

Pay to Park and Play in SNRA

The Sawtooth National Recreation Area and Ketchum Ranger District "Trailhead Parking Pass Project" charges a fee for recreationists entering the SNRA. Passes are required at 38 parking lots and trailheads.

There are two type of passes: a $5 three-day pass and a $15 annual pass. The three-day pass expires at midnight three days following purchase. The annual pass expires one year from date of purchase.

A Trailhead Parking Pass is only required for vehicles parked at specific trailheads on the Sawtooth National Recreation Area and Ketchum Ranger District. The fees collected from the program will be used for trailhead facility and trail maintenance on these two units.

Passes are available from any Sawtooth National Forest office and at a number of local, private businesses. Passes can also be purchased by mail.

Hikers and campers entering the Sawtooth National Recreation Area should also be aware of rules regarding fires. Campfires are not permitted at a number of wilderness campground sites, and some entire drainages are closed to campfires. Where campfires are allowed, they can be built only on fire pans or fire blankets.

Dog must be on leashes on wilderness trails between July 1 and Labor Day.

For more information, call 737-3200 or visit the Ketchum Ranger District's SNRA info web page: www.svguide.com/frstinfo.htm

Almost all of the larger lakes on the trails have trout that are relatively easy to catch. Although the season starts late in the high country, with ice often lingering into early July, alpine lakes offer one of the most consistently dependable fly fishing opportunities in the West.

Excellent trails to higher lakes start out from the larger ones of the Stanley Basin, including Alturas, Petit, Redfish, and Stanley. All of these lakes hold rainbows, kokanee, and, in some cases, bull trout. But they are not really great fly fishing waters. Long casts with attractor flies will sometimes yield good results. The season on Redfish Lake is limited to January 1 to August 7. Elk Lake and the Valley Creek Lakes are catch-and-release.

On the east side of the basin, the White Cloud Mountains dominate the horizon. They get their name from the white, limestone rocks of the interior peaks of the range. The White Clouds also have dozens of excellent alpine lakes to choose from. Several that feed the headwaters of various Salmon River tributaries also boast healthy wild populations of cutthroat trout that spawn in late-July. Trailheads enter the White Clouds from the west and north at turnoffs on Highway 75, and from the east at the end of the road that extends up the East Fork of the Salmon River.

The best trail guide for both of these ranges is *Trails of the Sawtooth and White Cloud Mountains* by Margaret Fuller. Also see the *Hiker's Guide to Idaho* by Jackie Johnson Maughan.

North of the White Clouds in the Middle Fork of the Salmon River drainage are the Big Horn Crags, another wilderness mountain range with many trout-filled lakes. Trailheads for most of these lakes are located north of Challis and west of Salmon. Ask for maps and directions to the Morgan Creek and Panther Creek roads at the Land of the Yankee Fork Historic Area Interpretive Center at Challis or at the Forest Service offices in Challis and Salmon.

The Lemhi Mountains, southeast of Salmon, the Pioneer Range east of Sun Valley, and the Lost River Range southeast of Challis also have excellent alpine lakes awaiting fly fishers.

Stock up with supplies and have a full gas tank before embarking for trailheads or base camps in any of these remote regions.

Idaho Fish and Game stocks more than 100 of the central wilderness lakes in a three-year rotation with cutthroat, California golden trout, and grayling. This keeps the fishing quality high on lakes that would otherwise be unable to sustain wild populations because of lack of spawning habitat and freeze-out.

The best way to seriously fish the high country lakes is on horseback with a guide. They can get you and your float-tube deep into the backcountry away from the more crowded lower lakes. However, some lakes only a couple of miles from the road offer excellent fishing. Bull Trout Lake, northwest of Stanley, once managed as a trophy trout fishery is now a "family fishing water."

The Salmon River's larger tributaries offer a host of additional fly fishing opportunities. Valley Creek, which runs through Stanley, is stocked and is fishable on public land west of town and at its mouth. Only rainbow missing an adipose fin may be harvested. Wild rainbow and cutthroat are catch-and-release. The Yankee Fork, the Pahsimeroi, the Lemhi, and Panther creeks are all good fishing destinations after spring runoff ends.

Cutthroat harvest was banned in 1996 on all main stem rivers in the upper Salmon drainage, including the Yankee Fork, West Fork of the Yankee Fork, East Fork, Pahsimeroi, Lemhi, and North Fork. Legal minimum size for wild rainbows with adipose fins is 14 inches on the Pahsimeroi and Lemhi Rivers.

Bull trout in all Idaho waters are catch-and-release.

Fly fishers who come to Idaho only to fish famous waters like Silver Creek and the Henry's Fork are missing a memorable fishing experience when they pass up the wilderness lake country. It is the side to Idaho angling that makes it the hidden gem of the fly fishing world.

See the Upper Salmon River Map for an overview of this area.

Goat Lake, west of the Craig Mountains in the Frank Church River of No Return Wilderness, is as far away as you can retreat in the Lower 48 states. Bob Sherwood photo.

*On the Middle Fork, it's not uncommon to have those beautiful cutthroats
come out of the water and take the fly on the way down.*

Stephen Stuebner,
Outdoor writer and river god

The Middle Fork of the Salmon River

Idaho's Wild Heart

Idaho's millions of acres of pristine wilderness—the biggest sections left in the Lower 48—set it apart from all states.

The largest is the Frank Church-River of No Return Wilderness. This 32 million acre federally designated wilderness has streams that don't see anglers all year. At the heart of the Frank lies the Middle Fork of the Salmon River. This river, designated wild under the Federal Wild and Scenic Rivers Act, is known as a whitewater paradise, with dozens of rapids and falls that please rafters and kayakers alike.

Less recognized but just as superlative is the Middle Fork's fishery. Idaho's beloved wild river has an abundant population of westslope cutthroat trout that are only fished

Upper Middle Fork in late summer offers great pocket water fishing for hikers.

by 2,000 of the 10,000 people who float the length of the Middle Fork each year. This strain of westslope cutthroat, Idaho Fish and Game fisheries biologists say, is pure and unique among westslope cutthroat. They are emerald green, mimicking the color of the clear waters of the Middle Fork, perhaps the clearest river in the region. They also have a distinctive red tint that matches the red rocks of the Idaho Batholith within which the Middle Fork carves its way to the main Salmon. The native fish and river are as one. The Middle Fork of the Salmon also supports healthy numbers of bull trout that are becoming rare throughout much of the Northern Rockies.

Once the Middle Fork was one of America's finest salmon and steelhead rivers with thousands of hogs up to 80 pounds making the 800-mile trip from the ocean to spawn in its tributaries. As late as the early 70s, thousands of anglers from around the world would make the long, hard trip into the wilderness to fish for these anadromous giants in places like the deep, clear Pistol Creek Hole, and the river's tributaries. The annual chinook harvest exceeded 2,000 fish in the late 1960s. Today, returning salmon are counted in the dozens as the series of eight dams erected on the Columbia and Snake rivers choke off the migration, especially of the young fish leaving the spawning grounds for the ocean.

Over-harvest very nearly destroyed the cutthroat population until the Idaho Department of Fish and Game put in place catch-and-release regulations on the Middle Fork in 1970. As it has elsewhere, this action proved to be extremely successful, and today cutthroats are numerous and easy to catch along the entire 115 miles of the river.

The only problem for anglers is that most of the river is difficult to reach except by airplane, raft, long hike, or horseback. The only road access on the entire river is at Dagger Falls on its upper stretch, and secondary roads to the upper ends of a few tributaries.

All reservations and fee payments to float the Wild and Scenic Middle Fork of the Salmon River as a private, non-commercial party must be made online. Make all pre-, post-, and controlled season arrangements with www.recreation.gov or call 1-877-550-6777.

Lottery applications will be accepted only online, beginning December 1 and ending January 31. The lottery control season is May 28 to September 3, and group size determines trip length: For non-commercial groups size 21 to 24, maximum trip length is six days, five nights; size 11 to 20, maximum trip length is seven days, six nights; size one to 10, maximum trip length is eight days, seven nights. Outside the Lottery Control Season the maximum group size is 24 and maximum trip length is eight days. For complete details on rules and regulations for floating the Middle Fork of the Salmon, find link to it at www.fs.fed.us/r4/sc/recreation/4rivers

Additional information is located at the end of this section of the book and in the appendix.

The two main launch sites for the Middle Fork are Boundary Creek, below Dagger Falls, and a fly-in strip at Indian Creek, on the lower river.

Boundary Creek is accessed by dirt road from Idaho State Highway 21, and is often closed by snowdrifts until late May or early June. The turn-off to Boundary Creek is located 23 miles west of Stanley or 107 miles northeast of Boise between mileposts 109 and 110. This road is commonly referred to as the Bear Valley Road. This road is rough and narrow. Your vehicle and/or trailer should be prepared for 25 miles of single-lane driving.

From April 1 through June 15, driving is usually limited by snowdrifts and trees on the road. Depending on the amount of snow and the spring weather and temperatures, the road to Boundary Creek may not open until sometime in early June.

High water levels may also be a concern for boaters once spring runoff begins.

Indian Creek is a fly-in location only. Several flights are often required for large groups. The In-dian Creek launch site usually becomes operational in early May and typi-cally stays open through October.

In the spring and fall, Boundary Creek Guard Station may not be open, depending upon condi-tions. If it is not open when you launch, you need to stop at Indian Creek to obtain your permit. Until you get to Indian Creek, campgrounds will be first-come, first-served.

If your launch date occurs when Indian Creek is not open or if you plan to launch from an airstrip or tributary below Indian Creek Guard Station, you will need to contact the Middle Fork Ranger District to obtain your permit. In these situations, call 208-879-4101 to make arrangements to secure your permit at least a week before your launch.

The Boundary Creek launch site closes in late summer or early fall when water levels drop and the majority of the floaters begin launching from Indian Creek. The camp-grounds remain open until cold tem-peratures threaten the water system. The boat ramp is accessible until snow closes the road.

Even experienced drift-boaters and rafters should not attempt to float the Middle Fork without going with an outfitter or someone else with a lot of experience on this river. There are people who run the Middle Fork in drift-boats, but its Class IV falls and rapids are dangerous. In low water years, the upper portion of the wilderness stretch can be hard to negotiate late in the season.

The trip takes anywhere from five to eight days depending on the location of the entry point and the pace. High water makes fishing problematic early in the season, so the fisher-floater should plan the trip after July 1. Early in the season, outfitters put in at Boundary Creek in the Boise National Forest just below Dagger Falls. In low water years and late in the season, floaters fly their rafts into the Indian Creek airstrip, 25 miles downriver.

Idaho outfitter Doug Tims says if God were to set out to design the perfect river for wilderness river trips, he'd make sure there were series after series of exciting but nego-tiable rapids and falls, schools of trout waiting to take the first fly they see, and hot springs all along the route in which to soak at the end of a hard day. That describes the Middle Fork perfectly.

The river doesn't sport a lot of large fish, but 12- and 14-inchers are common. Occasionally fishers will hit an 18-inch trout. Of course there is always the possibility of hooking into one of the large steelhead that may have come upriver early or stayed late. Large bull trout are also taken sometimes, especially below larger tributaries such as Big Creek. Since these fish are often bottom feeders, fishers would be most likely to inadvertently hook these rare fish on a nymph or a streamer. Smaller chinook and steelhead smolts also may be caught along the way.

Make no mistake, there are times when the cutthroats are simply not feeding. After a short rain or when the weather has just changed, sometimes the trout will just shut down. Also, in the lower 10 to 15 miles of the river in a really hot August when the river is low, water temperatures can rise high enough to drive most of the fish to colder waters. If this happens look for the mouths of tributaries for colder water and pockets of fish.

The Middle Fork is formed by the confluence of Bear Valley and Marsh Creeks. Bear Valley is already catch-and-release with only brook trout allowed in the creel. Just last year, Marsh became catch-and-release along its entire length.

Pocket waters on the Middle Fork of the Salmon harbor a multitude of westslope cutthroat.

Several of the tributaries also offer excellent fishing and have the same catch-and-release regulations. Loon Creek can be reached by taking the Yankee Fork Road north from Highway 75 at Sunbeam to the Jordan Creek Road and onto the Loon Creek Road. Loon Creek Ranger station is 40 miles northwest of Highway 75 on mostly dirt roads. Camas Creek can be reached by taking the Morgan Creek Road northwest from Highway 93, 12 miles east of Challis. After about 45 miles, the road turns into Panther Creek Road. Turn left on Silver Creek Road, which ends at the wilderness boundary.

The Middle Fork is not a place where you have to pay great attention to the hatches. In June, a salmonfly hatch moves up the river and in early July anglers report a nice green drake hatch. Afternoon caddis come off for most of the season.

Effective patterns for the Middle Fork of the Salmon

Most anglers stick to attractor flies, royal Wulffs, humpies, renegades, stimulators, and elk hair caddis. Try larger caddis patterns, 8-12, with yellow bodies. Muddler minnows and grasshopper patterns are also dynamite.

Campgrounds are located all along the Middle Fork's length and permittees must register for the campgrounds they choose before they leave. Several have hot springs nearby. Campgrounds are located at Boundary Creek and Dagger Falls. The take-out spot is located at Cache Creek on the Main Salmon three miles down from the mouth of the Middle Fork. River Rat Express Shuttle Service in Stanley (774-2265) will pick up boaters and drop them off.

TRIBUTARY ACCESS TO MIDDLE FORK

Big Creek floaters must obtain a Tributary Permit from the Krassel Ranger District, but they are not required to obtain a Middle Fork of the Salmon launch reservation and permit if they will go all the way out in one day with no overnights.

Contact the Krassel District at 208-634-0600.

Other access points to the Middle Fork are Bear Valley and Marsh creeks, Thomas Creek Airstrip, Lower Loon Airstrip and Creek, Camas Creek, Bernard Airstrip and Big Creek. The airstrips are located at mile 35, 50 and 68, respectively, and are primarily used for river access when the road to Boundary Creek is closed by snow, or when water levels are low to very low.

Camas, Loon and Big creeks are tributaries to the Middle Fork and are usually only navigable during higher water/spring runoff. Marsh Creek is sometimes used to access the Middle Fork before the road opens in the spring, since it can be accessed just off Highway 21.

These creeks are ever changing and swift runs. They should only be used if you have small craft and excellent boating skills. Use extreme caution. They frequently have debris and log jams, and if the water is too high, you may not be able to get under the pack bridges.

For more information, go online to www.fs.fed.us/r4/sc/recreation/4rivers/ and follow link to the Middle Fork of the Salmon.

Middle Salmon River

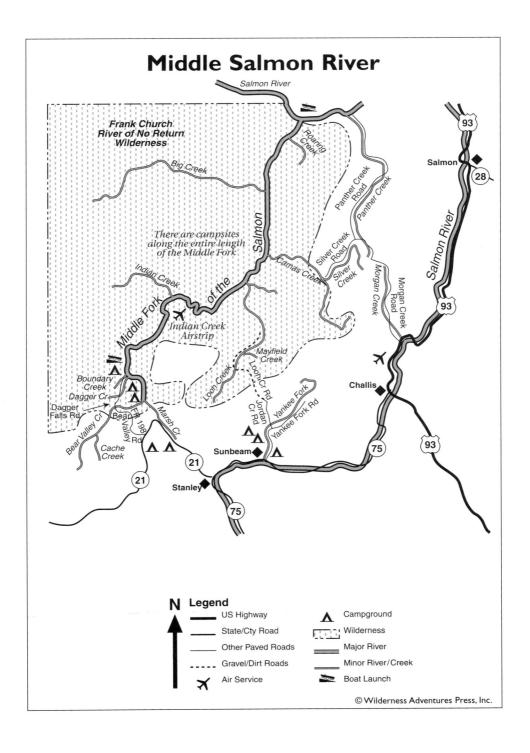

Stream Facts: Middle Fork of the Salmon River

SEASONS
- From the mouth of Roaring Creek, Saturday of Memorial Day weekend through September 30
- From Roaring Creek to Bear Valley Creek, Saturday of Memorial Day to November 30
- Posted area at Dagger Creek, closed all year
- From Dagger Creek to the confluence of Bear Valley and Marsh Creeks, Saturday of Memorial Day to November 30

SPECIAL REGULATIONS
- Catch-and-release entire drainage for trout upstream to the confluence of Marsh and Bear Valley Creeks, including tributaries. Whitefish may be kept only during general season
- Barbless hooks recommended; no bait

TROUT
- Unique westslope cutthroat in 10" to 18" class
- Some rainbows in the lower river and healthy population of bull trout
- Also steelhead and remnant chinook salmon population

RIVER MILES
Total 112 miles, 96 from Boundary Creek to the mouth. One mile between Boundary and Dagger Creeks and 15 miles from Dagger Creek to the confluence of Marsh and Bear Valley Creeks.

RIVER FLOWS
- Spring runoff can exceed 12,000 cubic feet per second and affect the river through July
- Summer flows drop to under 2,000 cfs in dry years

RIVER CHARACTERISTICS
The Middle Fork is one of America's most pristine wild rivers, with big shouldered whitewater even at low flows. Large rubber rafts are recommended, but drift-boats are used by highly experienced boatmen. We recommend no one float the river the first time without an experienced guide or outfitter.

BOAT RAMPS
- Mile 16—Boundary Creek, south side, down a hill by hand on log ramp.
- Mile 115—Cache Creek, Mainstem, Salmon River three miles west of the mouth of the Middle Fork. North side, concrete.

MAPS
- Middle Fork River Map, U.S. Forest Service
- Middle Fork Salmon River 11x17 flyfishing map, by Wilderness Adventures Press. Available at http://store.wildadvpress.com.

Floater Guide: Middle Fork Salmon

All reservations and fee payments to float the Wild and Scenic Middle Fork of the Salmon River must be made online. Make all pre-, post-, and controlled season arrangements with http://www.recreation.gov or call 1-877-550-6777

Lottery applications will be accepted only online, beginning December 1 and ending January 31.

For complete details on floating Middle Fork through the wilderness, visit the Four Rivers Lottery web site: www.fs.fed.us/r4/sc/.

See page 195 for more details.

For shuttle and flight services, equipment rentals, and other businesses, contact Chambers of Commerce at Challis 208-879-2771; www.challischamber.com; Stanley Chamber 800-878-7950; www.stanleycc.org; Salmon Chamber 208-756-2100; www.salmonchamber.com

Trip Duration

During the Lottery Control Season, May 28 to September 3, group size determines trip length:

See page 195 for more details.

Recreation Fees

A $6 non-refundable Lottery Application fee is required for each lottery application submission.

If a permit is purchased outside of the lottery a $6 non-refundable reservation fee is required for each reserved permit.

All persons floating the Wild Section of the Main Salmon River must pay a Recreation Fee in the amount of $4 per person per day (or any part of a day) or be a valid Middle Fork/Main Salmon Rivers Sea-son Pass holder. A fee reduction of 50 percent is available to Senior or Access Pass holders (formerly Gol-den Age or Golden Access Passports). Season pass holders and persons using a Senior or Access Pass for a fee discount must present their pass, along with their photo ID, to the launch personnel issuing the permit.

Permit holders will be responsible for payment of fees for their entire group. Payment will be made to www.recreation.gov. Final payment must be made three days prior to the actual launch date. Please read the refund policy carefully before submitting payment.

The permit holder must acknowledge any pass holders (season, senior or access) at the time of final payment for the group. Refunds will not be made if the permit holder overpays for pass holders.

Season Passes are available for purchase from the Middle Fork and North Fork offices for $40. An order form is posted at www.fs.fed.us/r4/sc/.

Purchases of maps and season passes need to be made ahead of time from the North Fork Ranger District. (Also see order forms posted at www.fs.fed.us/r4/sc/) The launch site will still supply the permit holder with one free map.

Campground fees will be accepted in the fee tube at the campground.

The America the Beautiful Interagency Annual Pass is not accepted on the Middle Fork or the Wild Main Salmon rivers.

Refund Policy

Payments can be adjusted until three days prior to the launch date. Refunds will be credited back to the credit card within a few days. No shows will not receive refunds of prepaid fees.

Invasive Species Boat Sticker Required

Idaho State Boating Law requires that all vessels (motorized and non-motorized) display the Idaho Invasive Species Fund sticker to legally launch and operate on Idaho waters. Inflatable, non-motorized vessels less than 10 feet long are exempt. Go to http://parksandrecreation.idaho.gov or call 800-247-6332 for more information and purchase options.

Conditions of Float Permit

The permit holder will sign a permit affirming that they have read and understand the definition of a private float trip. The permit holder is then authorized to enter onto the Middle Fork of the Salmon Wild & Scenic River subject to the following conditions:

Permit holder signs the permit and becomes responsible for the group and must be present and accompany the group at all times while on the river.

Observe all local, state and federal laws and regulations.

Camp in the assigned camps listed on the permit. (River camp sites will still be assigned at the launch site.)

Carry and display permit upon request of any Forest Officer.

Carry a porta-potty with sufficient carrying capacity for the number of persons in your group. If you have a pet, you must transport out all pet feces.

Use a firepan or ash container to carry out all campfire ashes and charcoal. Build fires only in safe locations within a fire pan. Tend them with extreme care and completely extinguish prior to retiring for the night or leaving the area. Do not build fire rings.

Pick up all garbage including foil, plastic bottles, cans, cigarette butts, and pop tops, and carry them out of the area to a provided dump site and recycling station.

Do not use soap, not even biodegradable soap, in any stream, river, lake or hot springs.

Carry a mesh strainer fine enough to filter coffee grounds. This should be used to strain food particles and other materials from your dish- and gray-water.

Carry a bucket and a shovel for fire fighting.

Riding the Middle Fork of the Salmon's spectacular whitewater is part and parcel of incredible fishing. Jeff Haller photo.

Passenger List

A formal, complete passenger list will be required on the day of the launch. At that time each person will be required to sign a document certifying that their trip is a private trip. A river trip is not commercial if: (1) There is a bona fide sharing of actual expenses, including transportation to and from the site; (2) The trip does not include any costs for payment of salaries or expenses of any person to help with the trip or logistics of the trip; (3) Costs shared by trip members include the costs of damaged or lost equipment, renting or buying minor equipment or the acquisition of new equipment to the advantage of an individual or an organization. Persons involved in unauthorized commercial operations are subject to fine and/or imprisonment.

Cancellation Policy

A reservation is not transferable (exceptions may be made on a case-by-case basis for medical or special circumstances; call the Middle Fork District office if you have questions about your situation).

If you cannot make the trip, you must always provide a cancellation to the reservation system; no exceptions. Cancellations should be entered at the recreation. gov as soon as possible, but have to be re-ceived no later than 21 days prior to your launch date.

There will be no exceptions to the 21-day cancellation requirements during normal water flows. When water levels exceed 5.0 feet, or if the road to Boundary Creek is not open, the time requirements may be waived, but a cancellation must always be submitted.

When submitting your cancellation, please go to your existing reservation with recreation.gov and follow the instructions.

Failure to provide timely cancellation will trigger a no-show penalty. No-show status restricts you from holding a permit for three years.

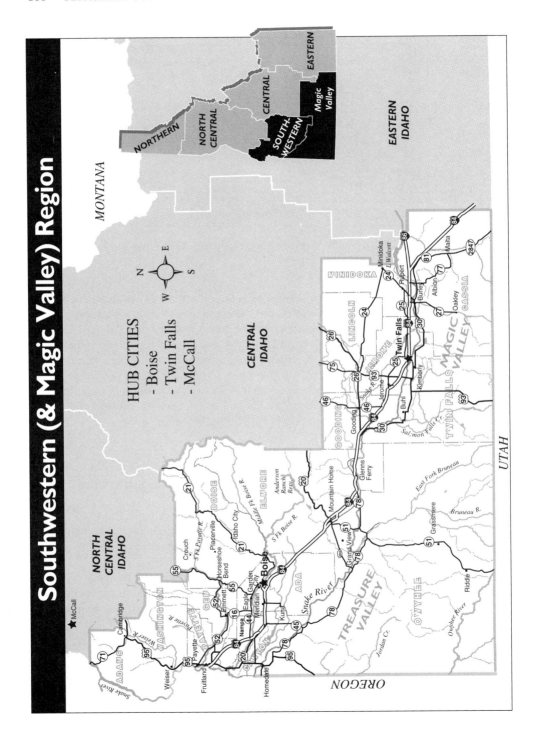

SOUTHWEST IDAHO

Southwestern Idaho is the fastest growing corner of the state, and it's no wonder. With Boise serving as the corporate headquarters of companies like timber titan Boise-Cascade, computer chip marvel Micron, and grocery giant Albertsons, it has become a New West metropolitan center. Along with its urban amenities, Boise's appeal is its proximity to miles of mountain trails, wild rivers, and public lands perfect for camping, hunting, boating, fishing, mountain biking, skiing, and hiking.

Boise residents can leave work and be playing in the back country in a matter of minutes.

For fly fishers the destination is often the South Fork of the Boise River, 60 miles east. Or they may try their hand at bass fishing on Lucky Peak or Little Camas Reservoirs.

On weekends they load up their campers and head into the Boise National Forest where the upper Boise River and its tributaries, the North Fork, the upper South Fork, the Middle Fork, and Big and Little Smoky Creeks offer easy wading and hundreds of miles of pocket water fishing.

To the north lies McCall, only two decades ago a lumber town. Today McCall is filled with art galleries and real estate brokers, booming as a recreation center on the edge of central Idaho. Hundreds of alpine lakes dot the mountains of the Payette National Forest and fly fishers can catch big trout and find solace in the wilds of Idaho at the same time.

Many of the ponds and reservoirs dotting the sagelands of the southwestern Snake River Plain hold some of the best warmwater fisheries in the state. The three largest reservoirs in the region are Oxbow, Brownlee, and C.J. Strike on the Snake. But the premiere bass water in the region is Lake Lowell, southwest of Nampa.

Several of the desert impoundments, as well as the crystal-clear waters of the Thousand Springs area west of Twin Falls, are preferred destinations for early spring and late fall trout fishing.

Upper Boise River

Backcountry pocket water pleasures

Man has left his mark on the Boise River watershed.

The Boise River starts on the western slopes of the Sawtooth and Smoky Mountains of central Idaho at elevations of 10,000 feet and more. By the time it empties into the Snake River it has traveled 200 miles through a part of Idaho that is the home of a third of its citizens.

The river and its tributaries have a combined runoff of just over two million acre-feet of water, much of which is captured to irrigate more than 250,000 acres of cropland. Even before the farmers laid eyes on the productive Treasure Valley as it is called, miners had already dammed and diked and dug up the Boise, leaving tailings, toxic chemicals, and other telltale signs of their trade. Early logging, especially in the highly erodible soils of the northern forks of the river, also took its toll on the river's fisheries.

Despite these limitations, Idaho's Department of Fish and Game has done well with what it has. The South Fork of the Boise has national stature and several other tributaries offer excellent wild trout fishing opportunities. Even where habitat limits wild trout production, strategic hatchery stockings have allowed fishers to spread out over the hundreds of miles of fishing waters available.

What makes much of the Boise River drainage attractive is that the Boise National Forest has developed a series of campgrounds along the roads that provide excellent access to the river's many tributaries. Camping fly fishers can sample the upper Boise's many tributaries and spend a few days on the South Fork of the Boise, camping near backwoods communities like Featherville and Atlanta.

Starting in the east, Big Smoky and Little Smoky Creeks run into the upper section of the South Fork above Anderson Ranch Reservoir. Both are coming on strong as wild trout fisheries that attract the guides from Ketchum. These are fisheries passed over by many of Idaho's most savvy fly fishers.

Little Smoky is 20 miles long and is known as one of Idaho's last strongholds of the rare bull trout. It also has wild rainbow trout. But that hasn't stopped Fish and Game from supplementing the fishery with stocked rainbows.

It can be reached easiest by driving Warm Spring Road or Forest Road 227 west out of Ketchum for 45 miles. This turns into Carrie Creek Road before it connects with the Little Smoky Creek Road, Forest Road 015. Fishermen can work the entire creek both right and left here. Downriver FR015 hits the Big Smoky Road, Forest Road 227.

Big Smoky Creek also has bull trout and self-sustaining wild rainbow populations. It runs 19 miles into the South Fork of the Boise. Both Big and Little Smoky are pocket water fisheries. They have three Forest Service campgrounds. All of the campgrounds are nice but the best is Baumgartner, which sports a cement hot springs.

The South Fork from Big Smoky Creek down to Featherville is 35 miles of excellent pocket water with a series of six campgrounds that attract hundreds of families from around the region each weekend. The stretch above Beaver Creek to Big Smoky Creek is limited to artificial flies and lures with one barbless hook to encourage the wild trout fishery. This reach also has a two-fish limit, none under 14 inches. However, the entire stretch is heavily stocked to allow for the demand of catch-and-keep fishers.

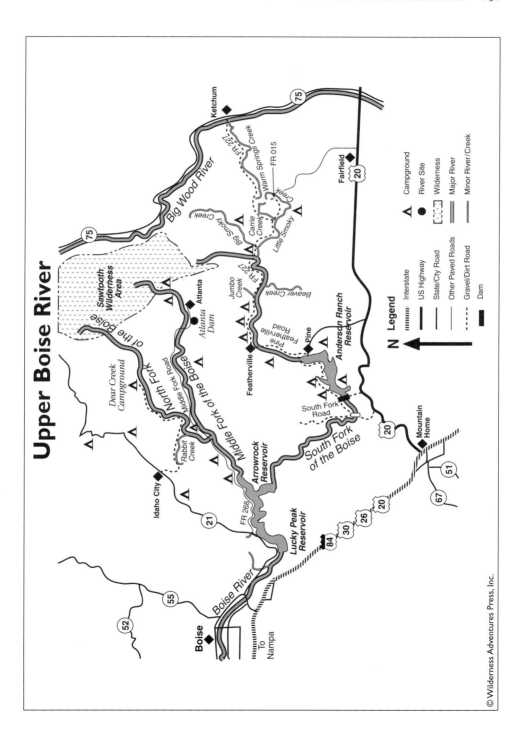

Upper Boise River

Legend

- Interstate
- US Highway
- State/Cty Road
- Other Paved Roads
- Gravel/Dirt Road
- Dam

- Campground
- River Site
- Wilderness
- Major River
- Minor River/Creek

N

Ketchum

75

Big Wood River

FR 227

Warm Springs Creek

FR 015

Fairfield

20

Carrie Creek

Big Smoky Creek

Little Smoky Creek

Sawtooth Wilderness Area

75

North Fork of the Boise

Atlanta

Atlanta Dam

Jumbo Creek

FR 227

Beaver Creek

Pine Featherville Road

Anderson Ranch Reservoir

Dear Creek Campground

Middle Fork Road

Featherville

Pine

South Fork Road

Rabbit Creek

Middle Fork of the Boise

Arrowrock Reservoir

South Fork of the Boise

Mountain Home

20

Idaho City

21

FR 268

Lucky Peak Reservoir

51

67

20

26

30

84

55

52

Boise River

Boise

To Nampa

© Wilderness Adventures Press, Inc.

Know Your Bull

Rare trout must be released

In an effort to protect bull trout, which was listed as a threatened species in 1998, Idaho Fish and Game is trying to make sure anglers know their trout. The trout is native to Idaho, but a lot of folks have trouble identifying it. And Fish and Game says anglers need to know—or let it go. Idaho banned harvest of bull trout in 1996 on state waters.

In 1998, Fish and Game biologists gave anglers a friendly "trout test" as they fished along the Middle Fork of the Boise River. It was a research project designed to find out just how well anglers could identify bull trout. They showed life-like models of six different trout species mounted on a display board with a burlap cover. Anglers were asked to identify each trout one at a time.

"Last year for bull trout on average, 35 percent of the people could identify it from our board." Research Biologist Tony Lamansky said. "Sixty-five percent of the people couldn't identify it."

This has biologists concerned. Obviously, the best way to recover the species is to leave fish in the river. In addition, since the fish is listed as a threatened species, there's a pretty stiff fine—$200—for anglers who have a bull trout in possession.

"We don't want to write those kinds of tickets, so if people can learn how to identify them and just let them go, then they'll be safe and the bull trout will be better off," Lamansky said.

So what are the identifying factors on trout? Lamansky lists the key factors:

- The bull trout doesn't have any spots on any of the fins and (pale) pink or salmon-colored spots (on its flanks).
- Rainbow has a red stripe down the side.The cutthroat has a red slash under the chin. The brook trout has worm-like markings on the fins and three colors on the bottom fins, white, black and red. And the brown trout has large black spots with red spots down the sides with pale halos.
- Lamansky said the folks who took the "trout test" loved it, enjoying the challenge.
- Biologists are hoping there will be an increase in anglers who can identify bull trout with the help of 30 news signs that have been placed along the upper Boise river drainage.
- It's part of a media campaign that Fish and Game has launched called "Know Your Bull!" It includes posters and stickers with a color image of a bull trout to put on your tackle box or coolers to help you identify bull trout. And scientists say the most important thing to remember is: If you don't know, let it go.

Mike Retallick briefly displays a rare bull trout, a threatened species that must be released unharmed.

From Featherville to Pine, the river flows past many cabins kept by Boise residents who fill the area for most of the summer. Despite all the pressure and activity, bull trout survive and kokanee salmon can be taken in the fall when they run out of Anderson Ranch.

North of the South Fork, the Middle Fork of the Boise River starts high in the Sawtooths and runs nearly 70 miles into the North Fork of the Boise River. The first 30 miles are inside the Sawtooth Wilderness area and require a good walk to fish. However, anglers who have made the trip say the fishing for rainbow, cutthroat, bull, and brook trout is excellent. The 32-mile stretch from the Atlanta Dam downriver to the confluence with the North Fork has turned into a good wild fishery with artificial-barbless hook rules and a two-fish limit, none under 14 inches, beginning to bear fruit.

The Middle Fork is reached by several backroad routes to Atlanta. The straightest route is to take Highway 21 east from Boise 20 miles to the Middle Fork Road, Forest Road 268, a right turn just past Lucky Peak Reservoir. The road follows the Arrowrock Reservoir on its north side and then the combined waters of the North and Middle Forks of the Boise. Forty miles east the rivers split with the road continuing up the Middle Fork.

The North Fork is reached by continuing on Highway 21 to Idaho City. Turn right on the Rabbit Creek Road three miles north of this old mining town and drive 20 miles on a dirt road into the North Fork. Below Rabbit Creek the river runs seven miles through mostly roadless country and offers a good wild rainbow trout fishery in pocket water. The 13 miles along the Rabbit Creek Road is a popular fishery that gets some pressure. At Deer Park Campground, the road ends and the North Fork runs another 41 miles into roadless country that ought to be protected as wilderness. On the Middle Fork, from the North Fork upstream to the Atlanta Dam there is a two-trout limit, none under 14 inches.

All of these tributaries have good caddis hatches, so anglers should carry a lot of elk hair dry flies. The hare's ear nymph is the standby, but all sorts of mayfly patterns will pay off, as will attractors for cutthroats and streamers and sculpins for the deeper feeders.

Effective patterns for Upper Boise and tributaries

Elk hair caddis; hare's ear nymph; various mayfly patterns; attractors for cutthroat; streamers such as Mickey Finn and sculpins for deep feeders.

Far and away the best fishery in southwest Idaho is the South Fork of the Boise.
- Andy Brunelle, former Idaho member, Northwest Power Planning Council

South Fork of the Boise

Wild trout under pressure

The South Fork of the Boise River has been the prime example of the wisdom of wild trout management for more than 30 years. It remains the major draw for flyfishers from the state's largest urban area, Boise, and the surrounding communities of more than half a million people. The fishery remains strong, especially for larger fish, in the face of this population growth. But there are disturbing signs that have made the Idaho Department of Fish and Game and dedicated anglers seek answers.

First, the wild rainbow trout population has been trending downward in the 21st Century. Trout densities for wild fish smaller than 9 inches have shown the most decline, while medium-sized trout also show a decline.

Fish and Game's 2006 survey showed a low number of medium-sized trout in the 10- to 16-inch range, which is confounding fisheries biologists because the numbers of larger fish appear to be hanging steady. In fact, Fish and Game reported it had taken, through electro-fishing, some the largest rainbows it had ever seen in the river.

They surmise that the South Fork's stable flows, excellent habitat and fantastic insect hatches may be attracting larger fish from the Boise River's other two branches, the North Fork and Middle Fork, as well as other tributaries. They may be coming down through Anderson Ranch Dam as well.

For anglers, there is a noticeable drop in the number of medium-sized fish being net-ted on the South Fork, especially in the 10 miles above Danskin Bridge. But the big fish are still there and can keep an angler busy all day in a good hatch.

The South Fork's productivity ultimately is a product of its geology. Much of the southwestern mountain country of Idaho is sterile batholith, a granite-based rock forma-tion older than 50 million years. Rivers running through this rock, such as the Payette, are far less productive than those that run through the rich volcanic basalts of the Snake River Plain. The Boise River has drainages in the batholiths, but the South Fork lies on the edge of the Snake River Plain, providing a bounty of mineral nutrients for its rich insect hatches.

The South Fork's other secret for a bountiful fishery is winter flows. The Anderson Ranch Dam holds back waters necessary for irrigation throughout the arid Boise River Valley. Yet, despite the pressures of irrigation farmers, the Bureau of Reclamation keeps the winter flows from the dam above 300 cubic feet per second. This is more than enough to provide trout with necessary holding pools and habitat to ensure winter survival. It's also a tailwater fishery that offers better trout rearing and living conditions than if the dam wasn't there.

In spring, flows may rise to more than 3,000 cubic feet per second during the runoff. When it's this high, the ability of waders to fish the most productive waters, starting about two miles down from the dam, is hampered. But dam operators bring the flows down to around 1,500 cfs as soon as possible because the excess water can't be harassed for hydro-electricity production. In summer, at 1,500 cfs, waders have full run of the first 10 miles. Late in the season, when the irrigation season ends and the flows are dropped below 1,000, floating the upper stretch above Danskin becomes difficult but the fishing really turns on.

Boaters and rafters need to check with the Boise National Forest to ensure the water level is high enough to navigate. The first two miles below Anderson Ranch, the river runs a little fast through the canyon into a wider cottonwood-lined, freestone stream. Another two miles down, the river opens up into a meadow stretch that runs for another two miles. From the Cow Creek Bridge to Danskin, it straightens and widens again.

Fish and Game and the U.S. Forest Service, which controls the land along the river, have attempted to limit the number of boats, primarily by prohibiting outfitting. This hasn't prevented some illegal outfitting but it has made the South Fork harder for a visiting fisherman to learn quickly. Still, the river's fishing is worth the trip to Boise in itself.

Boise flyfishers have been leaving work early and catching the evening caddis hatches for years. Even Sun Valley fishers make the 130-mile trip to the South Fork – while they drive past the Big Wood River and Silver Creek to get the South Fork.

To get to the South Fork from Boise, fishers must drive southeast on Interstate 84 for 35 miles to Mountain Home's second exit to reach U.S. Highway 20. Turn northeast, or left, onto Highway 20 and drive 20 miles to the Anderson Ranch Dam-Dixie Road and turn north, or left. An eight-mile drive down into the canyon takes fishers to Forest Road 113. Turn left, or west, and for the next 10 miles the road follows the river, providing access all along it to the Danskin Bridge. Seven miles downriver is the Cow Creek Road, which runs back up to Highway 20, about 10 miles west of Anderson Ranch Dam road. However, this dirt road takes a little longer time because the driving is slower and the road, true to its name, often is full of cows.

The 17-mile stretch of river below Danskin is only fishable by drift boat or raft and it takes good boating skills to float it. But for proficient boaters, it's worth it.

With the lower pressure comes more medium-sized fish, but all are a little less educated and more eager to take flies. Many anglers float the stretch in a day but there are some good campsites to stretch out the trip through the remote canyon.

Raspberry Rapid is a class IV rapid, so beware - it has been deadly in high water.

The lower South Fork runs through a large, deserted canyon and empties into Arrowrock Reservoir. The take out is at the Neal Bridge on Black's Creek Road, which is reached by taking Exit 64 off I-84, southeast of Boise.

The South Fork of the Boise's hallmark mayfly hatch is the "pink Albert" cahill. Known scientifically as Epeorus albertea, the pink Albert comes off on the river throughout the day from July through September. The Pink Albert fly is tied primarily in a size 14 and 16 and is a must-have fly selection for South Fork anglers.

Don't forget the salmonfly. These big stoneflies come off around the end of June and continue through July.

In June, caddisflies are the major hatch but an occasional early small yellow stonefly will work. These stoneflies come off in July and August. A Yellow Sally pattern in size 12 to 16 works well.

From August through October, blue-winged olive hatches carry the angler into the late season. Craneflies are around from September through October. There also is an orange caddis in October.

A mountain whitefish season is open during the winter, when trout are to be released. Since most fishermen release all trout anyway there is little effect on the population. March brown nymphs are popular among these "whitefish anglers". Prince nymphs and Hare's Ear nymphs also can be effective when the hatches turn off. A Stimulator in size 16 or 14 also is deadly.

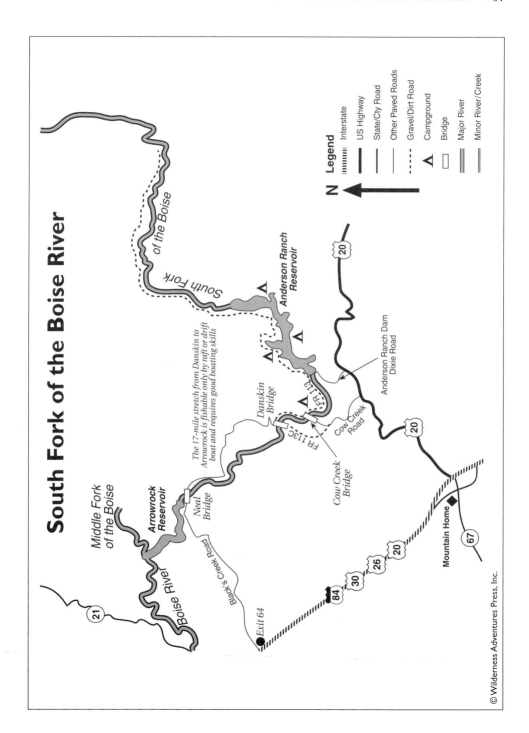

South Fork of the Boise River

Middle Fork of the Boise

Boise River

Arrowrock Reservoir

Neal Bridge

Black's Creek Road

Danskin Bridge

The 17-mile stretch from Danskin to Arrowrock is fishable only by raft or drift boat and requires good boating skills

South Fork of the Boise

of the Boise

Anderson Ranch Reservoir

FR 113

Cow Creek Bridge

FR 113C

Cow Creek Road

Anderson Ranch Dam Dixie Road

Exit 64

Mountain Home

21

20

20

84

30

26

20

67

Legend

N

▬▬▬▬	Interstate
▬▬▬	US Highway
—	State/Cty Road
⋯⋯	Other Paved Roads
-----	Gravel/Dirt Road
▲	Campground
□	Bridge
▬	Major River
	Minor River/Creek

© Wilderness Adventures Press, Inc.

WINTER FISHING

While the South Fork of the Boise ranks as one of the best rainbow trout tailwater streams in the West in late-summer, some hard core flyfishers are convinced its better fishing occurs in winter. For awhile longer, perhaps, it remains a relatively undiscovered fishing option.

"If you want to have the South Fork all to yourself, this is the time of year to do it," says a spokesman for Idaho Angler, a Boise fly shop and outfitter.

"One more tip—if the weather is sunny but cold and windy, try another spot. But if the weather looks dark and snowy and cold or rainy, say goodbye to your family and burn for the river. The fish get easy this time of year."

The river's trout feed heavily on midge larvae and adults (often considered the standard fare of winter fishing) and blue-winged olives hatch well on cloudy days through December. *Baetis* mayflies on the surface can be matched by No. 18 or 20 olive sparkle duns, cripples, or a parachute Adams. Other anglers report good success with pheasant tail nymphs, beadheads, brassies, and any dry fly size 20-22.

But its big rainbows (17 to 20+ inches) are also fond of stonefly nymphs, cranefly larva patterns, woolly buggers, egg-sucking leeches and olive rabbit-strip leeches.

With flows in the 300 cubic feet per second range, the South Fork is easiest to wade during its low winter flows. A dirt road parallels the river for 10 miles below Anderson Ranch Reservoir, where excellent wading access produces the best fishing.

Given the region's milder climate, chances of reaching the river from the highway often remain good through much of the winter. Wise anglers pack car chains, however. The road can be very slick after the sun is gone.

Winter fishing on the South Fork of the Boise is a popular getaway for Boise flyfishers.

Stream Facts: South Fork of the Boise

SEASON
- From Neal Bridge (Forest Road 189) upstream to Anderson Dam, Memorial Day Weekend through Nov. 30
- Dec. 1 to March 31 no-harvest winter trout season

SPECIAL REGULATIONS
- Artificial flies and lures with one barbless hook
- Two fish limit, none under 20", from Neal Bridge upstream to Anderson Ranch Dam
- Above Anderson Ranch Reservoir, two-fish limit, none under 14", from mouth of Beaver Creek upstream to Big Smoky Creek

FISH
- Rainbow over 20 inches

RIVER MILES
- Mile 0, Anderson Ranch Dam
- Mile 7, Cow Creek Road
- Mile 10, Danskin Bridge
- Mile 27, Neal Bridge

RIVER CHARACTERISTICS
- The first two miles of the river below the dam runs a little fast through a canyon then widens to a cottonwood lined free-stone stream.It turns into a meadow stretch and then straightens and widens again to Danskin. Below Danskin, the river is only fishable by drift-boat or raft and it takes good boating skills to float it. It runs through a large deserted canyon and empties into Arrowrock Reservoir.

FLOWS
- Early in the season flows can exceed 2,000 then drop to 1,500 steadily until the late season when they drop below 1,000, making boating difficult.

BOAT RAMP
- Below Anderson Ranch
- Cow Creek
- Danskin Bridge
- Neal Bridge

MAPS
- Boise National Forest
- South Fork Boise River 11x17 flyfishing river map by Wilderness Adventures Press
- Idaho's Best Fishing Waters mapbook by Wilderness Adventures Press

SOUTH FORK OF THE BOISE RIVER MAJOR HATCHES

Insect	J	F	M	A	M	J	J	A	S	O	N	D	Flies
"Pink Albert" Cahill								█	█				Pink Albert #14–16; Pink Cahill #14–16; Light Cahill #14-16; cream dun #14-16; red quill #14-16
Caddis					█								Hemingway Caddis #14–16; Emergent Sparkle Pupa #14–16; Spent Wing Caddis #14–16
Small yellow stonefly							█	█					Stimulators #12–16; Yellow Humpy #12–16
Blue-winged olive										█			Olive Sparkle Dun #16–20; BWO Cripple #16–20; Pheasant Tail Nymph #16–20
Midges	█										█		Palomino midge #16-22; chironomid larvae #18-22; brassie #16-20

Andy Brunelle enjoys the South Fork of the Boise River.

Rocky Barker photos.

A scenic float trip down the South Fork of the Boise River covers more water.

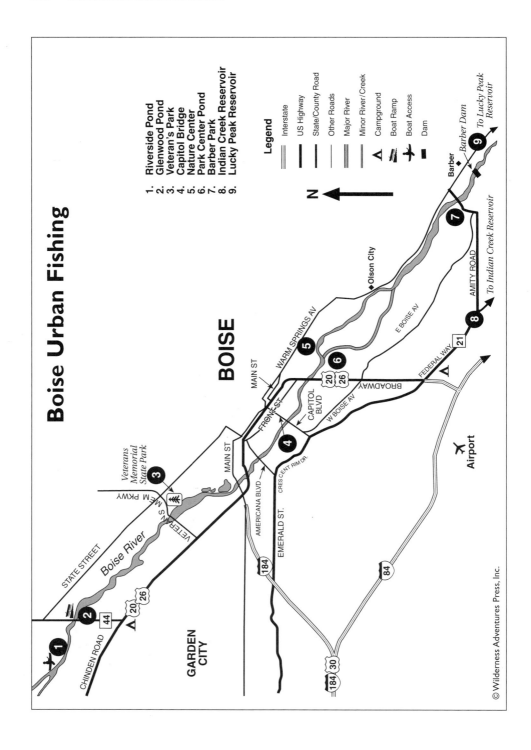

Boise Urban Fishing

BOISE

1. Riverside Pond
2. Glenwood Pond
3. Veteran's Park
4. Capitol Bridge
5. Nature Center
6. Park Center Pond
7. Barber Park
8. Indian Creek Reservoir
9. Lucky Peak Reservoir

Legend

Interstate
US Highway
State/County Road
Other Roads
Major River
Minor River/Creek
Campground
Boat Ramp
Boat Access
Dam

N

GARDEN CITY

Veterans Memorial State Park

Boise River

STATE STREET

CHINDEN ROAD

MAIN ST

AMERICANA BLVD

EMERALD ST.

CRESCENT RIM DR.

FRONT ST.

CAPITOL BLVD

W BOISE AV

BROADWAY

WARM SPRINGS AV

E BOISE AV

FEDERAL WAY

AMITY ROAD

MAIN ST

Olson City

Barber

Barber Dam

To Lucky Peak Reservoir

To Indian Creek Reservoir

Airport

To Indian Creek Reservoir

© Wilderness Adventures Press, Inc.

Urban Fishing

Below Lucky Peak Dam and through the city of Boise, the fishing can be surprisingly good at times in the Boise River—boosted by a healthy stocking program while efforts continue to enhance its wild trout fishery.

The river and several urban ponds provide a good diversity of fishing challenges in downtown Boise. Short drives out of town are additional small ponds and Lucky Peak Reservoir, one of three large impoundments in the Boise River drainage.

There are four kinds of cool water fish to pursue—rainbow, brown and cutthroat trout, and kokanee salmon. Steelhead trout are planted in the Boise River in fall and winter after state and federal agencies collect their quotas of hatchery fish. Whitefish also provide a popular winter fishery on the river.

Largemouth and smallmouth bass, crappie and bluegill are warmwater species found in the region. They like shallower, warmer waters of ponds and reservoirs. Smallmouth bass also are the most popular game fish in the lower Snake River and its large impoundments in the Hell's Canyon Recreation Area.

Warm water pan fish provide a great fishery for kids just starting out. They can be found readily just off docks, near vegetation, and in the shallower water where the young angler's line is often located.

Anglers should check reservoir levels and the availability of launching facilities before heading out of town by calling the Idaho Power Company (1-800-422-3143) or the U.S. Bureau of Reclamation (334-9134).

Political news conferences decrying the loss of Idaho's wild anadromous fisheries highlight the debate concerning retention or removal of dams on the lower Snake River.

Boise River

Fishing in the shadow of the Capitol

The Boise River is a popular year-round fishery in Idaho's fastest growing and most fast-paced city.

Despite its urban setting, the river offers numerous opportunities to escape the hustle and bustle of the rat race. Wildlife sightings are common. Anglers can see numerous waterfowl and songbirds during the summer. Bald eagles and waterfowl are common in winter.

The Discovery area just below Lucky Peak Dam provides access to the upper river's pocket waters in its rocky canyon, which offers another source of reflections on western natural wonders and rare opportunities for solitude.

Below Barber Park the river meanders through downtown Boise, which has one of the longest and most attractive greenbelts in Idaho. The river tenders virtual doorstep angling to visitors on tight schedules. Local anglers favor it when they want to relax after work or stay home on weekends and holidays.

Popular fishing access areas include Barber Park, Eagle Island, and the Boise State University greenbelt stretch between Broadway and Capitol.

The Boise is stocked with rainbow trout monthly at the major bridges, such as Barber Park, Capitol and Glenwood. A growing number of wild rainbow and a small population of brown trout also are present in the upper river. Whitefish are common.

A late fall through spring fishing bonus is steelhead. Idaho Fish and Game plants hatchery bred steelhead in the Boise after egg collection goals have been accomplished and there is a surplus of captured fish at their weirs. The steelhead are trucked to release sites on the river, including several close to downtown Boise.

"Boise River anglers are very passionate about the resource and some have raised concerns about the number of anglers and the associated fish harvest that occurs in the river," said Art Butts, fisheries biologist. "In response to these concerns, Fish and Game conducted a year-long creel survey to measure fishing activity and fish harvest. From June 2007 through June 2008, anglers were surveyed along the river from Barber Dam downstream to the Americana Boulevard Bridge."

During the creel survey, 1,358 anglers were interviewed and nearly 700 angler counts were conducted on 109 separate dates. Anglers spent an estimated 33,056 hours fishing the Boise River during the year. About 89 percent of the fishing effort was by anglers using bait and lures.

Rainbow trout comprised the bulk of the catch, said Butts. The average catch rate for rainbow trout was 0.6 fish per hour. During the survey, 20,704 rainbow trout were caught and of those, 4,277 were harvested. Nearly 80 percent of the rainbow trout caught in this section of river were released even though harvest is legal in most of the section.

Brown trout were caught less frequently, and the average catch rate was 0.01 fish per hour, which resulted in an estimate of 330 fish caught throughout the survey period. No brown trout were recorded as harvested during the creel survey and thus brown trout had an estimated release rate of 100 percent, Butts said.

"Observed harvest rates do not appear to be high in relation to the number of fish in the river," Butts said.

Wild fish population density estimates for the creel survey area, include 13,908 wild rainbow trout, 2,398 wild brown trout, and 34,754 mountain whitefish.

In addition, about 20,000 hatchery rainbow trout are stocked annually throughout the year (population estimates noted above do not include hatchery rainbow trout). Using the 2007 estimates, roughly 5 percent of the wild rainbow trout population is being harvested over the course of one year.

"Not surprisingly, creel survey results reveal that the Boise River is indeed a very popular destination for local anglers," Butts said. "It also suggests that a majority of anglers prefer to release fish to be caught again rather than take them home. In the future, Fish and Game biologists will be applying some statistical modeling for estimated catch and harvest rates in relation to existing population data to gain a better understanding of the trout population dynamics within the Boise River."

While brown trout often present a challenge to most anglers, many Boiseans marvel at the "big one" that didn't get away.

Ed Hedges, of Boise, caught the third-biggest brown trout recorded in Idaho on Veterans' Day 1992 on the Boise River, within sight of the Capitol. The brown was a recently spawned female 35 inches long, weighing 20 pounds, 6.5 ounces.

The longest held Idaho record was recorded in the South Fork of the Snake River in 1981. The Henry's Fork now claims the record brown trout – 37 inches, 27.3 pounds – caught in 2007 by West Chase of Ashton in the Ashton Reservoir.

There is a two-fish bag limit on rainbow, none under 14 inches, from the East Boise River Footbridge upstream to Loggers Creek diversion, one mile below Barker Park Bridge. A steelhead permit in addition to a fishing license are required to fish for steelhead.

The river's flows are regulated by releases from Lucky Peak Reservoir. A long series of riffles, pools and runs, it fishes best for wading anglers in early spring and late-summer through winter. Currents can be swift year-round in chutes. Summer anglers often share the river with flotillas of inner-tube floaters.

The special-regulations area is designed to improve the urban trout population located upstream from Municipal Park to the Loggers Creek diversion, but anglers are encouraged to practice catch-and-release to speed the recovery of wild trout.

Effective flies include woolly buggers, beadhead nymphs, caddis larva and emerger patterns, elk hair caddis and other attractor patterns, and grasshoppers.

Below Eagle Island the river becomes warmer and water quality is poorer. But it has one local secret—the surprising opportunities for hooking large brown trout.

These secretive fish don't feed much during the day but come out at night even in the most urbanized stretches. A late-evening angler, armed with a Mickey Finn or other streamer pattern could hook into one of these 20-inch plus fish, especially in autumn.

The lower Boise also is an untapped source of great smallmouth bass fishing.

For best results for better-than-average-sized bass, concentrate on deeper, rocky pools below fast-water heads. Early evening often is most productive during late-season, low-water conditions.

Due to access problems, fishing from a raft or canoe is considered the best option in approaching the lower Boise fishery.

Winter Fishing

The Boise River in town offers good fishing during the winter months until the water rises in the spring, according to the folks at Idaho Angler fly shop. Whitefish and hatchery rainbows make up most of the fish, but steelhead plants continue as long as there is a constant influx into the hatcheries and the river in town doesn't get too high.

Midges hatch throughout the winter, especially on cloudy days, offering good dry fly fishing. The bread and butter of winter fishing, though, is nymphing with olive caddis larva and beadheads in size 14 and 16, said an Idaho Angler spokesman. Steelhead prefer dead drifted Dr. Suess or Boss flies. Because the river is low, a floating line with a long leader will suffice.

Downtown Boise Ponds

Boise's fishing ponds are the ideal place for the beginning angler to learn the basics, or the more experienced angler to practice new skills. The ponds are the ideal place to take the kids. Easy access and frequent stocking increases the likelihood of success.

Rainbow trout are regularly stocked in Riverside Pond, Glenwood Pond, Veteran's Park and Park Center Pond.

Sportsplex Pond, a one-acre lake in the West Boise Sportsplex located near the corner of Eagle and McMillan Roads, may be another option for young anglers. Check with local fly shops or Fish and Game for information on its rainbow stocking schedule.

At Park Center and Veterans Park, you can also try your skill and luck with largemouth bass, crappie or bluegill. Riverside Pond has rainbow and bluegill.

Remember, when fishing for warmwater fish such as bass, crappie and bluegill you will have best success around structure, such as the docks, at any of the ponds, or the underwater brush structures at the southeast corner of Veterans Park.

MK Nature Center

The MK Nature Center, located next to Municipal Park behind Idaho Fish and Game's state office, is worth a visit, but not to fish. It is an education center which features a detailed replication of an Idaho stream.

Viewing windows allow you to observe fish, aquatic insects and natural fish habitats. Visiting the center will help you to better understand an aquatic ecosystem, and watching and learning more about fish will make you a more successful angler.

The center is open daily from sunrise to sunset.

URBAN RESERVOIRS

Indian Creek Reservoir

Located 19 miles east of Boise, just south of Interstate 84, this popular pond has a mix of cold and warmwater species. Rainbow trout, largemouth bass, crappie, bluegill, bullheads and channel catfish all contribute to the diverse, year-round fishery.

Shore access is limited and float-tubing is one way to increase the amount of the reservoir which can be fished. Some large trout and bass can be caught in this small reservoir.

From January 1 to June 30, the bass limit is 0, catch-and-release. From July 1 to December 31, the bass limit is 2, none between 12 and 16 inches.

Lucky Peak Reservoir

The largest of the urban fisheries is Lucky Peak. The reservoir is 12 miles long, with 45 miles of shoreline, most only accessible by water craft. When full, it is 258 feet deep, but water levels may change radically, season to season.

Located 8 miles east of Boise on Highway 21, the 28,050-acre reservoir is a very popular trout and kokanee salmon fishery. Fall rainbow fishing is excellent.

Early summer smallmouth bass fishing is also coming on strong. For smallmouth bass, look for rocky shorelines or outcroppings. The area southeast of Spring Shores has been productive.

Shore anglers can find success fishing for trout, perch and smallmouth bass. The best fishing, however, is from a boat.

Float-tubing is a popular activity on some areas of the reservoir and is definitely worth trying to reach some otherwise inaccessible areas. Be sure to use tubes designed for safe fishing.

Lucky Peak State Park

This day-use-only park is located on and near Lucky Peak Reservoir. The park consists of three units providing a wide variety of recreational activities, but there are no camping sites:

• Sandy Point Beach—A 20-acre site at the foot of Lucky Peak Dam, located nine miles east of Boise along Highway 21, is a popular family recreation area.

• Discovery—A seven-acre site located eight miles east of Boise just off State Highway 21, this park unit is situated along the waters of the Boise River just downstream from Lucky Peak Dam. Discovery is a great place to picnic, fish and relax among the magnificent trees and the rocky canyons.

• Spring Shores Marina—Spring Shores, located 18 miles east of Boise off State Highway 21, is a 213-acre unit on the shore of Lucky Peak Reservoir. The site includes marina, a restaurant and store, boat ramps, boat trailer parking, picnic areas and a swimming area.

Snake River Birds of Prey National Conservation Area

This unique 483,000-acre wildlife preserve, on the south bank of the Snake River, in spring supports the densest nesting concentration of birds of prey in North America and perhaps the world.

Located along a quiet, isolated stretch of the Snake River, about 40 miles south of Boise, the site of most interest to adventurous trout anglers is the pocket waters below Swan Falls Dam, east of Melba. These waters have produced trophy trout and devoted bass anglers rave about its smallmouth bass fishery.

Several outfitters in Boise and Mountain Home, who cater to bird watchers interested in the raptors, also offer float trips for anglers.

No overnight camping facilities are available within the park area at the Swan Falls Dam operated by Idaho Power Company. A picnic area is provided, and hikers can cross the river on the dam. A portage trail around the dam and a rafting ramp below it provides access to the lower river.

For more information, contact the BLM Bruneau Resource Area, 384-3300.

LOWLAND PONDS AND RESERVOIRS

For excellent warmwater pan fish and trophy bass fishing, the many ponds and reservoirs dotting the sagelands of the southwestern Snake River Plain are magnets for fly casting float-tubers, canoers and boaters. Several of the desert impoundments are preferred destinations for early spring and late fall trout fishing.

On a series of small ponds full of largemouth bass, bluegills and crappie, budding fly fishers and experts, alike, flex their casting arms and perfect their presentation skills. Many youngsters get their first lessons on Caldwell's small ponds, which hold smallmouth bass and rainbows.

Lake Lowell

Four miles southwest of Nampa is Lake Lowell, the state's premiere warmwater fishery. Located on the Deer Flat National Wildlife Refuge, the shallow irrigation impoundment holds strong populations of bluegills and crappie and harbors trophy smallmouth and largemouth bass.

The reservoir is approximately 9,000 acres at full pool, and is fed by water out of the Boise River through the New York Canal. The water in the lake is manipulated for irrigation purposes, which usually results in broad mud flats on parts of the refuge by autumn.

Lake Lowell is open to fishing on a year-round basis. During the non-boating season, Oct. 1 through April 14, fishing is restricted to the area in front of the Upper and Lower Embankments. Limits are set by the Idaho Fish and Game.

From Jan. 1 to June 30, the bass limit is 0, catch-and-release. From July 1 to December 31, the bass limit is 2, none between 12 and 16 inches.

During drought conditions, late-summer bass fishing in Lake Lowell may be restricted as fish become concentrated and vulnerable in low water.

Fishing action usually picks up in mid-May, with bass being caught in flooded vegetation. Crappie and bluegill action follows as water temperatures rise. Late in the season fishing below the outlets of the lake can be productive.

Also in the Nampa area, four ponds at the Wilson Springs IDFG property were changed to general regulations in 2000. What this means to anglers is the trout limit has been increased from 2 to 6 fish. These areas include the North and South Ponds, Beach's Pond, and Wilson Drain. The Trophy Pond regulations remain catch and release, no bait or barbed hooks allowed.

Paddock Valley Reservoir

Paddock Reservoir is located about 70 miles northwest of Boise at the end of a very rough road, but the drive is worth it.

Float-tubers like it for its strong crappie and largemouth bass populations. The four-mile-long, 1,300-acre reservoir also contains bluegills and punkinseed sunfish.

"The best flyfishing is on the east side of the reservoir, where a float-tube or canoe is very helpful," said a spokesman for Idaho Angler in Boise. "We like fishing Paddock in late April through the first couple weeks of June. As soon as the daytime temperatures hit 80 degrees in Boise, the fishing is good to go."

Take woolly worms, woolly buggers, Stayner ducktails, black-brown leeches, jigs and small spider patterns.

To reach Paddock Valley Reservoir, drive west on Highway 52 from Emmett about 25 miles to Little Willow Creek Road (6 miles east of Payette) and turn north. It's another 20 miles over a rough dirt road to the reservoir.

HELL'S CANYON RESERVOIRS

Below Weiser on the Snake River strict regulations are producing trophy smallmouth bass on Oxbow Reservoir, where it is catch-and-release for bronzebacks prior to July 1. The rest of the season there is a 2-bass limit, none between 12 and 16 inches.

Brownlee Reservoir, upstream from Oxbow, also harbors good populations of small-mouths. Hell's Canyon Reservoir, downstream from Oxbow, is lightly fished but offers excellent bass fishing, too. During the April-May spawning period in these waters, bass anglers are encouraged to also stick to catch-and-release fishing.

All three reservoirs contain rainbow trout, and varying populations of largemouth bass, crappie and bluegills. Brownlee also has whitefish. Sturgeon are a protected fish, and must be released immediately.

The reservoirs fish best from March to October, although the extreme heat of the canyon in July and August may produce a summer doldrums period. Concentrate on stream outlets, rocky structures along the shores, and cove inlets.

Shore access is largely limited to campground areas and along the canyon road, which dips into Oregon on the west side of Oxbow.

Boaters like to work the banks and stream inlets. Float-tubing flyfishers can safely tie into fish on these huge deep-water impoundments by staying within the wind-sheltered waters of the coves along the cliffs.

If you fish up into stream mouths on the Oregon side of Brownlee, you need an Oregon license. An Oregon license also is required to fish from the west shore of Oxbow.

To get to the Hell's Canyon Reservoirs from Boise take Interstate 84 west to Payette and drive north on U.S. 95 to Weiser, where the Old Ferry Road leads to the upper end of Brownlee Reservoir. Continuing northwest past Weiser on U.S. 95 to Cambridge and turning west on State Highway 71 leads to the lower end of Brownlee Reservoir. Oxbow and Hell's Canyon reservoirs are downstream, and the road ends at Hell's Canyon Dam.

The upper end of Brownlee can be reached on the Oregon side by driving west from Boise on Interstate 84 to Ontario. The lower two reservoirs can be reached on the Oregon side from Baker City via a scenic drive into the canyon on Highway 86

The canyon is remote country with only a few small shops at crossroads. It is a good idea to stock up on supplies and top off the gas tank before leaving civilization.

Brownlee Reservoir

A deep, narrow, 40-mile long impoundment, Brownlee is the oldest and largest of the three Hell's Canyon Reservoirs.

Many consider it one of the best smallmouth fisheries in the West. Of the three reservoirs, it is the most exposed to winds, which can create high waves.

Southern end access to the reservoir is available at Farewell Bend State Park, via I-84, on the Oregon side, and downstream at Spring Park Camp.

Steck Park near Weiser is the main Idaho access point to the upper backwaters of the reservoir.

On the north end of Brownlee, west of Cambridge, Woodhead Park is located on the Idaho side of the river. It is the largest of four excellent Idaho Power Company parks and campgrounds in the Hell's Canyon complex.

These areas have good to excellent dock and ramp facilities for boaters and provide some shoreline access. Other shoreline access is limited by rough terrain —a problem typical to all three reservoirs.

Oxbow Reservoir

A 10-mile-long, very narrow impoundment, Oxbow's flow are regulated by Brownlee Dam. Summer anglers fishing the upper end of the lake benefit most from the cool flows provided by Brownlee, but should keep an eye out for increases in releases from the dam. Conversely, upper Oxbow anglers benefit from "warmer" releases in winter.

Idaho Power's McCormick Park Campground and boat launch is on the Idaho side of the river, about a half mile below Brownlee Dam.

Idaho Power's Copperfield Park Campground is located just below the Oxbow Dam on the Oregon side of the Snake River. There also are several Oregon State Campgrounds on its side of the reservoir.

From Jan. 1 to June 30, the bass limit is 0, catch-and-release. From July 1 to December 31, the bass limit is 2, none between 12 and 16 inches.

Hell's Canyon Reservoir

This deep, 25-mile-long reservoir is the most remote impoundment in the Hell's Canyon complex. The paved canyon road follows the Idaho side. A dirt road extends several miles below Oxbow Dam on the Oregon side.

Idaho Power's Hell's Canyon Park Campground and launch ramp is about half way down the reservoir and offers the best access to the lake. The road ends at a visitors center and boat launch below the dam.

Below Hell's Canyon Dam, the Snake River plunges down its last wild stretch in Idaho through the deepest gorge in North America. Designated a Wild and Scenic River below the dam, river running opportunities for both private and commercial rafters and jet boaters in the lower Snake are strictly regulated by federal agencies.

For information on fishing and boating the lower Snake River, see the Northcentral Idaho section of this guide book. Information also is provided on outfitters who cater to tourists and steelhead anglers.

Hell's Canyon below Brownlee Reservoir leads into the deepest gorge in North America.

Owyhee River

Oregon river's stellar dry fly fishing is irresistible

The Owyhee River's trophy brown trout fishery is a class act just west of the Oregon border that Boise flyfishers can't resist. Theirs may be about the shortest drive, but the Owyhee is gaining attention from a growing cohort of selective anglers, both nationally and internationally, willing to go the extra mile to test their skills as dry-fly anglers on this remote southeast Oregon tailwater fishery.

The South Fork of the Boise River remains southwest Idaho's flyfishing mecca, but for more than a decade Boise anglers in-the-know led the parade that crossed the Oregon border in late winter and spring to stalk the Owyhee in hopes of scoring on one of the West's best brown trout fisheries.

Years of drought had turned the tailwater fishery into a winter fishery, one to leave when the heat of summer came. That changed in 2005 when high floods washed away decades of accumulated silt and restored the stream's lava rock bottom to prime habitat for stoneflies and mayflies. Flows since have been relatively stable. The Owyhee River now fishes like a weedy spring creek.

Idaho flyfishers like Tim Burke, owner of the Riverkeeper fly shop in Boise, quit buying daily or short-term licenses and now cough up the fee for a non-resident annual license. The character actor has captured a starring role, and the Owyhee is a year-round fishery on par with any of the West's classic waters. Summer and fall are now the prime seasons.

Only a 50-mile drive west of Boise, the river flows out of the Owyhee Dam near Adrian, Oregon, through a rocky canyon in series of short riffles and long pools that favor sight-fishing for rising trout. The first 10 miles of the river that anglers key on are easily accessible from Snively Gulch Road and Lake Road out of Adrian. Routes to the river are well marked. The road along the river is a bit rough, but the slow driving aids anglers in scoping the river for risers.

The average brown trout runs 18 inches and many exceed 25 inches, but this is not your average brown trout fishery. You don't have to wait until nightfall to catch them on streamers. These brown trout love dry flies.

"These fish are very hatch oriented," Burke said. "They're not super-educated but they're not dumb."

It may seem to be equally beneficial that the river often runs a little off color, but what he means is you've got to match the hatch.

Long leaders, 5X or 6X, for downstream or down-and-across presentations in low-water situations often are the key to success. But it may not be all surface action when heads are popping. Pay attention to the life cycle of the hatch. Emergers save the day more often than not.

When in doubt when you keep getting tantalizing refusals, downsize your fly.

By the same token, nymph fishers have to read the water and maintain a delicate weight balance in following the flow when keying on riffles and pool tail-outs or stream troughs and flow seams.

From late March to early May, look for skwalas on the Owyhee.
Photo courtesy Joshua Bergan.

Nowadays, Owyhee Dam is operated in a way that protects the scarce water resources available in the basin, so very rarely will flows get heavy due to runoff. This means that the Owyhee is fishable throughout spring most years, when most other waterways in the region may resemble cafe au lait.

Typically in April, dam operators will raise flows to somewhere in the 200 to 300 cfs range. But even at those levels the river is perfect for wading. At the same time, these stronger flow aid hatches that can be thick throughout spring and summer.

Flows generally drop down to winter levels in October to perhaps as low as 30 cfs. That makes the fishing considerably more technical, aka spring creek like, but it helps preserve the resource along with the needs of irrigators to maintain reservoir levels.

Midges are the predominant fly drawing heads up in winter, but they hatch year round and many times, tiny subsurface midges will be the target of choice over the larger bug of the day for the river's more selectively feeding browns.

Beginning in March blue-winged olives and some callibaetis draw fish to the surface. These continue into April when the skawala hatch adds its tastier, short lived attractive powers to the action.

As the skwala hatch tapers off in May blue-winged olives continue to keep the fish's attention until the pale morning duns show up. This becomes the workingman's fly in May and June, when caddis also join the mix. Ants become effective as the summer turns hot and carry anglers into the prime grasshoppers action in late summer and early autumn.

In late August there's a small trico hatch that had been stronger before the flood, but will still divert some browns from hoppers. September is the transition month, returning to pale morning duns and introducing small mahogany duns and, finally, blue-winged olives return, carrying fall anglers into the winter. Then it's primarily midges as the circle turns again.

Trophy browns are the primary target, but that's not to say there aren't rainbows. The river is stocked and bait fishing is permitted. Rainbows may run to 17 inches or larger.

Hang on with whichever species you score. Shallow water runs like the Owyhee induce screaming runs from rainbows. The leaping frolics of browns may surprise anglers into letting their guard down. Maintain a gentle, tight line on the leapers.

The Owyhee River system meanders through some of the most desolate high desert country in the United States. It holds redband trout -- descendants of coastal rainbow trout that are native to the inland West -- that attract a special class of anglers seeking fish in their native haunts. The hardiest, most dedicated flyfisher who dare to take on grueling long drives in late spring can be rewarded by catching redbands in the deep canyons of the East Fork or the South Fork of the Owyhee.

But if you are serious, you really need a guide. You won't find Mr. Ranger anywhere close. The roads are bad and often cross private land. Guides will take you in an inflatable kayak or, in the lower stretch that ends at Owyhee Reservoir, in a raft.

Some redbands flow over the dam and contribute to the fly fishing on the main stretch of the Owyhee.

Owyhee River

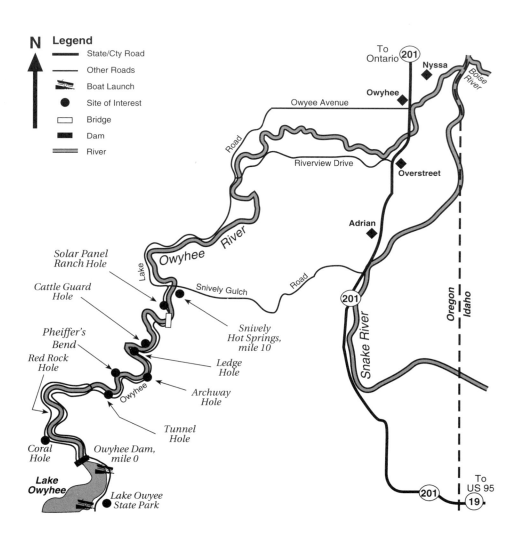

N

Legend
- State/Cty Road
- Other Roads
- Boat Launch
- Site of Interest
- Bridge
- Dam
- River

To Ontario 201

Nyssa

Owyhee

Owyee Avenue

Boise River

Riverview Drive

Overstreet

Road

Adrian

Lake Owyhee *River*

Snively Gulch

Road

201

Solar Panel Ranch Hole

Cattle Guard Hole

Snively Hot Springs, mile 10

Pheiffer's Bend

Red Rock Hole

Ledge Hole

Owyhee

Archway Hole

Tunnel Hole

Snake River

Oregon | Idaho

Coral Hole

Owyhee Dam, mile 0

Lake Owyhee

Lake Owyee State Park

To US 95

201

19

Stream Facts: Owyhee River

SEASON
- Open all year; need an Oregon fishing license.

SPECIAL REGULATIONS
- Catch and release for brown trout. Limit of five fish for rainbows.

FISH
- Brown trout averaging 18 inches, grow to 30 inches; wild redband trout; rainbows

RIVER MILES
- The prime stretch runs 10 miles between the dam and Snively Hot Springs.

RIVER CHARACTERISTICS
- Wadeable its entire stretch, but it has a sometimes slippery lavarock bottom that requires a staff. It runs through a dry rocky canyon in series of short riffles and long pool surrounded by sagebrush hills. Rattlesnakes are present, so be observant.

FLOW
- The highest flows come in the spring but it has become relatively stable.

MAPS
- Owyhee River 11x17 flyfishing river map, by Wilderness Adventures Press

Owyhee River Hatch Chart

Insect	J	F	M	A	M	J	J	A	S	O	N	D	Flies
Midge		▓	▓	▓	▓	▓	▓	▓	▓	▓	▓	▓	Griffith's Gnat #18-22; Parachute Adams #18-22; Palomino Midge #16-22; Chironomid larvae #18-22; Brassie #16-20
Baetis			▓	▓							▓		Parachute Adams #18-20; Olive Sparkle Dun #18-20; Pheasant Tail nymph #18-20
Skwala			▓	▓									Bullethead Skwala/black egg sac, Olive Stonefly, Parachute Stone, EZ Skwala, Skwala Stonefly Dry #10-12; Dark Stonefly Nymph, Brooks' Stonefly Nymph, Yak Skwala Nymph (dark) #8-12
PMD					▓	▓			▓	▓			Yellow Sparkle Dun #16-20; PMD Cripple #16-20; Poxyback PMD #16-20
Callibaetis				▓	▓				▓				Parachute Adams #14; Speckle Wing #14-16; Callibaetis spinner #16-18
Ants						▓	▓		▓				Cinnamon Ant #12-18; Foam Ant #14-16
Hoppers							▓	▓	▓				Henry's Fork Hopper #8-12; Meadow Hopper #8-12
Mahogany Duns									▓		▓		Mahogany Sparkle Dun #16-18; Pheasant Tail nymph #16-18
Tricos								▓	▓				CDC Trico #20-22; Polywing Trico #20-22
Caddis					▓			▓					Emergent Sparkle Pupa #14-16; Spent Wing Caddis #14-16; Hemingway Caddis #14-16

Shoshone Falls on the Middle Snake River marks the historic dividing line between upriver advances of anadromous salmon and rainbow, steelhead trout, and the Yellowstone cutthroat that eventually continued upstream to Yellowstone National Park and into the Missouri River drainage.

Magic Valley

Flyfishers who favor the flatlands of southcentral Idaho's Magic Valley seek trophy bass in ponds and reservoirs southwest of Mountain Home or hefty trout in the Hagerman-Thousand Springs area northwest of Twin Falls.

The Snake River, buried in a deep canyon, is a little known fishery outside the region. Seek help from local fly shops, outfitters and sporting goods stores.

Excellent big water fisheries are found on large impoundments of the Snake and the South Fork of the Boise River.

Anglers should check reservoir levels and the availability of launching facilities before heading out of town by calling the Idaho Power Company (1-800-422-3143) or the U.S. Bureau of Reclamation (334-9134).

TWIN FALLS / THOUSAND SPRINGS

Northwest of Twin Falls, the spring-fed ponds and creeks in the Thousand Springs area at Hagerman attract winter and early spring flyfishers who can't wait to kick off a new season. They're also a good option when other waters are less pliant during high spring runoff. Summer fishing for warmwater fish is another little known bonus.

From Twin Falls, take U.S. 30-Thousand Springs Scenic Byway through Buhl to the Snake River Canyon's south side, or take Interstate 84 to Wendell for quick access to the north side of the river and its tributaries.

To reach the Hagerman-Thousand Springs area from Boise or Mountain Home, drive east on Interstate 84, and turn south at the Bliss or Wendell exits.

Get tips on fishing conditions and help with directions at fly shops and sporting goods stores in Twin Falls, or check in at Simerly's General Store in Wendell. Either way, pick up a supply of Stayner ducktails, one of southwest Idaho's most productive stillwater flies.

The Thousand Springs region gets its name from the hundreds of springs gushing from the north canyon wall. They are fed by the Snake River Plain Aquifer, which collects the flows of the Big Lost and Little Lost rivers that sink 150 miles to the north into the lava flows of a vast volcanic-sagebrush desert.

These springs include 11 of the 65 springs in the United States with an average discharge exceeding 100 cfs. Water quality from the springs has been excellent, but continuing development by commercial fish farmers is lowering water quality in the Snake River.

Commercial hatcheries at Thousand Springs produce more rainbow trout for the table than anywhere else in the United States. There are several federal hatcheries in the valley and Idaho's largest state-owned hatchery is located on the Hagerman Wildlife Management Area.

This is Idaho's Banana Belt and fishing conditions often are pleasant year-round.

Riley and Billingsley spring creeks are local trout streams explored by only a few non-resident flyfishers. There are several bass and bluegill ponds that have good late-summer float-tube angling.

Clear Lake, a pay-to-play pond, is the place to be in the dead of winter when everything else is closed or frozen.

A worthwhile side trip is the Hagerman Fossil Beds National Monument. It produced one of the largest museum collections of Ice Age mammal fossils in the world that includes skeletons of ancient giant bison, horses and camels. Scientists continue to probe its crumbling slopes.

SNAKE RIVER

With the exception of spawning areas, trout habitat in the Snake River is good throughout most of the free-flowing reaches between C.J. Strike Reservoir, south of Mountain Home, and Lake Walcott, upstream of Rupert, state Idaho Fish and Game biologists.

Trophy size trout are caught in portions of the Snake River, such as the areas below Minidoka Dam, near Rupert, and Upper Salmon Falls Dam, below Twin Falls. Species of trout present are rainbow, brown, cutthroat, and rainbow-cutthroat hybrids. The cutthroat trout and rainbow-cutthroat hybrids are found mainly in the area between Milner Dam and Twin Falls Dam, an area seriously impacted by low flows during the irrigation season. Many of these hybrid trout attain large sizes, some reaching weights of over 6 pounds.

Vinyard Creek, an aquifer spring entering the Snake River on the north side just above Twin Falls, is the major spawning area for cutthroat trout and the rainbow-cutthroat hybrid trout.

Many of the minor tributary streams entering the Snake River also contain good trout habitat and support good populations of wild trout, primarily rainbow. Some of the streams, especially the springs, are utilized for spawning by trout from the Snake River.

The main Snake River contains seven reservoirs, which are suitable in varying degrees for trout: Bliss, Lower and Upper Salmon Falls, Shoshone Falls, Twin Falls, Milner, and Lake Walcott.

The trout fishery in Lower Salmon Falls Reservoir is the best of the six reservoirs, with the fishery being supported by releases of hatchery rainbow trout.

Areas with warmwater fisheries are fairly numerous in the main Snake River and minor tributary drainages, but a great demand exists for more waters of this type in the populated portions of the drainage. Major warmwater species present in the Snake River and surrounding waters are largemouth and smallmouth bass, and bluegill.

There is a no harvest restriction on smallmouth bass in the Bell Rapids area of the Snake, between the Upper and Lower Salmon Falls dams, from Jan. 1 through June 30. The rest of the year there is a two-fish bag limit on bass, none between 12 and 16 inches.

There is a two-trout cutthroat limit in the Snake upstream from Shoshone Falls.

MALAD RIVER

The Malad River sets out on a leisurely course across a rumpled sagebrush desert before it meets the Snake River Canyon and cuts a spectacular gorge through its rim in a final mad dash to the Snake.

The river is only 12 miles long, formed where the Big and Little Wood rivers merge near Gooding, northeast of Malad Gorge State Park.

Fishing the gorge is foolhardy, of course, but the upper and lower stretches of the Malad offer surprisingly good options for anglers to test relatively unexplored waters.

December 1 through Friday before Memorial Day weekend, from its mouth upstream to the I-84 bridge at Malad Gorge, the trout limit is 0, catch-and-release. From Saturday of Memorial Day weekend through November 30, the trout limit is 6.

Fishing the river's last dash through swift pocket waters is excellent for rainbows ranging from 12 to 17 inches. This short stretch can be reached at the bridge on U.S. 30, west of Hagerman, and from a dirt road along its west bank to its confluence with the Snake.

The Malad above I-84 to its source is open year-round.

This flat, meandering stretch of the river has a reputation for producing large brown trout exceeding 20 inches. For tips on fishing conditions and help with directions, check with fly shops and sporting goods stores in Twin Falls, or at Simerly's General Store in Wendell.

Brown trout are a premiere attraction for anglers on Billingsley Creek.

The Malad Gorge is just south of the I-84 Bridge over the Malad. The river crashes down stairstep falls and into the Devils Washbowl, then cuts through a beautiful 250-foot gorge on its way to the Snake River, 2.5 miles downstream. Views of the gorge are best from the sturdy footbridge that crosses the canyon in Malad Gorge State Park, reached from the north via the Tuttle exit on I-84.

There is no campground at the park.

BILLINGSLEY CREEK

Billingsley Creek, crossed by U.S. 30 just west of the town of Hagerman, is noted for top rainbow and brown trout fishing in a spring creek atmosphere in Idaho's newest state park.

The two miles of public access at the Billingsley Creek Wildlife Management Area is bordered by cattail marshes and difficult to wade. Fishing from a canoe or float-tube is the better option, although this requires negotiating around a water pipe crossing the creek. However, two new public access areas that make up the Billingsley Creek State Park, formed in 2001, will add nearly 8 miles of open water to anglers, along with more canoe access.

The former McFadden Farm is directly across from the wildlife management area and will eventually open to the public. Currently open to anglers and visitors is the Vardis Fisher section that is now called the Aqualife Property. It extends about 4 miles along Billingsley Creek, downstream from Tupper Grade Road. It holds Fisher Lake, a crystal-clear pond fed by one of the region's famous "Thousand Springs," and is popular with float-tubers.

From the old railroad crossing upstream to Tupper Grade Road, there is a two-trout limit, none under 20-inches, on Billingsley Creek, and on Fisher Lake. Flies and lures only; no bait.

Upstream from Tupper Grade to Vader Grade, the creek is fly fishing only, and somewhat easier to negotiate for wading anglers. Permission to fish must be obtained from the landowner, or arranged by outfitters.

"This beautiful little spring creek produces a surprising number of rainbow trout from about 10 to 20 inches. Dry fly fishing in clear, cold water to visible fish is the rule at Billingsley. Shallow wading and easy access make this stream a low-pressure treat," says a spokesman for Idaho Angler, a Boise fly shop and outfitter.

"A good population of brown trout in the 15- to 17-inch ranges, with occasional larger surprises, also haunt the creek's pristine waters," says Chuck Warren, an IDFG biologist.

HAGERMAN WILDLIFE MANAGEMENT AREA

The best public access to fish in the Thousand Springs area is at Idaho Fish and Game's Hagerman Wildlife Refuge.

Riley Creek is open year-round upstream from the hatchery. Downstream to Riley Falls the season is March 1 to Oct. 31. Most of the rainbows are in the 10- to 12-inch range, but be prepared for larger fish that escape from the hatchery and spawners moving upstream from the river in spring. Fishing season on the refuge's four small trout and bass

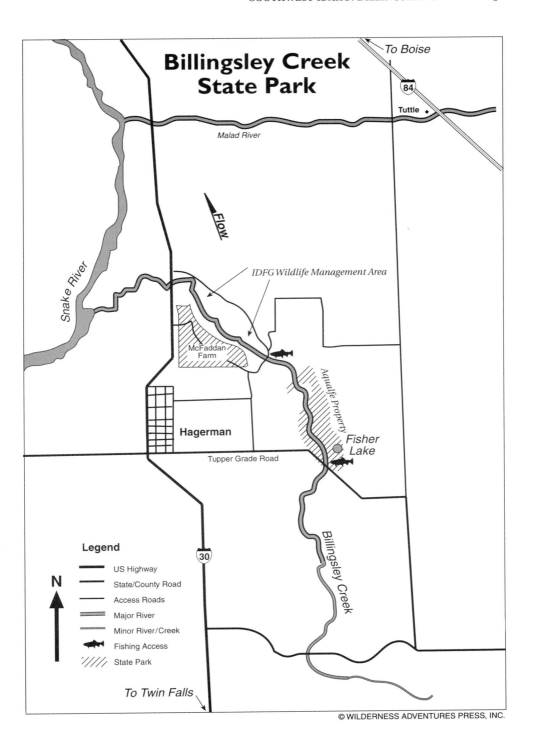

Billingsley Creek State Park

To Boise

84

Tuttle

Malad River

Flow

Snake River

IDFG Wildlife Management Area

McFaddan Farm

Aqualfe Property

Hagerman

Fisher Lake

Tupper Grade Road

Billingsley Creek

Legend

N

US Highway
State/County Road
Access Roads
Major River
Minor River/Creek
Fishing Access
State Park

30

To Twin Falls

© WILDERNESS ADVENTURES PRESS, INC.

ponds is July 1 to Oct. 31. Oster Lakes, which are on Riley Creek, offer good wading or float-tube fishing, and also are open from the first of March through Oct. 31 for trout and bass. Summer crowds are common at Hagerman WMA, especially on weekends and holidays. Better opportunities for solitude on the refuge's waters occur during the off seasons in early spring and late autumn.

NIAGARA SPRINGS

Tumbling down the north canyon rim at 250 cubic feet per second, Niagara Springs is a sight you won't soon forget. The churning water is the icy blue of glaciers. The springs are a National Natural Landmark and part of the world-famous Thousand Springs Complex along the Snake River.

The road from Wendell to Niagara Springs Park provides the best opportunity to drive down the north rim of the 350-foot-deep canyon, but be cautious. The road is narrow and steep. It is advised not to try it in a motorhome or while pulling a large trailer.

Once inside the canyon, you'll find year-round fishing in Crystal Springs Lake, a put-and-take rainbow pond, a half mile east of Niagara Springs, that includes a handicap-accessible site.

A federal steelhead hatchery is located at Niagara Springs. It is open to tours, and offers visitors and anglers a parking and picnic area.

Nearby is a small pond on the Niagara Springs outflow and its short tumbling course to the Snake open to year-round fishing. Small rainbows generally are the rule here, but large spawners migrate upstream from the river in April.

There are two wild rainbow ponds to the west on Idaho Fish and Game's Niagara Springs Wildlife Management Area that require a one-mile hike to fish. The bag limit on the ponds is two trout.

CLEAR LAKE COUNTRY CLUB

Clear Lake, located near Buhl in the Snake River Canyon in the upper Thousand Springs Valley, features year-round fly fishing in a 15-acre, spring fed lake for "king-sized" rainbow trout.

If you're worried about the "country club" setting of Clear Lake, don't be. It only costs $10 per day to fish, and it's cheaper for kids.

It's mostly a lake for float tubes or other small, non-motorized crafts that don't need a ramp. There are a few bank angling spots. The pro shop and its amenities also feature flies, complimentary air compressor for float tubes, boat dock, and helpful advice for beginners.

Hint: The Hagerman Valley, west of Twin Falls, is known as the "Banana Belt" of southern Idaho. It's a favorite destination of anglers seeking to dispel cabin fever blues in late winter or early spring.

Niagara Springs is one of numerous outflows into the Thousand Springs section of the middle Snake River Canyon.

In recent years, Clear Lake managers have become tired of dealing with escaped trout and feeding pelicans, and started stocking trout in the 4- to 5-pound range. There may even be a few "palomino trout" in the mix that have become "golden" moving targets for sight-fishers.

That's not to say they're all just bigger and dumber hatchery fish. The lake used to have a reputation for folks scoring dozens of fish on an outing, but in recent years, fishing has required a bit more finesse.

Angling is limited to catch-and-release, which means the lake is typically favored by flyfishers.

When you're done fishing, stop by the clubhouse for lunch or an early dinner before the drive home. The clubhouse is a warm, casual place where you can get a hearty meal and a beer for a reasonable price.

Or, you could make the trip a full weekend adventure with a round of golf.

The complex includes an 18-hole golf course, pro shop and restaurant, and an RV park open March through October.

Visitors may use showers, restrooms and picnic area bordering the RV park.

Address: Clear Lake Country Club, 403 Clear Lake Lane, Buhl, Idaho 83316
Phone: 208-543-4849
Website: www.clearlakecc.org

SALMON FALLS CREEK RESERVOIR

The Salmon Falls Dam, 20 miles south of Twin Falls via U.S. 93, creates a reservoir that provides an important source of recreation in this semi-arid sagebrush desert above the Idaho/Nevada border.

Game fish include rainbow trout, kokanee salmon, smallmouth bass, black crappie, and yellow perch as well as an occasional brown trout. Walleye were introduced into the reservoir in 1974 and provide a unique opportunity for anglers.

Rainbow trout are stocked in the reservoir twice per year. Fishing is especially good in the fall. Rainbow can be caught throughout the reservoir from shore, or by trolling from boats.

Kokanee fishing is best in the summer months and into the fall, between the dam and Grey's Landing. Fifteen to 20-inch kokanee are typical. In late summer, as kokanee come into shore to spawn, bank anglers may have some success. However, kokanee are open water fish, so fishing from a boat and trolling is most effective.

Walleye provide the most unique fishery in the reservoir. This long-lived fish, native to cool water lakes of the Upper Midwest, can reach up to 20 pounds. More typical here are 6- to 10-pound fish, but the reservoir produced an Idaho record 17-pound, 6-ounce walleye in 2006.

Smallmouth bass can be found in the mid-section of the lake along rocky shorelines. Best fishing is from boats.

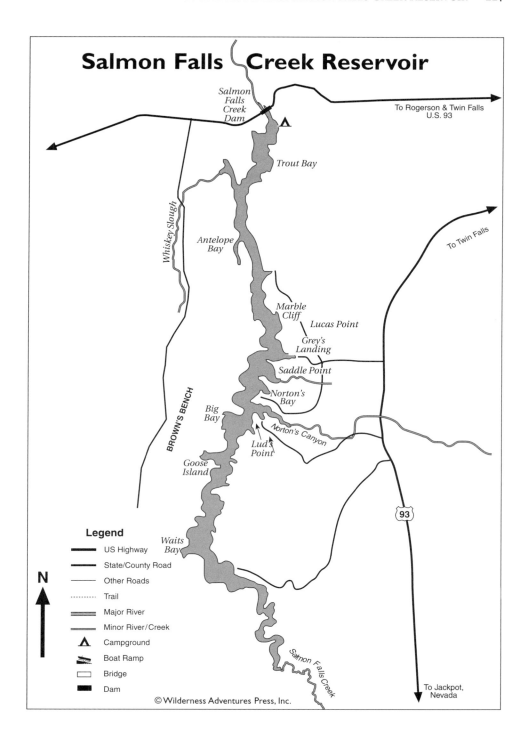

Salmon Falls Creek Reservoir

Salmon Falls Creek Dam

To Rogerson & Twin Falls U.S. 93

Trout Bay

Whiskey Slough

Antelope Bay

To Twin Falls

Marble Cliff

Lucas Point

Grey's Landing

Saddle Point

Norton's Bay

Big Bay

BROWN'S BENCH

Norton's Canyon

Lud's Point

Goose Island

93

Waits Bay

Salmon Falls Creek

To Jackpot, Nevada

Legend

▬▬	US Highway
▬	State/County Road
—	Other Roads
·········	Trail
▬▬	Major River
▬	Minor River/Creek
⬧	Campground
⬚	Boat Ramp
▭	Bridge
▬	Dam

N

© Wilderness Adventures Press, Inc.

Crappie fishing can be spotty. But it is a schooling fish, so once found they can provide quick action, especially on small streamer patterns.

Day-use and overnight facilities, including picnic tables and RV camp sites, are available at Lud Drexler Park. Developed recreation sites along the reservoir also are located at Greys Landing, Norton Bay, and Whiskey Slough.

For more information, contact the BLM Snake River Resource Area, 677-6641.

Mountain Home Environs

The main road to Mountain Home's three key fishing attractions, southwest of town, is State Highway 51. To reach the lakes, take the Highway 51 exit on Interstate 84 and proceed south about 15 miles to the Snake River Bridge. South of the bridge, follow the signs on Highway 78 east to Bruneau State Park or west to Crane Falls Lake and chosen destinations along the Bruneau Arm of C.J. Strike Reservoir.

Also south of Mountain Home are two little-known trophy trout ponds at the Duck Valley Indian Reservation which straddles the Idaho/Nevada border.

North of Mountain Home are Anderson Ranch Reservoir and the main road into the fabled lower canyon of the South Fork of the Boise.

C.J. Strike Reservoir

C.J. Strike Reservoir, southwest of Mountain Home on the Snake River, holds key sections of shallow waters amenable to fly fishing. It has jumbo largemouth bass, irascible smallmouths and tail-walking rainbows.

Bass hunters work the flats and shallow areas of its two arms as the water warms in spring and cools in autumn. Trout fishers work the reservoir year-round, but fall can be especially good when the rainbows come back to the surface.

Land surrounding the 7,500-acre C.J. Strike Reservoir is managed by Idaho Power Company and Idaho Fish and Game to maximize habitat for geese, ducks, pheasants, quail, deer, and other wild animals.

The stable reservoir pool results in a fertile and productive environment for both fish and aquatic insects, making this a very popular fishery. Each of three reservoir sections provides a unique fishing experience.

The main reservoir, near the dam, provides easy access for both bank and boat angling for trout. Boaters trolling along the face of the dam, the south shore or in the narrows, can be rewarded with excellent trout fishing, states Idaho Fish and Game.

Anglers find success in spring and early summer fishing for smallmouth bass along the dam, in shallow coves, and rocky banks.

Best fishing on the Snake River Arm is by boat, though some bank fishing can be found at the Cove Arm site. Look for smallmouth bass in the coves and sheltered area during the spring months.

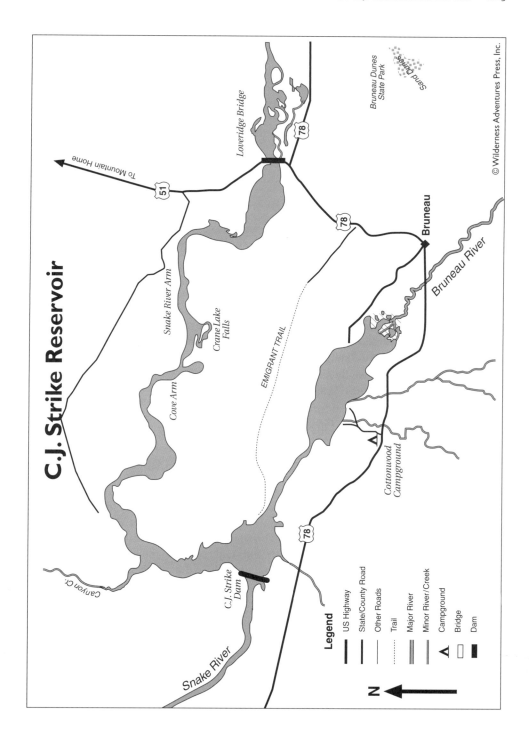

C.J. Strike Reservoir

To Mountain Home

51

Loveridge Bridge

78

78

Bruneau

Bruneau River

Snake River Arm

Crane Lake Falls

Cove Arm

EMIGRANT TRAIL

Bruneau Dunes State Park

Sand Dunes

Cottonwood Campground

Canyon Cr.

C.J. Strike Dam

78

Snake River

© Wilderness Adventures Press, Inc.

Legend

US Highway

State/County Road

Other Roads

Trail

Major River

Minor River/Creek

Campground

Bridge

Dam

N

The most diverse fishing can be found in the Bruneau Arm. The Cottonwood Campground and Jack's Creek access site provide both boat and bank angling for bluegill, perch, crappie, trout, largemouth and smallmouth bass. In the early spring, the narrows is a good area to troll for trout, and for smallmouth bass in May and June.

Fish for largemouth bass the same as for the smallmouth but look for heavy vegetation and perhaps use a weedless lure. Bluegill like the vegetation as well and the rocky shoreline. In May and June, crappie can be found in the shallows, usually in less than 6 feet of water.

Float tubers do well in the Bruneau Arm, especially in the vicinity of Cottonwood Campground. Try casting back toward overhanging brushy areas or rocky shores.

Access

- To reach the reservoir from Mountain Home, follow the signs to the Mountain Home Airbase, and turn south at the Bruneau turnoff (State Highway 51) and continue 14.3 miles to the Loverage Bridge access.
- To reach Cove Arm launch, continue 3.5 miles and turn north at the Cove Arm, Crane Falls sign. Follow the signs, down the hill and to the north for 6.5 miles. The last 1.5 miles is extremely rough gravel road.
- To reach Bruneau Arm and C.J. Strike Dam, continue through Bruneau and watch for signs for C.J. Strike Wildlife Management Area, and other destinations, including a campground and boat launch below the dam.
- C.J. Strike Dam can also be reached from Mountain Home by taking State highway 67 via Grandview, or gravel road cut-off to Strike Dam Road.
- Boat access only is found at Crane Falls, Loverage Bridge.
- Fishing access is possible at the C.J. Strike Wildlife Management Area.

CRANE FALLS LAKE

Nestled in the sagelands above a broad bend of the Snake River Arm of C.J. Strike Reservoir is Crane Falls Lake. A no-longer secret hideaway for old-time float-tubers, it is managed for trophy largemouth bass, with a two-fish limit, none under 20 inches.

The 84-acre lake also holds bluegill and crappie, and is stocked with rainbow trout.

Float-tubing is the best option because weeds and reeds rim the lake shore. The pond is open year-round and is an early season attractions since the region's climate is mild.

In late spring, action can be intense during spawning seasons of the warmwater species.

BRUNEAU SAND DUNES STATE PARK

About 15 miles south of Mountain Home is Bruneau Sand Dunes State Park, home-waters of another excellent warmwater fishery favored by float-tubers and canoers.

The Sand Dunes Lakes are open year round and offer good action on bluegills and bass. There is a two-fish limit for bass, none under 20 inches. No motors allowed.

The dunes at Bruneau Dunes State Park are unique in the Western Hemisphere. Other dunes in the Americas form at the edges of natural basins; these form near the center. Bruneau Dunes include the largest single-structured sand dune in North America, with a peak 470 feet above the lakes.

The park has one of the longest camping seasons in Idaho's state park system. Campers often start coming in March and continue to enjoy its warm weather late into the fall.

For more information, call 366-7919.

BRUNEAU/JARBIDGE RIVERS

Spectacular canyons that tower 1,200 feet high sharply dissect the plateau that surrounds the confluence of the Bruneau and Jarbidge Rivers, 12 miles southeast of the hamlet of Bruneau. The Bruneau flows into the Snake River at the south arm of C.J. Strike Reservoir, southwest of Mountain Home.

Headwaters of both rivers rise in isolated sections of Nevada. Remote and rarely explored, there are no paved roads in this section of either state. Both rivers offer challenging whitewater boating in primitive and isolated settings. Foot access into the canyons is strenuous and very time consuming.

For the very adventurous, small redband trout and smallmouth bass are plentiful. There is a two-trout bag limit on redbands.

The Bruneau and Jarbidge rivers flow through deep, narrow canyons from the mountains of northern Nevada through the remote high desert of Idaho's Owyhee Uplands to the Snake. The sheer-walled rhyolite canyons and rock spires provide a first-class wilderness experience for self-sufficient, experienced boaters. There are about 40 miles of Class II-V whitewater, which takes between two and six days to run. These rivers are only for experienced boaters, who are well-versed in self-supported wilderness travel.

This is a rugged and remote area for experienced wilderness explorers only. There are no trails or developed facilities. Four-wheel-drive vehicles are required for access to the Bruneau River put-in at Indian Hot Springs. Two-wheel drive vehicles are sufficient to reach the Jarbidge River put-in at Murphy Hot Springs.

The rivers are usually boatable by raft or hard-shell kayak from April 1 to June 15. In late June and early July, the rivers can usually be floated with inflatable kayaks.

The "Owyhee and Bruneau River Systems Boating Guide" is available from the Bureau of Land Management. The area is also serviced by commercial outfitters in Boise, Mountain Home and Twin Falls.

For more information, contact the BLM Bruneau Resource Area, 384-3300.

Duck Valley Indian Reservation

TROPHY TROUT RESERVOIRS IN THE HIGH DESERT

The Duck Valley Indian Reservation of the Shoshone-Paiute Tribes straddles the Idaho-Nevada border, about 95 miles south of Mountain Home on Highway 51.

The reservation has three reservoirs: Sheep Creek, Mountain View and Lake Billie Shaw. Sheep Creek and Mountain View are managed for catch-and-keep fishing. Billie Shaw is a trophy lake where anglers are limited to keeping one fish per day. A tribal fishing license is required on all three lakes.

Billie Shaw has become a favorite trophy-trout lake for fly anglers, and double-digit catches of big, hard-fighting rainbow trout are common from April through June.

The town of Owyhee, Nevada, is 98 miles north of Elko, Nevada, via Highway 225 and 97 miles south of Mountain Home, Idaho, via Highway 51. All three reservoirs are located within reservation boundaries, and signs are posted for direction to the reservoirs.

The East Fork of the Owyhee River is accessible for fishing for 10 miles along Highway 225 within the reservation. When traveling through the reservation, use caution as it has open range for livestock.

Permits may be purchased at:

The Fishin' Hole, Highway 51 Bruneau, Idaho; 208-845-2001

Sportsman's Warehouse, 3797 E. Fairview, Meridian, Idaho; 208-884-3000

Stagers Surplus, Commercial St. Elko, Nevada; 775-753-4333

Duck Valley Gas N Go, Highway 225, Owyhee, Nevada; 775-757-3301. (Note: Lake Billy Shaw Permits and RV electric hook-ups sold here only.)

Tribal Office: Highway 51, Owyhee, Nev.; 775-757-2921.

Call 208-759-3100 ext. 410 for automated fishing report.

Website: http://duckvalleyonline.com/Fishing_Information.htm

Mountain View and Sheep Creek

Seasons: Mountain View open year-round; Sheep Creek, April 1 - Oct. 31.

Adult Daily Fishing Permit: $7.50; Two Day Fishing: $13; Daily Fishing Permit 14 yrs. and younger: $5; Season Individual camping and fishing: $50; Season Family camping and fishing: $75

Daily Possession Limit: Adults, 5 trout daily, 8 in possession; Children under 14, 4 trout daily, 6 in pos-session.   No size limit . Hours: 1 hour before sunrise, 2 hours after sunset.

The use of live bait is prohibited.

Lake Billy Shaw

Season: April 1 - Oct. 31.

Daily Individual permit: $25; Season Individual permit: $275.

Catch and release only. Single-point barbless hooks. No live bait. Limit: 1 fish, 16-19 inches. All other fish must be retuned to water immediately, unharmed. No gas-powered engines.

In the Shadow of the Mountains

LITTLE CAMAS RESERVOIR

A popular prairie pond, Little Camas Reservoir is about 10 miles northeast of Mountain Home, via U.S. 20 and a short drive north from the highway.

When full it is more than 1,000 acres, but is relatively shallow throughout. It can be fished from motorized boats, float-tubes or pontoon boats. Casting from shore or wading the shallows during early morning or evening hatches also is productive.

Rainbow trout grow quickly in its fertile waters, and the population is maintained by stocking. The trout average 12 to 14 inches, with occasional fish to 18 inches.

Ice-out occurs as early as mid-April in mild years, so flyfishers can jump start their season.

ANDERSON RANCH RESERVOIR

A favorite camping and fishing destination for Magic Valley and Treasure Valley families, Anderson Ranch Reservoir is located on the South Fork of the Boise River approximately 25 miles northwest of Mountain Home.

To reach it, take U.S. 20 north about 5 miles to the turn off to the Anderson Ranch-South Fork Canyon Road to reach the dam, or continue east to Hill City and take the road to Pine and the backwaters of the reservoir.

The dam is the uppermost of three dams built on the Boise River. When full, it has an area of 4,700 acres, is 14 miles long and a mile wide with a depth of 315 feet. Due to irrigation demands, significant drawdown in late summer may affect ramp access. Curlew ramp on the upper end of the reservoir, and Elk Creek ramps, however, are nearly always available.

The shoreline is accessible to anglers along the northwest side from the dam to Fall Creek, where streams enter the reservoir. Bank anglers also have good access at the upper end of the reservoir from Lime Creek to the Pine boat ramp. Undeveloped camp sites are available along the shoreline near the road and several sites are accessible only by boat. Developed camp sites are available in resort areas of Pine, Deer and Fall creeks.

A variety of game fish can be found in Anderson Ranch, including rainbow trout, smallmouth bass, yellow perch, and the most popular kokanee salmon. Bull trout can also be found, but there is no harvest of bull trout and they must be released immediately.

Fishing for kokanee is best in the summer months and fall throughout the reservoir. Generally, kokanee are 10 to 12 inches long, with the occasional 20-incher in good years. As they are open-water fish, anglers have best success from a boat. In the spring and late fall, kokanee can be found near the surface. During the warmer summer months, water temperatures force kokanee to drop to deeper depths of 50 feet or more.

Anderson Ranch Reservoir

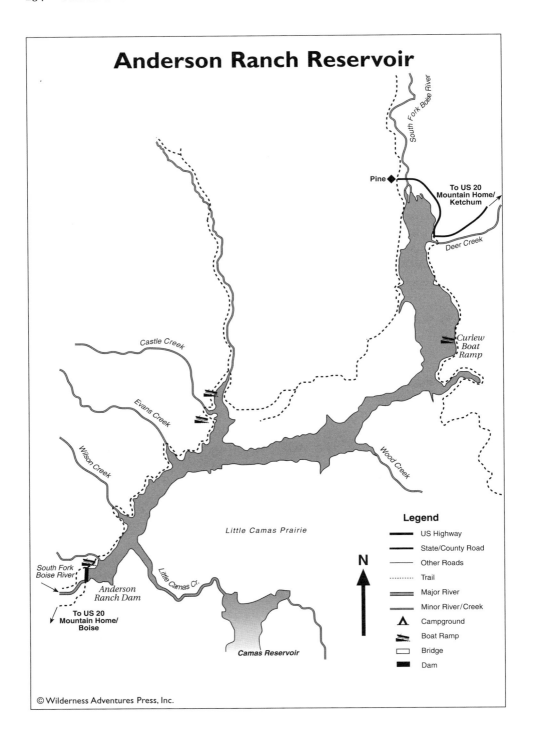

Pine

To US 20
Mountain Home/
Ketchum

Deer Creek

South Fork Boise River

Curlew
Boat
Ramp

Castle Creek

Evans Creek

Wilson Creek

Wood Creek

Little Camas Prairie

South Fork
Boise River

Anderson
Ranch Dam

Little Camas Cr.

To US 20
Mountain Home/
Boise

Camas Reservoir

Legend

▬▬▬	US Highway
───	State/County Road
───	Other Roads
······	Trail
▬▬▬	Major River
───	Minor River/Creek
▲	Campground
⚞	Boat Ramp
▭	Bridge
▬	Dam

N

© Wilderness Adventures Press, Inc.

Starting in August, kokanee migrate up the South Fork Boise River and other smaller tributaries to spawn. At this time the South Fork Boise River is closed to fishing between the slack water of the reservoir and the Pine Bridge to protect these spawning fish when they are concentrated. Six kokanee can be harvested above the Pine Bridge from the river using standard fishing methods. Snagging is not allowed.

Anderson Ranch Reservoir contains both wild and hatchery rainbow trout. Hatchery trout are stocked into the reservoir as both fingerling and catchable size fish, primarily in the spring. Wild rainbow trout move down into the reservoir from the river during early spring and late fall at about 6 to 8 inches long. Growth rates for both wild and hatchery trout in the reservoir are good and fish can grow to 5 pounds or larger.

Trout fishing is best during spring and fall months for shoreline anglers when surface water temperatures are cool. During the summer when surface temperatures warm, trout go deeper in the reservoir and are more difficult to locate. At this time, areas around springs and cool water streams are good.

Smallmouth bass can be found in rocky areas throughout the reservoir, with the best fishing in the area from the Narrows to the dam. Easiest fishing is from boats or float-tubes.

Bull trout, a native char found in Anderson Ranch Reservoir, South Fork Boise River and small tributaries are protected and must be released unharmed. They are normally caught when fishing for rainbow trout in the early spring by bank anglers near the upper end of the reservoir. If you catch one and it has swallowed the hook just cut your line and release the fish. Hooks will digest away within a couple of weeks.

Our main forte here is the high mountain lakes and, of course, all of the lakes have trout.
Richard Escott, former owner of the
Payette Lake Charters & Lick Creek Fly Shop

Payette River and Alpine Lakes

Western highlands harbor pristine lakes, bountiful streams

The pristine alpine lakes and churning mountain streams of the Payette National Forest surrounding the resort town of McCall, 100 miles north of Boise, offer wilderness adventures in one of the largest remaining undeveloped tracts of land in the Lower 48.

Thousands of acres of roadless areas in the forest abut the western boundary of the Frank Church-River of No Return Wilderness. The forest is bordered by two Wild and Scenic rivers—on the north, the Salmon and on the east, the Middle Fork of the Salmon. Its western border is the southern end of Hell's Canyon National Recreation Area, the wilderness section of the Snake River.

Public access is excellent. In addition to Payette National Forest lands, there are extensive tracts of state lands east of McCall and Payette Lake. The Boise National Forest extends north and east of Cascade.

Food, services, motels, RV parks, and private campgrounds can be found at McCall, Donnelley, Cascade, and New Meadows. Ponderosa State Park is just east of McCall on a peninsula extending into Payette Lake. Numerous national forest campgrounds can be found at various lakes and trailheads.

For fly fishers, the region's strongest drawing cards are the hundreds of trout-filled alpine lakes that capture the snows of the west-central mountains. Most dot the ridges between the South Fork of the Salmon and the North Fork of the Payette and the wilderness mountains above the Middle Fork of the Salmon. Another multitude of mountain lakes bedeck the Lava Ridge-Hard Butte area east of the Little Salmon River drainage, northwest of McCall. Eight of the alpine lakes—Brush, Crystal, Serene, Blackwell, Lake Rock, Long, Louie, and Tule—are managed as trophy fisheries for trout over 20 inches. They have received this distinction because they can produce and are popular and relatively easy to reach.

Optimum fishing waters can be found in mile-high Long Valley, north and south of McCall, too. The resort town circles the western shore of Payette Lake, the largest natural reservoir in the region and homewaters of trophy lake trout. A few miles upstream on the North Fork is Upper Payette Lake. Northwest of it, in the Little Salmon River drainage, is the trio of Hazard Lakes and Brundage Reservoir, another trophy fishery. Just to the southeast of McCall is Little Payette Lake, a trophy fishery for both rainbow trout and smallmouth bass that feeds into the North Fork via Lake Fork Creek. Cascade Reservoir, just south of McCall, is the major man-made impoundment stilling the flows of the North

The Payette River—optimum scenery and fishing. Art Today photo.

Fork en route to its juncture with the South Fork to form the main stem of the Payette River south of Cascade at the village of Banks.

The Payette River gathers the flows from a 3,300-square-mile drainage area and flows 55 miles from Banks to join the Snake River just west of the city of Payette. Its best fishing is on its tributaries. The flows of its numerous forks and minor tributaries rise at elevations of 10,000 feet in the Salmon River and Sawtooth Mountains east of McCall and north of Boise. The Payette and its tributaries descend through rugged mountain terrain, deep canyons, valleys, and river plains to an elevation of 2,125 feet at the mouth.

The length of the North Fork of the Payette is 55 miles; Gold Fork River, 20; Lake Fork Creek, 25; and the South Fork of the Payette, 60. Gold Fork and Lake Fork are tributaries of the North Fork. Two principal tributaries of the South Fork are the Middle Fork of the Payette and Deadwood River. The latter also has a major impoundment. Black Canyon Dam on the lower Payette blocked the drainage's access to sea-running steelhead trout and chinook salmon decades ago.

Feeding the Salmon River drainage north and east of McCall are Rapid River, Little Salmon River, Secesh River, the South Fork of the Salmon, the East Fork of the South Fork, and tributaries of the Middle Fork of the Salmon.

The South Fork flows north through the Idaho batholith, a gargantuan volcanic intrusion that thrust up the wilderness highlands, and enters the Salmon at Mackay Bar.

Its tributaries rise at elevations exceeding 9,000 feet and the South Fork descends to 2,166 feet at its mouth.

The mountainous topography is characterized by extreme changes in elevation and scenery within very short distances, varying from high peaks and bare, rocky ridges to steep canyons and narrow meadows. The batholith's soils are mostly weathered granitic sands that are very susceptible to erosion. Annual precipitation ranges from 30 to 70 inches. Most of it falls in the form of snow, although major storms can occur any time of year.

High alpine lakes are largely the headwaters of these major drainages, still essential spawning waters of steelhead and chinook. The South Fork historically had the largest summer chinook run in the state and once annually supported angler harvests ranging from 1,700 to 4,000 fish. Its historic steelhead spawning run once exceeded 3,000 fish.

Modern anadromous runs have declined drastically the past three decades and now number only in the hundreds. Chinook and steelhead have been off limits to South Fork anglers since the 1960s. Also off-limits on both the South Fork and Middle Fork are two of the three populations of B-run steelhead in the Columbia Basin. These fish are predominantly large steelhead, which also run up the Clearwater drainage. They spend two or three years in the Pacific Ocean, compared to the smaller one- and two-year A-run steelhead that inhabit much of the rest of the Salmon River drainage.

The two bright spots for fly fishers pursuing anadromous fish in the region are the superb spring run of steelhead on the Little Salmon River and the fall and spring steelhead opportunities on the Salmon above and below Riggins.

For non-anadromous fish anglers there are ample opportunities to pursue resident trout. Native westslope cutthroat, redband rainbow, bull trout, and whitefish, along with introduced strains of rainbow, brook trout, and a few brown and golden trout are in the rivers, small mountain streams, and alpine lakes of the western highlands. Lake trout, splake (brook-lake trout hybrids), and bass are in a few lakes.

"Take a 50-mile radius and you've got close to 200 mountain lakes. That's our main forte. We have lakes at elevations of 5,000 to 9,000 feet, and even higher," says Richard Escott, a former fly shop owner and the alpine fishing guru in McCall.

But lakes aren't the only cards on the table.

"The upper North Fork of the Payette is excellent fishing," Escott notes. That's when it has good flows. Water releases have been curtailed in recent years due to political wrangling over providing supplemental water to help flush endangered salmon to the sea."

"The Secesh River is fairly decent for cutthroat," Escott adds. The same goes for the East Fork of the South Fork of the Salmon for rainbows and cutthroat, and the South Fork for cutthroat. A mid-summer ban on fishing to protect spawning salmon was dropped in 1996.

"The Little Salmon is fairly decent early on, but it's too low later in the season [because of irrigation diversions]. It has excellent spring steelhead fishing."

"The Main Salmon [below Riggins] has excellent smallmouth bass fishing. Cast and blast floats in the fall for steelhead and chukars are very popular."

Escott also favors Lake Fork Creek when flows from Little Payette Lake are adequate. Above the lake to Brown's Pond, the creek is managed as a trophy fishery.

Big Creek, flowing into the Middle Fork of the Salmon east of Yellow Pine, is perhaps the most popular catch-and-release stream in the region for cutthroat—a secret many resident fishers would like to keep to themselves. Ditto for Johnson Creek, a major tributary of the East Fork of the South Fork, east of Warm Lake.

At these elevations, the past winter's snowpack and current weather conditions play major roles in summer fishing options. In a good water year, fishing can be excellent well into fall. Drought years can dry up smaller streams by mid-summer.

Check out current conditions ahead of time by visiting with the folks at T. Avery Outfitters or call a fly shop in Boise.

Dry flies recommended by Escott include the standard mayfly, caddis, midge, and terrestrial patterns. One of the most common mayflies on lakes is the *Callibaetis*. Generic patterns and attractors include Adams, renegades, humpies, stimulators, royal Wulffs, and Coachmans.

Effective wet flies and nymphs for high lakes include leech patterns, small streamers, and woolly buggers to bead head nymphs, *Chironomid* nymphs, soft-hackle nymphs, prince nymph, hare's ear, Sheep Creek Special, green caddis emerger, peacock emerger, pheasant tail, green scud, and pink or green shrimp patterns.

During some seasons, certain lakes have good damselfly hatches. In high mountain streams, stonefly nymphs are more effective than dry fly patterns because of the sporadic nature of the hatches.

Rod choices vary with conditions or the length of the hike into a lake. A three-piece, 8-foot 6-weight travel rod with a weight-forward line and medium sinking tip is handy on longer trips. For small lakes with windless conditions, you can get by with a 4-weight rod and floating line. Big lakes or windy conditions may require a 9-foot 6- or 7-weight rod and a sinking-tip line.

Fly fishers who tackle high lakes typically rate the experience as excellent to frustrating. Read that as "hot-and-frenzied" to "are-there-really-fish-in-this-lake?" Either way, this is central Idaho at its best. The scenery is great.

Fish and Game generally manages individual lakes for a single species, although each lake in a chain may contain several different species. Most have the colorful and accommodating westslope cutthroat. Sizes vary in each lake. The range runs from 22-inch cutthroat to 10-inch brook trout. Many of the lakes are stocked with trout or grayling fry by helicopter or airplane on a three-year rotation.

Some lakes are at the end of easy hikes and permit float tubing. Those that don't sometimes present more of a challenge in finding enough casting room. Practice your roll cast before setting out.

Dry fly action often is limited in mid-summer, and fly fishers can plan on mostly working the depths of a lake with wet flies. The key is to find at what depth the fish are feeding. Use a dropper fly to speed up your prospecting.

Given a choice, the fish seem to prefer to rise to adult flying insects. The sight of a lake dimpled like falling rain by scores of rise forms is a guaranteed adrenaline rush. Fly takes can be frenzied and almost non-stop. Look for surface activity shortly after dawn, as twilight falls, or on heavily overcast days. These also are the best times to work the shallows along the shoreline. Other good bets are to work the mouths and outlets of feeder streams and to cast to fallen logs and shoreline boulders or off rocky points.

When first approaching a lake, work the shallows, then plumb the deeper waters.

Three well-maintained gravel roads lead to backcountry service points and provide access to other forest roads and trailheads.

- The Warren Wagon Road just north of McCall goes northeast to the old mining town of Warren and follows the Secesh River east into the lower South Fork of the Salmon drainage.
- The Lick Creek Road out of McCall goes east to Yellow Pine on the East Fork of the South Fork and continues northeast to Big Creek.
- The Warm Lake Road out of Cascade goes east to Warm Lake, near the headwaters of the South Fork, and continues northeast to Yellow Pine.

All three are interconnected and loop trips are possible, starting from either McCall or Cascade on State Highway 55. Payette and Boise National Forest travel maps should be obtained before setting out. Always have a full tank of gasoline and carry extra water.

A more expensive alternative is to fly into the backcountry. There are numerous landing strips in the central highlands, including wilderness areas. Local Forest Service ranger district offices can provide information on outfitters and flight services. Some outfitters also provide guided trail rides by horseback.

Backcountry fly fishers and hikers should remember snow can occur any time of year at higher elevations. Pack accordingly to be prepared for spring or fall-like conditions even in mid-summer. Summer squalls, sometimes accompanied by intense lightning, are common at higher elevations and can drop temperatures 20 degrees in an hour. Always include rain gear, a sweater, extra wool socks, knit cap, and gloves or mittens in your day pack. Insect repellent is a must to combat pesky mosquitoes and deer flies.

Topographical maps are useful for realistically planning extended hikes, or fully appreciating the actual elevation changes in some shorter hikes. Take them along and know how to read them.

Extensive fires in 1994 scorched approximately 290,000 acres in scattered pockets of forest north and east of McCall and temporarily blocked access to one million acres. The following year, the Forest Service began working to reopen about 150 miles of hiking trails. Campers should avoid camping near dead or dying trees, especially during stormy or windy conditions.

Resident fish were essentially unaffected by the fires. Fishing might even be improved by the increase in nutrients being washed into the drainages.

Following are some lakes and streams to consider in the McCall area. Be sure to check current regulations.

Long Valley Lakes and Streams

Payette Lake

Referred to locally as the Big Lake, it is located in the center of Long Valley with McCall on its southwest shore. It is the largest natural lake in the area, about six miles long, with 20 miles of shoreline and a maximum depth of 300 feet. Cutthroat to 15 inches provide shoreline fly fishing opportunities. The biggest draw for non-fly fishers are lake trout 5 to 25 pounds. They are most accessible after spring ice-out and over spawning reefs in late fall; down-rigger fishing in summer. Payette Lake is also planted with rainbow trout and kokanee salmon. To produce more large lake trout in Payette Lake, the limit is 1 fish, none over 30 inches.

Little Payette Lake

Trophy fishery just east of McCall off Lick Creek Road. Only one boat ramp; partially surrounded by private property. Trophy hunters are after Kamloop and Pennask strains of rainbow and residual stock of smallmouth bass. Kokanee also planted. The bass limit is 2, none under 20 inches.

Upper Payette Lake

Higher in elevation than its sisters, located north of the Payette Lake on Warren Wagon Road in beautiful mountain scenery. Heavily stocked with hatchery rainbow 8 to 12 inches; also contains brook trout.

Upper North Fork of Payette

Scenic, serene canoe float between Upper Payette Lake and Big Lake; also easy wading. Contains mostly hatchery rainbows, some cutthroat and brook trout. Kokanee run upstream from Big Lake in late summer is off-limits. Canoe rental available in McCall.

Middle North Fork of Payette

Chance for large wild rainbows, plus hatchery rainbows 12 to 14 inches between McCall and Cascade Reservoir. Best access from roads on west side of Long Valley, but inquire locally. Shallow in places but can be floated in canoes or rafts; inquire locally for portages. Kokanee run upstream from Cascade in late summer is off-limits.

Brundage Reservoir

A quality fishery north of the ski resort along the road to the Hazard Lakes between McCall and New Meadows in the Little Salmon River drainage. Wild and hatchery rainbow average 10 to 18 inches. Limit is two fish, none over 14 inches.

Lake Fork Creek

It is the source and outlet of Little Payette Lake. Upstream along Lick Creek Road, from lake to Brown's Pond, it was previously managed as a trophy fishery. It is now a full-year fishery with a 6-trout limit. Inquire locally for access sites downstream to the North Fork; kokanee are off-limits there.

Valley County Ponds

Good opportunities for family outings, teaching youngsters to fish. Inquire locally for locations and access; some on private property. Stocked mostly with rainbow, some contain cutthroat and brook trout. Holdover rainbows can grow to good sizes.

Trophy Alpine Lakes

Tack a Payette or northern Boise forest map to the wall, toss a dart at it and the missile will land near a mountain lake. Some are strung out in chains, making loop trips possible.

Some of the hike-in lakes popular with fly fishers are Josephine Lake, Twenty Mile Lake, Box Lake, and Boulder Lake. Trailheads are relatively easy to find, but check first with Lick Creek Fly Shop in McCall or use Forest Service and topo maps.

Eight of the west-central highland lakes are managed as trophy fisheries. Limit is two fish over 20 inches; single barbless hook on flies or lures. They are:

Brush Lake

In North Fork of Payette drainage east of Upper Payette Lake, south of Warren Wagon Road. Contains rainbows.

Crystal Lake

In the North Fork of the Payette drainage, northeast of Little Payette Lake and west of Lick Creek Road summit. Contains cutthroat.

Blackwell Lake

In the North Fork of the Payette drainage, north of Little Payette Lake and east of Big Payette Lake, above Lick Creek Road. Contains rainbows.

Lake Serene

In Hazard Creek drainage, northwest of the Hard Creek Guard Station on the Brundage-Hazard Lakes Road. Contains cutthroat.

Lake Rock Lake

In Secesh River drainage east of Warren Wagon Road, north of Upper Payette Lake. Contains cutthroat.

Long Lake

South of Warm Lake and east of headwaters of South Fork of Salmon drainage. Contains cutthroat and rainbow.

Louie Lake

In Boulder Creek drainage southeast of Little Payette Lake. Contains cutthroat.

Tule Lake

Southwest of Warm Lake in South Fork of Salmon drainage. Contains cutthroat.

Really Off the Beaten Path

Opportunities for quality-time, laid-back solitude, and good fishing are virtually unlimited in Idaho's central highlands and designated wilderness areas. Getting there requires time and effort. The golden pots at the end of the rainbow are wild, accommodating trout and fabulous scenery. Consult local outfitters, guides and fly tackle shops for other quality options. Two suggestions follow:

Big Creek

The upper trailhead and Big Creek Ranger Station are 25 miles northeast of Yellow Pine. Another trailhead is located five miles downstream at Smith Creek, where Big Creek enters the Frank Church-River of No Return Wilderness, and the best fishing begins.

The 35-mile stream drops from 5,500 to 3,400 feet in elevation, cascading into deep plunge pools and down stair-step pools, moderately stilled in stretches by long, crystal-clear runs, and cuts through a deep gorge above its confluence with the Middle Fork of the Salmon. Volume grows to small river size as it is joined by Monumental Creek, ten miles downstream, and Cabin Creek, 20 miles downstream. The spring runoff usually winds down by early July. The stream can't be floated. A trail follows it all the way to Middle Fork.

Big Creek is managed as catch-and-release fishery for westslope cutthroat. Surveys indicate more than half the trout exceed 14 inches, some in the 20-inch range. Fly fishers report catches of 20 to 40 fish a day. Also contains bull trout and steelhead smolts.

Pinnacle Lakes

The trailhead is at Belvidere Creek, southeast of Profile Gap summit, on the road between Yellow Pine and Big Creek. The cluster of lakes on the headwaters of Belvidere and its tributaries are nestled on the slopes dominated by 9,273-foot Pinnacle Peak. The climb to a lake may require an overnight camp on the trail for some hikers because of elevation gains of 2,500 to 3,000 feet.

Ice breakup usually occurs after mid-June. Best fishing is in July and August for cutthroat trout up to 16 inches, most in the 8- to 12-inch range. Sizes depend on three-year stocking program and number of holdover fish. Consult topo maps and inquire locally about current conditions.

Lower North and South Fork Payette

Cascade Reservoir, nestled in the majestic mountains of west-central Idaho, is a major fishing center south of McCall, adjacent to the small towns of Cascade and Donnelly. Rainbow trout, coho salmon and smallmouth bass can be caught from the shore or by boat and float-tube.

South of the reservoir are the cascading flows of the North Fork and South Fork of the Payette River. Both ranked as top whitewater adventures for kayakers and rafters, their turbulent waters also offer prime pocket water fishing for rainbow close to roads. Cutthroat and brook trout are found in the South Fork's headwaters.

Trout and bass in remote tributaries of the Payette drainage and backcountry lakes and reservoir also await anglers who go further afield.

Cascade Reservoir

Cascade is a large reservoir, nearly 30,000 acres, on the North Fork of the Payette River. Known for its consistent fisheries and convenient location, only 70 miles north of Boise, it is one of the most popular and heavily used fisheries in Idaho. At one time, Cascade was rated the No. 1 fishery in the state.

Cascade Reservoir is just west of Highway 55, between Donnelly and Cascade, and recreational development adjacent to the lake makes it a great destination for family outings for a day or the weekend. Shoreline access is excellent around the entire reservoir, especially near camping and picnicking areas provided by Cascade State Park. Numerous docks and ramps are available for boater access.

Cascade offers a good diversity of angling opportunity. Fish species range from rainbow trout and coho salmon, with a few kokanee salmon, to the warmwater species of smallmouth bass and crappie. It also is loaded with perch.

Cascade is most popular for trolling for the big trout and coho salmon. During the spring, anglers fishing from shore during the ice-out can pick up large spawners using Mepps spinners and Little Cleo's, but flyfishers can get in on the action with woolly worms and other flies.

Though smallmouth bass are not yet a major fishery on Cascade, they provide great excitement when found. Look for broken rocks, docks or some type of cover. The Crown Point area, among other areas, is good for bass.

Coho are an excellent eating fish that has become extremely popular with anglers. They were initially stocked in the early 1970s to offset reduced kokanee populations. Today, both coho and kokanee are caught. They are very difficult to tell apart.

Cascade State Park

The park surrounding most of Cascade Reservoir offers 300 tent and RV camp sites scattered around the reservoir, and two group camp areas, Snowbank and Poison Creek, for small to medium-sized groups.

Osprey Point is the secluded, yet accessible, site of the park's three yurts for group camping without roughing it. The yurts feature wood stoves for heat, propane lighting, a propane stove for cooking, beds and other furniture. You won't find a better view on the lake.

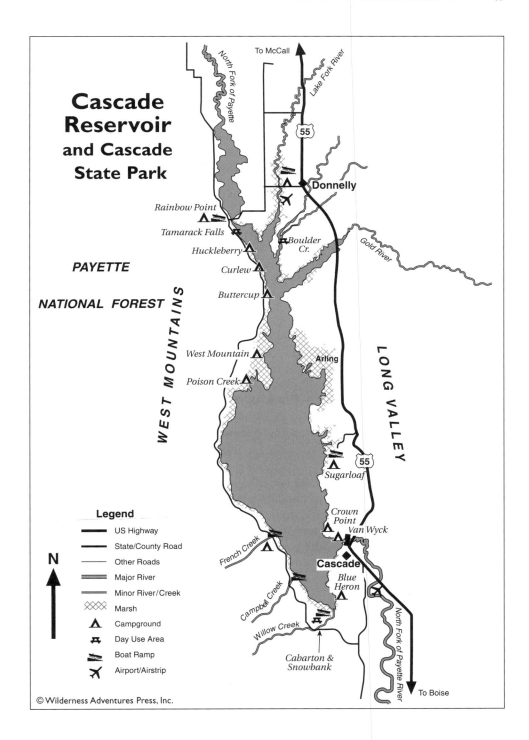

Cascade Reservoir and Cascade State Park

To McCall

Lake Fork River

North Fork of Payette

55

Donnelly

Rainbow Point

Tamarack Falls

Boulder Cr.

Huckleberry

PAYETTE

Curlew

Buttercup

NATIONAL FOREST

Gold River

WEST MOUNTAINS

West Mountain

Arling

Poison Creek

LONG VALLEY

55

Sugarloaf

Crown Point

Van Wyck

Legend

──	US Highway
──	State/County Road
──	Other Roads
──	Major River
──	Minor River/Creek
✕✕✕	Marsh
▲	Campground
⌗	Day Use Area
≈	Boat Ramp
✈	Airport/Airstrip

N

French Creek

Cascade

Blue Heron

Campbell Creek

North Fork of Payette River

Willow Creek

Cabarton & Snowbank

To Boise

© Wilderness Adventures Press, Inc.

For more information, contact the park at 382-4258; Fax: 382-4071; or Email: CAS@ idpr.state.id.us

Lower North Fork of Payette

The North Fork of the Payette River, with its world-class kayaking rapids, flows to the south from Cascade Reservoir to Banks, where it joins the South Fork to create the Payette River.

The tailrace below Cascade Dam is away from roads and more remote. A moderate whitewater float from the dam to Cabarton Bridge, it also can be fished from boats. Inquire locally for put-in sites and bank fishing access.

Boat anglers should leave the swift canyon stretches along Highway 55 below Cabarton and below Smiths Ferry to kayakers and other whitewater enthusiasts.

Shore anglers who tackle the river's boiling rapids and pocket waters along the highway need to scramble down steep rocky banks and riprap boulders. Do not wear waders. The quiet flat flows between Cabarton Bridge and Smiths Ferry are essentially barren of fish.

Fishing the river's pocket waters for 12- to 14-inch rainbows is productive with attractor dry flies, streamers and nymphs. The North Fork also holds whitefish.

High spring runoff and summer irrigation releases from Cascade may hinder fishing until late-July. The river fishes well in late summer through late autumn, and it is open to anglers year-round.

South Fork of Payette

The South Fork of the Payette cuts its 60-mile course through the ponderosa pine forests of central Idaho along one of the most scenic backcountry drives in the state. A rare treat, virtually its entire dash down the mountains is paralleled by a state highway and Forest Service road.

Approaching it from the top on the west slopes of the Sawtooths, you can watch the South Fork Payette grow from a high mountain runnel into a tumbling whitewater playground below Lowman, where it picks up the Deadwood River. Pocket water fishers have to share this popular downstream stretch with kayakers and rafters. Below Couch, where it picks up the Middle Fork, the South Fork flattens out and meanders through a high valley en route to its confluence with the North Fork at Banks.

There are three routes to the South Fork Payette. From its mouth at Banks on Highway 55, a paved secondary road follows the river east through Garden Valley to Lowman. This historic mining town is 35 miles northeast of Boise on State Highway 21. The other route to the upper river is to take Highway 21 west from Stanley and cross over Banner Summit to Lowman.

The South Fork Payette provides excellent pocket water fishing for native redband rainbow in the 9- to 14-inch range.

The wild Payette River. Art Today photo.

The river is managed as a wild rainbow fishery with a two-trout bag limit. Westslope cutthroat, bull trout and brook trout may be found in its higher reaches, and whitefish are present throughout the river. Bull trout must be released immediately. The South Fork is open in May from Memorial Day weekend through November 30.

The river's prolific caddis hatches make it a good dry fly stream, so anglers should carry a selection of elk hair caddis, stimulators and other attractor patterns, as well as grasshoppers in late summer. A variety of mayfly patterns pay off during sporadic hatches. Also watch for the giant stonefly hatch as spring runoff starts to wane in late spring.

Hare's ear nymphs, small woolly buggers and stonefly nymphs are standbys in pocket waters, and streamers and sculpin patterns can be tried for deeper feeders.

Spring runoff usually subsides by mid-July and the South Fork Payette's best fishing continues into October.

Access to the river from a road is best east of Couch and on upstream past Lowman. In many places the river cuts a deep course and anglers have to scramble down very steep banks. There are no side roads into its headwaters stretch.

Tributaries of the South Fork Payette worth exploring include the Middle Fork Payette and Deadwood River. Deadwood Reservoir has one of the most mixed-bag fisheries in the state, including rainbow and cutthroat trout, and kokanee salmon, landlocked fall chinook salmon and Atlantic salmon.

Pay to Park and Play

Passes are required to park and use facilities at eight river access sites along the South Fork and mainstem Payette River. Boaters and other river users can purchase either a season pass for $30 or a day pass for $3 per day.

A pass is required to park at the Danskin, Banks, Banks Beach, Chief Parish, Beehive Bend, Porter Creek, Deadwood River, and the Lower Confluence ("Worm Farm") river access sites.

Day passes can be purchased at the river access sites.

Season passes can be purchased at the Forest Service - Bureau of Land Management Interagency Visitor Center in Boise; Boise National Forest District Offices in Emmett, Lowman, and Garden Valley; Ponderosa Sports; Banks Cafe and Store; Garden Valley Store; Boise Army Navy Store; Cascade Outfitters; Cascade Raft Company; Idaho River Sports; and REI.

All of the funds generated by sales of the passes will be used to maintain and enhance recreational facilities and services along the river corridor.

Payette River season passes also are valid at fee sites on the South Fork of the Snake River in eastern Idaho, and season passes for that river are valid at Payette fee sites.

Backcountry Lakes and Reservoirs

Warm Lake

Warm Lake is a 640-acre lake about 25 miles east of Cascade on Forest Service Road 22, which is also known as Warm Lake Highway.

The lake is open year-round and general bag limits apply to all species. Excellent facilities make Warm Lake a great family fishing destination. The U.S. Forest Service maintains a campground, day-use area and boat ramp on the north shore. Two private lodges also provide services.

Rainbow trout are stocked throughout the spring and summer and provide the primary fishery on Warm Lake. Brook trout, whitefish, kokanee salmon, lake trout, and bull trout are also present. Anglers should note that there is a statewide no harvest rule on bull trout, they must be released immediately.

Bank anglers will do especially well along the rocky northwest shores. Shoreline fishing will be best early in the morning and evenings when fish are feeding in closer the banks.

Boat and float-tube anglers have success with lures and flies as well. Trout will tend to seek deeper depths during the hot summer months. Fly anglers will have best success in the morning and evening as the trout begin to surface feed.

Lake trout (mackinaw) were stocked into Warm Lake in 1976. Though they never really took off, there is still a small population in the lake and the occasional 15-pounder is caught by the persistent angler. Lake trout tend to school in deep water, but may be accessible to flyfishers around ice-out.

An under-utilized fish in Warm Lake is the abundant mountain whitefish.

Horsethief Reservoir

A popular float-tubing fishery, less than 10 miles east of Cascade, the 1,270-acre Horsethief Reservoir is on the comeback trail.

The reservoir was drained for a perch eradication project in 1999. Rainbow trout were planted in spring 2000 to bring the reservoir back to its productive trout fishery. In the past it produced respectable rainbows in good water years, and also was planted with brown trout. Brook trout in its tributaries also are expected to return to the lake.

Horsethief can be reached by driving east from Cascade on the Warm Lake Road about 5 miles and taking a side road south about 3 miles to the reservoir.

Sagehen Reservoir

Above the town of Smiths Ferry, southwest of Cascade, lies Sagehen Reservoir, another excellent float-tube fishery.

The scenic 180-acre pond is a popular camping and fishing destination for Boise families, so it gets heavy pressure during summer. The draw is holdover rainbows that reach 16 inches in good water years.

Small but deep due to its steep banks, Sagehen fishes best from a boat or float-tube in its creek channels and along flat shelfs near shore. Ice-out occurs in early May and fishing often is excellent.

A sinking line and a leech are a good bet most of the time. Damsel fly emergers also work in May and June, and mid-summer offers some great surface fishing with *Callibaetis*, big black ants and beetles.

To reach Sagehen take Highway 55 south from Cascade or north from Boise to Smiths Ferry, and watch for the road sign just north of town. The reservoir is about 15 miles northwest on a gravel road.

Deadwood Reservoir

The Deadwood Reservoir is a 3,000-acre impoundment on the Deadwood River, a tributary of the South Fork of the Payette. It is reached by taking the South Fork road about 5 miles west from Lowman to the Scott Mountain Road, and following the Deadwood River north about 20 miles. The reservoir also can be reached by taking the Bear Valley Road north out of Lowman.

Deadwood Reservoir has one of the most mixed-bag fisheries in the state, including rainbow and cutthroat trout, kokanee salmon, and landlocked fall chinook salmon and Atlantic salmon. According to reports, the lake's fish range from 10 to 16 inches. A 13-pound Atlantic salmon was netted in 1995.

Six-trout limit; 25 kokanee.

Bull trout caught in the reservoir or river must be released immediately.

FINAL NOTES

All the principal rivers in the Payette and South Fork of the Salmon drainages are paralleled for major stretches by roads, including bigger tributaries like Johnson Creek. Fasten your seatbelts, some are more bumpy than others. The last ten miles of the South Fork to the Main Salmon has to be hiked.

Bull trout are protected on all Idaho waters and must be released. Cutthroat must be released on the Salmon River and its major tributaries, including the South Fork, Middle Fork, East Fork of the South Fork, Secesh, and Little Salmon rivers, and Johnson, Big, and Squaw creeks. There is a two-trout limit on Chamberlain Creek and its tributaries.

Rapid River, a tributary of the Little Salmon, also has a two-trout limit.

Rainbow trout over 20 inches in the Salmon and Snake drainages are considered steelhead and can be taken only in their designated seasons.

Effective patterns for high mountain lakes and streams

Nymphs: *Callibaetis*, No. 16-14; Sheep Creek Special, Carey Special or soft-hackle nymphs, 16-8; Chironomid, 16-10; olive damselfly, 10-12; hare's ear, 16-10; green caddis emerger, 12-8; peacock emerger, 16-10; pheasant tail, 16-10; olive or pink freshwater shrimp, 16-10; olive scud, 16-10; black or brown leech, 10-8; midge pupa, 20-16; beadhead nymphs, 16-10; black or brown stonefly and black rubber legs, 10-6.

Streamers: Muddler minnow, 10-2; rabbit leech, 8-2; royal Coachman, 14-8; spruce fly, 10-8; marabou muddler, 8-4; woolly bugger, 12-4; Zonker minnow, 8-4; Zug bug, 12-8; Stayner ducktail, 12-8.

Dry flies: *Callibaetis*, 16-10; Adams, 20-14; parachute Adams, 20-14; light or pink Cahill, 20-14; elk hair or deer hair caddis, 18-12; Henryville caddis, 18-12; yellow or orange stimulators, 16-12; humpies, 12-10; flying ant, 18-14; grasshopper, 14-8; royal Wulff, 16-12; renegade, 18-12.

McCall Area

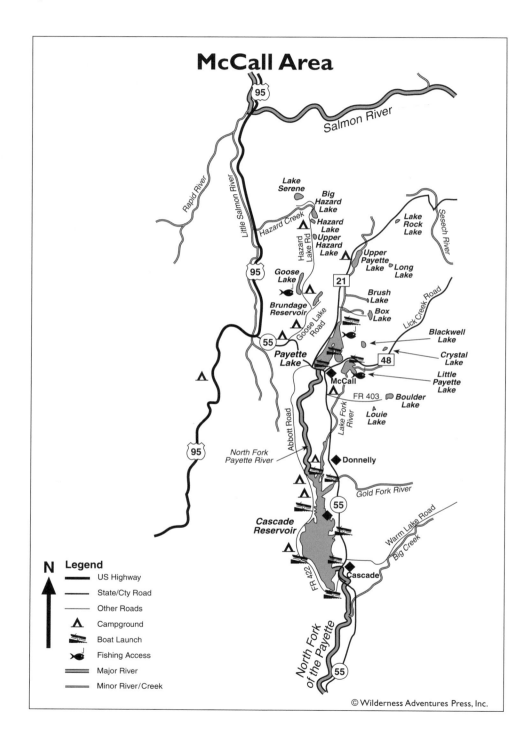

Salmon River

Rapid River

Little Salmon River

Lake Serene

Big Hazard Lake

Hazard Creek

Hazard Lake

Upper Hazard Lake

Hazard Lake Rd

Lake Rock Lake

Seseech River

Upper Payette Lake

Long Lake

Goose Lake

Brundage Reservoir

Goose Lake Road

Brush Lake

Box Lake

Lick Creek Road

Blackwell Lake

Crystal Lake

Payette Lake

McCall

Little Payette Lake

FR 403

Boulder Lake

Louie Lake

Lake Fork River

Abbott Road

North Fork Payette River

Donnelly

Gold Fork River

Cascade Reservoir

Warm Lake Road

Big Creek

FR 422

Cascade

North Fork of the Payette

N

Legend
- ▬ US Highway
- ▬ State/Cty Road
- ▬ Other Roads
- ▲ Campground
- 🛶 Boat Launch
- 🐟 Fishing Access
- ▬ Major River
- ▬ Minor River/Creek

© Wilderness Adventures Press, Inc.

McCall Area (cont.)

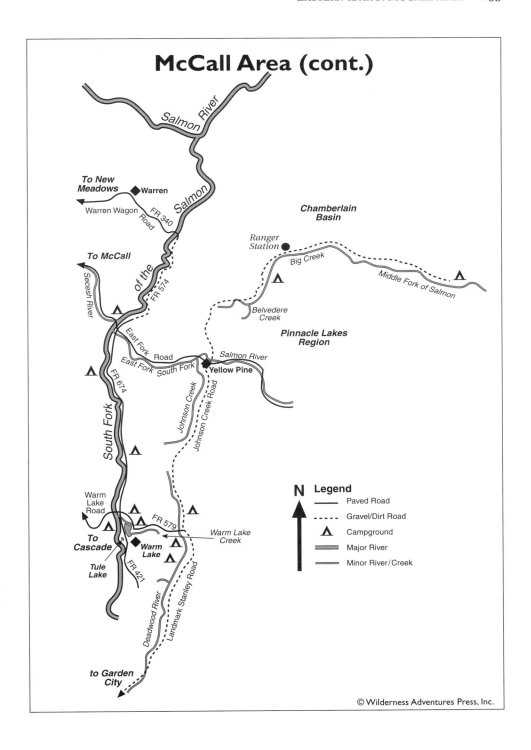

© Wilderness Adventures Press, Inc.

Northcentral Region

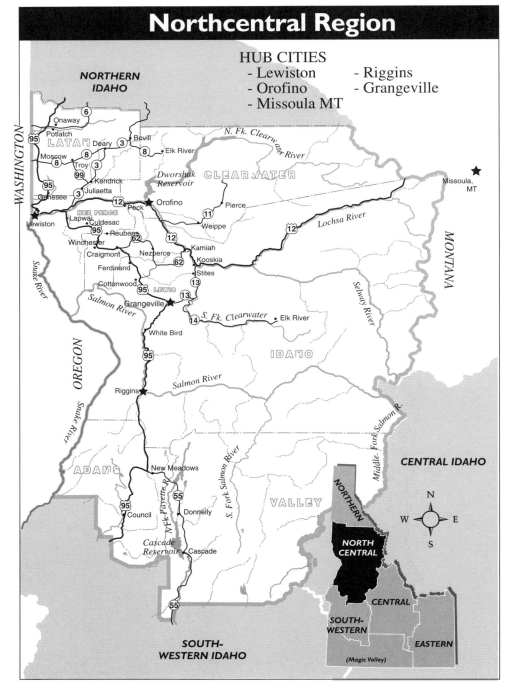

HUB CITIES
- Lewiston
- Orofino
- Missoula MT
- Riggins
- Grangeville

© Wilderness Adventures Press, Inc.

NORTHCENTRAL IDAHO

The homewater of giant steelhead

Northcentral Idaho's Clearwater River is at the top of the list of a growing host of fly fishers who pursue the sea-running rainbows. Fresh from the Pacific Ocean, they are the ultimate challenge for adventurous casters who tote tall, powerful rods to match the brawny strength of the tail-walking brutes.

Idaho's two steelhead runs split at Lewiston, a landlocked seaport on the Snake River. The larger B-run fish head up the Clearwater and their smaller A-run cousins head up the Snake and Salmon rivers. Steelheaders follow them from autumn to early spring, ascending the Snake and Salmon through the two deepest river gorges in North America.

The prime summer attraction of the region's piscatorial smorgasbord are its native westslope cutthroat trout. Thanks to special regulations to protect them these finned jewels are synonymous with the alpine beauty and backcountry wonders of the Lochsa, Selway and North Fork of the Clearwater Rivers, Kelly and Cayuse Creeks.

Flowing off the Bitterroot Mountains, the Lochsa is still as wild and free as when Lewis and Clark first saw it on their voyage of discovery. The Selway rampages through one of the most pristine wilderness areas in the Lower 48. Kelly Creek rises at the top of a broad expanse of roadless forest lands, its narrow canyon carved through the eons by cascading, clear waters.

The purity of these mountain streams holds a second surprise for newcomers. Beware, wading can be difficult in the deceptive depths of their riffles and pools. They are much deeper than they first appear because the crystal clarity of the water distorts depth perception. Watch your step or you may fill your hip waders—perhaps even your chest waders.

Spring and fall anglers also pursue smallmouth bass on the Clearwater, Snake, and Salmon, and a string of lowland lakes are popular sites for family outings throughout the year for rainbows and largemouth bass.

Most of the region's cities and towns are in the lowlands; its backcountry still unsettled. Anglers headed for remote mountain streams and alpine lakes are advised to stock up first at Lewiston, Orofino, Grangeville or Riggins. Those who enter the backcountry from the east can get supplies at Missoula, Hamilton, or Superior, Montana.

Outfitters and guides are based at the region's principal towns as well as in some of its more isolated environs.

Steelhead top the menu of the area's piscatorial smorgasbord, and the big fish are taken from September through April by drift fishing, trolling and fly fishing.

Dewey Haeder,
Lewiston Chamber of Commerce

Clearwater River and Lowland Lakes

Armadas of colossal steelhead return home from the sea

The spawn of its many celebrated tributaries is the historic bounty of the Clearwater River.

Historically, it was chinook salmon. Today, it is its fabled steelhead trout, the largest in Idaho and much of the Pacific Northwest. Some of the Clearwater's B-run steelhead that spend one to three years in the ocean grow to 40 inches in length and surpass 20 pounds. Many range from 12 to 16 pounds and the low end of the scale is a respectable eight pounds.

Waiting to greet the sea-running rainbows at the end of their 460-mile run up the Columbia and Snake rivers from the Pacific Ocean is an international legion of fly fishers. The clan begins to gather in August to test the river for early arrivals. Fishing improves in September and often peaks in October as the crescendo of the run passes over Lower Granite Dam, 30 miles below Lewiston on the Snake River.

Rainbow trout longer than 20 inches are considered steelhead and may be kept only during the open steelhead harvest season.

Early season action often includes A-run steelhead. Smaller in size than their B-run cousins, they average four to eight pounds and return earlier in the year for their longer migrations up the Snake and Salmon rivers. When Hell's Canyon flows are too warm, they will move up into the colder water of the lower Clearwater to wait out the thermal block on the Snake.

The official catch-and-release season, July 1 to Oct. 5, is the best time for fly fishing on the Clearwater. Through a gentlemen's agreement, officials maintain water flows out of Dworshak Dam on the North Fork of the Clearwater at a moderate 1,000 cubic feet per second or lower. The river at this level is comfortable wading in many places and a pleasant float for drift-boaters and canoers.

After Oct. 5, the catch-and-keep season opens, dam releases often increase and the river is invaded again by hordes of large jet boats. Local anglers refer to this period as the "aluminum hatch."

A hearty breed, many steelheaders continue to fish the river through winter, which can be relatively mild at these elevations. Others return in early spring, when water temperatures get above 40 degrees, and fish until the season closes.

Only hatchery-bred steelhead may be taken. They are marked by a missing adipose fin. A steelhead with an adipose fin is a wild fish and must be released.

The majority of the B-run steelhead are headed for the Dworshak Hatchery at Ahsaka, 40 miles above Lewiston and just below Orofino. An open season on steelhead continues upstream to Kooskia, where the Middle Fork and South Fork merge to form the main stem of the Clearwater. Steelhead continuing as much as 200 miles to upstream headwaters are considered wild fish and off-limits to anglers.

To tackle one of the Clearwater's brawling brutes, come prepared. A 9-foot rod rated for an 8- or 9-weight line and a reel that can handle 200 feet of backing are recommended. Weight-forward or shooting-head floating lines work in low waters. For deeper waters, attach a sinking tip.

Effective steelhead patterns

Traditional steelhead flies come in both wet and dry patterns, but there are no guarantees. Persistence is often the major component of the game.

Wet fly patterns tend to be dark and somber, sometimes with bright accents, or they are super bright with colors that rival the rainbow, although orange predominates. Favorite dark patterns are the Black Skunk, Green Butt Skunk and Purple Peril. Traditional bright patterns are the Thor, Skykomish Sunrise and Brad's Brat.

Fished deep at eye-level to the fish, the axiom is: "Dark day, dark fly. Bright day, bright fly." These are heavy patterns tied in No. 1/0 to No. 10 for fast to slow waters. Other options already in your vest pockets are stonefly nymphs, woolly buggers, and flashy streamers.

Sparsely tied streamer patterns that float just under the surface replicate the Spey flies perfected on Atlantic salmon waters. Most western versions—March Brown, Silver Doctor, Lady Caroline, Silver Blue—are tied with hair wings on shorter shanks in No. 1 to 12 Neutral patterns and bright or silver ones work best in low-water or bright conditions. Black or darker patterns are more visible on dark days or in faster waters.

Dry steelhead patterns, like the October Caddis, Waller Walker and Rusty Bomber, are designed to skate across the water on the downstream swing and make a commotion. They are big and buggy-looking with stiff wings or tails. Also try large dry flies you already have at hand like irresistibles, humpies, muddler minnows, grasshoppers, or royal Wulffs in No. 4 to 8. Wet flies tied with a riffle hitch can be skated across the surface, too.

Joe Norton of Twin Rivers Anglers in Lewiston recommends darker wet fly patterns, like the skunks and Purple Peril, while noting that skating fly patterns are also popular on the Clearwater.

Unlike rainbows, look for resting steelhead at the flowing lower end of a pool above a riffle or waterfall. They have come up through the same type of heavy water and prefer to rest in the tail outs and along the lower sides of pools before continuing upstream. When water temperatures are warm or a pool doesn't provide enough cover, you may find resting steelhead in upstream riffles.

One of the Clearwater's first holding pools is just upstream from Lewiston at the "Stink Hole" across from the Potlatch paper mill. It isn't a pretty place to fish, but an island and gravel bar permit easy wading. Further upstream, anglers often wade deep across broad flats to reach the fish.

Scout the river from U.S. Highway 12 or inquire locally to determine which holding areas are hot. The stretch just below the North Fork can be very crowded at times.

The third largest tributary of the Snake, the Clearwater joins it at Lewiston, where the Snake leaves the state at its lowest point, 725 feet. The slack water impoundment behind Lower Granite Dam extends up into both rivers and makes the city a landlocked sea port. Cargo ships and barges reach it through the locks on four Columbia River dams and four Snake River dams. Hydropower generators on each dam also have contributed to the decline of Idaho's anadromous fish runs.

While its mouth has been tamed, the Clearwater is still a big river with a mean annual discharge of 15,000 cubic feet per second. Spring runoff can exceed 30,000 cfs., falling below 7,000 cfs by summer and to 2,500 cfs or much less by autumn. Lower river flows fluctuate with releases from Dworshak Dam on the North Fork of the Clearwater.

The Clearwater's fabled steelhead, the largest in Idaho and much of the Pacific Northwest. Art Today photo.

The Clearwater runs 75 miles through a deep, semi-arid valley that becomes more desert-like along the 45 miles below Orofino. Despite today's towns and highways, the prevailing characteristics of the river are much the same as when the Lewis and Clark Expedition reached its mouth.

"...the water of the South Fork (Snake River) is greenish blue, the north (Clearwater) as clear as cristial...not one stick of timber on the river near the forks and but a few trees for a great distance up the river we decended...," Capt. William Clark recorded in his journal on Oct. 10, 1805.

The lower river is broad and flat, with occasional riffles and numerous deep pools. Above Orofino, its grade is slightly steeper and flows are rumpled and swirled by a rocky bottom and numerous boulders. Pools and other holding waters harbor both migrating steelhead and resident trout and smallmouth bass. By legal definition, a steelhead is any rainbow over 20 inches and may be kept only during an approved harvest season.

U.S. Highway 12 winds and twists with the river along its entire length. There are numerous pull-outs and public access is excellent.

All but the last 8 miles of the river runs through the Nez Perce Indian Reservation. In 1994, the tribe exercised its authority and established its own steelhead fishing season on the mainstem. Idaho Fish and Game agreed to honor the tribe's regulations. Anglers with either a state or tribal permit can fish for steelhead in the river.

During the spawning runs, an angler may tie into a rare chinook. Listed as an endangered species, all anadromous salmon must be released immediately. The tribe also marks the locations of salmon spawning redds with large, bright buoys. Anglers should avoid these waters.

"The lower Clearwater holds decent rainbows, if you know the time and places to look for them, but it is primarily a steelhead fishery. You can find a few cutthroat and steelhead smolts all season," says Tim Cochnauer, fisheries manager for Idaho Fish and Game's Clearwater Region. There is a 6-trout limit. Only trout with a clipped adipose fin may be kept.

The river also contains bull trout, a protected species, and some landlocked kokanee salmon, which are flushed through Dworshak Dam. Warmwater, summer fishing for smallmouth bass has become a popular attraction upstream from Orofino.

Check locally for the best times and places for summer fishing opportunities. Outfitters and guides specializing in steelhead fishing can be found at Lewiston and Orofino.

Both towns, as well as smaller ones along the river, have excellent accommodations, restaurants, and services. Private campgrounds and RV parks are located along the river.

A large public campground is available at Hell's Gate State Park, on the southwest edge of Lewiston on the Snake River. Dworshak State Park, northwest of Orofino, is located on the lower west bank of the reservoir.

National forest campgrounds along U.S. 12 are above Syringa on the Middle Fork and on the Lochsa River.

The region's mild winters and a four-month whitefish season also permit anglers to escape cabin fever blues.

Some of the region's best and most overlooked fishing can be had during the whitefish season, December 1 to March 31 on the Loshsa River below Wilderness Gateway, the Selway River below the Selway Falls cable car, and the North Fork Clearwater above Dworshak Reservoir.

These waters have excellent populations of whitefish up to 18 inches. Some granddaddy whitefish—up to 22 inches—can be found in the Clearwater River below Orofino.

Wet flies tipped with maggots are the most popular bait.

Two choices for steelhead permit

A license reciprocity agreement between Idaho Fish and Game and the Nez Perce Tribe allows steelhead anglers to buy a license and permit from either the Nez Perce Tribe or Idaho Fish and Game to fish for steelhead on the Clearwater River within the Nez Perce Indian Reservation boundary. The agreement does not extend to any other waters or species.

Steelhead anglers with a valid Nez Perce Tribal steelhead fishing license may fish the Clearwater River within the reservation, from its western boundary near the mouth of Hatwai Creek to the upstream boundary above Kooskia.

The Nez Perce Tribe began issuing fishing permits regulating steelhead fishing on the portion of the Clearwater River running through the reservation in 1994.

The Idaho Fish and Game Commission and the Nez Perce Tribe Executive Committee mutually establish the steelhead fishing season on the Clearwater River so that regulations are consistent.

For information on where to buy a license and steelhead permit to fish the Clearwater River, contact Idaho Fish and Game at 334-3717 or the Nez Perce Tribe at 843-2383.

If a salmon answers, hang up

When you're fishing for steelhead and a chinook salmon answers, hang up.

This advice comes not from your friendly telephone company but Idaho Fish and Game as a reminder to steelhead anglers that any fall-run chinook salmon they get on the end of the line must be released immediately.

A remnant run of the seagoing salmon returns to Idaho each year about the same time as steelhead. Similar in size and appearance, they differ sharply in legal status. Fall chinook are protected under the federal Endangered Species Act, while hatchery steelhead may be caught and kept during the steelhead season.

Fortunately, distinguishing a chinook from a steelhead is much easier than deciphering your phone bill. The easiest way to tell them apart is by checking the lower gum line.

If the lower gum is white or light colored, it's a steelhead. If the lower gum is black or dark-colored, it's a chinook. Using the gum line test, identification can be made quickly without taking the fish out of the water.

Another feature that helps differentiate chinook salmon from steelhead is the spotting on the back and tail.

The dark spots on the back of a chinook are blotchy and irregular in shape. On a steelhead, the spots are rounded and more uniform. The black spots on the upper part of the tail fin of a chinook are large in comparison to the spots on the tail of a steelhead.

By November, though, most fall chinook salmon are so dark in color the spots have become obscured. Fall chinook spawn in November in the lower mainstem Snake, Clearwater and Salmon rivers. Most have spawned and disappeared from the rivers by the end of the year.

In recent years, there have been limited mid-summer seasons for chinook. Watch for IDFG press releases on season options, or check with local fly shops and outfitters.

HELL'S GATE STATE PARK

Lewiston is often called Idaho's Banana Belt because of its low elevation and mild autumn and winter temperatures. Hell's Gate State Park, just south of Lewiston, includes 200 developed acres that border the Snake River.

There are 93 campsites within 100 yards of the Snake River that are open year-round. Power and water hookups are available at 64 sites. All sites include picnic tables and barbecue grills. There are modern restrooms with showers and a nearby dump station.

The Snake River is perfect for personal watercraft, jet boats, power boats and water skiing. Hell's Gate Marina has more than 100 slips available on a daily to yearly basis. There is also a public boat launch, store, restrooms and plenty of parking.

Outfitters offer jet boat trips into Hell's Canyon.

For more information, call the park office at 799-5015, or the marina at 799-5016.

Clearwater River

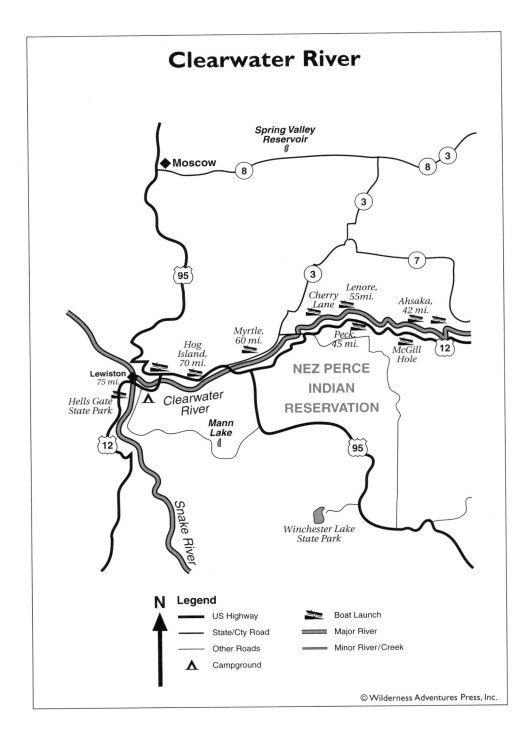

Spring Valley
Reservoir

◆ Moscow ⑧

⑧ ③

③

95

⑦

③

Cherry
Lane

Lenore,
55mi.

Ahsaka,
42 mi.

Myrtle,
60 mi.

Peck,
45 mi.

McGill
Hole

12

Hog
Island,
70 mi.

Lewiston
75 mi.

NEZ PERCE

Hells Gate
State Park

▲ Clearwater
River

INDIAN

RESERVATION

Mann
Lake

95

12

Snake River

Winchester Lake
State Park

N

Legend

—— US Highway

—— State/Cty Road

—— Other Roads

▲ Campground

Boat Launch

Major River

Minor River/Creek

© Wilderness Adventures Press, Inc.

Clearwater River (cont.)

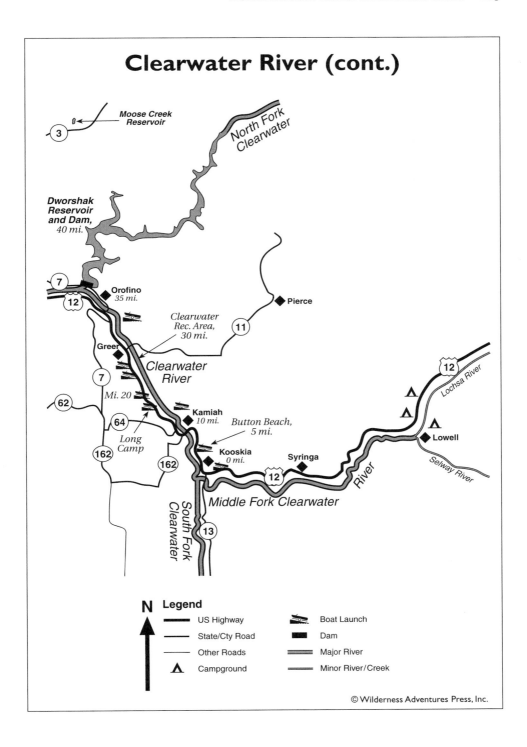

Moose Creek Reservoir

3

North Fork Clearwater

Dworshak Reservoir and Dam, 40 mi.

7

12

Orofino 35 mi.

Pierce

Clearwater Rec. Area, 30 mi.

11

Greer

Clearwater River

7

62

Mi. 20

64

162

Long Camp

Kamiah 10 mi.

Button Beach, 5 mi.

162

Kooskia 0 mi.

Syringa

12

12

Lochsa River

Lowell

Selway River

Middle Fork Clearwater

River

South Fork Clearwater

13

N

Legend

━━━	US Highway	🚤	Boat Launch
━━	State/Cty Road	▬	Dam
—	Other Roads	━━━	Major River
▲	Campground	═══	Minor River/Creek

© Wilderness Adventures Press, Inc.

Source of the Clearwater

The two other major streams in the western Clearwater Drainage are the Middle Fork and South Fork of the Clearwater. Lewiston also is the northern gateway to the Snake River flowing through Hell's Canyon.

MIDDLE FORK OF THE CLEARWATER

A Wild and Scenic river, the Middle Fork collects the flows of the Locsha and Selway. It runs 23 miles from Lowell to Kooskia to join the South Fork and form the main stem of the Clearwater. It is broad and flat, and spring runoff can exceed 30,000 cubic feet per second. By mid-summer, it is a very comfortable canoe float through Class II waters.

Fishing is best in spring and fall for resident cutthroat and rainbow. In fall or early spring, you may latch into a migrating steelhead but it must be released immediately.

U.S. 12 parallels the river, east of Orofino.

From December 1 through the Friday before Memorial Day weekend, the trout limit is 0, catch-and-release and from Saturday of Memorial Day weekend through Nov. 30, the trout limit is 2, none under 14 inches. No boat motors allowed from Sept. 1 through April 30.

SOUTH FORK OF THE CLEARWATER

This tributary of the Clearwater headwaters is in one of the most remote, picturesque regions of the state. Its gradient and characteristics mirror the wild and free flows of its famous sisters to the northeast, although the lower stretch runs mostly through private lands.

But the South Fork drainage has suffered much from gold dredging and placer mining and loss of riparian habitat from overgrazing by livestock. Its cutthroat is only a remnant population and mostly small in size. Fall and early-spring fishers may tie into a catch-and-release steelhead.

It is spectacular country and worth the drive to Elk City and Red River. At the end of the maintained roads is the Red River Wildlife Management Area, recently purchased, with the aid of wildlife conservation organizations like Trout Unlimited, from a local rancher. It is operated as an educational project for habitat restoration for anadromous fish and wildlife.

Elk City also is the western gateway to the Magruder Corridor, a primitive road that leads to the headwaters is of the Selway River and its fantastic cutthroat fishing. The road skirts the Selway-Bitterroot Wilderness and crosses the Continental Divide into Montana. Snow may block the road until the end of June.

To follow the South Fork, turn south off U.S. 12 at Kooskia onto State Highway 13 and turn east on State Highway 14, northeast of Grangeville, to reach Elk City and Red River.

The trout limit is 6, but only trout with a clipped adipose fin may be kept. Only single pointed barbless hooks are allowed while fishing for steelhead or salmon.

Clearwater Memories

A brief history of the rise and fall of its steelhead fishery

By Keith Stonebraker

Nobody knows when the first sportsman caught a steelhead on the Clearwater River. There was a little activity for anadromous fish—mostly summer chinook—in Idaho rivers prior to World War II. Most summer chinook angling was done in the South Fork of the Salmon River. In fact, during the 1950s, more Idaho anglers chased salmon than steelhead.

GIs returning from Europe in the 1940s brought back with them the spinning reel, revolutionizing steelhead fishing. It allowed shorebound anglers easy access to steelhead lairs in large rivers such as the Clearwater.

The first fly fisherman on the Clearwater that I recall was Eddie Ward, husband of actress Jane Wyatt of "Father Knows Best" fame. Eddie and his wife would fish for steelhead in the Lenore stretch as soon as the fish counts were over 300 per day over the old (now removed) Washington Water Power dam in Lewiston. Eddie would explain that he picked the Clearwater over more publicized rivers in Canada because the fish were just as large and ferocious as their Canadian counterparts. Eddie said the Clearwater steelies would take a fly even more aggressively than their northern cousins, and had the advantage of more even temperature weather conditions. So Eddie, along with a handful of Disney Studio fly fishers, was a regular on the Clearwater in the early days.

There were no hatchery clones in those days. All of the Clearwater steelhead were wild, averaging about fourteen pounds. Some would reach twenty pounds or more, laying to waste insufficient equipment.

Bill McAfee came along in those early days. In his Volkswagen bus with his yellow canoe attached to the roof, Bill managed to wander off in his rig to Argentina and Chile chasing sea-run browns and turn around to drive thousands of miles to fish for Atlantic salmon in Quebec or chase Pacific salmon in Alaska. That VW bus wore out three engines in its master's quest to find that perfect, secret spot to cast his sparse flies over the ultimate reel burning fish. He always ended up back on the banks of the Clearwater.

I asked Bill why he spent so much of his time on the Clearwater when he could be wading around in more exotic waters. He looked at me with his wry smiling eyes and rhetorically asked, "where in North America can you hook twenty-pound wild rainbow trout on a dry fly other than the Clearwater?"

He was right, of course. Here in my own backyard I had the best fishing in the hemisphere. What could possible go wrong?

Then Ice Harbour and Lower Monumental Dams on the Lower Snake River were built without much fanfare. The promoters of the Lower Snake Project—which eventually also included Lower Granite and Lower Goose Dams—gleefully told service clubs and Chambers of Commerce that they would boost local economies to a level that mortals could not fathom. The Lewiston Chamber of Commerce chortled that Lewiston would be a seaport city of over 125,000 happily employed residents. The Idaho Legislature was convinced that the Port of Lewiston would be "self-sufficient within a decade."

These promises, of course, never came true. But the worst lie that we were told was that these "run of the river dams" were not detrimental to the salmon or steelhead. In fact, we were told by the Corps of Engineers, the run of the river dams would make it easier for the fish to get to the sea and back. We accepted the fish gospel from the Corps as the truth. Fish hatcheries such as Dworshak were being built not only to mitigate but to enhance and increase the runs. I was told by a civilian engineer for the Corps of Engineers, Donald Baskin, that he loved building these dams because he could be "a part of helping to improve the fishing."

The public was giddy believing the Corps' story that we would have a thriving economy and a better than ever fishery. With claims like "the Dworshak fish hatchery is the most advanced in the world," the Corps successfully sold the community on the idea that a techno-fix would improve all the fish runs.

Only the Nez Perce Tribe remained skeptical of the promises that were being made. Is it any wonder why the Nez Perce and other tribes remain doubtful that current promises such as barging the fish to the ocean and other techno-fixes will restore the runs?

What history dictates to us, if we are to learn from it, is that we need a techno-unfix. Remove the four dams!

(Keith Stonebraker, a former commissioner on the Idaho Fish and Game Commission, is an Idaho Rivers United Board Member. He lives in Juliaetta, Idaho.)

Stream Facts: Clearwater River

SEASON
- Open year-round from mouth at Lewiston upstream to South Fork of Clearwater

SPECIAL REGULATIONS
- Rainbow over 20" considered steelhead
- Sept. 1 to Oct. 15, barbless hooks only
- Catch-and-release Sept. 1 to Oct. 15, most years, and hatchery steelhead open to harvest thereafter; check regulations for dates and restrictions
- Must have special steelhead permit from either Idaho Fish and Game or Nez Perce Indian Reservation
- No motors above Orofino Bridge, Jan. 1 to April 30 and Sept. 15 to Dec. 1
- In years of large return runs, special salmon seasons may be permitted
- Six-trout limit. Only trout with clipped adipose fin may be kept.

FISH
- B-run steelhead, range from 8 to 16 lbs, may exceed 20 lbs.
- A-run steelhead, 4 to 8 lbs.; generally near the mouth of the river
- Hatchery rainbows, steelhead smolts, a few cutthroat and bull trout
- Smallmouth bass present in lower river, more common above Orofino

RIVER MILES
- 75 miles from merger of South Fork and Middle Fork to mouth at Snake River
- Mile 0, Kooskia
- Mile 10, Kamiah
- Mile 30, Geer
- Mile 35, Orofino
- Mile 55, Lenore
- Mile 75, Lewiston

RIVER CHARACTERISTICS
- Upper river is low-gradient mountain stream, flowing through narrow wooded valley. Rocky channel is filled with numerous boulders. Enters broad semi-arid valley near Orofino, where river becomes wider and flatter with a few riffles and gravel bars, and many long, deep pools.

FLOWS
- Mean annual discharge of 15,000 cubic feet per second
- Spring runoff may exceed 30,000 cfs
- Summer flows average 7,000 cfs and drop to about 2,500 cfs by fall
- Autumn storms can bump up flows, occasionally cause flooding.

BOAT RAMPS

Above Orofino, ramps located at:
- Kooskia
- Button Beach
- Kamiah
- Long Camp
- Clearwater Recreation Area
- Orofino Bridge.

Downstream ramps at:
- Ahsaka
- McGill Hole
- Lenore
- Cherry Lane
- Myrtle Beach
- Hog Island
- Lewiston

Author Rocky Barker landing a nice rainbow.

LOWLAND LAKES AND RESERVOIRS

While the Clearwater Region's late summer fishing for cutthroat on its mountain streams and lakes attracts the most attention of out-of-staters, there are excellent opportunities in the lowland environs around Lewiston, says Tim Cochnauer, regional fisheries manager.

"Most of the really good fish are on the special regulations streams to protect westslope cutthroat, but most of the fishing load is on local reservoirs and ponds. These offer good family-oriented fishing, and they are also good float-tube lakes for fly fishers. We get a terrific return (to the creel) from catchable (hatchery) trout, and if they survive over the winter, they get to be good size."

Lowland lakes and reservoirs in the Lewiston area provide some of the most popular and heavily used fisheries in Idaho. These areas are generally found close to highways or major roads so they are easy to find, they are open year-round, provide easy access to water for both boaters and shore anglers, and have available good to excellent facilities for day use, or in some instances camping. All of this makes for great family fishing opportunities.

Though varieties of fish differ somewhat from area to area, the "bread and butter" fish is the rainbow trout. Where conditions permit, rainbow are stocked on a regular basis throughout the season.

Fishing for trout is best early in the season, April, May, June, slacking off with the hot July and August weather, and picking up again in September as the water begins to cool.

When fishing for warmwater fish such as bass and crappie, both wet and dry flies must be fished actively, casting and retrieving repeatedly. These fish will be found closer to shore near some type of cover such as rocks, plants, stumps or docks.

Fly fishing from a boat, canoe or float-tube can be exciting. Start the early season with nymph patterns and sinking lines, then moving toward more dry fly patterns and floating lines in the middle to later summer when the hatches come on. Specific flies will depend upon the conditions and time of year, and local retailers will be glad to help you choose what's hot.

Using Lewiston as a base, day trips and overnighters to consider include:

Winchester Lake

An 103-acre lake in Winchester State Park, it is best known for its early spring rainbow and late-summer largemouth bass fishing. Trout angler show up here as soon as the ice begins to break up and fish through June. After the summer doldrums, they return in September. Summer is the time for bass fishers, who have landed largemouth exceeding 6 pounds. Only electric motors are permitted on boats.

Nestled in the heavily forested foothills of Craig Mountain, the park is one of the prettiest in the state. It is about 50 miles southeast of Lewiston. Turn west off U.S. Highway 95 at the sign for the the town of Winchester.

Lowland Lakes and Reservoirs

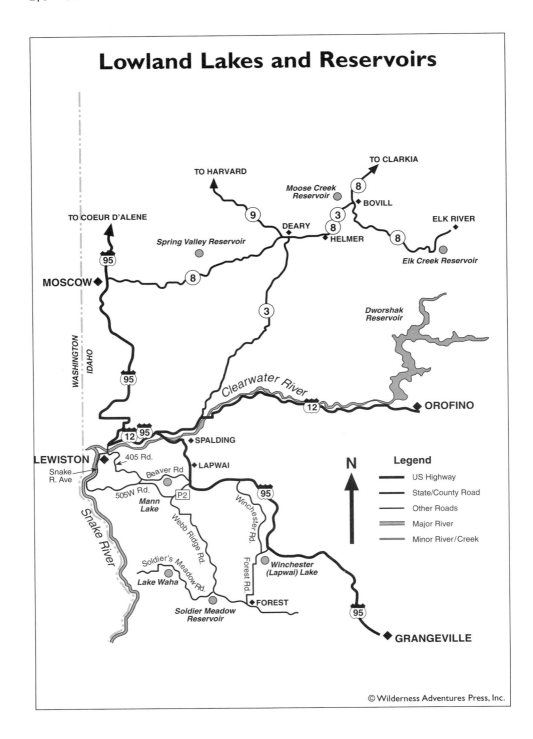

TO CLARKIA

TO HARVARD

Moose Creek
Reservoir

⑧

◆ BOVILL

TO COEUR D'ALENE

⑨

③

ELK RIVER
◆

DEARY

⑧

Spring Valley Reservoir

◆ HELMER

⑧

Elk Creek Reservoir

㉟ 95

MOSCOW ◆

⑧

Dworshak
Reservoir

③

WASHINGTON
IDAHO

95

Clearwater River

⑫

◆ OROFINO

⑫ 95

◆ SPALDING

LEWISTON ◆

405 Rd.

◆ LAPWAI

Snake
R. Ave

Beaver Rd

95

505W Rd.

P2

Mann
Lake

Webb Ridge Rd.

Winchester Rd.

N

Legend

US Highway

State/County Road

Other Roads

Major River

Minor River/Creek

Snake River

Soldier's Meadow Rd.

Forest Rd.

Winchester
(Lapwai) Lake

Lake Waha

◆ FOREST

Soldier Meadow
Reservoir

95

95

◆ GRANGEVILLE

© Wilderness Adventures Press, Inc.

Mann Lake

Just southeast of Lewiston, this 130-acre lake can offer fast action on rainbows and largemouth bass, as well as crappies and bluegills. Six-fish limit on bass, none under 12 inches.

Ask locally for directions to county road that connect with Powers Avenue in Lewiston.

Spring Valley Reservoir

Only 55 acres in size, its action on rainbow and largemouth bass can equal Winchester's, and follows about the same time table.

The picturesque lake is located in the rustic, low-elevation mountains northeast of the town of Troy, east of Moscow. Continue east past Troy on State Highway 8 and turn north at the sign for the lake.

Moose Creek Reservoir

Another mixed-species fishery, this 50-acre lake contains largemouth bass, rainbow, crappie and sun fish.

It is about 45 miles northeast of Lewiston and west of State Highway 3.

Dworshak Reservoir

A 50-mile impoundment on the North Fork of the Clearwater above Orofino, it is best known for its kokanee salmon fishery. It also contains cutthroat, bull trout, rainbow, smallmouth bass, and a few largemouth bass.

Due to its steep, rugged banks, it is fishable for the most part only from a boat or float-tube. Check locally for fly fishing options and times.

Lake levels have fluctuated radically in recent years because it has been drawn down to provide flushing waters for migrating anadromous salmon and steelhead.

The reservoir is 53 miles in length, has 16,000 surface acres, a maximum depth of 636 feet with 183 miles of shoreline.

Primitive campsites, accessible by boat only, are located in isolated coves along the shoreline. Additional camping and access information can be obtained through the Corps of Engineers visitor center located at the dam.

Kokanee salmon, introduced in 1972, is the most predominant species of angler interest. Dworshak kokanee have been noted for their good size. These open water fish are most effectively caught while trolling from a boat. Daily limit: 25.

Rainbow trout, stocked as fingerlings, grow rapidly and provide for a healthy winter fishery.

A good smallmouth bass population provides an exciting fishery for anglers who get out to the steep, rocky shoreline areas. The reservoir produced the Idaho State record smallmouth bass in 1995, weighing 8 pounds .5 ounce.

If fishing from a boat, cast into the rocky shore-line and retrieve in an irregular pattern.

Early season flyfishing for smallmouth, with nymphs and poppers, can add a thrill to your fishing experience.

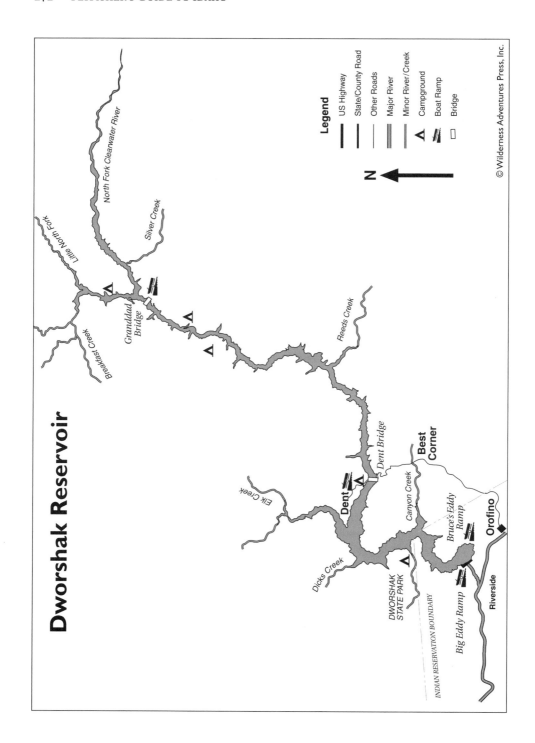

Dworshak Reservoir

North Fork Clearwater River

Little North Fork

Silver Creek

Breakfast Creek

Granddad Bridge

Reeds Creek

Elk Creek

Dent Bridge

Dent

Canyon Creek

Best Corner

Dicks Creek

DWORSHAK STATE PARK

Bruce's Eddy Ramp

Orofino

INDIAN RESERVAITON BOUNDARY

Big Eddy Ramp

Riverside

Legend

US Highway
State/County Road
Other Roads
Major River
Minor River/Creek
Campground
Boat Ramp
Bridge

N

© Wilderness Adventures Press, Inc.

The reservoir also has limited populations of largemouth bass, native cutthroat and crappie, which adds to the angler opportunity year-round. Bull trout are also present and anglers should note that there is a no harvest regulation on bull trout, and if caught must be released immediately.

Upstream of Grandad Bridge, trout limit is two, no cutthroat under 14 inches.

Dworshak State Park

Dworshak State Park is located among trees and open meadows on the western shore of Dworshak Reservoir. The area is known for its moderate summer nights and mild winter temperatures.

The park is about a one-hour drive from Lewiston or Moscow and 45 minutes from Orofino. The final two miles of road to the park entrance are a paved, twisting, narrow, 10-percent downgrade.

A boat ramp and handling dock provide easy launching most of the year. A fish-cleaning station is nearby, and parking and picnic facilities are available.

Their are 105 campsites at Freeman Creek Campground, 46 have water and electrical hookups. Twenty-five sites are provided at lakeside for tent camping. Sites are also available for use by the disabled.

There are three group-camping loops, designed to accommodate camping groups who desire a more private setting. These loops may be reserved by contacting the park office.

Three Meadows Group Camp, nestled in a lush forest, is perfect for organized retreats and other functions. It offers a spacious lodge with modern kitchen facilities and eight bunk-style group cabins. Reservations can be made through the park office.

The Dworshak National Fish Hatchery and the Idaho Department of Fish and Game's Clearwater Anadromous Hatchery are located one mile downstream of the dam. Both provide information and viewing opportunities to learn more about the native chinook salmon and steelhead trout of the Clearwater River.

For information, contact the park office at 476-5994; Fax: 208-476-7225; Email: DWO@idpr.state.id.us

The Lochsa River is one of northern Idaho's best westslope cutthroat fisheries.

Much of the year (the Lochsa) is either snowbound or raging with spring runoff. But from early summer to fall, devotees of the wild little westslope cutthroat, which rarely weighs more than a pound, come here to pay homage.

Bill Loftus,
Former outdoors editor, *Lewiston Morning-Tribune*

Wild and Scenic Gems

Lochsa and Selway rivers preserve treasures of the past

The rampaging beauty of the Lochsa River was first revealed to the outside world in journal entries by Capt. William Clark of the Lewis and Clark Expedition. Tired and frustrated from the Corps of Discovery's arduous trek over the crest of the Bitterroot Mountains, he still managed to capture in a few words its compelling nature: "... Encamped opposite a Small Island at the mouth of a branch on the right side of the river which at this place 80 yards wide, Swift and Stoney..."

Clark penned his notation on Sept. 13, 1805, at the site of the present-day Powell Ranger Station on U.S. Highway 12. The island is still there; the side stream is not.

The next day the explorers "...proceeded on down the right Side of the River over Steep points rockey and buschey as usual for four miles to an old Indian fishing place..."

The Lochsa's wildness endures almost two centuries later. Chinook salmon and steelhead runs have not fared as well, but fat, sassy westslope cutthroat abound in today's fishing places.

Its snow-fed waters plunge 65 miles down a rugged mountain canyon and narrow glaciated valley to join the Selway River and form the Middle Fork of the Clearwater, 70 miles east of Lewiston. The headwaters of the Lochsa rise at 6,000 feet on the western slopes of the Bitterroot Mountains. The elevation at its mouth is 1,250 feet.

A rich variety of wildlife still reside in the dense thickets of pine, fir, and cedar of the temperate rain forest flanking the river. Its upper 30 miles are federally protected as Wild and Scenic. Towering, weather-grayed snags stand as mute reminders of the Great Fire of 1910.

Until U.S. 12 was punched over Lolo Pass, old-timers say a fishing trip to the upper reaches of the Lochsa was almost as strenuous as it was for Chief Joseph's Nez Perce on their ill-fated flight for freedom to Montana. Today, fly fishers have virtually unlimited public access along 60 miles of the river skirted by the highway.

Cutthroat above the Wilderness Gateway Campground just upstream from Fish Creek have made a remarkable recovery since catch-and-release regulations were imposed in 1988. The potential for continued improvement on the river's lower 30 miles will depend more on nature than people. It was placed under wild trout management in 1992—two-trout limit, none under 14 inches.

"Weather and drought are a bigger factor than angling pressure," says Tim Cochnauer, fisheries manager for Idaho Fish and Game's Clearwater Region. "We're seeing cutthroat over 14 inches with three good-water years.

"Kelly Creek, the Selway, and Lochsa all have responded very well to special regulations. But it was the cutthroat in the tributaries that brought the Lochsa back once special regulations were imposed."

All tributaries of the Lochsa are under wild trout management. On Crooked Creek, from its mouth to Brushy Fork Creek, cutthroat are catch and release. Upstream from Brushy Fork Creek, and including it and all other tributaries, there is a two-trout limit. All other tributaries of the Lochsa have a two-trout limit.

Most of the cutthroat netted in upper Lochsa are in the 10- to 14-inch range. Fish 16 to 18 inches provide occasional tussles, along with a rare few over 20 inches. Rainbow catches average 10 to 14 inches, and may include steelhead smolts. A good population of bull trout also is present.

Some anglers rate the Lochsa more by the number of cutthroat caught than by the size of individual fish netted. Reports of 30-fish days are not uncommon; a favored few push the envelope past 50 fish. These are mostly in the 10- to 12-inch class. Big fish here, as elsewhere, take more effort and know-how—and patience.

The westslope cutthroat is one of the most combative of the so-called docile species.

Lochsa River

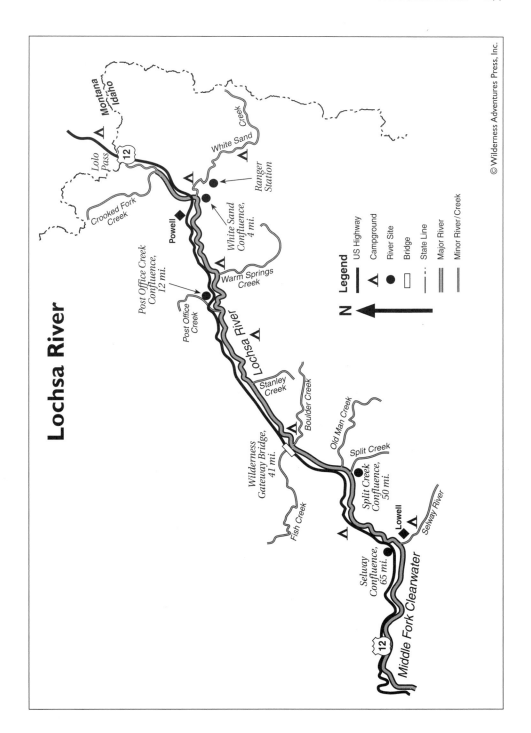

© Wilderness Adventures Press, Inc.

Montana
Idaho

Lolo Pass

Crooked Fork Creek

White Sand Creek

White Sand Confluence, 4 mi.

Ranger Station

Powell

Post Office Creek Confluence, 12 mi.

Warm Springs Creek

Post Office Creek

Lochsa River

Stanley Creek

Boulder Creek

Old Man Creek

Wilderness Gateway Bridge, 41 mi.

Split Creek

Split Creek Confluence, 50 mi.

Lowell

Selway River

Fish Creek

Selway Confluence, 65 mi.

Middle Fork Clearwater

Legend

N

- US Highway
- ▲ Campground
- ● River Site
- ▢ Bridge
- State Line
- Major River
- Minor River/Creek

Fantastic fishing can occur just before spring runoff peaks, if it doesn't happen before the general season opener. Most anglers fish the river after flows subside in late June or early July and on into fall. In low-water years, the trout bail out of the lower river for its tributaries in mid-summer and return with the cooler temperatures of autumn.

Flows can peak at 10,000 cubic feet per second in June, but usually fall to 2,200 cfs by July and to 800 cfs by August. Heavy summer rains also can raise the river dramatically and turn it off-color.

A whitewater rafters dream, the Lochsa has plenty of holding waters for its native trout. Look for them around the breakwaters and eddies of its many boulders, in deep pools, and the rock gardens of its long riffles and slick-water runs. Watch your step—wading is difficult in some places. The pools are much deeper than they look because of the clarity of the water.

Effective patterns for the Lochsa River

Like its sister westslope streams, matching the hatch is not a major fishing strategy for the Lochsa. Early fishers may score on a sporadic golden stonefly hatch, although nymph patterns generally produce better than dry flies. The standard bearers are elk hair caddis, humpies, and stimulators. Pack along a few grasshopper patterns and a basic assortment of generic mayflies like Adams and Cahills and attractor patterns, including renegades, western Coachman, Wulffs, and Trudes. Size selection generally ranges from 12-16, but a larger caddis pattern, 10-8, can be effective. Generic nymphs can include hare's ear, prince, woolly bugger, and golden stoneflies.

Excellent National Forest campgrounds are spaced out the entire length of the river. Lodging and services are available at Lowell and Powell on U.S. 12 The nearest towns to the west are Kooskia, Orofino and Lewiston. Lolo, Hamilton, and Missoula, MT are east of Lolo Pass on U.S. 93.

Stream Facts: Lochsa River

SEASON
- From mouth to Wilderness Gateway Bridge, Saturday of Memorial Day weekend through Nov. 30; catch-and-release winter season, Dec. 1 to March 31
- Upstream from Wilderness Gateway Bridge, Saturday of Memorial Day weekend through Nov. 30; no winter season

SPECIAL REGULATIONS
- From mouth to Wilderness Gateway Campground Bridge, two-trout limit, none under 14"
- Artificial flies and lure with only one barbless hook
- Above Wilderness Gateway and including lower Crooked Creek, catch-and-release all trout
- All tributaries, two-trout limit
- Posted area at hatchery fish weir near Powell closed to fishing

FISH
- Westslope cutthroat in 10" to 14" class, a few 16" to 20"
- Rainbows average 10" to 14"
- Also steelhead smolts and bull trout

RIVER MILES
- 65 miles from headwaters to confluence with Selway to form Middle Fork of Clearwater
- Mile 4, Powell
- Mile 12, Post Office Creek
- Mile 41, Wilderness Gateway
- Mile 50, Split Creek
- Mile 65, Lowell

RIVER CHARACTERISTICS
- The Lochsa is protected as a Recreation River under the Wild and Scenic Rivers Act and is very popular with rafters and kayakers who run its Class III and IV rapids. It plunges through narrow canyon from elevation of more than 6,000 feet in Bitterroot Mountains to 1,205 at mouth. Upper river swift and rocky with numerous fast runs and pocket waters between boulder-choked rapids. Lower river also filled with large rapids but holds more pools, rock-garden glides, and a few gravel bars.

FLOWS
- Spring runoff peaks around 10,000 cubic feet per second in June, falls to about 2,200 cfs in July and to 800 cfs by August
- Summer storms can turn water off-color; occasional autumn storms may cause flooding

BOAT RAMPS
- Indian Grave Creek
- Wilderness Gateway
- Split Creek
- Major Fenn Recreation Area
- Lowell

The Selway River in the Selway-Bitterroot Wilderness is a backcountry fishing paradise.

Selway River

One of the most protected rivers in Idaho, the Selway is a wilderness experience unmatched in the state or elsewhere in the Lower 48.

A Wild and Scenic river, its tumbling rapids hurl through a boulder-choked canyon in the Selway-Bitterroot Wilderness to join the Lochsa 75 miles downstream at Lowell. Its descent plunges from 6,000 feet in the Bitterroot Mountains to 1,250 feet at the mouth.

The 18 miles of river below Selway Falls are outside the wilderness and accessible by road from Lowell.

A journey into the wilderness headwaters requires advance planning. The isolated launch site at the Paradise Guard Station is at the end of a rugged mountain road, 55 miles from civilization.

For floaters, gaining a permit is like winning the lottery. Only 78 permits a year are issued; 16 for commercial outfitters and 62 for private floating parties. Launches are restricted to one a day to preserve the wilderness experience.

Permits are issued by the Bitterroot National Forest's West Fork Ranger District at Darby, MT, 406-821-3269. They also have information on shuttle services and commercial flights into the wilderness.

To reach the Selway from Montana, take Forest Road 473 west from Conner, just south of Darby on U.S. Highway 93. High-clearance vehicles are required for this primitive forest road, known as the Magruder Corridor. It follows the southern boundary of the wilderness and continues west to Elk City on the South Fork of the Clearwater.

The permit season runs from May 15 to August 1, but early-season permit holders may find Nez Perce Pass blocked by snow. The road east out of Elk City can be blocked by snow through June.

Flows peak around 14,000 cubic feet per second in May or June and fall rapidly to about 4,000 cfs by July and below 1,000 cfs in August.

Floaters can cast to trout when running the river, but it is a challenging prospect during high flows. After rafters and kayakers can no longer play in its Class III and IV rapids, the Selway becomes a backcountry fishing paradise. A late-summer trip into the wilderness is a popular excursion among Clearwater Basin fly fishers, but watch out for rattlesnakes. Most years, a stunning population of cutthroat holds in the upper river through August before beginning its annual migration to downstream wintering waters.

Thirty-fish days are routine, mostly on 10- to 13-inch cutthroat, although 18-inchers are not uncommon. Rainbows and steelhead smolts also may pepper your dry flies, and the Selway has one of the strongest populations of bull trout in the state.

This is not rocket-scientist fishing. "Way up in these three rivers (the Selway, Lochsa, North Fork), all are about the same for patterns," says Joe Norton of Twin River Anglers in Lewiston.

Fish the big holes below the rapids and the edges of the boulder-strewn rapids with parachute Adams, stimulators, elk hair caddis, or hoppers. The river also holds golden stoneflies; look for these earlier in the season.

Hit it right and you can hook a small fish on virtually every cast. The upper river's larger denizens require a bit more finesse in fly selection and presentation, but not as much as the ones downstream.

Catch-and-release regulations on the wilderness stretch have made a remarkable difference. Below Selway Falls, the river is now under wild trout management—two-fish limit, none under 14 inches—but fishing pressure is still intense and the big trout are more wary.

The lower river is flatter, wider, and more accommodating to boaters and waders. It contains a few Class II rapids in the first 10 miles below the falls, but in late-summer it is a beautiful canoe run. Its best seasons are in spring and fall. In low-water years, summer temperatures can become almost lethal and the trout run up into its tributaries.

Selway tributaries, regulated under wild trout management, have a two-trout limit.

There is a stonefly hatch in late May and June and sporadic mayfly hatches later in the season. Caddisfly hatches predominate.

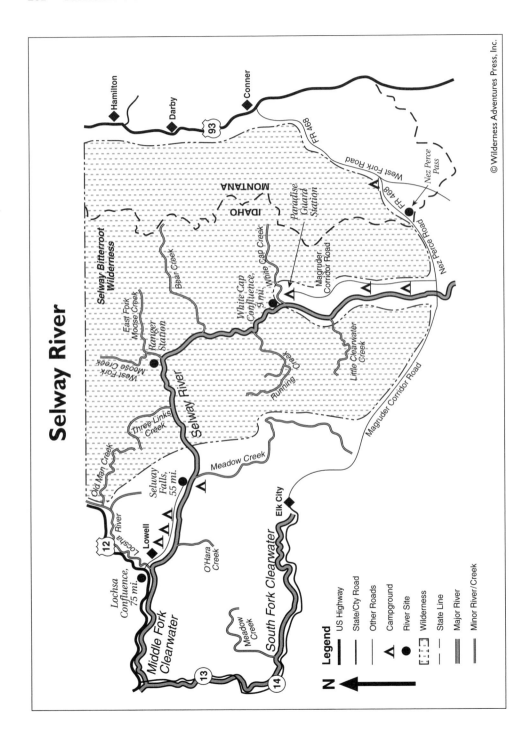

Selway River

Hamilton

Darby

Conner

93

FR 468

West Fork Road

Nez Perce Pass

Selway Bitterroot Wilderness

MONTANA

IDAHO

Paradise Guard Station

Bear Creek

White Cap Creek

White Cap Confluence, 9 mi.

Magruder Corridor Road

Nez Perce Road

FR 468

East Fork Moose Creek

Ranger Station

West Fork Moose Creek

Little Clearwater Creek

Running Creek

Selway River

Three Links Creek

Magruder Corridor Road

Old Man Creek

Meadow Creek

Selway Falls, 55 mi.

Lowell

Lochsa River

12

O'Hara Creek

Elk City

South Fork Clearwater

Meadow Creek

Lochsa Confluence, 75 mi.

Middle Fork Clearwater

13

14

© Wilderness Adventures Press, Inc.

Legend

US Highway

State/Cty Road

Other Roads

Campground

River Site

Wilderness

State Line

Major River

Minor River/Creek

N

Effective patterns for the Selway River

Parachute Adams, stimulators, elk hair caddis, hoppers; early in the season look for golden stoneflies.

The lower wilderness section of the river can be reached on foot. An easy, well-maintained trail follows the north bank above the falls and gains little elevation in the first six miles. Designated campsites are located along the trail.

A number of National Forest campgrounds are located at both ends of the Selway. Lodging and services are available at Lowell.

Idaho Cutthroat Numbers are Healthy

Every one of Idaho's native trout species is currently either listed under the federal Endangered Species Act or proposed for listing, including the westslope cutthroat, but Fish and Game biologists do not think westslope cutthroat are in trouble in Idaho.

Years of data show healthy populations of westslope cutthroats on the Selway, the Lochsa, the St. Joe, Kelly Creek and the Middle Fork of the Salmon. This documentation was included in Fish and Game's official comments to the U.S. Fish and Wildlife Service as the federal wildlife agency considered the possibility of listing this trout under the Endangered Species Act.

Bill Hutchinson, manager of Idaho's resident fish, said, "We feel from our standpoint, from all the data we've seen so far, that Idaho should be excluded from the listing. The other states will have to look at their own populations, but we in Idaho feel very strongly that the species as a whole is not in any danger of extinction. It should not even be listed as a threatened species."

Since the 1970s, catch-and-release has been the regulation on rivers like the Selway and Middle Fork of the Salmon.

Commenting on the Selway Hutchinson said, "...the water's clean, clear, cold. It doesn't take a rocket scientist to figure out that if we maintain this kind of habitat for these fish, they'll do what Mother Nature's been letting them do for thousands and thousands of years. And it's our job to protect them and to give them that type of environment so they can prosper."

Stream Facts: Selway River

SEASON
- Saturday of Memorial Day weekend through Nov. 30; no winter season

SPECIAL REGULATIONS
- From mouth to Selway Falls, two-trout limit, none under 14"; artificial flies and lures with only one barbless hook
- Above falls in wilderness, catch-and-release all trout
- All tributaries, two-trout limit
- Posted area at falls closed to fishing

FISH
- Westslope cutthroat in 10" to 13" range, growing number in 16" to 18" class.
- Steelhead smolts common and a few rainbow
- Strong population of bull trout

RIVER MILES
- 75 miles from headwaters to confluence with Lochsa to form Middle Fork of Clearwater
- Mile 9, Paradise Guard Station
- Mile 55, Selway Falls
- Mile 75, Lowell

RIVER CHARACTERISTICS
- Top 55 miles protected as a Wild and Scenic River. Falls from more than 6,000 feet in headwaters to 1,250 feet at mouth. In wilderness stretch, river plunges through narrow, boulder-choked canyon filled with Class III and IV rapids, deep pools, long swift runs, and pocket waters. Below Selway Falls, the river is wider, flatter with only a few Class II rapids.

FLOWS
- Spring runoff peaks around 14,000 cfs in May or June; falls to about 4,000 cfs by July and below 1,000 cfs in August
- Summer and autumn storms may turn water off-color

BOAT RAMPS
- Paradise Guard Station, with pull-out above falls
- Below Selway Falls Cable Car
- Lowell

Floater Guide Selway River

All reservations and fee payments to float the Wild and Scenic Selway River must be made online. Make all pre-, post-, and controlled season arrangements with http://www.recreation.gov or call 877-550-6777.

Lottery applications will be accepted only online, beginning December 1 and ending January 31.

Permits

Permits are not required outside of control season, but if on the river during pre-season, you may not be on the river May 15.

Control season May 15 through July 31: no more than 1 party is allowed to launch each day.

Outside of control season August 1 to May 14: unlimited number of launches per day. You must take off the river on May 14.

Recreation Fees

A $6 non-refundable Lottery Application fee is required for each lottery application submis-sion. If a permit is purchased outside of the lottery a $6 non-refundable reservation fee is required for each reserved permit. There are no other recreation fees for the Selway River.

Invasive Species Boat Sticker

Idaho State Boating Law requires that all vessels (motorized and non-motor-ized) display the Idaho Invasive Species Fund sticker to legally launch and operate on Idaho waters. Inflatable, non-motorized vessels less than 10 feet long are exempt. Go to http://parksandrecreation.idaho.gov or call 800-247-6332 for more informa-tion and purchase options.

Group Size

Maximum party size is 16, but maximum trip duration can vary.

Recommended Equipment

Porta-potty (preferably washable) toilet with appropriate capacity
Fire pan (3-inch sides); ash container (preferably metal); strainer; shovel; bucket

Camp Sanitation

All dish/waste water must be strained and broadcast above high water mark
All human and pet feces should be packed out in porta-potty
Absolutely nothing but human/pet waste in porta-potty, no sanitary wipes, tam-pons, sticks etc. Foreign objects aren't compatible with RV dump stations
All fire ash should be packed out in ash container

All urination can be above the high water mark

No soaps, even biodegradable, in any streams, river or water source

Camp on already hardened sites, avoid packing vegetation down

All litter, food particles, including micro-trash must be packed out

Camp Etiquette

Use only dead and downed wood or charcoal for fire

Return any rocks to where found if used for tent, tarp, or boat anchors

Leave beaches unmarked, smooth disturbed surfaces

Do not disturb or harass wildlife

Leave camp in pristine state

Heritage Resources

Do not touch, remove or damage any heritage resources (e.g. historic cabins, pictographs, artifacts, etc.) Oils from fingers can contribute to deterioration of pictographs.

Campsites

All members of group must camp together

Please plan lay-over days in less used sites

Camps at Moose Creek may need to be shared with other groups

Tid-Bits

Permit holder signs the permit and becomes responsible for the entire group and must be present and ac-company group at all times while on the river

Observe all local, State and Federal laws and regulations

Carry and display permit upon request of any Forest Officer

Public nudity is discouraged

Respect private property, do not enter unless acknowledged or invited, contain dogs at boat or on leash.

Be courteous and efficient at put-in/take-out sites, no camping at boat ramp.

Call ahead on road conditions and campfire restrictions

Contact Information

West Fork Ranger District, Bitterroot National Forest, 6735 West Fork Road, Darby, MT 59829; Phone: 406-821-3269

"Kelly has everything I look for in an ideal trout stream—solitude, wild beauty, sparkling clear water, and plenty of fish!"

Dave Engerbretson,
Idaho's Top 30 Fishing Waters

Kelly Creek

International Mecca for wild westslope cutthroat trout

The allure of Kelly Creek's cutthroat is irresistible to fly fishers dedicated to wild trout in wild country. A 23-mile tributary of the North Fork of the Clearwater River, its crystal clear waters harbor the most famous population of westslope cutthroat in the West. Their comeback from the ravishes of overharvesting is a renowned accolade to catch-and-release management.

Almost as pure as rainwater, Kelly Creek flows like liquid glass on its serpentine westerly course through the Bitterroot Mountains. The steep, rugged "V" of its canyon is carpeted by pine, fir, and cedar. Its rocky banks are flanked by lush ranks of ferns, wildflowers, and deciduous shrubs.

Looking into one of its deep pools below a galloping rapids is like gazing into an emerald aquarium. The water is so translucent that trout lazily finning in the subtle current appear to be suspended in mid-air. If you are lucky, you will watch with suspended breath as a "tanker" rises to your fly.

"The big cutthroat like to cruise long, deep pools with large rocks," says Tim Cochnauer, fisheries manager for Idaho Fish and Game's Clearwater Region. "When we see them, we say the tankers are cruising. There are no cutthroat in the pocket waters. You'll find rainbows there."

While Kelly's cutthroat prefer its deep pools and long, flat runs strewn with boulders and broken cobble floor, they are not bashful. These feisty native trout of northcentral Idaho pepper dry flies with the savagery of a rainbow. Their determined first runs are equally reminiscent of their red-banded cousins. The comparison ends there. The fight of most westslopes quickly fizzles.

When the fishing is hot, they rise with abandon to a basic selection of dry flies and attractor patterns. Joe Norton of Twin River Anglers in Lewiston recommends elk hair caddis, humpies, parachute Adams, and royal Wulffs in No. 10 to 16.

A selection of grasshopper patterns and back-up dry flies like stimulators, renegades, or royal Trudes are good to have along, too. Beadhead hare's ear or prince nymphs and small marabou streamers or woolly buggers are worth trying when dry fly action tapers off.

Don't be leader-shy, especially if you want to bring a trout to hand quickly so that you can release it and catch another. Under most conditions, you can get by with a three- or four-pound tippet.

The aggressive feeding nature of westslope cutthroat was almost their downfall in Kelly Creek. They were on the brink of disappearing in the late 1960s before Kelly was declared Idaho's second catch-and-release stream in 1970. The Middle Fork of the Salmon River was the first.

Other westslope streams like stretches of the St. Joe, Lochsa, and Selway have joined its ranks, but Kelly's success story captures the attention of anglers everywhere. A University of Idaho graduate student conducting a 1995 census for Fish and Game was surprised at the number of out-of-state anglers he checked. He was more amazed when fly fishers from Canada and Europe told him they had read about the creek and came to test it. They weren't disappointed—although the stream's popularity has increased pressure and made the trout more challenging to catch since its peak years in the 1980s.

Recent studies indicate the westslope species is vulnerable only up to a point. It is much less gullible than Yellowstone cutthroat. Once bitten by a hook, westslope cutthroat are prone to depart that area for safer waters. Also, as the season progresses, they become conditioned to the pressure and fewer fish can be enticed into taking a fly. Yellowstone cutthroat studies show they come to the net an average of nine times in a season—although intense pressure may be changing that scenario, too.

Most of the action in Kelly Creek is on 10- to 14-inch cutthroat; 16-inchers are not uncommon and an occasional 20-inch beauty is netted. Its smaller population of rainbows run mostly in the 10- to 14-inch range. A rare bull trout may add to the day's tally.

But ghost fish haunt these hallowed waters. The last steelhead and chinook salmon smolts went to sea from Kelly Creek and the North Fork in 1970. When the 717-foot Dworshak Dam blocked the North Fork in 1967, it cut off one of the most productive salmon and steelhead spawning and rearing streams in Idaho. The backwaters of the reservoir extend 50 miles upstream. Returning runs of North Fork anadromous fish now only make it as far as the Dworshak Hatchery.

Pause to reflect whenever a large cutthroat is netted in this drainage. Lack of competition from the spawn of their sea-running brethren has contributed much to the growth potential of trout reared by the North Fork, Kelly Creek, and other tributaries.

Either way, life as a westslope cutthroat is a tough job. They have evolved to take advantage of a coldwater environment low in nutrients and productivity. Food sources are limited, the growing season is short. They eat whatever they can get, but their preference is definitely floating insects.

Kelly Creek cutthroat are typical of the westslope species in taking advantage of an entire drainage. The annual cycle begins with the upstream run on the spring flood to spawn in the headwaters. Fly fishers have to bide their time at this point. The water is too high most years for good fishing and roads into this remote area may be blocked by snow into June. Kelly's flows peak around 1,000 cubic feet per second in May and stabilize by July. The trout linger through the summer, and the best fishing usually occurs from early-July through August. In high-water years, delightful fly casting may continue into September as the cutthroat drop downstream in stages to the North Fork. In low-water years, they may bail out of Kelly Creek sooner. Their goal is their wintering waters in the big pools above the Dworshak Reservoir, 50 miles downstream on the North Fork.

The hike into the upper Kelly Creek Canyon is a true wilderness experience.

The clear water pools of Kelly Creek harbor some of its largest cutthroat.
Michelle Retallic photo.

In 1994, a regulations change ended a late fall requirement for catch-and-release on the North Fork. The remoteness of the fishery remains as one safeguard. Distractions like the elk hunting season is another.

Rule number one when heading for Kelly Creek is to stock up on provisions and have a full tank of gas. It is about 60 miles on gravel roads from the nearest towns at either end of the route into the Clearwater National Forest.

To reach the stream from the west, turn north off U.S. 12 onto State Highway 11, about eight miles east of Orofino, and drive 20 miles to Pierce. From Pierce take Forest Road 250 to the North Fork of the Clearwater and then upstream to Kelly Creek. Just upstream from the North Fork Bridge you will pass the mouth of Weitas Creek, a major tributary that attracts a lot of angler attention.

To reach the headwaters of the North Fork and upper Kelly Creek from the east, cross over Hoodoo Pass south of Superior, MT, about 70 miles northwest of Missoula on Interstate 90. At Superior, take the Trout Creek road over the pass to Forest Road 250. At the intersection with Forest Road 255 at Cedars Campground you can turn south to Kelly Creek or continue on 250 down the North Fork to the Kellys Fork Campground.

Pick up an Idaho fishing license at Superior or Missoula, Montana, before heading over Hoodoo Pass.

If you are into real rocky road trekking, you can reach Kelly Creek on a series of primitive forest roads that run northwest from the Powell Ranger Station on U.S. 12. Be sure to take a good map if you choose this route. Forest Road 581 crosses Cayuse Creek, a backcountry tributary much favored by fly fishers, and intersects with the Kelly Creek Road at Ruby Creek.

Camping is permitted at the Ruby Creek parking lot, but there are no tables and only a single outhouse. Good Forest Service campgrounds are just upstream on Ruby Creek and 10 miles downstream at the mouth of Kelly Creek. There are four large campgrounds on the North Fork, or you can pull over and pitch a tent where it strikes your fancy.

The 10-mile Kelly Creek Road parallels premiere trout waters and the fish drop down through the system throughout the season.

Those interested in Kelly's more remote fishing waters hike upstream from Ruby Creek on a narrow rocky trail that dips and climbs along the north side of the stream. About five miles upstream is the mouth of Cayuse Creek, where Kelly narrows and the trail continues along its winding course to Hanson Meadows. Three forks branch like tendrils on a vine and flow down from the crest of the Bitterroots to join at the meadow and form the main stem of the creek.

The general consensus is that Kelly just keeps getting better as you progress upstream. Depending on your stamina, upstream jaunts can be done as long day-hikes. The more productive option is to hike in and camp. Wildlife viewing opportunities also improve as you continue into the backcountry.

Cayuse Creek is a blue-ribbon fishery that is catch-and-release, too. "Hiking down the (Cayuse Creek) canyon to Kelly Creek while fishing for westslope cutthroat trout is an experience in primitive Idaho that no one can forget," says Richard Moran, a Boise fly fisher and member of Idaho Rivers United.

The U.S. Forest Service in 1995 made a preliminary recommendation for protection of Kelly Creek as a wild river under the Wild and Scenic Rivers Act. It recommended scenic status for Cayuse Creek and the North Fork of the Clearwater. Idaho Rivers United considers the North Fork of the Clearwater Basin a national treasure and endorses the recommendation for Wild and Scenic protection.

Stream Facts: Kelly Creek

SEASON
- Saturday of Memorial Day weekend through Nov. 30; no winter season

SPECIAL REGULATIONS
- All trout, catch-and-release
- Artificial lures and flies, single barbless hook; no bait

FISH
- Westslope cutthroat in 10" to 14" class, a number in 16" range and a few to 20"
- Rainbow 10" to 14" and a few bull trout

RIVER MILES
- 23 miles from headwaters to merger with North Fork of Clearwater
- Mile 0, Hansen Meadows
- Mile 7, Cayuse Creek
- Mile 12, Ruby Creek
- Mile 23, Kelly Forks

RIVER CHARACTERISTICS
- Narrow, churning mountain stream below Hansen Meadows that tumbles through boulder-filled pocket waters, a few fast glides, and shallow riffles. Canyon widens at Cayuse Creek and Kelly flows in long, sweep-ing curves to Ruby Creek, where canyon narrows again as it plunges through cascading rapids, long, deep pools, and swift, rock-garden glides.

FLOWS
- Spring runoff peaks around 1,000 cfs in May or June, falls to about 200 cfs or less by fall.

BOAT RAMPS: N/A

The mouth of Cayuse Creek, flowing into Kelly Creek, is an easy day hike adventure.

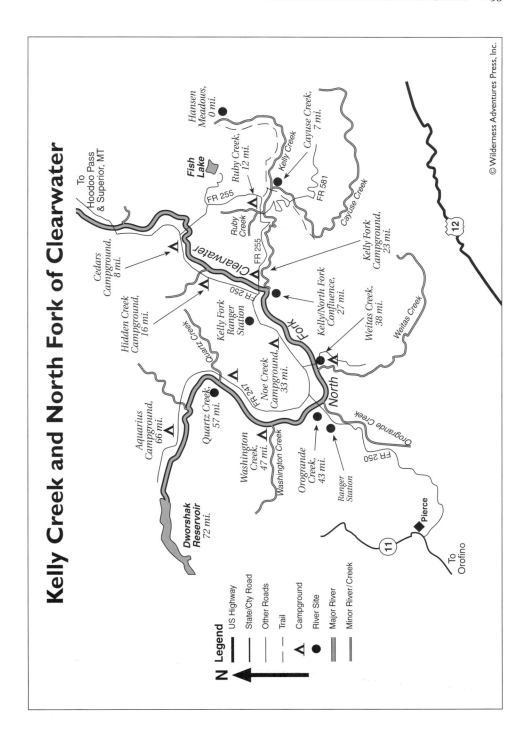

Kelly Creek and North Fork of Clearwater

North Fork of the Clearwater

The North Fork should not be overlooked in the rush to get to Kelly Creek. Plan a trip that allows enough time to fish it while you are in the drainage.

Fat, healthy cutthroat and rainbow reside in the river, and most fly fishers will tell you they are more accommodating than the residents of its famous tributary. Look for lots of action on fish averaging 10 to 14 inches. Anticipate surprises.

"There are bigger fish in the North Fork," says Joe Norton of Twin River Anglers in Lewiston. "Some are over 20 inches, and there are some big bull trout."

The North Fork's long, deep pools are where to hunt for its bigger fish. "They really like grasshoppers, muddlers, and sculpin streamers," Norton adds.

A protected fish, all bull trout must be released immediately. North Fork wild trout regulations permit a two-fish limit, none under 14 inches, on cutthroat and rainbow. Single barbless hooks are required on all flies and lures; no bait

Caddis flies are the predominant dry fly hatch on the river and throughout the central mountains. Elk hair caddis, stimulators, and humpies in No. 10 to 16 are the standard searching patterns in summer. The fall caddis, with its bright orange body, is an autumn favorite. Parachute Adams and attractor patterns like renegade, royal Wulff, and royal Trude also are standard fare. Small, basic nymphs like the hare's ear, prince, and woolly bugger can round out the wet fly selection.

The headwaters of the North Fork rise at elevations exceeding 6,000 feet on the western slopes of the Bitterroots. The altitude 90 miles downstream at its confluence with the Clearwater River is 965 feet.

The upper North Fork mirrors the challenges and opportunities of Kelly Creek. Its twisting run through a heavily forested canyon courses down a mix of boulder-strewn rapids, deep clear pools, flat, smooth runs and fast-flowing shallow riffles. All contain infinite hiding places for trout, especially around boulders and log jams and the stone gardens of the long runs. The pattern continues below Kelly Creek, where the river doubles in volume and width. Tributaries like Weitas Creek contribute to the volume and pools increase in depth and length.

Spring runoff peaks around 12,000 cubic feet per second in May, and flows fall to about 2,400 cfs by July and to 1,000 cfs by September. Fly fishers can start prospecting the river by June if the roads are open, fish it through the summer, and have a truly wonderful experience in late fall, as long as the roads stay open.

Along with the 1994 change to wild trout management, the river was reopened to continued fishing to the end of the general season on Nov. 30.

"The North Fork is a blue-ribbon opportunity in late September and October," says Tim Cochnauer, fisheries manager for Idaho Fish and Game's Clearwater Region. "It is a little known, greatly missed opportunity."

You bet, agreed Herb Pollard, former regional supervisor: "Think about it. Low water, big hungry fish, lots of hunters and fewer anglers. All of the cutthroat drop out of the tributaries to overwinter in the lower river. It's the typical pattern of the westslope cutthroat. They start dropping out by mid-September. By October, they are down in the main stem."

Restraint is the key word in this equation. The health of this basin's remarkable fishery is based on the principles of catch-and-release on an easily exploited species.

Access to the North Fork is excellent. Forest Road 250 follows the upper 50 miles of the river. Forest Road 247 parallels the bottom 25 miles to just above the Dworshak Reservoir slack waters and then cuts south to State Highway 11 and Pierce.

North Fork of the Clearwater. Photo by Michelle Retallic.

Stream Facts: North Fork of Clearwater River

SEASON
- Upstream from Dworshak slack waters, Saturday of Memorial Day weekend through Nov. 30
- Whitefish only, Dec. 1 to March 31

SPECIAL REGULATIONS
- Upstream from Dworshak Reservoir slack waters, two-trout limit, none under 14"; artificial flies and lures, single barbless hooks; no bait; no Kokanee harvest
- All tributaries—except Kelly, Lake and Sheep Creeks—two-trout limit
- Kelly, Lake and Sheep Creeks all cutthroat catch-and-release

FISH
- Westslope cutthroat and rainbows average 10" to 14"
- Some cutthroat and bull trout exceed 20"

RIVER MILES
- About 72 miles from headwaters to Dworshak slack waters
- Mile 8, Cedars
- Mile 27, Kelly Fork
- Mile 38, Weitas Creek
- Mile 43, Orogrande Creek (road to Pierce)
- Mile 57, Quartz Creek
- Mile 72, Dworshak backwaters

RIVER CHARACTERISTICS
- Upper river is a carbon copy of Kelly Creek. Below Kelly Forks, canyon widens and river runs through long, deep pools, cascading boulder-choked chutes, and swift rock-garden glides. River volume increases with tributary flows, and pools become longer and deeper below Orogrande Creek.

FLOWS
- Spring runoff peaks around 12,000 cubic feet per second in May or June, falls to about 2,400 cfs in July and to 1,000 cfs in September

BOAT RAMPS: N/A

Over four days of fishing we hooked powerful, beautiful steelhead that sometimes succumbed to the net and sometimes humbled the angler. And we watched wildlife that people from most parts of the country only see on cable TV or in a zoo.

Paul Emerson,
Managing Editor, Lewiston Morning Tribune

Hell's Canyon

Last burst of freedom by mighty Snake River

Cascading out of Hell's Canyon Dam, the Snake River makes its most dramatic, last free run as a living river, churning through a gorge more than a mile deep.

The deepest river gorge in North America, Hell's Canyon is more than 2,000 feet deeper than the Grand Canyon of the Colorado. It has whitewater thrills to match and much better fishing.

Bisecting the 652,488-acre Hell's Canyon Recreation Area on the Idaho-Oregon border, the Snake is protected as a Wild and Scenic River. The 31-mile stretch from the dam to Pittsburg Landing is classified as a wild river. The next 40 miles to the Oregon-Washington state line, about nine miles below the mouth of the Salmon River, is classified as a scenic river. The river flows another 35 miles to merge with the Clearwater River and leave Idaho at Lewiston.

Two tributaries also in the recreation area and adjacent 215,000-acre Seven Devils Wilderness Area in Idaho are protected as Wild and Scenic, the Rapid River in Idaho and the Imnaha River in Oregon.

The highest point on the Idaho side of the canyon is 9,393-foot He Devil Peak, which is 8,043 feet above the Snake. On the Oregon rim, 6,982-foot Hat Point is 5,632 feet above the river. Average width of the canyon is 10 miles, with no roads or bridges crossing the river. On its final run through the state, the river drops from an elevation of 1,688 feet at the dam to 725 feet at Lewiston.

Water volumes can be gargantuan and fluctuate radically. The upper canyon run is not a river for inexperienced boaters. At high flows it tests the mettle of even expert whitewater runners. Floatboaters also must share the river with jetboats and other powered watercraft. Permits for all watercraft are required year-round.

Releases from Hell's Canyon Dam vary from a low of 5,500 cubic feet per second to an extreme of 86,000 cfs. Most years, spring runoff releases peak around 50,000 cfs and by mid-July flows drop to around 20,000 cfs. Late-summer and fall flows may drop to 13,000 cfs or less. But the river can rise and fall significantly at any time of year. In a 24-hour period, flows can fluctuate 10,000 to 15,000 cfs and result in a three- or four-foot change in the high-water mark.

Boaters should always check on river levels before turning in for the night. Many tie off their watercraft with double lines, one to each individual boat or raft and a second that holds all the vessels in a floating party.

Steve Steubener plays a stubborn fish in the depths of Hell's Canyon.

Most of the whitewater is above Pittsburg Landing. There are 11 major rapids in the 18 miles between the dam and Rush Creek Rapids. Several are rated Class V or IV, depending on flows, and there are numerous Class III rapids in between. Below Pittsburg Landing, the river is flat with only a few rapids, but rowing can be tough when winds are blowing up the canyon.

Big water for a big country. The breathtaking, panoramic vistas of Hell's Canyon encompass a vast, remote region with sensational changes in elevation, terrain, climate and vegetation communities that range from alpine forest and wildflowers to desert shrub. A host of wild creatures—deer, elk, bighorn sheep, mountain goats, moose, bear, cougars and bobcats, waterfowl and shorebirds, songbirds, grouse and chukars, eagles and hawks—haunt the canyon at all elevations. Rattlesnakes are common. Ditto poison ivy.

But fish are one of Hell's Canyon's major drawing cards. The lower Snake is rated as the state's best mixed-species fishery. Fly fishers can pursue steelhead and rainbow trout and smallmouth bass. Other anglers also tackle its huge white sturgeon and channel catfish.

Idaho's second subspecies of steelhead, the smaller A-run strain, turns south at Lewiston and continues its fall spawning run up the Snake. A-run steelhead, which spend one to two years in the Pacific Ocean, average four to eight pounds.

They may start showing up as early as August, but if water temperatures are too warm, they will stack up around Lewiston. Many will move up into the Clearwater, which runs colder than the Snake, and wait for water temperatures out of Hell's Canyon to drop to 65 degrees or lower.

Most A-run steelhead head for the headwaters of the Salmon River and its tributaries, although a few continue up the Clearwater. The Snake's anadromous runs that now end at Hell's Canyon Dam once extended upstream to Shoshone Falls. Historically, it produced some of the largest summer chinook salmon in the Northwest. The rare angler who encounters one today must release it immediately since Idaho salmon are protected as endangered species.

Only hatchery-bred steelhead, whose adipose fins have been clipped off, may be taken. A steelhead with an adipose fin is a wild fish and must be released.

Steelhead anglers concentrate most heavily on the Lower Snake steelhead run in late fall, although some pursue the rockets from the sea through the winter. A favorite fall outing for wingshooters and fly fishers is a "cast and blast" trip that combines hunting for chukars and grouse and fishing for steelhead.

Taking a steelhead on a fly in big, deep water like this can be a challenge. They rarely rise to the surface, so fly fishers have to work hard to get a fly deep enough for a strike. A more effective option is to cast to promising spots along the edges of the steep river banks.

Summer boaters also fish the edges of the cliff walls, probing pocket waters, eddies and pools and tributary mouths for rainbows and smallmouth bass.

"I find when water levels drop to 18,000 cfs or less, fishing can be real solid," says Steve Stuebener, a Boise whitewater rafter who runs the canyon several times a year. "It also can be good in April before the river starts honking from spring runoff."

Most of the larger rainbows below the dam are residual steelhead that never made it to the ocean. They average 16 to 18 inches and are streamlined fighters like their seafaring brethren. The river is also stocked with hatchery rainbow.

Although not generally known, the lower Snake's smallmouth bass fishing is among the best in the Pacific Northwest. It has a strong population of the pugnacious bronzebacks in the two- to four-pound class, with occasional specimens topping the scales at five pounds.

The best action is in early spring as water temperature climbs above 40 degrees. It accelerates when the water tops 50 degrees and continues until spring runoff blows out the river. Dedicated bass anglers return to the river in fall after the high flows of summer drop.

Effective bass flies are weighted nymphs, crayfish imitations, white marabou muddlers and black marabou streamers for pools and riffles. Cork or elk hair popping bugs and hair-wing dry flies produce when surface action is occurring.

To reach bank wading stretches of the lower river during low-water periods, some fly fishers cross it at Lewiston and take Washington State Highway 129 from Clarkston upstream to Asotin or to Heller Bar at the mouth of the Grande Ronde River. This is a strategy employed by both bass and steelhead anglers. If you wade the west bank, you need a Washington license, or you can boat or kayak across the river and fish with your Idaho license on the east bank.

Idaho, Washington, and Oregon honor fishing licenses from each of their neighbors for anglers who fish the Snake from a boat. Only one bag limit is permitted even though an angler may be carrying more than one state license. All three states require special steelhead fishing permits.

Permits are required year-round to run the river in rafts, floatboats, or jetboats. Private floatboat parties running from the dam to Rush Creek are required to obtain reservations from the Friday before Memorial Day to Sept. 10. Self-issue permits are required below Rush Creek during this period and at other times of the year.

Wild River non-motorized periods have been designated for the 21-mile section between Wild Sheep Rapids and the upper landing at Kirkwood Historic Ranch. These periods are Monday-Tuesday-Wednesday beginning the first Monday in June and continuing every other week through the end of August. If the July 4th holiday falls in a non-motorized period, the non-motorized period will be the following week and every other week thereafter.

Floatboaters can arrange commercial shuttle service to have their vehicles waiting at their pull-out sites. Some floaters elect to have their rafts pulled back upstream to their launch site by jetboats. Another option, if you only want to fish the lower end of the canyon, is to be pulled upstream and float back to your vehicle.

Licensed guides and outfitters, offering both floatboat and jetboat services on the lower Snake and Salmon rivers, are located in Lewiston, Grangeville, White Bird, Riggins, and McCall, as well as Clarkston, Washington. Similar Hell's Canyon services are provided by outfitters operating out of Boise, Payette and Weiser, as well as Ontario, Baker City and Enterprise, Oregon.

For information on fishing and shuttle services, contact the Idaho Outfitters and Guides Association or the U.S. Forest Service. River reservations are issued by the Forest Service's Clarkston office, 509-758-1957. The Hell's Canyon National Recreation Area headquarters is at Enterprise, 503-426-5546. There is also a Forest Service visitor information center at Riggins, 208-628-3916.

Roads to the river bank are few and far between. Only three offer access in Hell's Canyon, two on the Oregon side and one on the Idaho side. A fourth extends upstream into the lower canyon on the Washington side. Several other roads lead to canyon overlooks, campgrounds, and trailheads.

RIVER ACCESS SITES

Hell's Canyon Recreation Site

Boat launch is one mile below dam on Oregon side. Limited parking; vehicle-trailer combinations over 35 feet not recommended.

Reach it from Cambridge, Idaho, via State Highway 71, or Copperfield, Oregon, on State Highway 86. Dam is 23 miles below Copperfield on paved Forest Road 493.

Dug Bar

Boat ramp is 27 miles from Imnaha, Oregon, via County Road 785 and Forest Road 4260 at end of steep, rugged, and slippery-when-wet gravel road. High-clearance, four-wheel-drive vehicles recommended.

Imnaha is northeast of Enterprise.

Pittsburg Landing

Boat ramp is 19 miles from White Bird, Idaho, via Forest Road 493. One-lane improved gravel road crosses Pittsburg Saddle and winds down steep grade to river. Vehicles pulling trailers should have good breaks.

White Bird is midway between Grangeville and Riggins.

Heller Bar

Boat ramp is 22 miles upstream from Asotin, Washington, near mouth of Grande Ronde River. Take State Highway 129 south from Clarkston.

This road connects with Oregon Highway 3, which leads to Enterprise and Imnaha.

Salmon River and the town of White Bird.

Hells Canyon Floater Guide

Note: If you have been on the Snake River on a previous trip, please read this carefully. There have been many important changes that have taken place as a result of the Wild and Scenic River Recreation Management Plan that may effect how you plan to conduct your trip.

THE PRIMARY SEASON extends from the Friday preceding Memorial Day weekend through September 10.

THE SECONDARY SEASON extends from September 11 through the Thursday before Memorial Day.

WILD RIVER RESERVATIONS – from Hells Canyon Dam to Upper Pittsburg Landing – are required for the issuance of a trip permit, seven days a week during the primary season. There are three private permit launches each day. These reservations can be obtained through the four rivers lottery or by picking a cancellation once the lottery reservations have been allocated.

Both processes can only be done through the website www.recreation.gov or by calling 877-550-6777.

Float reservations can only be made through www.recreation.gov website or by calling their toll free number at 877-550-6777.

A $6 non-refundable Lottery Application Fee is required for each lottery application submission. If a permit is purchased outside of the lottery a $6 non-refundable reservation fee is required for each reserved permit.

SCENIC RIVER RESERVATIONS – from Pittsburg Landing and Dug Bar – are required for the issuance of a trip permit on Fridays, Saturdays, Sundays and Holidays during the primary season. Two private permit launches are available each day. Additional reservations/permits are not required for a float party continuing into the scenic river from a reserved and permitted Wild River launch. Scenic River launches on Monday through Thursday except Holidays do not require an advance reservation. Self-issue permits must be completed at a permit station at the portal of entry.

SELF-ISSUE RIVER PERMITS are required for the entire river corridor during the secondary season, but do not require an advance reservation. They can be self-issued at any river portal. They cannot be used in place of a reserved launch in the Wild River between Hells Canyon Dam and Upper Pittsburg Landing during the primary season.

SPECIAL USE PERMITS FOR OUTFITTING AND GUIDING are required for all commercial float trips in the entire river corridor year round.

WILD RIVER NON-MOTORIZED PERIODS: Possessing or operating a motorized rivercraft is prohibited in the section of the Wild River between the top of Wild Sheep Rapids and the upper landing at Kirkwood Historic Ranch during the non-motorized periods. These periods are Monday Tuesday Wednesday beginning the first Monday in June and continuing every other week through the end of August. If the July 4th holiday falls in a non-motorized period, the non-motorized period will be the following week and every other week thereafter.

MAXIMUM PARTY SIZE is 24 persons, including overnight use at river campsites. Multiple parties (float and/or power) may camp together as long as the maximum party size is not exceeded.

MAXIMUM NUMBER OF FLOAT CRAFT is 8 per party.

All boats must carry at least one U.S. Coast Guard-approved personal floatation device for every person on board.

Overnight camping is prohibited at the Hells Canyon Creek Recreation Site, Pittsburg Administrative Areas, Cache Creek Administrative Site and those areas under Special Use Permit – Sheep Creek and Temperance Creek.

Camping for one night only is permitted at either one of the Granite Creek sites or Saddle Creek during the primary season. All other sites have a two-night stay limit in the Wild River and a three-night stay limit in the Scenic River during the primary season.

SOLID HUMAN WASTE carryout equipment and its use is required at all times in the river corridor.

The burning of wood in firepans is prohibited in the river corridor from July 1 through September 15 each year. Gas stoves and charcoal in a firepan or barbeque are acceptable. Firepans are required yearlong and open campfires are no longer allowed. All firewood for camp use must be packed in. The use of chainsaws is prohibited.

Fireworks are prohibited yearlong.

All garbage and trash must be packed out.

Kicker motors may not be used in the Wild River but can be used in the Scenic River.

Cultural Resources are protected by law from vandalism, destruction or theft. Collection of historic and prehistoric artifacts is prohibited.

If you are planning to use an outfitter and guide, be sure that person has the proper license. Licensing is for the protection of the public.

Trip leaders are responsible for the conduct of the members of their party during the entire trip. Inappropriate behavior resulting in complaints from other river users can result in loss of access to the permit system.

Reservation information: 509-758-1957

All other business and general information: 509-758-0616

Mail: Hells Canyon National Recreation Area, P.O. Box 699, Clarkston , WA 99403

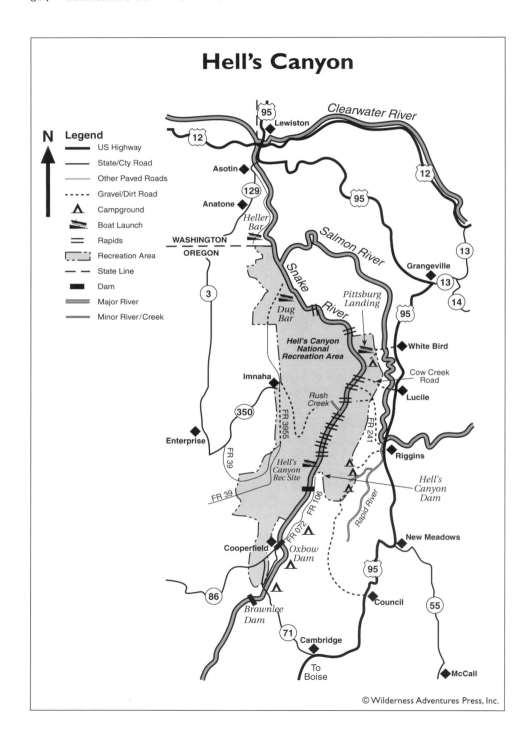

Hell's Canyon

Legend

▬▬▬	US Highway
———	State/Cty Road
———	Other Paved Roads
- - - -	Gravel/Dirt Road
▲	Campground
🚤	Boat Launch
═══	Rapids
░░░	Recreation Area
— —	State Line
▬	Dam
▬▬▬	Major River
▬▬▬	Minor River/Creek

© Wilderness Adventures Press, Inc.

We were after (steelhead) the kind of fish that bend a heavy fishing rod in half before they erupt from the water and tail-walk across the surface, attempting to dislodge the bite of the lure.

Paul Emerson
Managing Editor, *Lewiston Morning Tribune*

Lower Salmon River

Seafaring rainbows and pugnacious bass entice anglers

In fall, as the days grow short and frost paints cottonwood leaves golden-yellow, Riggins switches gears.

The tiny resort town on the Lower Salmon River says goodbye to its summer crowds of laid-back whitewater thrill seekers and hello to a steely-eyed host of anglers with visions of giant tail-walking trout dancing in their dreams. Armed with tall, powerful rods, the steelheaders begin showing up in September. By October, the hunt gets really serious as the seafaring rainbows funnel upstream to their headwater birthplaces, a 900-mile return journey from the Pacific Ocean.

Its size, beauty, and fighting ability make the steelhead the favorite game fish of Idaho anglers. And for many, Riggins has become the prime gathering place for a first shot at the leviathans. Midway between Boise and Lewiston on U.S. Highway 95, it is nestled in a bend of the Salmon at its confluence with the Little Salmon River.

Lower Salmon fly fishers can vie for both strains of Idaho steelhead. The smaller fish of the more prolific A-run average four to eight pounds and the larger B-run giants average 12 to 16 pounds, but often exceed 20 pounds.

A-run steelhead are predominantly "one-salt" fish, with 60 to 80 percent spending only one year in the ocean. Their return migration begins earlier and most are headed for the Upper Salmon. The principal destination of B-run steelhead, which are 70 to 80 percent two-salt fish, is the Clearwater River, but a small run of wild fish heads for the Middle Fork of the Salmon.

Fresh from the sea, steelhead entering the Salmon are scrappy fighters. Early fish zip upstream but the run continues through autumn until water temperatures drop below 40 degrees and the steelhead find holding places to wait out the winter. Their spring dash to the spawning grounds erupts in earnest when the river climbs above 40 degrees again.

Steelhead fishing on the Salmon and other streams can be hot or cold from year to year, depending on the size of a returning run. In low-water, high-temperature years, thermal blocks on the Columbia can sometimes stall a run's return to Idaho until the water cools. Always call ahead first for a conditions report and update on the progress of a run.

To enhance spring steelhead fishing on the lower Salmon, Idaho Fish and Game established a hatchery fish run on the Little Salmon River, which merges with the mainstem at Riggins.

The only tributary of the Salmon open to fishing during the steelhead season, the Little Salmon has had one of the hottest spring catch-rates in Idaho in recent years. But the rocky, narrow stream is a tough challenge for fly fishers because it is difficult to get a fly deep enough in the small pools of its rampaging pocket waters. Its anadromous fish run is halted 21 miles upstream by cascades at Round Valley Creek.

The Little Salmon is paralleled much of its length by U.S. 95. Summer fishing for resident trout doesn't open until July 16.

Rapid River, one of Idaho's most important chinook salmon spawning tributaries, enters the Little Salmon about four miles above its mouth. A few times in the early 1990s it was opened to salmon fishing on surplus hatchery fish. But recent return runs have been so low that some years the hatchery has been barely able to meet its egg collection goals. The Wild and Scenic river also is a major spawning stream for bull trout, a protected species.

Rapid River has a two-fish limit on resident trout during the general fishing season. It is closed to fishing from its mouth to the hatchery trap until Sept. 1. A primitive road follows the river upstream from the hatchery.

Fishing guide Jeff Vermillion and his dog Buddy examine a wild steelhead caught on the Lower Salmon with a Waller Waker dry fly. Photo by Jeff Vermillion.

Lower Salmon

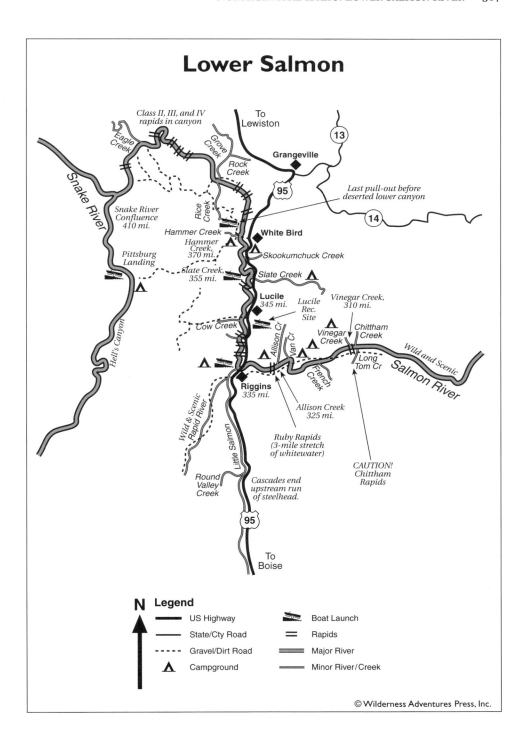

Class II, III, and IV
rapids in canyon

To
Lewiston

13

Eagle
Creek

Grove
Creek

Rock
Creek

Grangeville

95

Snake River

Last pull-out before
deserted lower canyon

14

Snake River
Confluence
410 mi.

Rice
Creek

Hammer Creek

White Bird

Pittsburg
Landing

Hammer
Creek,
370 mi.

Skookumchuck Creek

Slate Creek,
355 mi.

Slate Creek

Lucile
345 mi.

Lucile
Rec.
Site

Vinegar Creek,
310 mi.

Cow Creek

Allison Cr.

Van Cr

Vinegar
Creek

Chittham
Creek

Hell's Canyon

Long
Tom Cr

Wild and Scenic

Salmon River

Riggins
335 mi.

French
Creek

Wild & Scenic
Rapid River

Allison Creek
325 mi.

Little Salmon

Ruby Rapids
(3-mile stretch
of whitewater)

CAUTION!
Chittham
Rapids

Round
Valley
Creek

Cascades end
upstream run
of steelhead.

95

To
Boise

N

Legend

—— US Highway

—— State/Cty Road

- - - - Gravel/Dirt Road

⋀ Campground

Boat Launch

= Rapids

—— Major River

—— Minor River/Creek

© Wilderness Adventures Press, Inc.

Westslope cutthroat fishing on the Lower Salmon is strictly catch-and-release, although summer flows often are too warm for them and they run up into its tributaries. But, in addition to its steelhead fishery, the river is highly regarded for its excellent smallmouth bass fishing. The limit on bass is six fish.

The best times to tackle smallmouths mirror those on the Lower Snake River—in early spring before runoff blows out the river and in early fall when water levels drop.

During the lower flows of the fall steelhead season there are good bank fishing opportunities at Riggins and upstream, a rare treat on this deep-water river. A gravel road extends upstream about 25 miles through a broad valley to the edge of the Frank Church-River of No Return Wilderness. The best steelhead fishing is from exposed gravel and sandbars, although some can be reached only by boat.

Below Riggins, U.S. 95 parallels the river about 30 miles north to White Bird, where the Salmon swings west and enters a high-cliffed desert gorge on its final 50-mile run to the Snake. Tackling the river along the highway requires some rock scrambling. A few roads lead into the remote canyon below White Bird. Inquire locally for directions if you want to try the river on this stretch.

Even at low flows, the Salmon is a big, turbulent river. Inexperienced boaters would be wise to take their first venture up or down it with a professional guide or a friend who knows it well.

Jetboaters going upstream should put in above Ruby Rapids, a three-mile continuous stretch of whitewater about five miles above Riggins. Other rapids to watch out for upstream are at Vinegar and Chittam Creeks, at the edge of the wilderness, and at Long Tom Creek and Dry Meat Rapids. Long Tom marks the bottom end of the Wild and Scenic stretch of the Salmon. There is no permit requirement to run it after the first week of September.

Whitewater also churns the river below Riggins, but fall floats can be rewarding for more than steelhead and smallmouth bass. Wingshooters like to make "cast and blast" trips by combining chukar hunting with fishing. There are several boat ramps above and below Riggins. The last pull-out before entering the isolated lower canyon is at Hammer Creek, west of White Bird.

Even during autumn flows under 5,000 cubic feet per second, the deep gorge has Class II and III rapids and one Class IV, Snow Hole Rapids, but experienced boaters find it to be a fun float. The first pull-out below the mouth of the Salmon is Heller Bar, 20 miles downstream on the Washington bank of the Snake and about 30 miles south of Clarkston.

Outfitting and guide services, motels, RV parks, and restaurants are available at Riggins, Lucile, White Bird, and Grangeville.

There are three Forest Service campgrounds upstream from Riggins at Allison Creek, Van Creek, and Vinegar Creek. Downstream campgrounds are located at the Skookumchuck Recreation Site and Hammer Creek.

Stream Facts: Lower Salmon River

SEASON
- Open all year.

SPECIAL REGULATIONS
- Rainbow over 20" considered steelhead; special permit required, check regulations for dates and restrictions
- Cutthroat are catch-and-release; six-fish limit on rainbow with no adipose fin
- Bass, six-fish limit
- All tributaries—except Crooked Creek, Little Salmon and South Fork of Salmon—two-trout limit
- Little Salmon open to steelhead fishing, also salmon when numbers warrant

FISH
- A-run steelhead, average 4 to 8 lbs, with hatchery fish open to harvest
- A few wild B-run steelhead, 12 to 16 lbs, catch-and-release
- A few cutthroat and bull trout, catch-and-release
- Strong population of smallmouth bass in 1 lb. to 3 lb. range, some over 5 lbs

RIVER MILES
- About 95 miles from edge of wilderness to confluence with Snake River
- Mile 310, Wilderness (road's end)
- Mile 335, Riggins
- Mile 345, Lucile
- Mile 370, Hammer Creek (below White Bird)
- Mile 410, mouth (Hell's Canyon)

RIVER CHARACTERISTICS
- Big-water river with strong, powerful currents and numerous Class I to IV rapids, long deep pools, rocky riffles, occasional gravel bars. Inexperienced boaters should not run river, even at low flows, without first going with a guide or friend who knows it well. Lower 50 miles run through isolated, desert gorge inaccessible by road; floatboat and raft pull-out is another 20 miles downstream on Snake. Upstream from Chittham Rapids, the Salmon is protected as a Wild and Scenic River past the Middle Fork.

FLOWS
- Spring runoff peak in June can exceed 40,000 cubic feet per second
- Falls to below 20,000 cfs by July and under 9,000 by August
- Fall through early spring flows may drop to 5,000 cfs or less

BOAT RAMPS
- Vinegar Creek
- Allison Creek
- Riggins
- Lucile Recreation Area
- Slate Creek Recreation Area
- Ham

Northern Region

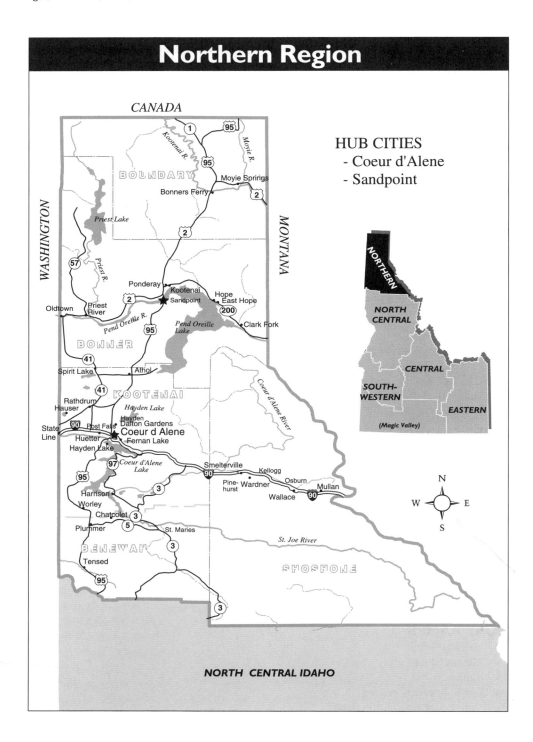

CANADA

Kootenai R.

Moyie R.

BOUNDARY

Moyie Springs

Bonners Ferry

WASHINGTON

Priest Lake

MONTANA

Priest R.

Ponderay

Kootenai

Hope

East Hope

Oldtown

Priest River

Sandpoint

Clark Fork

Pend Oreille R.

Pend Oreille Lake

BONNER

Spirit Lake

Athol

Coeur d'Alene River

Rathdrum

Hauser

KOOTENAI

Hayden Lake

State Line

Post Falls

Hayden

Dalton Gardens

Coeur d Alene

Smelterville

Kellogg

Huetter

Fernan Lake

Pine-hurst

Wardner

Osburn

Mullan

Hayden Lake

Coeur d'Alene Lake

Wallace

Harrison

Worley

Chatcolet

Plummer

St. Maries

St. Joe River

BENEWAH

SHOSHONE

Tensed

HUB CITIES
- Coeur d'Alene
- Sandpoint

NORTHERN

NORTH CENTRAL

CENTRAL

SOUTH-WESTERN

EASTERN

(Magic Valley)

N
W — E
S

NORTH CENTRAL IDAHO

When the carpenter ants pop everything fishes.
Joe Roope, Coeur d'Alene guide and fly shop owner

NORTHERN REGION

North Idaho is the state's lake country and fly fishers used to fishing the lake country of northern Wisconsin and Michigan will feel at home here. Nearly a century ago the Weyerhaeuser family moved its extensive logging operations from the North Woods of the Midwest to this area. Lumberjacks and their families found familiar country. The only difference is that the mountains added to the challenge of logging and amplified the scenic beauty of the northern forests.

Fly fishers attracted by the St. Joe and North Fork of the Coeur d'Alene can find ample diversions on Lake Coeur d'Alene and Hayden Lake. Pend Oreille and Priest Lake offer pleasures of their own. Several other streams and rivers offer limited fly fishing action. The alpine lakes of the Selkirk Mountains round out the fly fishing opportunities of Idaho's panhandle country.

Scenic wonders of Idaho's northern lakes attract tourists from around the world.

North Idaho Lakes

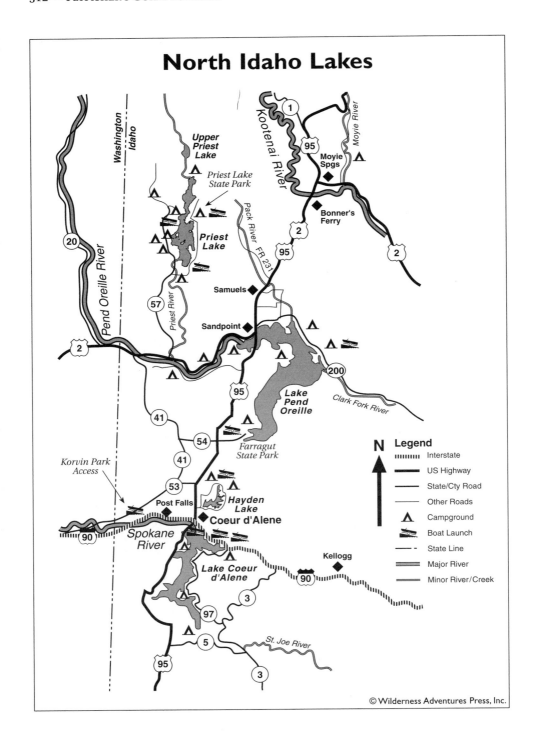

© Wilderness Adventures Press, Inc.

North Idaho Lakes

Coeur d'Alene Lake

Coeur d'Alene Lake is 31,487 acres of clear water with 100 miles of mostly wooded shoreline. Only 30 miles from downtown Spokane, WA, the lake gets heavy pressure from water skiers, sail boats, jet skis, and anglers. The city of Coeur d'Alene sits on its northeastern shore with scenic beaches and the luxurious Coeur d'Alene Resort dominating the waterfront.

Few lakes offer such a mixed bag of species. The lake still has good populations of native westslope cutthroat, bull trout, and kokanee, the dominant fish of the lake. The lake also has healthy rainbow and brook trout populations, chinook salmon that exceed 20 pounds, largemouth bass, crappie, perch, and huge northern pike.

The time of the year local fly fishers key on Coeur d'Alene is during the early season when spring runoff makes the rivers nearly unfishable. Two important hatches trigger heavy feeding by cutthroats, the most sought-after fish of fly anglers here. A March brown hatch starts around May 1 and lasts through June 15. These burrowing nymphs emerge from the lake bottom and swim toward the shoreline.

Fly fishers use March brown nymphs along the southern exposure's extensive rip rap by cruising with canoe or float-tube. Shore casters also can find success around the lake's many public access points.

Lake Coeur d'Alene still has good populations of cutthroat trout. Art Today photo.

The other major hatch is the carpenter ant hatch that runs for two to five days around the end of May through early June. It is not limited to Coeur d'Alene Lake. Hayden Lake, a smaller lake just five miles north of Coeur d'Alene, and Pend Oreille also have carpenter ant hatches at this time that trigger a trout feeding frenzy. Red ant patterns match this hatch as do specialized patterns that can be found locally.

One other hatch in the fall seems to turn the Coeur d'Alene and Hayden Lake fish on for one last major feed. A stink bug beetle that locals call "leptos" infests trees around the lakes. They fall into the water in October and cutthroats especially have learned to key on this phenomenon.

Through the rest of the summer woolly buggers, leeches, a wide variety of nymphs, royal Wulffs, elk hair caddis, renegades, and other attractors work well.

Bass, perch, and crappie can be found in weedy bays and are best sought with poppers. Coeur d'Alene's northern pike grow unusually large—over 20 pounds—so fly fishers seeking them need heavy tackle like steelhead equipment. Large bucktail streamers like the Dahlberg Diver are the fly of choice for these toothy tacklebusters.

There is a 6-trout limit on the lake, but none may be cutthroat or bull trout. The chinook salmon limit is 2 fish, none under 20 inches. The kokanee salmon limit is 15. The bass limit is 6, both species combined.

The Coeur d'Alene Indian Tribe manages the southern portion of Coeur d'Alene Lake. Anglers who are not members of the tribe are required to obtain a tribal fishing permit, in addition to a state license, to fish reservation waters.

COEUR D'ALENE LAKE FISHERY SURVEY

Jim Fredericks
Regional Fishery Manager

Coeur d'Alene Lake is one of Idaho's most heavily used fisheries. In 2003, an IDFG economic sur-vey indicated anglers spent approximately $6.7 million fishing Coeur d'Alene Lake, making it an extreme-ly valuable fishery both in terms of recreation and impacts to the local economy. Chinook salmon are the trophy species, with kokanee being the "bread and butter" fish. Increasingly, warm and cool water fish, such as largemouth and smallmouth bass and northern pike have become a major part of the fishery.

Creel Survey Helps Understand Fishery

There are several types of surveys that help us understand a fishery. Many focus on fish population assessment. However, assessing angler use, catch rates, and harvest can be equally as important. Unfortunately, these surveys, known as "creel surveys" are costly, so we typically only conduct them every 5 to 10 years on important fisheries. The last creel survey on Coeur d'Alene Lake was completed in 1996. So, in 2009, IDFG partnered with the Coeur d'Alene Tribal Fisheries Program to conduct a year-long survey of Coeur d'Alene Lake and the lateral lakes.

Boats and anglers were counted from an airplane at randomly selected times throughout the week. Anglers were interviewed at boat ramps or on the water to provide information such as hours fished, type of equipment used, species caught, and the number harvested.

Over 2,600 anglers from 19 states and Canada were interviewed in 2009, with 83 percent being from Idaho. Washington had the second most number of anglers, with 13 percent of the total. Anglers fished an estimated 95,000 hours on Coeur d'Alene Lake and an additional 56,000 hours on the chain lakes from January 1 to December 31. Of the Coeur d'Alene Lake effort, 34 percent was in the northern section (north of Arrow Point), 52 percent was in the middle section (Arrow Point to tribal boundary), and 14 percent was in the tribal waters.

Forty-two percent of the total fishing effort was directed toward Chinook salmon and 35 percent towards kokanee. Twelve percent was directed towards northern pike, 6 percent towards large-mouth bass, and 3 percent towards small-mouth bass.

Anglers caught an estimated 877 Chinook and harvested 729 of them. Harvested Chinook ranged from 14 to 35 inches, with an average of 23 inches. Chinook catch rates were best from late August through December, when anglers caught a Chinook for every 5 to 15 rod hours, and slowest in June-July, when an average of 60-80 rod hours was spent on each fish. Anglers caught an estimated 8,841 kokanee and har-vested 6,770 for catch rates of .68 fish/hour and .52 fish/hour respectively.

Chinook/kokanee Populations Finding Balance

So what is the latest on kokanee? For more than a decade, adult kokanee have been well below our desired levels of about 12 to 24 adult kokanee per acre of water. In the three years prior to 2009, the lake had about 1.2 adult kokanee per acre. These low densities made it difficult for anglers to find the adult fish and kept catch rates low. The kokanee grew large, but the low numbers impacted the kokanee fishery and forced emer-gency closures to protect spawning adults. Chinook growth was also affected by the low ko kanee densities (their main food source), with few mature fish exceeding 15 pounds. Chinook stocking was greatly reduced and the limit was liberalized to help reduce preda-tion on kokanee and allow the popu-lation to recover.

As hoped, we saw a significant rebound in the kokanee population in 2009. Adult densities have increased ten-fold to 12 adults per acre of water. This puts them right at the lower end of our desired range. One and two year old kokanee have also rebounded to levels not seen since before the mid-1990s. With this improvement, we kept the kokanee fishery open this fall for the first time in three years, and resumed stocking Chinook salmon.

The one low year class is kokanee fry. We estimated the lake contained only 3.6 mil-lion of them. That may seem like a lot, but it is one of the lowest estimates on record. Why? It seems the low numbers of adult kokanee in 2008 produced very low numbers of fry in 2009. We will be keeping a close watch on this year class and may need to adjust Chinook stocking to accommodate them.

How are the Chinook salmon faring? With the kokanee population increasing, Chinook growth is up as well. Several fish over 20 lbs were taken in 2009. We resumed stocking in 2009 with 20,000 fingerling Chinook. We are in the midst of an effort to refine our stocking program as well. Specifically, we are evaluating June vs. October releases.

Coeur d'Alene Indian Reservation

The Coeur d'Alene Indian Reservation covers 350,000 acres in Idaho's Panhandle southwest of the resort town of Coeur d'Alene. Tribal headquarters are located at Plummer.

The tribe manages the southern portion of Coeur d'Alene Lake. Benewah and Lake creeks on the reservation are closed to fishing to help restore westslope cutthroat trout populations.

Anglers who are not members of the Coeur d'Alene Tribe are required to obtain a tribal fishing permit, in addition to a state license, to fish reservation waters, including the southern end of Lake Coeur d'Alene: Youths, 14-17, $10 annual license; Adults, 18 to 55, $25 annual license; Seniors, 55 or older, $5 annual license.

Licenses are available at the Coeur d'Alene Tribal Fish & Wildlife Office at Plummer. Additional information can be obtained by calling the Fish, Water, Wildlife, Lake Management Office at 208-686-5302.

Commercial vendors for tribal licenses include:
- Blue Goose Sport Shop, St. Maries
- St. Joe Sport Stop, St. Maries
- Fins & Feather Tackle Shop, Coeur d'Alene
- HiWay Motel, Plummer
- Steamboat Trader, Harrison

Coeur d'Alene Tribe Trout Ponds

The Coeur d'Alene Tribe Fisheries Program has planted three trout ponds with rainbow trout in the 11- to 14-inch size range. Daily catch limit is five fish per day.

The pond locations are:

Worley: Go south of Worley turn right off of US 95 near Or at the billboard Sign go about 300 yard and turn right the pond will be right there.

Agency: Located behind the Tribal Court building (Old Agency) at Plummer. Instead of turning at the Agency keep going to the right on the main road around the corner and the pond will be on your left side of the road.

DeSmet: Approximately two miles west of DeSmet on the Saltese/DeSmet road, turn left after you pass the Tee Pee house on your right side of the road.

FERNAN LAKE

Fernan Lake, located on the eastern outskirts of Coeur d'Alene, provides one of the finest natural urban fisheries in the state. This 300-acre lake receives heavy angling pressure. Nearly 23,000 fish per year are harvested. Aggressive management strategies, such as diversifying the fishery with non-native, compatible species, has kept Fernan Lake a high success fishery.

Shoreline and boat anglers alike fish Fernan. There are two public boat launches, one at the east end and one on the west end of the lake. Shoreline access can be found in these areas around the docks and along the roadside on the northwest side of the lake.

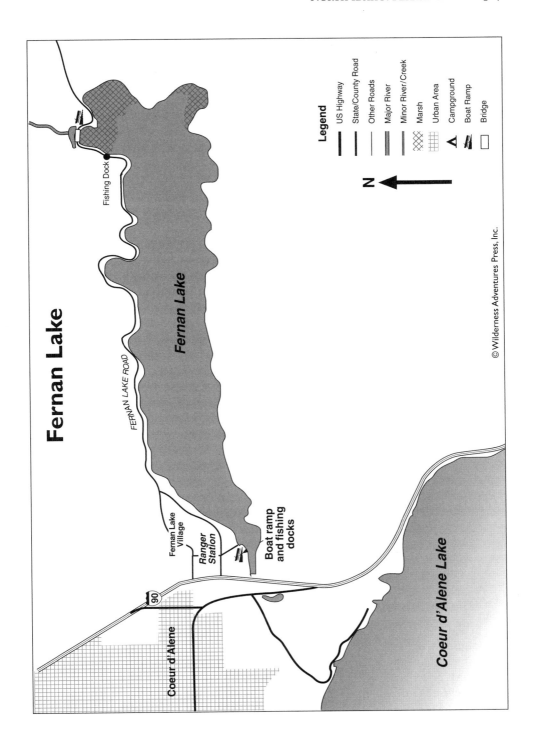

Fernan Lake

Fernan Lake

FERNAN LAKE ROAD

Fishing Dock

Fernan Lake Village

Ranger Station

Boat ramp and fishing docks

Coeur d'Alene

90

Coeur d'Alene Lake

Legend

US Highway
State/County Road
Other Roads
Major River
Minor River/Creek
Marsh
Urban Area
Campground
Boat Ramp
Bridge

N

© Wilderness Adventures Press, Inc.

Wild cutthroat trout, brook trout and stocked rainbow trout account for over 40 percent of the catch in Fernan. Warm water species also play a critical role. With an average depth of only 12 feet, water temperature rise quickly and provide good habitat for species such as largemouth bass, bullhead catfish, channel catfish, crappie, perch, and pumpkinseed sun fish. Northern pike can also be found in Fernan.

Trout are cool water fish so as surface temperatures begin to rise you will find them in Fernan's deeper more protected waters.

Fishing for pumpkinseed sun fish and crappie is ideal for kids. These fish can be found in the shallows.

Largemouth bass are doing well in Fernan. Some up to 21 inches have been caught. Bass like heavy cover, so seek out vegetation or artificial structure.

Tiger muskie record falls

Four times in 1998, the Idaho record for tiger muskie fell to Hauser Lake fish.

Hauser Lake, northwest of Coeur d'Alene and west of Rathdrum, is one of a few Idaho waters where the sterile hybrid tiger muskies have been planted. They can only be planted where there is no chance of escape into other fishing waters where these voracious predators could damage desirable species. The record fish caught in Hauser Lake in 1998 were planted in 1989 or 1990.

The lake yielded a tiger muskie of more than 24 pounds in March. That record only lasted until July when record-book fish started coming into the Panhandle Region Fish and Game office about once a week.

On June 16, 2001, a 38-pound, 7-ounce tiger muskie with a length of 48.25 inches and girth of 22.5 inches was presented to Fish and Game for verification. This fish may be hard to top any time soon.

Patricia Jennen of Post Falls was fishing for crappie with ultralight tackle when she hooked the muskie. With only 60 feet of line on the reel, she had to hang on for about one-and-a-half hours while her husband followed the fish with the boat.

The tiger muskie is a sterile hybrid, a cross of a northern pike and a muskellunge. The fish also has been stocked in Shepherd, Freeman, Blue and Dawson lakes in northern Idaho. The limit on tiger muskies is two fish, 40-inch minimum size.

LAKE PEND OREILLE

In 2013, for the first time since 1999, anglers were again allowed to harvest kokanee salmon in Lake Pend Oreille as a result of the success of the Lake Pend Oreille Fishery Recovery Program. Anglers may harvest six kokanee per day in the lake and Clark Fork River.

In addition, the increase in kokanee has made it possible to move back towards trophy rainbow trout management. A size and bag limit has been reinstated for rainbows: six rainbow trout, only one more than 20 inches long, and the $15 per head angler harvest incentive is no longer in effect for rainbow trout. Also, the Clark Fork River and tributaries are now closed to trout harvest from Dec.1 to the Friday before the Memorial Day weekend to protect spawning rainbows.

Restoration of the kokanee salmon population in northern Idaho's Lake Pend Oreille is crucial to preserving its fabulous trophy rainbow fishery.

The $15 incentive remains in place for harvest of lake trout in Lake Pend Oreille. There is no limit on harvest of lake trout in the lake.

"The change in direction for rainbow trout management was possible because of the success of predator removal efforts (i.e., fewer lake trout) and increased kokanee abundance," stated Jim Fredericks, regional fishery manager. "Over time, these rule changes will allow more rainbows to reach trophy size, especially now that they have a more abundant kokanee food supply.

"There is still a lot of work to be done to reach fishery recovery goals, but the positive response of the fishery in recent years is evidence that we are making great progress. Anglers have played a major role in helping to improve the fishery and we thank you for your efforts."

Pend Oreille is the largest and deepest natural lake in Idaho, covering 85,960 acres with a 111-mile shoreline.

Tall mountains surround the shores of this great lake that drains much of Montana's storied rivers, including the Clark Fork, Flathead, Bitterroot and Blackfoot. The quality of this immense fishery therefore is highly dependent on the water quality of these waters. And of even more importance in recent years has been the detrimental affect of fluctuations in lake levels for increased power generation.

The resort town of Sandpoint lies on the lake's northwest shore. It can be reached by taking Highway 95 north from Coeur d'Alene. Farragut State Park is located at the end of the southeast arm of the lake, and there are a number of resorts and marinas along its shores.

The lake is a big water fishery averaging 538 feet in depth, dropping to 1,152 feet in the deepest hole. It is 43 miles long and six miles wide.

Effective fishing requires a boat.

Historically, westslope cutthroat made up the bulk of the Pend Oreille fishery. Today, introduced strains of Kamloops rainbow trout from British Columbia are its biggest draw. Its trophy trout reputation rests on its consistent production of Kamloops pushing 20 pounds or more, and occasional large lake trout.

But, unfortunately, Pend Oreille's storied kokanee salmon fishing faced virtual collapse and anglers were again permitted to harvest them in the lake or the Clark Fork in 2013 aftger a fishing ban of nearly 15 years.

The lake still has healthy populations of bull trout, a rarity in the region, and it produced a world record 32-pound fish in 1949. But since 1996, harvest of bull trout is banned on all Idaho waters. The U.S. Fish and Wildlife Service listed it as a threaten species in 1998.

The best fly fishing occurs during the carpenter ant hatch in late May and early June and the fall for the large Kamloops rainbow. Streamers are the most effective flies.

However, since kokanee are an important forage fish for the rainbows, a cloud of uncertainty hangs over the lake's legendary trophy fishery.

The kokanee population in Lake Pend Oreille has been at a record low level since the 1997 flood—a 100-year event—practically wiped out the population.

Pend Oreille's kokanee fishery was once the largest fishery in the state with over a million fish harvested annually, but the fishery declined concurrently with deeper drawdowns of the lake to provide for additional power generation in winter. The drawdowns exposed kokanee spawning beds and killed tens of thousands of eggs. A lower regiment of drawdowns negotiated with Avista power company has helped mitigate this problem, but the first hint of a rebound in kokanee populations has taken more than a decade

The huge lake also holds whitefish, perch, and a variety of warmwater species, including largemouth and smallmouth bass, crappie, and pumpkin seed sunfish.

Often overlooked, largemouth bass can be found in the shallows around the mouth of Pack River and farther east in the waters around Denton Slough near the mouth of the Clark Fork River. The lake's smallmouth bass concentrate along rocky underwater ledges. There is a six-fish limit on bass.

Cutthroat trout and bull trout are catch-and-release. Harvest of lake trout remains unlimited, and as an added incentive anglers are paid $15 for the head of each lake trout and each rainbow over 13 inches turned into Fish and Game.

Another key component of the kokanee recovery program is decreasing the number of predators in the lake. The rapid expansion of the lake trout (mackinaw) population in the 1990s, combined with depressed kokanee populations, has thrown predator-prey populations out of balance, threatening the world-famous trophy rainbow fishery and the federally protected bull trout population.

Biologists are hopeful anglers can help keep the kokanee population in Lake Pend Oreille from collapsing by reducing lake trout while enjoying what may be spectacular fishing for large fish. They see this as one of the few situations in which predation by one fish species on another can be the controlling factor in survival of a population.

At the same time, while large rainbow trout were previously targeted for reduction, biologist note that getting kokanee populations closer to historic levels will ultimately preserve the lake's storied trophy rainbow fishery.

Kokanee recovery shows positive signs

Biologists and anglers working to recover the kokanee population in Lake Pend Oreille first found reasons to be encouraged by progress seen in 2009, said Jim Fredericks, regional fisheries manager.

After more than a decade of lake level management to benefit shoreline spawning by kokanee and four years of an aggressive predator reduction program, the kokanee population is showing some positive signs, Fredericks said.

The first encouraging sign came in the fall with the annual population estimates. Each year fishery researchers use hydroacoustics and trawl nets to estimate the population of each age-class of kokanee. The estimates can be compared with previous years to evaluate survival. Though overall abundance was still low, juvenile kokanee survival was the highest seen since 1996. More than 70 percent of the 2009 class of one-year-old kokanee survived to become two-year-olds in 2010.

"This represents a seven-fold increase from a low of 10 percent survival in 2008," Fredericks said.

No one was happier to see those results than Andy Dux, the research biologist charged with monitoring the population.

"Last year we saw an increase from 10 percent survival to 30 percent survival, and we were pleased with that. So, to see it more than double this year, is really exciting," he said.

More good news came later in the fall during the kokanee spawning season. Each year a trap is set up in Granite Creek to collect kokanee returning to spawn. Eggs are stripped from many of the fish. The resulting offspring are raised in Cabinet Gorge Hatchery and later released into the lake.

Typically, 10 to 15 million eggs are collected each year at the trap. In 2007 and 2008, however, it was nowhere close to that, with just over 1 million eggs taken between both years combined.

"Although the hatchery is not the key to recovery of the Pend Oreille fishery, it represents one very important component," said Fredericks. "Getting 8.25 million eggs is a real boost this year."

The juvenile survival rates and the increased number of kokanee spawners are solid evidence the efforts to reduce predators are paying off, Fredericks said. Since 2006, Idaho Fish and Game has used a two-pronged approach consisting of netting and angler harvest incentives to reduce the number of lake trout and rainbow trout.

Mitigation funds from Avista and Bonneville Power Administration are used to contract commercial netters from Lake Michigan to help control the expanding lake trout population. Their specialized equipment and decades of experience netting deepwater lakes make them uniquely qualified to work on Pend Oreille. To date, they've removed nearly 40,000 lake trout.

Avista mitigation funds are also used to fund the Angler Incentive Program, which pays anglers $15 for each lake trout and rainbow trout harvested from Pend Oreille. Since 2006 anglers have turned in nearly 50,000 lake trout and 25,000 rainbow trout.

Anglers have been extremely valuable in this effort, Fredericks said.

"They've removed a lot of lake trout, but they've also removed a lot of rainbow trout," he said. "The nets don't capture rainbow trout, so the angler catch is critical to the success of the predator control program."

Although the Pend Oreille fishery recovery effort has not been without controversy, Fredericks said the one thing nearly all Pend Oreille anglers agree on is that kokanee are the key to restoring a healthy fishery.

"Not only do they provide a popular fishery, they are the foundation for the world famous trophy rainbow fishery as well," he said. "Kokanee are also essential to a healthy bull trout population, so everyone ought to be pretty excited with what we saw in 2009."

While the biologists are confident in saying the increased survival rates are a direct result of decreasing the number of predators in the lake, they're quick to point out that predator removal is not the whole key to recovery in Pend Oreille.

"Although many may think the Pend Oreille Fishery Recovery effort is all about the commercial netting and harvest reward programs, the effort really began with, and still relies on, lake level management," Dux said.

Research in the early 1990s demonstrated a full 11.5-foot winter drawdown on Pend Oreille left the best kokanee spawning gravel high and dry, and that the loss of those important spawning gravels was a big reason the kokanee population had been in decline since the 1960s. As a result of the research and the im-portance of kokanee to the Pend Oreille bull trout population, the U.S. Army Corps of Engineers has kept the lake at a higher level (7.5-foot drawdown) the majority of years since 1996. Modifying winter lake level management has more than doubled the survival of kokanee eggs to fry in the wild. Because wild kokanee production drives the fishery, maintaining high survival rates for all ages of kokanee - including eggs - is critical to recovery of the fishery.

The decision on extent of drawdown is based on several factors including pre-cipitation forecast, previous year elevation, and the number of wild kokanee spawners expected to use the shoreline. Periodically lowering the lake can actually benefit kokanee by allowing winter wave activity to redistribute and clean the shoreline gravels, as is the case this year.

The predator problem began developing in the late 1990s -- just as the solution to the spawning habitat problem was being implemented, Dux said.

Commercial netting and angler harvest appear to be reversing the expansion of the lake trout population. Fredericks notes they've seen the lake trout population show defi-nite signs of over harvest, which is exactly what they hope to see.

Anglers who catch lake trout of any size from Lake Pend Oreille may submit the heads for payment to one of the following locations: Holiday Shores Marina, Hope Marine Services, Anchor Gas (Garfield Bay), Hudson's Bay Marina (Bayview), Fish and Game Bayview Research Station, Fish and Game regional office (Coeur d'Alene).

Bull trout's listing won't limit fishing

Idaho Fish and Game has been joined by Washington Water Power Co. and The Panhandle Chapter of Trout Unlimited in an all out effort to protect bull trout in the Pend Oreille drainage. Information, education, and protection will be the backbone of a project implemented by conservation officers to work with the public and private industry to restore historic numbers of this indigenous species of fish, which was listed as a threatened species in 1998.

Bull trout numbers have become perilously low in most river systems of the West and are under consideration by the U.S. Fish and Wildlife Service for listing as threatened and endangered. To help protect and restore bull trout Idaho closed the take season on bull trout in 1996.

Panhandle Fish and Game officers and biologists in conjunction with sportsman's groups have made efforts in the past to protect bull trout in northern Idaho. Money donated by Lake Pend Oreille Sportsman Association was used to print wallet size color prints of bull trout and other trout species to help fisherman identify their catch. This hopefully has helped prevent new or uninformed anglers from taking bull trout by mistake.

So what are the identifying factors on bull trout?

The bull trout doesn't have any spots on any of the fins, but has pale pink or salmon-colored spots on its olive-green body.

By comparison, the rainbow has a red stripe down the side.The cutthroat has a red slash under the chin. The brook trout has worm-like markings on the fins and three colors on the bottom fins, white, black and red. The brown trout has large black spots with red spots down the sides with pale halos. The lake trout has light gray to white spots on its dark gray or gray-green body, and its tail has a deep fork.

Fish and Game officers have increased patrols and called upon volunteers and reservists to watch certain streams and lakes when bull trout are particularly vulnerable. Several cases have been made but it has become apparent that much more needs to be done in the areas of informing the public to prevent accidental take, and enforcing the laws to stop intentional poachers. That is where the partnership with private industry and sportsman's groups has now come to help an imperiled species.

State officials were disappointed by a federal decision to list the bull trout for Endangered Species Act protection, but stress anglers will not suffer because the native fish were placed on the list. The U.S. Fish and Wildlife Service decision to list Pacific Northwest bull trout as a threatened species was forced by a 1997 federal court decision in a suit brought by conservation groups.

People had feared this would result in severe restrictions on sport fishing. In this case, however, USFWS decided that "Because the 1994 record demonstrates that the states of Montana, Idaho, Oregon, and Washington have made their angling regulations more restrictive to protect bull trout, the Service also proposed to relax the Endangered Species Act prohibition against incidental taking of a listed species for the Columbia River population segment."

Idaho Fish and Game banned harvest of bull trout in 1996. Anglers are responsible for making sure they can recognize the species and for following the no-harvest regulation.

FARRAGUT STATE PARK

Farragut State Park offers a large selection of individual and group campsites and day-use shelters, and numerous opportunities to play and fish in Lake Pend Oreille.

It is located near the town of Athol on the tip of the southeast arm of Lake Pend Oreille. It can be reached by taking State Highway 54 east at its intersection with U.S. 95, about 25 miles south of Sandpoint.

One of the most popular destinations in northern Idaho, it sees heavy use in summer.

For information on campsite reservations, contact the park office at 683-2425; Fax: 683-2975; or Email: FAR@idpr.state.id.us.

ROUND LAKE STATE PARK

The 58-acre lake at Round Lake State Park, about 10 miles south of Sandpoint, is relatively shallow, approximately 37 feet at its deepest point. But it provides food and habitat for brook trout, rainbow trout, largemouth bass, pumpkinseed sun fish sunfish, yellow perch and black crappie.

Small boats and canoes are permitted, however, the lake is restricted to electric motors only. A gas motor can not be attached to the boat.

Round Lake has a small campground designed for smaller RVs and tent camping. There are no electrical hook ups.

The parks is just south of Sagle, and 2 miles west of U.S. 95.

For more information, call 263-3489.

COCOLALLA LAKE

Cocolalla Lake, located approximately 10 miles south of Sandpoint, just off of U.S. 95, provides an easy access year-round fishery. Total size of Cocolalla Lake is about 800 acres, with an average depth of nearly 26 feet. Feeding the lake is Cocolalla Creek, which also provides spawning habitat for brown, rainbow, cutthroat and brook trout.

Fishing access to Cocolalla for the shoreline angler is primarily limited to the northeast end and the east shoreline. Private ownership limits access on the southern end and west side. Boat access is available on the northeast end adjacent to the campground.

Although the primary fishing pressure on Cocolalla Lake has been for trout, opportunities for warmwater species really sets this lake apart from other north Idaho lakes. Channel catfish, largemouth bass, crappie and an abundance of perch are present.

Trout fishing Cocolalla can be slow, but fish can be found from shore, or by trolling from a boat.

Bass over 17 inches have been found and crappie in the 12-inch range are not uncommon. These fish are found near the shoreline, look for shallow weedy areas.

Priest Lake

Priest Lake is another popular North Idaho gem.

Lying at about 2,400 feet above sea level, it has an abundance of beautiful scenery and recreational opportunities. Visitors enjoy the dense cedar-hemlock forests and the wildlife, such as whitetail deer, black bear, moose and bald eagles. The stately Selkirk Mountain Range towers nearby and numerous streams tumble down the slopes.

The 23,360-acre lake runs north and south along Idaho's extreme northwest corner, due north of the town of Priest River, on U.S. 2 To reach the lake turn north on State Highway 57 and drive about 25 miles.

Noted for its clear water, Priest Lake extends 19 miles and is connected to the smaller 1,400-acre Upper Priest Lake by a placid, two-mile-long water thoroughfare.

Priest Lake is best known for its lake trout fishery, but it offers fine fly fishing for 12- to 15-inch westslope cutthroat, with the largest fish going to 20 inches.

The cutthroat are catch-and-release. There is a 6-fish limit on lake trout and a 6-fish limit on kokanee. The lake also holds whitefish and bull trout, another catch-and-release species.

Since shore access is limited, flycasters do best working the lake's coves, shallow shelfs, bays, and headlands sticking out into the lake from a boat or canoe.

Surface trolling "hot spots" on the east side are along the east side of Cavanaugh Bay, and off the end of Pinto Point. Bank fishing is best along the east side of Cavanaugh Bay, and where the East Lakeshore Road runs beside the lake.

Most tributary streams are closed to fishing except in July and August, but Soldier and Hunt Creeks are open during the regular season.

There are a number of resorts on the lake and Priest Lake State Park has four separate units around the lake, which offer additional shore access.

Primitive camping is available on Upper Priest Lake, but can only be reached by canoe or on foot. The Thoroughfare River and Upper Priest Lake tributaries are closed to fishing.

Upper Priest Lake also has an excellent population of westslope cutthroat, but it is strictly catch-and-release fishing—for all species in the lake.

Idaho Fish and Game, however, is conducting a lake trout population reduction program on Upper Priest Lake in an effort to maintain bull trout in the Priest River drainage. Gill nets are being employed to capture lake trout, a voracious predator on other fish species, including bull trout. Bull trout were listed as a threatened species in 1998.

An extensive study of both the lake trout and bull trout populations in Upper Priest Lake was conducted in 1997. This study indicated that lake trout were rapidly increasing and bull trout showed an alarming decline.

Biologists recommended not to open the lake to angler harvest of lake trout because gill nets are more efficient. They also were concerned about the accidental take of bull trout.

Fish and Game is actively involved in bull trout restoration in Upper Priest Lake for several reasons. Upper Priest Lake offers the last best hope to save bull trout in the Priest Lake ecosystem. If it cannot be accomplished there, there is no sense in attempting bull trout restoration in Priest Lake where the task is far more difficult.

Cutthroat fishing on Upper Priest Lake and all Priest Lake tributaries is catch-and-release. The bag limit on Priest River below the lake and on its tributaries is 6 trout, no cutthroat.

Priest Lake State Park

The park's camping and recreation facilities are located at four separate units around the lake:

Dickensheet—Located four miles south of Coolin, the Dickensheet Unit is nestled beside the pristine Priest River. Open from May 1 through Sept. 30, Dickensheet has become a popular entry point for raft and canoe float trips down the Priest River. This unit offers only primitive camping.

Indian Creek—This unit is located 11 miles north of Coolin on the east side of Priest Lake and is open year-round. Park headquarters are located here.

Lionhead—Located 23 miles north of Coolin on East Shore Road, the Lionhead Unit rests along the northern tip of Priest Lake. Located near the thoroughfare to Upper Priest Lake, Lionhead is a convenient departure point for boaters who wish to explore those pristine waters. Open from May 1 through Sept. 30, it was developed with tent camps in mind and offers a primitive camping experience.

Squaw Bay—Group camping for up to 50 people is available at this rustic, isolated retreat that has kitchen and shower facilities.

For more information and reservations, call 443-2200 or 443-2929 (Lionhead Unit); or Email: PRI@idpr.state.id.us.

North Idaho Streams

The Idaho Panhandle's two mountain stream fishing gems are the remote St. Joe River, southeast of Coeur d'Alene, and the North Fork of the Coeur d'Alene, east of the region's popular lake resort.

Upstream from the town of St. Maries at Avery, the St. Joe is a Wild and Scenic river filled with wild westslope cutthroat well worth the long drive into the wilderness.

Closer to civilization there are several other options for flyfishers who delve into moving waters in this corner of the state dominated by lakes.

SPOKANE RIVER

The Spokane River exits Coeur d'Alene Lake on the eastern edge of the popular resort town and flows northwest into Washington.

A notable fishery for large wild rainbow and brown trout is present in the lower river, but it offers limited fly fishing opportunities below Post Falls Dam. However, since rainbows do grow fast in the six-mile stretch between the dam and the state line, the effort rewards persistent anglers.

Drift boaters can put in at the Korvin Park Access, which can be reached by taking Interstate 90 west 3 miles past Post Falls to Exit 2 and turn south until you reach the river. The short, two-mile float ends at State Line Bridge.

Flows range from 20,000 to 25,000 cfs and most of the action is on nymphs and streamers, especially for the brown trout here. What dry fly fishing that is done usually is with caddis patterns.

There is a two-fish limit on trout in the river from the Idaho-Washington state line, upstream to Post Falls Dam. From the dam upstream to Coeur d'Alene Lake the river is open all year and cutthroat are catch and release. There is a six-fish limit for other trout.

KOOTENAI RIVER

The Kootenai River originates in British Columbia, flows south and west through Montana and then northwest into Idaho before returning to British Columbia, flowing through Kootenay Lake and eventually into the Columbia River.

In Montana it is a great trout stream, attracting floaters from around the country. But when it reaches into Idaho it begins to widen and slow down. The only stretch marginally of interest to fly fishers is the 19-mile stretch along U.S. 2 from the Montana border. The river flows through a canyon here dropping about three feet per mile.

Inland redband rainbow trout are native to the Kootenai River drainage and are present in the mainstem Kootenai and above barriers in some tributaries. Hatchery rainbow trout have been widely introduced throughout the drainage. Other native salmonids include westslope cutthroat trout, bull trout, and mountain whitefish. Introduced eastern brook trout are present throughout the drainage, and a few remnant early spawning kokanee salmon from Kootenay Lake, British Columbia, are present in the mainstem Kootenai River and some west side tributaries during the summer and fall. Kokanee salmon also enter the river from Montana's Libby Reservoir during some years.

The Kootenai River is the only drainage in Idaho where burbot, also called freshwater ling, are native. It is also home to the white sturgeon. Fisheries for both of these species have been closed in response to major declines in these populations. The Kootenai River white sturgeon was listed as an endangered species in 1994.

Numerous tributaries drain the Selkirk and Purcell mountain ranges and enter the Kootenai directly or through larger tributaries. Due to past glaciation, most of the tributaries are blocked by falls near their mouths, and recruitment of fish from tributaries is limited.

Selkirk Mountains contain numerous alpine lakes west of Bonner's Ferry. The primary trailheads leave the Pack River Road (Forest Road 231) to the south and a series of forest roads running north out of Naples. The Pack River Road junction with U.S. Highways 2 and 95, 17 miles north of Sandpoint, just past Samuel.

The lakes are stocked with trout fry on a rotating basis. Westslope cutthroat, Kamloops rainbow and brook trout are found in most lakes. A few have grayling and golden trout.

The trout limit on the Kootenai River is six, no rainbow or cutthroat trout under 16 inches.

MOYIE RIVER

The best fly fishing opportunities in Idaho's extreme northeast corner lie on the Moyie River, the major tributary of the Kootenai River.

It originates at Moyie Lake in British Columbia and flows 58 miles through Canada before entering Idaho. Its 26 miles in Idaho are marked by fast whitewater rapids and pocket waters in its lower sections.

The 17 miles of river above Meadow Creek has a relatively flat gradient with relatively few pools and virtually no tributary streams to provide wild trout production. This section is also roaded and the fishery is supported by stocking put-and-take rainbow trout. There is a two-trout limit.

Bank access on this stretch is limited, but it is a pleasant canoe float down to Meadow Creek Bridge. From the bridge to Meadow Creek Campground there are several Class II rapids.

The river gradient below Meadow Creek is much steeper, providing much better trout habitat. This eight-mile river section is mostly unroaded, and Deer and Meadow creeks provide enough wild trout production to maintain a trout fishery without stocking. The river also contains westslope cutthroat and a small population of eastern brook trout. There is a two-fish limit on the Moyie.

The best site to enter the river's lower pocket waters is at the campground. Downstream, the road climbs high from the river and hike-ins down steep slopes is strenuous.

An 80-foot waterfall and dam near its mouth isolates Moyie's fish population from the Kootenai.

To get to the river take U.S. 2 east from Bonner's Ferry to Moyie Springs and turn north on the Moyie River road. The first five miles or so is a very steep climb and not recommended for vehicles towing trailers.

The top end of the river is reached by U.S. 95 at the Canadian border.

KOOTENAI NATIONAL WILDLIFE REFUGE

The Kootenai National Wildlife Refuge, five miles west of Bonners Ferry, offers another easily accessed stream opportunity for Panhandle anglers.

A small population of trout lives in Myrtle Creek, including rainbow, eastern brook trout and westslope cutthroat. A small run of kokanee salmon spawns in the creek each fall.

Only Myrtle Creek is open to fishing where primarily trout are caught. Boats, float-tubes, or other flotation devices are not permitted in Myrtle Creek. Open dates and bag limits are concurrent with the state's general fishing season.

All anglers 14 years of age and older must have a state fishing license.

To reach the refuge from Bonners Ferry, take the dike road on the south bank of the Kootenai River westward for five miles to the refuge.

For further information, call 267-3888.

If you get up on the romanticism of fishing, you'll love the Joe. It's the definitive pocket water dry fly stream.

Joe Roope, Coeur d'Alene guide and fly shop owner

St. Joe River

Rediscovered wild trout haven

When most Idahoans think about the St. Joe River, visions of lumberjacks, cant hooks, and log drives come to mind.

Rafts of logs towed by tugs boats are still a common sight on this big-shouldered river below St. Maries, a timber town that still doesn't take well to tourists. The St. Joe has a rich fly fishing history but there was a time when more logs floated down the St. Joe than dry flies. The construction of a paved road for most of its length opened it up to heavy fishing pressure in the 1960s. There might have been more logs in the river than cutthroats in the 1970s.

Not today. The St. Joe has turned into one of the finest cutthroat fisheries in a state loaded with good cutthroat waters. Despite its easy access, fishing pressure is still low on large portions of the river. Only in the walking-and-wading upper stretch has the St. Joe gained proper respect as a fly fishing destination. With respect comes reputation and with reputation comes numbers. No longer is the St. Joe undiscovered.

Casting on the Joe.

The St. Joe flows out of the Bitterroot Mountains on the Montana border into Lake Coeur d'Alene 140 miles northwest. It starts as only a trickle at nearly 10,000 feet and grows into a wide, navigable river by the time in enters the lake. The first 26 miles to the Spruce Tree Campground are protected under the Wild and Scenic Rivers Act as a Wild River. The 39-mile stretch from Spruce Tree to the North Fork of the St. Joe is designated as a National Recreation River under the act. Much of this stretch is popular among kayakers and rafters. It does not lend itself to fly fishing floating except in the lower end near Avery and even here there are dangerous rapids that require scouting. Most of the fly fishing pressure is concentrated in the 15-mile-stretch from Gold Creek southeast to just beyond Spruce Tree Campground.

The resurgence of the St. Joe has been relatively recent. The Idaho Department of Fish and Game designated the upper 50 miles of the St. Joe above Prospector Creek as catch and release in 1989.

Even though the cutthroat grow relatively slow here, they responded well to the special regulations. Where Fish and Game snorkelers found only four or five cutthroats in transect sites in the 1970s, they were finding 50 in the early 1990s. In the 1970s fewer than five percent of the cutthroat were 13 inches or larger. Today, 30 percent exceed 12 inches, said Ned Horner, Idaho Department of Fish and Game biologist in Coeur d'Alene. Joel Hunt, a researcher from the University of Idaho, estimated there were 7,100 cutthroat in a 35-mile stretch of the catch-and-release section in 1990. One particularly dense stretch sported 700 fish per mile. Hunt found nearly twice as many cutthroats per mile than in nearby and much more famous Kelly Creek. Even below Prospector Creek in the catch-and-keep section of the river, Hunt estimated 4,400 cutthroats in a 37-mile stretch.

And the count goes on.

Despite recent heavy flood events, which can significantly reduce cutthroat numbers, the St. Joe population remains strong and able to support a quality fishing experience. More restrictive regulations, mild winters, and habitat improvements have contributed to higher fish densities.

In 2008, catch-and-release fishing for cutthroat was applied to the entire Coeur d'Alene and St. Joe drainages. Although the population can withstand some level of harvest, it would come at the expense of catch-rates and the number of quality-size fish in the population.

The 2008 survey of the St. Joe River counted a total of 1,127 cutthroat trout, 9 rainbow trout and 1,333 mountain whitefish. Cutthroat trout were observed in all transects and were the most abundant trout species.

Densities of cutthroat trout (all size classes) at these transects ranged from 0.00 to 6.09 fish per 100 square meters with an overall average of 1.02 fish per 100 square meters. About 24 percent of the cutthroat trout observed were estimated to be 12 inches in length and their overall density was calculated to be 0.25 fish per 100 square meters.

St. Joe's cutthroat leave the lower river in the early spring as water temperatures rise to spawn upstream and in its tributaries. Most of the fish remain in the upper stretch through the summer. They begin to school in September and migrate from the upper river into the deep pools of the lower river. Fish and Game extends the catch-and-release regulations river-wide in early September to protect them.

For anglers, the season on the St. Joe doesn't really get going until July, after the relatively long runoff ends. It peaks in late July and August, then tapers off in the upper sections as the cutthroat migrate downstream. Then the lower sections get hot and provide excellent late-season action.

The stretch from Gold Creek east is classic pocket water, with a few deep holes thrown in for good measure. The best way to fish it is to walk upstream and work down, fishing a riffle or pool until the fish are reasonably well-educated.

The best time to arrive is early morning before the sun rises high and into the canyon. Fishermen of all ages and ability can catch cutthroat all day long. But the larger fish—15 to 20 inches—are harder to find after 9 a.m. and before 3 p.m.

Below Gold Creek, the canyon narrows and the river picks up, whipping itself into a whitewater swirl that kayakers love. The roughest rapids on the entire river are in the seven-mile section to Bluff Creek Bridge and with the heavy rapids come deep holes. From Bluff Creek to Turner Flats Campground, the river flows through a series of mild rapids that experienced canoers can run. The catch-and-release section ends at Prospector Creek only a couple miles down from Bluff. There are good holes and riffles throughout this stretch. Just below Turner lies Skookum Canyon, a violent series of rapids no one but the most expert kayaker or rafter should attempt.

The 38-mile stretch from Packsaddle Campground through Avery is a good canoe float, with good fishing all along the route. Below Avery, the river becomes navigable by drift-boat. As the river widens and slows, the bass fishing picks up and eventually takes over.

The upper river has a small population of bull trout that must be released. There also are brook trout in the system, which is one of the reasons the bull trout numbers are low. When these two similar char species occur together, they interbreed and destroy the genetic base of the native bulls.

Effective patterns for the St. Joe River

Cutthroat here will take just about any dry fly. Renegades, hoppers, humpies, Adams, elk hair caddis, stimulators, and Royal Wulffs are among the most popular. The St. Joe cutthroat fishery has always had its fans as demonstrated by the development of two excellent flies that bear its name. The St. Joe Favorite has a green wool body, golden pheasant-tip tail, grizzly hackle, and gray mallard wings. The St. Joe Special has an orange body, the same tail, and grizzly hackle wings. Both are deadly on cutthroat, but not readily available. Ask the fly tiers at Joe Roope's Castaway Fly Fishing Shops in Coeur d'Alene to tie up a few specials the day you arrive so they will be ready for your trip. Nymphs, such as the prince and hare's ear also work well.

Getting to the St. Joe is not hard, but take along provisions because there are few services in this part of northern Idaho. From Coeur d'Alene, take Interstate 90 east to Highway 3 Turn south and drive to St. Maries. Turn left on the St. Joe River Road, which follows the river east for 100 miles through Avery to Gold Creek. The road is paved to Avery with an oiled gravel road running to the Red Ives Ranger Station. From there, a Forest Service Road goes to Spruce Tree Campground. A second route from Coeur d'Alene is to drive to Wallace on the Interstate and turn south on Placer Creek Road.

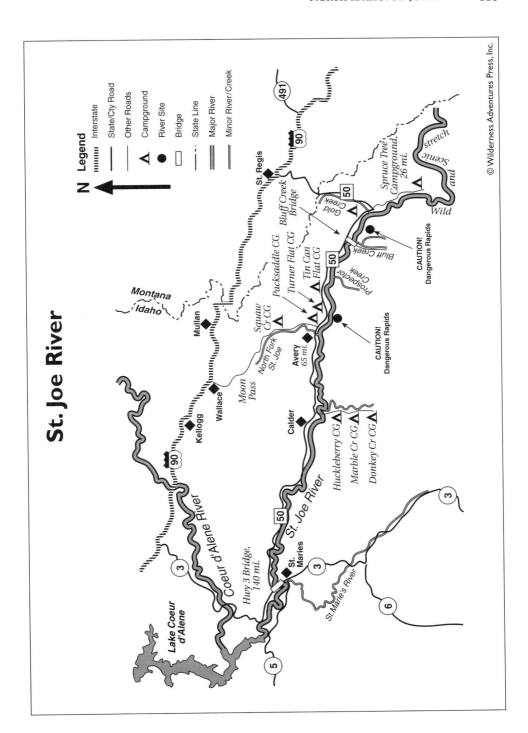

St. Joe River

Follow it as it turns into Moon Pass Road all the way to the North Fork of the St. Joe. Take the North Fork Road to Avery.

The other two routes, through Montana, are particularly convenient for getting to the upper stretches. Both leave Interstate 90 as exits that say "fishing access." One is located just west of St. Regis, MT. The second is just east of Lookout Pass on the border. Idaho fishing licenses can be purchased in St. Regis, Superior or Missoula before leaving Montana.

The St. Joe has many excellent campgrounds along the river but few accommodations. The St. Joe Lodge is located west of Avery. However, the best way to experience the river is at the St. Joe Hunting and Fishing Camp on the river's extreme upper stretch. The camp can only be reached by foot or horseback via the trail at the Spruce Tree Campground.

Stream Facts: St. Joe River

SEASON
- Memorial Day weekend through Nov. 30 above the town of St. Maries

SPECIAL REGULATIONS
- St. Joe and all tributaries upstream to Avery, two-cutthroat limit, none between 8" and 16"; 2 chinook in lower river and tributaries
- St. Joe at Avery and upstream, including all tributaries except mountain lakes, all cutthroat catch-and-release

FISH
- Cutthroats up to 20 inches, rainbow trout, brook trout, bull trout

RIVER MILES
- Mile 26, Spruce Tree Campground
- Mile 41, Gold Creek
- Mile 50, Prospector Creek
- Mile 65, North Fork of the St. Joe
- Mile 66, Avery
- Mile 140, Coeur d'Alene Lake

FLOWS
- Peaks at more than 3000 cubic feet per second in whitewater stretches and drops to as low as 500 cfs

BOAT RAMPS
- Heller Creek
- Spruce Tree Campground
- Conrad Crossing Campground
- Bluff Creek Bridge
- Turner Flat
- Packsaddle Campground
- Avery
- Calder

The North Fork is puzzling. It has genetically bigger fish than the St. Joe but it's in horrible disarray in terms of habitat.

Joe Roope, Coeur d'Alene guide

North Fork of the Coeur d'Alene

Bruised but not beaten

Once the Coeur d'Alene was considered among the finest trout streams in North America. That was long ago before some of the most destructive industrial activities known to man battered and crippled this once great fishery.

Yet despite overwhelming habitat destruction, portions of the Coeur d'Alene present at least a glimmer of its former brilliance. Nowhere is this more obvious and more surprising than in the North Fork of the Coeur d'Alene, a rising star in Idaho's fly fishing universe.

Like much of the drainage, the North Fork has suffered from stream channelization, sedimentation, pollution, and just downright poor management. Early loggers built splash dams to raise the water levels of many of the North Fork's tributaries so they could float them downstream. The logs would be piled behind the dams until the water level was high enough, then the dam would be busted, sending water and logs to scour out the river bed. Placer miners simply dug up the gravels of the river to sift out the gold and silver.

Heavy clearcuts and fires increased the spring runoff contributing to the streambed destruction. Later poorly built roads prevented the river channel from meandering naturally. Fish and Game officials added insult to injury in the 1960s by removing large logs and brush that helped hold the gravels and rocks upstream and contributed to the pool and riffle complexity.

"Right now we have such simplified channels that when we get high water we get massive movement of material downstream," says Ed Lider, a Forest Service fisheries biologist in Wallace.

In 2008 transect surveys, biologists counted a total of 1,413 cutthroat trout, 232 rainbow trout, 5 brook trout and 3,685 mountain whitefish in the North Fork Coeur d'Alene River system. Cutthroat trout were observed in 40 of the 43 transects snorkeled. Densities of cutthroat trout (all size classes) in these transects ranged from 0.00 to 7.86 fish per 100 square meters with an overall average of 0.84 fish per 100 square meters. About 21 percent of the cutthroat trout observed were estimated to be 12 inches in length and their overall density was calculated to be 0.17 fish per 100 square meters.

As in the St. Joe, the overall, cutthroat densities in the North Fork Coeur d'Alene River system are on the increase. The last two survey years have been the highest densities of cutthroat recorded since the surveys began in 1973.

Despite the high water events experienced in the N.F. Coeur d'Alene River system in the spring of 2008, cutthroat densities have remained strong. Past favorable weather patterns, restrictive fishing regulations, and vast habitat improvements may help explain why this increase occurred. A series of mild winters (1998-2005) and a lack of flood events may have increased survival of the larger adult fish.

In fact, aside from 2008, the warmest winters on record in Kellogg have occurred over the last several years (1998-2006). Future surveys will indicate whether this increase in the number of large cutthroat trout is a temporary or long-term trend and how average or below average winter temperatures and flood events will effect cutthroat trout densities.

No cutthroat harvest is allowed in the Coeur d'Alene drainages. The sections above Yellow Dog Creek (North Fork) and Laverne (Little North Fork) are no bait, barbless hook, catch-and-release waters.

Fishermen don't take as many larger cutthroat—those larger than 18 inches—as they do in the St. Joe. Still, the Coeur d'Alene's strain of westslope cutthroat genetically grow faster than the St Joe's—a 10.8-inch average for a four-year-old on the Coeur d'Alene to 768 inches for a four-year-old on the St. Joe. Most of the fish caught run in the 10- to 14-inch class.

The Forest Service, with the support of the timber industry, has embarked on an ambitious habitat restoration plan on the North Fork, actually sticking large logs back into the river bed in an attempt to improve trout habitat. If this effort is even moderately successful, look for the North Fork of the Coeur d'Alene to steadily improve in the coming years.

Fly fishers concentrate their efforts on the 30-mile upper stretch of the North Fork above Yellow Dog Creek. They don't just limit themselves to the main river, though. Tributaries like Jordan Creek and Tepee Creek offer similar pocket water pleasures protected by the catch-and-release regulations. In all, more than 200 miles of river and tributaries, including the Little North Fork above Laverne Creek, offer wild cutthroat fisheries. However, the best fishing lies in the Upper North Fork as far away from the road as a fisherman is willing to walk.

One place of special note is the mile stretch of river just above Yellow Dog Creek where Trout Unlimited members, the U.S. Forest Service, and Idaho Department of Fish and Game staff placed structures in the stream and rehabilitated the streambanks.

Fish numbers drop off dramatically below Yellow Dog as the river grows into a series of rapids and long deep pools. Here you are allowed to take one cutthroat larger than 14 inches. There are also rainbow and brook trout in this area. This 12-mile stretch south to Shoshone Creek can be good seasonally. Years of high flows and cool weather seem to keep more cutthroats in the lower river.

From Shoshone Creek down the river flattens out and offers floaters some opportunity. But few local fly fishers waste their time in this section, preferring to float the Clark's Fork River. Seasonally, kokanee and even chinook salmon that swim out of Coeur d'Alene Lake can be found in the lower river.

Like many of the westslope cutthroat rivers, the fish in the upper North Fork and its tributaries assemble in schools in September and move downstream into the catch-and-keep areas where there are deep holes for winter survival. The state stops all harvest in early September.

The North Fork can be reached easiest by driving 35 miles east from Coeur d'Alene on Interstate 90 to the Kingston exit. Take Forest Highway 9 north along the river to Forest Road 208. Turn north past Prichard and follow 208 into the upper stretches.

From the east, take Interstate 90 to Wallace and head north on Forest Road 456 It joins with Forest Road 208 about 22 miles north of Wallace.

A whole network of forest roads take you to the various tributaries. The Forest Service has obliterated more than 35 miles of road in the drainage already so make sure you get an up-to-date map if you plan to explore.

There are two National Forest campgrounds just south of Yellow Dog and another north of there near Miner's Creek. Much of the forest lends itself to rustic camping.

LITTLE NORTH FORK COEUR D'ALENE RIVER

The Little North Fork Coeur d'Alene River is one of the most remote rivers in the Panhandle Region. It provides an important fishery for westslope cutthroat trout and valuable habitat for an increasing bull trout population.

The Little North Fork is special to many people looking for quality trout fishing and solitude. Road access to the it is limited to the upper portion, with over 15 miles of the river accessible only by trail and another 15 miles of the river without trail access at all.

Unlike the St. Joe and Coeur d'Alene rivers, which have been surveyed every year since the 1970s the Little North Fork surveys didn't begin until 1997. Because of the relatively low angler use and difficulty of access we generally survey the it every three years.

Fish and Game biologists snorkeled 48 transects in the river in 2009. A total of 513 cutthroat trout, 153 rainbow trout, and 406 mountain whitefish were counted. Fourteen bull trout were also observed. Cutthroat trout were observed in all of the 48 transects. Densities of cutthroat trout (all size classes) ranged from 0.16 to 14.7 fish per 100 square meters with an overall average of 1.66 fish per 100 square meters. About 24 percent of the cutthroat trout observed were estimated to be 12 inches in length and their overall density was 0.39 fish per 100 square meters. Cutthroat densities were very similar to 2002 and 2005, but about four times higher than 1997.

Based on snorkeling surveys, the population did not appear to be overfished.

Since 2008, cutthroat have been protected by catch-and-release restrictions.

North Fork of the Coeur d'Alene

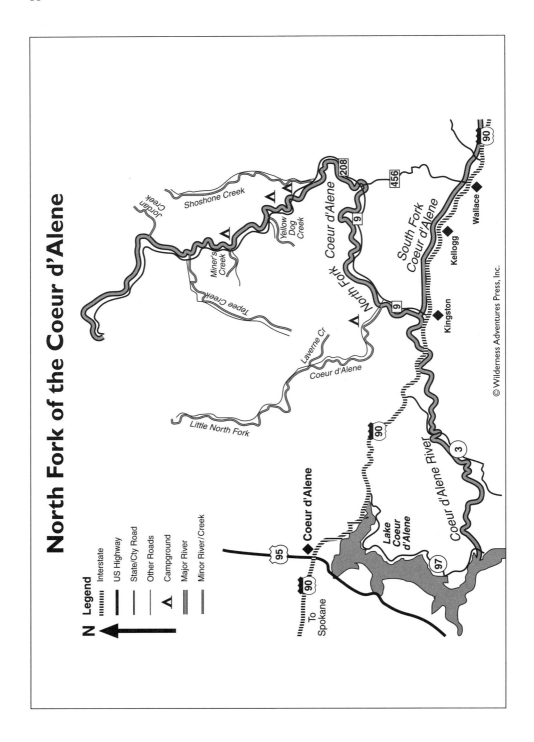

Legend

N

- Interstate
- US Highway
- State/Cty Road
- Other Roads
- Campground
- Major River
- Minor River/Creek

© Wilderness Adventures Press, Inc.

Stream Facts: North Fork of the Coeur d'Alene

SEASON
- Entire drainage upstream from and including Yellow Dog Creek, open year-round.
- Little North Fork, entire drainage upstream from and including Laverne Creek, open year-round.

SPECIAL REGULATIONS
- From the mouth upstream to Laverne Creek: Trout limit is 6, no harvest of any trout with a red or orange slash below jaw
- From and including Laverne Creek upstream: Trout limit is 6, no harvest of any trout with a red or orange slash below jaw; no bait allowed, barbless hooks required

FISH
- Westslope cutthroat up to 20", rainbows, brook trout, bull trout

RIVER MILES
- Mile 30, Yellow Dog Creek
- Mile 42, Shoshone Creek
- Mile 80, Little North Fork
- Mile 90, confluence with South Fork

RIVER CHARACTERISTICS
- Upper river, classic pocket water with pools and small riffles. Below Yellow Dog, it turns into deeper pools and larger rapids. Flattens below Shoshone Creek

FLOWS
- Peaks at more than 2000 cubic feet per second and drops to as low as 200 cfs

MAPS
- Panhandle National Forest
- *Idaho's Best Fishing Waters* mapbook, by Wilderness Adventures Press

Idaho Game Fish

CUTTHROAT TROUT: NATIVE SONS OF THE WEST

The favorite trout of dry fly purists and Idaho's state fish, the cutthroat rises lustily to fur-and-feather imitations and gladdens the hearts of novice and expert fly fishers alike.

Cutthroat usually fight stubbornly underwater and use stream flows to their advantage, sometimes even rolling with the current and twisting the line around themselves. But it is often a short-lived fight if your terminal tackle is not too delicate and you are not forced to prolong it.

The Yellowstone cutthroat is the native trout of eastern Idaho's Snake River drainage above Shoshone Falls. The westslope cutthroat is native to the Salmon River drainage and other major rivers north of the Salmon. Two other subspecies found only in eastern Idaho are the Snake River finespotted cutthroat and the Bonneville cutthroat.

A status review under the Endangered Species Act has been requested for the Bonneville cutthroat, which is known to occur only in the Thomas Fork drainage of Bear River and in Bear Lake in the southeast corner of the state. It also occurs in central and western Utah.

All other species of Idaho cutthroat are considered at risk. They are listed as Species of Special Concern because of their sensitivity to habitat changes.

Until other species were introduced in the late-1800s, the cutthroat was the only trout in much of the vast interior of the West, from the western slopes of the Sierras in California, up through Utah, Idaho, and Montana, and south to northern Mexico. The rainbow, the other native trout of the West, was historically a Pacific slope fish.

Originally, the cutthroat and rainbow were considered to be descendants of the Atlantic salmon, *Salmo salar*. Taxonomy specialists agreed in 1990 that western trout are more closely related to the Pacific salmon. Descendants of this genus are described as *Oncorhynchus*, which means "hooked snout."

Ironically, the taxonomists only recently caught up with the 1804-1806 Corps of Discovery. Meriwether Lewis first recorded the cutthroat for science in 1805 in western Montana. The men of the Lewis and Clark Expedition and later mountain men referred to the fish as the "trout salmon" because of its rich, orange flesh. The Yellowstone or interior cutthroat is now known by biologists as *Oncorhynchus clarki bouvieri*. The westslope cutthroat's scientific name, *Oncorhynchus clarki lewisi*, honors both captains sent west by President Jefferson to discover a route to the Pacific Ocean.

The Yellowstone cutthroat is a beautiful fish, with rouge-colored gill plates, a rose wash running across its golden flanks, and fins tinted with a translucent salmon-orange. Hundreds of round, black spots are sprinkled across it back, with somewhat larger and more heavily concentrated spots on its tail. Its name, and fame, comes from the bright orange-red slashes under its jaws. It is the ancestral parent stock of all the many interior subspecies that evolved in the Intermountain West.

It is evident the Yellowstone cutthroat once had a much broader historical range. Its taxonomic placement is based on the scientific species description made by a U.S. Army officer in 1882 from fish taken from Waha Lake, a now isolated basin north of Lewiston. After Shoshone Falls formed a barrier in the Snake River 50,000 years ago, the rainbow apparently replaced Yellowstone cutthroat in the lower Snake drainage.

The westslope cutthroat is native to a huge historical range that once included the entire upper Missouri River drainage in Montana and extended into Alberta and British Columbia, and a few rivers or lakes in Oregon and Washington.

As an environmental barometer of the mountains, the cutthroat is like the canary in the mine—it is the first species to be eliminated. Most of the 15 subspecies of this vulnerable, colorful fish are now largely restricted to the uppermost, coldest, headwater tributaries. A few that adapted to lower, warmer water conditions of Utah and Nevada's Basin and Range alkaline lakes and streams are largely gone or only shadows of their former glory.

Stronghold of the cutthroat is Yellowstone National Park, where the Yellowstone or interior cutthroat reigns supreme. This species spilled over into the Snake River drainage when Yellowstone Lake emptied into the Snake during one of Yellowstone's glacial periods. It's the fish that's making eastern Idaho's South Fork of the Snake famous.

The South Fork also contains Snake River finespotted cutthroat, a subspecies little studied by biologists. Its spotting pattern is heavier, and composed of much smaller spots than the Yellowstone species. It is unique in its ability to co-exist with its ancestral parent species in the Jackson Hole stretch of the Snake River in western Wyoming, where it is the predominant trout.

The finespotted cutthroat is stocked in Palisades Reservoir from the Jackson hatchery brood stock. Some biologists maintain it is present in the South Fork because it has been flushed through the dam. In the South Fork, though, the finespotted is a wild fish and there is evidence it is interbreeding with Yellowstone cutthroat. Spotting patterns of South Fork cutthroat vary from large-spotted to finespotted, with gradations in between.

Healthy cutthroat populations in the South Fork and Henry's Lake and their presence in eastern Idaho's other fine cutthroat streams like the Teton, upper Fall, Blackfoot, and lower Henry's Fork rivers are largely the success of special regulations to restrict harvest.

Studies show the cutthroat can be easily overexploited by anglers. Even with light fishing pressure, up to half the legal-sized cutthroat in a stream are often caught. But Idaho State University studies in Yellowstone show the fish are amazingly hearty. Cutthroat on the upper Yellowstone are caught and released an average of nine times during the river's short fishing season from mid-July to mid-October.

For this reason, the fish responds well to special regulations, such as size or bag limits, or catch-and-release restrictions. In Idaho, cutthroat populations have increased six to 13 times after special regulations were imposed. Yellowstone Park has experienced similar trends.

Steps taken in the mid-1980s to protect the cutthroat population on the South Fork of the Snake is Idaho's newest success story. The river's density of 3,000 adult fish per mile, 75 percent cutthroat, rivals the Yellowstone River's. The catch rate is as good or better.

The state learned its lesson in cutthroat preservation on Kelly Creek, a tributary of the North Fork of the Clearwater River in northern Idaho's Panhandle. Westslope cutthroat were all but eliminated in the drainage during the 1960s. In 1970, catch-and-release regulations were imposed in an attempt to save this vanishing species. The westslope cutthroat made a resounding comeback. Today, Kelly Creek is a classic, high-mountain native trout stream with a blue ribbon reputation.

Other strong pockets of westslope cutthroat are on Cayuse Creek and the upper Clearwater, Lochsa, Selway, St. Joe, St. Marie's, and Coeur d'Alene drainages. For the ultimate wilderness encounter with this native fish, float the Middle Fork of the Salmon River or hike in along one of its tributaries.

Unlike Idaho's sea-running steelhead, its cutthroat are a landlocked species. To test the anadromous species of this fine game fish, anglers have to go the coastal waters of the Pacific Northwest and British Columbia.

Idaho's cutthroat were imperiled through indiscriminate stocking of non-native species, particularly rainbow trout, and habitat loss—a story repeated throughout the West. While steps are being taken to eliminate or reduce hybridization, the threat may now be here forever. Attempts to make Henry's Lake cutthroat-rainbow hybrids sterile have been renewed by Idaho Fish and Game. Transplants of Yellowstone cutthroat are no longer made from Henry's Lake into key northern Idaho streams occupied by the westslope race.

The threat of hybridization and competition from other species is unfortunate. As the native trout that evolved in these waters, cutthroat grow at a better rate in a shorter period of time than their introduced brethren, including rainbow, brown, brook, and lake trout. Under wild trout management, cutthroat provide fish of remarkable size for the angler in all but the smallest streams. They have been known to live to 11 years of age, although six or seven is more common.

Cutthroat evolved to spawn on the spring floods common to the Northern Rockies. For this reason, a number of key tributaries with major spawning runs are off-limits to anglers during the earlier part of the fishing season, extending to late-summer on some creeks.

Spawning normally occurs in April or May; the same period rainbow spawn, which accounts for the threat of hybridization. The Yellowstone race of cutthroat spawn at three or four years of age. The westslope cutthroat is usually five when it first spawns.

The westslope cutthroat also differs from the Yellowstone race in its food choice. It primarily consumes insects and rarely feeds on other fish. This was probably an evolutionary adaptation to allow it to coexist with the predatory bull trout that shared the same waters. Fish form a sizable portion of the diet of larger Yellowstone-Snake River cutthroat, which also rely heavily on aquatic and terrestrial insects.

The effects of these feeding preferences are reflected in the size differences between westslope and Yellowstone-Snake River cutthroat.

Twelve to 15 inches is considered a good-sized westslope, although occasional larger fish occur. Maximum growth is about 3 pounds, but it rarely exceeds 2 pounds because of its non-piscivorous nature.

Twelve to 17 inches is the average size of Yellowstone-Snake River cutthroat, with some growing more than 20 inches. It often grows to 5 or 6 pounds, and in lakes may exceed 20 pounds. A Henry's Lake guide boasts of landing more than 35 fish over 28 inches in a season. Cutthroat-rainbow hybrids can top the 35-inch mark.

Idaho's record cutthroat—18 pounds, 15 ounces—was taken from Bear Lake in 1970. Its cutthroat-rainbow hybrid record, 24 pounds and 35.5 inches, was taken from Pend Oreille Lake in 1991.

Cutthroat are most active in water temperatures between 50 and 65 degrees Fahrenheit. They can be found in both fast and slack water, although they are less fond of exceptionally fast waters than rainbows. Like all trout, they take advantage of whatever structural protection a stream provides, from over-hanging, willow-lined banks to mid-stream boulders, logjams, stream bed depressions and deep pools at the base of riffles.

Never pass a logjam or a bank side feeding lane protected by an over-hanging tree without working it closely. Riffles also are prime feeding grounds of cutthroat and provide prodigious action, especially at the lip of a deep pool.

The cutthroat's reputation for eagerly rising to a dry fly remains paramount in most fly fishers' minds. Larger cutthroat will hit a stonefly or hopper pattern with slashing strikes rivaling the ferocity of rainbows or browns. Casting to the feeding frenzy on the lip of a riffle during a heavy caddis or mayfly hatch can bring a host of fish between 8 and 20 inches to the net. At the same time, a hit during selective, sipping rises to tiny mayflies will startle the angler who hooks a lunker lurking beneath the still waters.

A standard set of dry flies to attract cutthroat should include elk hair caddis, stimulators, yellow sallies, humpies, Adams, pale mourning dun, blue-winged olive, light Cahill and parachute hare's ear. Nymph and emerger patterns for each of these can be equally effective, especially on riffles. Effective sizes for both dry and wet caddis and mayfly patterns can range from No. 10 to 16 in spring and early summer. By late fall, you may have to go as small as No. 18 and 22.

When all else fails, or on big or heavy waters, you can always fall back on standard attractor flies like the renegade, royal Wulff, royal coachman, royal Trude, Goddard caddis, or irresistible.

Cutthroat also succumb to the usual assortment of small streamers, muddlers, weighted nymphs, woolly buggers, super renegades and rubber-legged patterns. Sizes No. 8 to 14 generally work best.

Cutthroat can be the least shy of the trout family. Occasionally, you can get amazingly close to feeding fish. On some streams, they may even be right underfoot, feeding on nymphs your boots stir up from the gravel.

But never underestimate the cutthroat. It is not a brown trout with a lobotomy, as some would disparage this remarkable fish. It can be easy to catch and it can be exactingly selective as it keys in on a specific mayfly or caddis hatch with the resolute intensity of one of its so-called educated brethren.

Either way, cutthroat are a joy to catch and behold.

CUTTHROAT TROUT IDENTIFICATION

Yellowstone cutthroat trout *(Oncorhynchus clarki bouvieri)*

The body coloration on the back ranges from silver-gray to olive-green, with yellow-brown flanks, orange-tinted fins, and reddish gill-plates. The large round spots on the body are more closely grouped toward the tail, which is slightly forked. The spotting is less dense than on a rainbow, particularly at the tail. The pale-crimson wash along the flanks is often bright-red during spawning. Cutthroat-rainbow hybrids display most of the rainbow's coloration and spotting, and the throat slashes are light-orange to almost indistinct. The Yellowstone cutthroat is the native trout of streams and tributaries of the Snake River above Shoshone Falls. This is the subspecies found in Henry's Lake, and it has been widely transplanted in Idaho and other states.

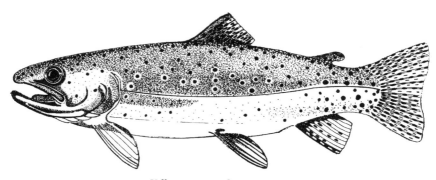

Yellowstone cutthroat trout

Westslope cutthroat trout (*Oncorhynchus clarki lewisi*)

The coloration of a westslope cutthroat is richer than a Yellowstone cutthroat's, with many small, irregularly shaped black spots across the back, concentrating on the tail and rarely extending below the midline. The westslope variety is generally steel-gray on the flanks with an olive back and a white belly. Gill-plates are dusky-red and a pale-crimson swath extends along the flanks. The belly may be bright red during spring spawning season. An oval parr mark is also seen along midline. Its native range in Idaho is the Salmon River drainage and the major river systems north of the Salmon River.

westslope cutthroat trout

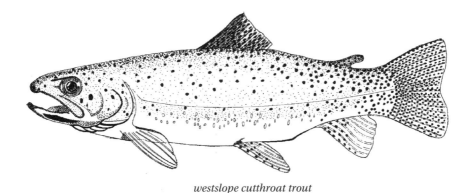

average length of a four-year-old cutthroat trout

River	Length
St. Joe River	7.68
Coeur d/Alene River	7.96
Middle Fork Salmon	8.52
Kelly Canyon	9.64
S. Fork Salmon	10.8
Snake River (Shelley, ID)	12.76
South Fork of the Snake	13.72
Teton River	15.12

Westslope cutthroat — Yellowstone cutthroat

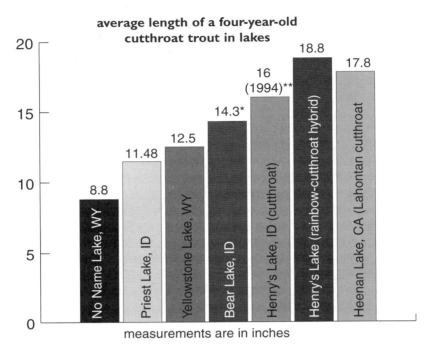

average length of a four-year-old cutthroat trout in lakes

measurements are in inches

* State record set in 1970; 18lbs, 15 oz
** 1950s = 20; 1977 = 18.6; 1986 = 17.2

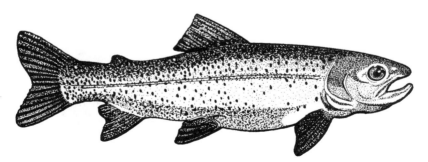

Snake River finespotted cutthroat trout

Snake River finespotted cutthroat trout
(Oncorhynchus clarki sp)
The Snake River finespotted is similar to the Yellowstone cutthroat in body conformation and coloration. Its profuse spotting pattern is more similar to coastal species than interior cutthroat. Its many small spots concentrate toward the tail and extend below midline. The tail and lower fins are sometimes darker orange. Found primarily in the upper Snake River in Jackson,Wyoming, and Palisades Reservoir in Idaho, finespotted cutthroat numbers are increasing in the South Fork of the Snake.

Bonneville cutthroat trout
(Oncorhynchus clarki utah)
The characteristics and coloration of the Bonneville are similar to Yellowstone cutthroat, but generally lighter and tending toward silvery white on belly. The black spots across the back and tail are larger, fewer, and more spaced out. Parr marks may be present along midline. Listed as a species of special concern by Idaho Fish and Game, the Bonneville cutthroat occurs only in the Thomas Fork drainage of Bear River and in Bear Lake in the southeast corner of state.

RAINBOW TROUT—MIGHTY LEAPER

Far and away the most exciting fighter of the trout family, the rainbow always pulls something from its bag of tricks, from cart-wheeling leaps to reel-sizzling runs to repeated dashes away from the net.

In waters containing other trout species, there's no doubt in an angler's mind when a rainbow is on the end of the line. A rainbow never hesitates in its frenzied quest for freedom. It often leaps more than once in its desperate panic to throw the hook. Even small fish offer a strong and agile fight. Large fish hooked on light tackle or a delicate leader tippet leave the angler only one—give the fish its head and hope the line is long enough for the first run. Your prayers won't always be answered, even on the second or third run. A rainbow rarely comes to the net willingly.

Anglers should use the heaviest terminal tackle conditions permit to make the fight as short as possible and not unduly tire out the fish. Use a good-sized, soft-meshed net so you aren't inclined to manhandle the fish as you attempt to land it.

The feisty rainbow's acrobatic leaps and speckled, multi-hued beauty—described once by a whimsical writer as "sheened like a Kang Shi porcelain vase" — make it one of the most popular game fishes in the world. A Native of coastal drainages of the north Pacific, it has been transplanted throughout North America, Europe, and South America.

It gets its name from the crimson to pinkish-red band along the midline of its flanks. This reddish band may be absent in lake dwellers, which are generally more silver in total appearance. It is marked across its head, back, and upper flanks with many small, irregular black spots that are concentrated the heaviest on its squarish tail.

The rainbow trout, *Oncorhynchus mykiss*, was reclassified as part of the western salmon genus, *Oncorhynchus*, in 1990. Its former classification was with the Atlantic salmon genus, *Salmo*. Its former species name, *gairdneri irideus*, was replaced with *mykiss* because the Japanese description of the rainbow preceded descriptions made in the western United States in early 1800s.

The redband rainbow was once thought to be common only to the desert water of southwestern Idaho. New studies show the redband may be the native species of central Idaho and north of the Salmon River drainage.

In Idaho, steelhead, the anadromous or sea-running form of this species, were originally native to the Snake River and its tributaries upstream to Shoshone Falls, near the town of Twin Falls. Dam construction for irrigation and hydropower production reduced that range to below Hell's Canyon Dam on the Snake River and the Salmon and Clearwater drainages. Steelhead numbers have fallen drastically in recent years, primarily from dam obstructions and habitat losses throughout the Columbia drainage. It may well join Idaho's Snake River salmon stocks on the endangered species list.

The Kamloops, a landlocked steelhead from British Columbia, was introduced in Pend Oreille Lake, Idaho's largest lake, in 1941. It flourished there, but other transplants elsewhere in the state experienced no better growth than other strains of rainbow. As early as the late 1880s, through fish cultural practices, these other rainbow strains have been widely distributed in Idaho in drainages outside the steelhead's native range. It does well under a wide range of temperatures in lakes, reservoirs, and streams. It's the fish that made the Henry's Fork of the Snake River in Island Park world-renown as a fly fishers' mecca.

The rainbow is also an important aqua culture species. Idaho is the largest commercial producer of trout in the United States. Most of the production occurs at Thousand Springs hatcheries on the Snake River.

A case can be made, however, that exploitation of the rainbow as a hatchery fish is overdone. Rainbows have been introduced in virtually every drainage in Idaho. Thus, on many reservoirs and smaller streams, the average rainbow taken by an angler is a hatchery-bred fish 8 to 12 inches in length. Its fins are ragged or deformed from rubbing against concrete hatchery raceways; its flesh pale and unsavory from its pellet-food diet.

But the modern trend toward wild fish management continues to gain acceptance in Idaho. It is exhibiting promising results. A number of Idaho streams where past rainbow plantings have taken hold are producing remarkable fish under wild trout, quality management, or trophy management policies. No new plantings are made in these waters. Under these policies, harvest is either strictly limited or catch-and-release only.

An eastern Idaho fishing lodge routinely extols in its newsletter the clients who win monthly big fish/catch-and-release contests netting rainbows in the 20- to 25-inch, 5- to 6-pound class in the Henry's and South Forks of the Snake and the Teton rivers. The bad news side of this glorification is that the South Fork and Teton are prime cutthroat trout waters, too. The aggressive rainbow often takes over streams it haunts. Hybrids of the two species are predominantly rainbow in characteristics.

It will take an act of Solomon on the part of Idaho Fish and Game to preserve the native cutthroat while fulfilling the desires of rainbow devotees. Still, it is basically playing a game of Russian roulette as it continues to plant "catchable" rainbows in the upper Teton and Willow Creek drainages and the headwaters of westslope cutthroat streams.

Shifting hatchery rainbow plantings away from wild trout populations to designated "put-and-take" streams and reservoirs is a policy of appeasement. It helps spread out angling pressure by offering enhanced opportunities to the general public for the waters "negated" by the stricter regulations on wild trout streams.

Discontinuing hatchery plants in restricted management streams is a biological decision, too. The disruptive, negative effects of hatchery rainbows on wild populations is well documented. It is a bit like dumping the cast from "West Side Story" into the serenity of a classical ballet.

Other southern Idaho waters rated by Idaho Fish and Game as significant wild rainbow fisheries include the upper Big Lost, Little Lost, Pahsimeroi, Big Wood, South Fork of the Boise, and upper Payette Rivers, as well as a number of spring creeks in the Silver Creek-Sun Valley and Thousand Springs-Hagerman areas. Public access on some of the latter may be difficult, except for Silver Creek.

In northern and central Idaho, significant wild rainbow streams include the Spokane, upper Kootenai and North Fork of the Clearwater Rivers, as well as the Snake from the Salmon River to Hell's Canyon Dam and the Salmon from the North Fork to the East Fork.

Generally, in streams where wild fish predominate or lakes and reservoirs with good holdover potential for hatchery fish, the average rainbow is 12 to 16 inches, with the potential in nutrient-rich waters for fish over 24 inches. In trophy lakes, a rare rainbow can reach 20 pounds. Landlocked monsters approaching this size take on the appearance of a potbellied pig, unlike the streamlined, typical rainbow characteristics that steelhead maintain by necessity.

Idaho's record fish are a 37-pound Kamloops from Pend Oreille Lake in 1947, a 19-pound rainbow from Hayden Lake the same year, and a 30-pound 2-ounce, 44-inch steelhead from the Clearwater River in 1973.

The rainbow is a spring spawner, like the cutthroat, which leads to hybridization when the species co-exist. The rainbow also reaches sexual maturity earlier, at ages two or three years. In hatcheries, they often spawn at one year of age. The life span of the rainbow is fairly short. Few live beyond five or six years of age.

Rainbow waters can be fast or slow, but chances are they will be found in faster moving and more turbulent waters than cutthroat or browns. Larger fish are found in the prime holding areas favored by all trout, like overhanging banks, obvious feeding lanes or sheer lines, in front of or behind mid-stream structures, or at the head of deep pools. While more active in morning or evening, they will move far up into a riffle even at high noon during a prime hatch, using the moving water as cover. Dark, cloudy days will set the fish on the prowl at any hour. The heaviest mayfly hatches regularly occur on these types of days, too.

The rainbow is most active in waters 45 to 75 degrees Fahrenheit. Peak activity is in waters around 60 degrees.

They are highly aggressive fish and will vigorously defend a feeding territory, especially against other salmonids of the same size.

Rainbows eat anything they can catch and swallow. All sizes of rainbows depend heavily on aquatic and terrestrial insects. Larger fish prey on smaller fish, too, and are known to take small mammals like mice or meadow voles. While opportunistic, larger rainbows tend to be very selective and key in on a particular food source, especially during a multi-hatch of mayflies or caddisflies. They also may concentrate on a particular stage of a hatch, keying on the nymph, emerger or adult flying form, or, later, the dead, spinner form. Lake dwellers tend to be more piscivorous.

The selective-feeding nature of large rainbows requires more patience and skill of a fly fisher. For those willing to be patient, it boils down to approach and presentation. Approach a feeding fish slowly and quietly to present a fly into its feeding lane. The key is a short-as-possible cast and a drag-free float through that lane. Most rainbows will not move to intercept a fly outside their feeding paths, so keep trying to put your fly right on the mark. Often, presentation is more critical than a perfect hatch match. If a fish shows an interest, present the fly again immediately. If your first choice doesn't work, rest the fish and try a different pattern. Above all, don't let your expectations cloud your appreciation of the challenge. A day on the stream is valuable, no matter how many fish you net.

Of course, all bets are off during major fly hatches, like the salmonfly or western green drake. These "Big Macs" of the aquatic insect world bring up trout of all sizes. Wariness is abandoned. This also applies during prime grasshopper activity.

The standard set of dry flies to attract rainbows is much the same as for cutthroat but, again, presentation is more of a factor. It should include elk hair caddis, stimulators, yellow sallies, humpies, Adams, pale morning dun, blue-winged olive, light Cahill, and parachute hare's ear. Nymph and emerger patterns for each of these can be equally effective, especially on riffles. Effective sizes for both dry and wet caddis and mayfly patterns can range from No. 10 to 16 in spring and early summer. By late fall, you may have to go as small as No. 18 and 22. Micro patterns of midges, callibaetis, and tricos also produce amazing results when that's the action on a particular stream, like Silver Creek and other spring creeks. Sometimes small terrestrial patterns, like ants and beetles, work best, even during an aquatic insect hatch.

Standard attractor flies like the renegade, royal Wulff, royal coachman, royal Trude, Goddard caddis, or irresistible work as well, particularly in faster waters.

Larger streamers, muddlers, weighted nymphs, woolly buggers, super renegades, and rubber-legged patterns can be very effective for rainbows. Waders fish them deep, dredging the bottom; float-boaters pound the banks. Leech, dragonfly nymphs, woolly bugger, and freshwater shrimp patterns are effective in lakes. Sizes can range from No. 2 to 14.

Most often a rainbow will hook itself. Just hang on when your fly scores.

REDBAND TROUT

Inland Columbia Basin redband trout
(Oncorhynchus mykiss gairdneri)

Recent expansion in knowledge about the inland redband trout marks it as a new species of special concern in Idaho and other states.

The rainbow trout species, *Oncorhynchus mykiss*, is now considered one of the most taxonomically complicated groups in the Pacific Northwest. The species probably consists of multiple subspecies, none of which have been formally recognized. The most recently published treatise on the species was by prominent fisheries biologist Robert Behnke in 1992, where three subspecies are proposed: *Oncorhynchus mykiss irideus*, or coastal rainbow and steelhead trout; *Oncorhynchus mykiss gairdneri*, or inland Columbia Basin redband and steelhead trout; and *Oncorhynchus mykiss newberrii*, or Oregon Basin redband trout.

The inland redband subspecies in Idaho was long recognized as uniquely adapted to streams with extreme water flow and temperature variations and high alkalinity in the high desert of southwest Idaho. Additional studies by taxonomists have concluded, however, that the native rainbow throughout nearly all of southwest and southcentral Idaho are redband trout.

Redband populations have remained genetically isolated in areas of extreme environmental conditions, where other rainbow trout strains, races, or subspecies have been unable to survive. And, like other native species, land management practices have threatened their status. Hybridization with other rainbow trout stocks has also diluted the remaining gene pool.

The redband trout is the only subspecies expected to survive in these types of environment and provide a viable fishery. Therefore, it has a higher value in its native environments and should receive management priority by the Idaho Department of Fish and Game, state and federal land management agencies.

The redband was petitioned in 1995 for listing under the Endangered Species Act. The U.S. Fish and Wildlife Service is in the process of addressing the petitions. The outcome will possibly direct future action.

RAINBOW TROUT IDENTIFICATION

Rainbow trout—nonmigratory
(Oncorhynchus mykiss)

The rainbow's common name comes from a broad swath of crimson to pinkish-red usually seen along the midline of its flanks. The reddish band may be absent in lake dwellers, which are generally more silver in appearance. River rainbow coloration ranges from olive to greenish-blue on back, with white to silvery belly. They are marked with many irregularly shaped black spots on the head, back, and tail that extend below the midline.

The rainbow was introduced to Idaho outside the steelhead's historic range.

STEELHEAD TROUT: ROCKETS FROM THE SEA

The steelhead, Idaho's native rainbow, is the anadromous form of this magnificent western trout. Like the salmon, it has migrated for eons to the Pacific Ocean and returned in a resolute, revolving cycle of life, death, and rebirth.

Until the 20th century, the Pacific Northwest's seafaring salmon and trout were impeded only by geological obstacles in the rivers and the power of voluminous currents cascading over stepping-stone waterfalls and rampaging through whitewater rapids. The region's natural predators and first people barely made a dent in the millions-upon-millions of steelhead and salmon coursing upstream in ancient spawning runs.

Today, many of the runs have been strangled to trickles by dams and further decimated by habitat loss, pollution, mismanagement, and continued harvest.

Hardest hit were Idaho's sockeye salmon. They were declared endangered in 1991, the year only five sockeye returned to Redfish Lake in the Stanley Basin, headwaters of the Salmon River.

Idaho banned sport fishing for wild chinook salmon in 1979, but the number of returning adults continued to plummet and fell to less than 21,000—two-thirds of them hatchery fish—by 1990. Snake River spring, summer, and fall chinook were listed as threatened in 1991. A very restricted fishing season for hatchery bred chinook, at Rapid River, occasionally occurs when there is a surplus after egg collection.

Some feel Idaho steelhead's status as a sport fish may be in equal jeopardy. The number of returning adults fell to less than 50,000 in the mid-1990s. The majority are hatchery-bred fish still available to anglers, with an average annual harvest of 30,000. Taking wild steelhead was banned in 1987, but by 1992 their numbers still fell to around 16,000. The runs continue to decline and in 1997 federal officials listed Snake River steelhead as a threatened species.

But before an Idaho angler can get a try at one, even hatchery steelhead have to relentlessly run a gauntlet of eight downstream dams to make it back to their natal waters. En route to their return to the Snake, Clearwater, and Salmon drainages, they also have

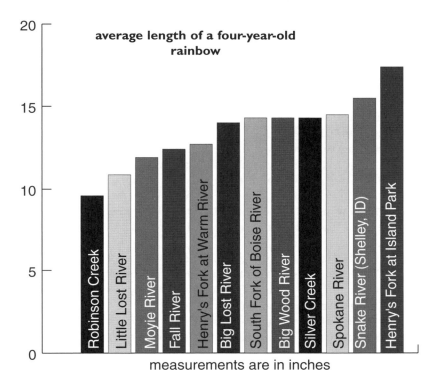

average length of a four-year-old rainbow

20 — 15 — 10 — 5 — 0

- Robinson Creek
- Little Lost River
- Moyie River
- Fall River
- Henry's Fork at Warm River
- Big Lost River
- South Fork of Boise River
- Big Wood River
- Silver Creek
- Spokane River
- Snake River (Shelley, ID)
- Henry's Fork at Island Park

measurements are in inches

rainbow trout

to escape deadly drift nets and purse seines at sea and gill nets straddling the Columbia River.

The length and breadth of the Idaho steelhead's peregrinations are extraordinary among this seafaring race.

Their perilous return journey covers 980 miles from the mouth of the Columbia to the Salmon River headwaters. The upstream swim from the Pacific to the upper Stanley Basin is a gain of more than 6,300 feet in elevation. Migrations to the Clearwater drainage above Lewiston and into the Snake River as far as Hell's Canyon Dam are equally staggering, with swims up to 700 miles.

In the Pacific, the steelhead's wanderings range from northern California to Alaska. A fish tagged at Adak Island in the Aleutian Islands was later caught in the Salmon River.

The evolutionary strategy behind these phenomenal migrations is a gamble that pays off in stupendous growth and spawning strength. Idaho produces some of the largest steelhead in the western United States. Thirty-pound summer steelhead have been taken from the Snake River. The state record was a 30-pound 2-ounce, 44-inch steelhead caught in the Clearwater River in 1973.

An angler needs a stout line and stout heart to bring one of these rockets from the sea to the net. The legendary strength of the rainbow pales by comparison to the energy and agility of its anadromous brother. The steelhead's ability to strip a line causes heart palpitations in even the most stoic of anglers.

Recent placement of the rainbow, steelhead, and cutthroat trout in the same genus as the western salmon, *Oncorhynchus,* is only just. All are unique to the Pacific Northwest, and the steelhead is the most salmon-like in its strength, endurance, and streamlined speed. The romance of its circular life cycle mirrors the salmon's.

Its former classification was with the Atlantic salmon, *Salmo salar.* For the rainbow and steelhead, the salar, or leaper, part still applies. In its prespawning adaptation, a male steelhead develops the longer, hooked jaw common to the five western salmon species. But the steelhead differs from Pacific salmon and mimics the Atlantic salmon in its ability to spawn more than once. This rarely occurs in Idaho's two strains of steelhead because of the arduous lengths of their journeys from the sea.

The historic native range of the steelhead extended from southern California coastal streams to the Kuskokwim River in southern Alaska. It also naturally occurs in Siberian streams. It has been transplanted to many waters around the world, including the Great Lakes and Atlantic Coast in the United States, but no true anadromous runs have developed outside the Pacific Coast.

In Idaho, the steelhead was originally native to the Snake River and its tributaries upstream to Shoshone Falls, near the town of Twin Falls. Dam construction for irrigation and hydropower production reduced that range to below Hell's Canyon Dam on the Snake River, the Salmon and its tributaries, and the Clearwater drainage.

Instate problems, such as habitat loss and degradation, have contributed somewhat to the decline in Idaho steelhead numbers. But the major cause has been migration obstructions encountered at the eight Columbia and lower Snake River dams. Bonneville, the first of four dams on the Columbia that Idaho fish must negotiate, was completed in 1938. Lower Granite, the last of four dams on the lower Snake just downstream from the port of Lewiston where the river leaves Idaho, was completed in 1975. Many biologists feel the four lower Snake dams were the coup de grace to Idaho salmon and steelhead runs.

Ultimately, the steelhead's fate rides on the shirttails of governmental policies and efforts to preserve endangered Snake River sockeye and chinook stocks. But political, economic, and engineering concerns continue to drive the preservation debate more than recognized biological solutions.

The steelhead is caught on the horns of the same dilemma snaring Idaho salmon. As many as 75 to 95 percent of the state's salmon and steelhead are lost as juveniles in their downstream migration to the sea. Both species need increased water flows to ensure greater smolt survival. Herculean efforts to capture and barge juvenile fish around the dams has had only marginal success. The debate over whether to increase water spills over the dams, draw down their reservoirs in spring, or find other methods of smolt survival is a political battle not likely to be resolved in this century.

Contrary to popular opinion, anadromous fish do not swim to the sea. They are washed downstream as they drift with the currents raised by spring thaws and rains.

After two years in their nursery waters, the spring floods and lengthening days induce young fish to migrate and begin the transformation into smolts. The amount of time it takes the smolts to reach the Columbia estuary and adapt to a saltwater environment is critical.

But the historical spring flush of smolts to sea was drastically slowed by the long slackwater pools behind the dams. A migration that once took 10 days or less may now take two months or more. These delays mean many of the juveniles die or arrive in the estuary too late, no longer smolts able to adjust to saltwater and go to sea. A part of the spring toll is exacted by predators, disease, and the dams' turbines.

Some concern has been raised about how many of the 6- to 8-inch smolts are being taken by anglers. They are still considered rainbow at that size. By legal definition, a steelhead is any rainbow over 20 inches in waters where they naturally occur. Future changes in fishing regulations may be imposed to protect smolts.

After one to three years in the Pacific, adult steelhead battle their way upstream through the gauntlet of dams. All of them have one or more fish ladders, but a number of adults can't find or are unable to ascend the ladders. An estimated 30 to 55 percent of the adults die at the dams on the return migration.

Idaho steelhead enter the Columbia in summer to reach the Snake, Clearwater, and lower Salmon by late summer or early fall. They overwinter and gather at their redds to spawn in spring.

The steelhead sport fishery for Idaho anglers is driven by hatchery production of a harvestable population, while stressing release and natural spawning of wild fish. Current practice is to take eggs from only a third of the wild steelhead trapped at hatchery weirs. The remainder are set free to spawn naturally to retain an essential genetic pool to pass on the necessary strength and endurance to future generations.

Hatchery steelhead are marked by the removal of their adipose fins. Steelhead with an adipose fin are wild and must be released.

By the time steelhead reach Idaho, they have lost the silvery sheen that helped protect them at sea. Their coloration and spotting pattern continue to darken as they approach spawning stage. Gill plates may be dusky-rouge and lateral red bands relatively pronounced.

A steelhead can be distinguished from a chinook by its white mouth and gum line. A chinook has a black mouth and gum line and its teeth are well developed. The chinook's tail is more streamlined, with a deep fork.

Sockeye salmon are smaller than both steelhead and chinook. The male develops a humped back and protruding hooked jaw as it approaches spawning stage. Its body turns bright red and the head becomes dark green. Female sockeye often retain a rosy, silvery sheen. While Idaho anglers are unlikely to hook a sockeye, spawning kokanee salmon are common in many streams. The kokanee is a landlocked version of the sockeye. Their characteristics are the same.

Idaho steelhead belong to two races. The A Group fish, averaging four to eight pounds, enter the Columbia earlier and can be found throughout the Clearwater and Salmon drainages. The range of the B Group steelhead, which average 12 to 20 pounds in size, is restricted primarily to the North and Middle Forks of the Clearwater and the South and Middle Forks of the Salmon. B-run steelhead are larger because the majority spend more than one year in the Pacific. Most A-run, but not all, return after one year at sea.

Catching one of these guys can be a bit like winning the lottery.

Depending on weather conditions affecting the runs, catch rates in recent years have been as brutal as one fish in 60 hours. At other times, a rate of one fish in 24 hours has been touted as good. But until it again approaches one in eight hours, no one is going to say the catch rate is decent.

The general season extends from September 1 to April 30, but specific starting dates and season lengths vary on the Clearwater, Salmon, and Snake rivers. Surplus hatchery steelhead also are planted in the Payette and Boise rivers, extending that season to May 31.

A steelhead permit is required in addition to an Idaho fishing license. The Nez Perce Tribe also offers its own permit for the stretch of the Clearwater flowing through its reservation east of Lewiston. Either a state or tribal permit can be used on the Clearwater within the reservation boundaries.

The Middle Fork of the Salmon and a few other key havens for wild fish are off-limits to steelhead fishing. Check for changes in regulations each season.

The key to steelhead fishing is to follow a run's progression upstream. Low water and hot weather can slow or stall the migration in some years.

Fish the waters where steelhead hang out. Unlike salmon, steelhead prefer shallower water. They hold in the tail of a deep pool or along the shallow waters of its sides. Those on the edges often are under some sort of structural cover. They can occasionally be found in whitewater, but generally prefer to hold in smooth flowing runs three- to six-feet deep. They take advantage of midstream obstructions, such as large boulders, by holding

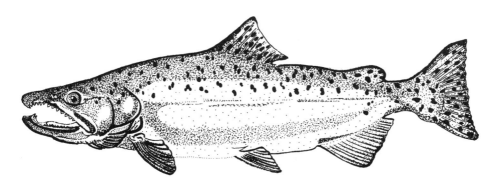

chinook salmon

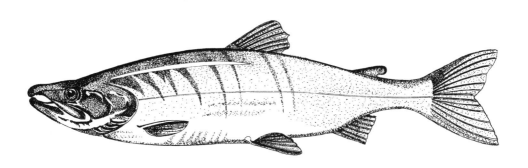

sockeye salmon

off to the sides or in front. In low, hot water conditions, they may move up into riffles to gain more oxygen and cover from the rippling waters.

After the winter layover, the renewal of the migration upstream speeds up when water temperatures reach 40 degrees Fahrenheit.

Always use tackle suitable to the task. A 9-foot, 7-weight fly rod is considered the minimum size. Going up to at least a 9½-foot rod and an 8- or 9-weight line is more realistic. Many fly fishers also prefer sinking-tip or shooting-head lines.

While bumper stickers declaring "Steelheaders Feel Bottoms Better" may seem to be the final statement on technique, steelhead do take dry flies.

Most western steelhead wet flies are generic affairs with weird names, such as the Rat-Faced McDougall. They range from brightly colored to black to a combination of the two. Usually, they are weighted and drifted just above the streambed. Weighting can be adjusted to float them in midwater or just under the surface.

Dry flies are heavily tied, buggy patterns, with flared wings or thick tails, usually made from undyed natural materials. A drag-free float is not a concern. In fact, a popular presentation is to skate them across the water.

Sparsely tied, thin-bodied streamer-like flies similar to those developed for the Atlantic salmon have evolved on Western waters. These flies vary in color choices but are generally more pragmatic than the elaborate patterns with exotic feathers traditionally used in the East or Europe.

Be sure to have a game plan. This is especially necessary for wading and bank anglers. The fish is going to run. You have to determine how far you can follow it, whether you have to cross the river to land it, or, regretfully, where you have to break off. Do this to be fair to the fish and to protect yourself.

On Idaho's extensive waters open to steelheaders, boat anglers have the advantage over waders. A boat is definitely needed to reach the upper sections of the Hell's Canyon on the Snake and to fish the wilderness section of the Salmon. Access for waders is found on the long, shallow stretches of the Clearwater, the lower entrance to Hell's Canyon, and the lower and upper stretches of the Salmon.

Good luck and tight lines!

STEELHEAD TROUT IDENTIFICATION

Steelhead trout-anadromous (Oncorhynchus mykiss)

Steelhead have lost their bright silver coloration by the time they return to Idaho after one to two years in the Pacific Ocean. Adults are generally 18-40 inches in length. They have a profusion of small black spots on the upper head, back, dorsal fin, and tail. The upper head and back are greenish-brown. A reddish tinge on the gill plates and a red lateral stripe are darker the longer the fish is in fresh water. The inside of the mouth and the gum line are white. These are black on chinook salmon.

Anadromous steelhead are native to Idaho below Shoshone Falls on the Snake River and the Salmon and Clearwater drainages.

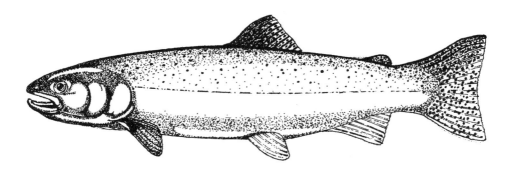

steelhead trout

BROWN TROUT:-CRAFTY BRUTES

The brown trout's well-deserved reputation for wariness demands a dedicated effort on the part of anglers seeking one of these crafty brutes.

Most fly fishers pursue browns with large, heavy nymphs or streamers, but they rise well to a dry fly when big flies like stoneflies or hoppers are present or a mayfly or caddis hatch is heavy enough to be profitable.

When hooked, browns run long and deep, although they will jump, especially in shallow-water runs or on riffles. It fights the hook with a bullheaded tenacity that can strip line from a singing reel more than once.

The brown's scientific name, *Salmo trutta*, declares it as the "true trout." It was introduced into the West in the late-1880s and in Idaho in 1892 from stocks originating in Scotland and Germany. Many anglers refer to it as a German brown.

Its basic coloration is an overall golden-brown, with its back ranging from dark-brown to greenish-brown, and its sides and belly ranging from light tan to lemon-yellow or white. The back and flanks are marked with many large black or brown spots. The few red spots on the lower flanks are surrounded by light blue-gray halos. There are very few or no spots on its squarish tail.

Turn of the century attempts to introduce brown trout in Idaho had limited success. Since the 1950s, however, they has become well established. Several river systems at lower elevations in southern Idaho and the northern Panhandle produce trophy fish.

Longer-lived than North American species, browns have been known to grow to sizes exceeding 30 pounds in the United States and up to 40 pounds in Europe. The U.S. record, 33 pounds, came from the Flaming Gorge Reservoir on the Green River on the southwestern Wyoming-northeastern Utah border. The South Fork of the Snake gave up Idaho's official record, 26 pound, six ounces and 36½ inches, in 1981. A larger South Fork brown, reportedly around 35 pounds, was disallowed as a record fish by Idaho Fish and Game in 1985 because of the method of take.

The older the fish, the bigger and more wary the brown trout. They normally grow about four to six inches a year the first three years. Growth slows to about two inches a year after this, but browns have been known to live up to 15 years. Still, depending on environmental variables such as water temperature and available food, size can range widely. Average fish on some streams may range from 10 to 12 inches and up to two pounds, which is still a respectable fish. On others, lunkers over 25 inches and five to 10 pounds may be common.

The preferred habitat of the brown is large rivers and lakes at lower elevations, although it can grow to remarkable size in small streams with adequate cover or deep pools. It is generally thought the brown is able to adapt to warmer waters than North American species, but the brown's most active periods mirror those of the rainbow. It is active in waters ranging from 45 to 70 degrees Fahrenheit, with activity peaking at 60 degrees.

Cold water, in fact, spurs the brown's autumn spawning runs. Late October through December are the times trophy hunters most heavily flog the waters.

Browns first spawn at three or four years of age. They can spawn in lakes in shallow waters, but most move up into tributary streams. In rivers, browns are known to make long upstream runs to tributaries, but also spawn in shallow waters of their resident streams. In rivers with dams halting their upstream runs, they will go to extraordinary lengths to spawn, even to the extend of turning over cobble-sized rocks to create their redds.

A large spawning male can be distinguished from a female by its hooked lower jaw. This morphological adaptation is called a kype.

Browns rarely hybridize with brook trout, which also spawn in fall. One case was reported in California on a tributary to Lake Tahoe. The hybrids are called "tiger fish" and are sterile. Some Western states now stock a few streams with hatchery-bred hybrids.

For the most part, anglers pursuing browns in Idaho will be going after wild fish. Once established in a stream, restocking is often unnecessary because they reproduce well and are difficult to catch. Stocking does continue on streams without the conditions to support reproduction, like Billingsley Creek in the Thousand Springs area and the Palouse River in the Panhandle.

In addition to the South Fork of the Snake, significant wild brown rivers in southern Idaho include the lower Henry's Fork above St. Anthony, the Snake below American Falls, the upper Portneuf, the lower Boise, and the Little Wood. The latter is the source of the browns in the fabled Silver Creek south of Sun Valley. In northern Idaho, significant wild brown waters include the Spokane and lower Clark Fork Rivers.

The typical realm of larger browns can be summed up in a single phrase, "Under the cover of darkness."

Small browns can be found in most waters common to other trout species. Larger fish prefer quieter waters than cutthroat or rainbows, and more than other species they hold up in areas where they feel safest and don't have to expend undo energy to feed.

By day, browns hide out in the darker cover provided by deep pools, overhanging banks, and bankside or mid-stream structures like log jams and large boulders. The other essential element to good brown hiding places is a steady supply of food streaming into or close by their hang-outs.

A big brown will lay claim to the same prime spot for years. When it succumbs to old age or an angler, another large brown fills the vacancy.

Older browns are nocturnal feeders as well as being very active during early-morning or evening hours and on heavily overcast days. At these times, they'll move out of the deeper waters of lakes to cruise the shallows, or come out of their stream side haunts on feeding excursions.

An angler planning to linger into the night should scout out the area first, or only attempt it on well-known home waters. He needs to know the obstacles to avoid when casting to things that go plunk in the night and, for his own safety, to prevent getting into a precarious situation.

Browns are known for their piscivorous nature, which contributes to their ability to obtain massive body weight. They even eat their own kind, but they also feed on a large variety of other organisms, including aquatic and terrestrial insects, mollusks, and crayfish.

To entice them from their deeper hiding places, a lot of anglers resort to the chuck-and-duck technique of casting large nymphs to large trout. These heavy patterns in sizes No. 6 to No. 2 include large stonefly nymphs, woolly buggers, zug bugs, and super renegades. They are bounced off the bottom or drifted just above it. Also effective in similar sizes are streamers, like marabou or bullet-head muddlers. Zonkers and spruce flies that imitate sculpin or other bait fish also are effective.

Both styles of wet flies can be used to pound the banks, too, by both drift-boat and wading anglers. The same goes for large, buggy styles of dry fly patterns. In either case, hit the places with the thickest cover the hardest.

Stonefly hatches bring large browns up in spring just like other trout. In mid-summer, a hopper bounced off a grassy bank or tossed up under an overhanging tree can be deadly. Smaller dry flies, including large drakes, caddis patterns, and stimulators in No.

10 to No. 14, occasionally bring up a good-sized fish if they float directly through a feeding lane. Browns will move the least of all the trout to intercept a fly. Still, under the right conditions, they will move up into a riffle to grub for nymphs or take emergers. And when there's a carpet hatch, they will slurp down huge quantities of micro-flies, like midges, tricos, and callibaetis. Western anglers pursuing these cruisers call them gulpers and revel in the experience of taking a 20- to 25-inch fish on a No. 20 or 22 hook.

Whether you use wet or dry patterns, you can expect to lose more than a few if you are getting them into the haunts where large browns reside. That is one of the costs of going after one. Also expect to spend more time on the water. Studies show that for every five rainbow or brook trout taken, one brown is caught.

It is sometimes easier to tie into one during the fall spawning season, but some anglers frown on this practice because the fish are more vulnerable at this time and their redds can be damaged by waders. Idaho has closed seasons early on a few streams to protect redds, like the one on the Warm River above the confluence with the Henry's Fork. More may be closed in the future if complaints continue to mount. Other trophy hunters attempt to intercept large browns in long, deep runs on their upstream migrations and in the tailwaters of dams blocking spawning runs. Autumn weather plays a major role in this pursuit. You can encounter conditions commonly associated with steelhead fishing, when days of spitting rain, or snow, prove to be the most rewarding.

Any time of the year, a brown in the net is a fly fisher's reward earned the hard way.

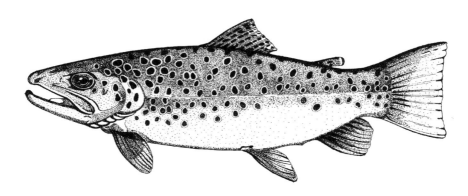

brown trout

Brown Trout Identification

Brown trout (Salmo trutta)

The coloration of a brown trout is generally golden-brown with a dark-brown to greenish-brown back. The sides and belly range from light brown to lemon-yellow. There are well-spaced large black or brown spots mixed with a few red spots on the sides with light blue-gray halos. The adipose fin usually has an orange border. There are very few or no spots on the squarish tail.

The brown was introduced to the United States from Europe in the 1800s.

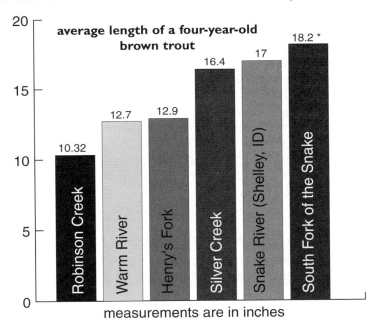

average length of a four-year-old brown trout

measurements are in inches

Robinson Creek	Warm River	Henry's Fork	Silver Creek	Snake River (Shelley, ID)	South Fork of the Snake
10.32	12.7	12.9	16.4	17	18.2 *

Brook Trout: High Country Brawlers

The flamboyant brook trout is the painted porcelain doll of the trout world. A beautiful fish, it is almost bird-like in the brilliance of its colors.

Brookies offer stubborn, scrappy fights with leaps rivaling the rainbow's and frantic, line-tugging runs.

Native to East Coast and Canadian waters, the brook trout, *Salvelinus fortinalis*, is actually a char-like lake trout, bull trout, Dolly Varden and Arctic char. Both trout and char belong to the same family, *Salmonidae*. The main difference between the two is that char have light spots on dark backgrounds. Trout have dark spots on light backgrounds. Both prefer cold water environments, but char seek out the coldest water.

Introduced into the West in the 1880s, the brook trout is a resident of pure cold waters of headwater mountain streams and alpine lakes. To find brookies in Idaho, head for the high country.

Unfortunately, its eastern reputation as a scrappy fighter is lost to most Western anglers because it tends to overpopulate the waters in which it occurs, thereby stunting its growth. The short growing seasons of alpine lakes also contribute to its diminutive size. But many high country hikers don't mind. They love to catch "plate-size" brookies because they are excellent table fare, often rated as the best among the trout species. Take advantage of it since Idaho provides anglers a very generous harvest limit on brook trout, except on Henry's Lake.

Average size in most Western waters is eight to 12 inches, although its potential is much greater. Brook trout sometimes take up residence in lower lakes, reservoirs, and beaver ponds, where they may grow to a substantial size and provide a tussle worthy of their renown as excellent game fish. A two- or three-pounder taken from one of these waters is considered a good-sized fish.

Attempts to develop prolonged trophy-sized populations, such as the introduction of the fast-growing Temiscami strain at Henry's Lake, have met with mixed success. Still, the lake is producing a 13- to 17-inch brook trout, a respectable size for Western waters.

Henry's Lake gave up the state record, seven pounds, one ounce and 23½ inches, in 1978. DeVere Stratton, the Idaho Falls angler who caught it, took another brookie just under seven pounds a week earlier but didn't have it officially weight. He often wonders whether he had two records in a row.

The world record, 14½ pounds and 31 inches, was taken from the Nipigon River in Ontario, Canada, in 1915.

Two other char species occurring in Idaho waters can be exceptionally large, capable of exceeding 20 pounds. Anglers should know the difference between these, since the bull trout, native to northern Idaho and the state's central highlands, is a candidate for endangered species listing.

The brook trout's most distinctive markings are white and black edges on the fronts of its lower fins. It is dark green or blue-black on its back, fading to white on the belly. Numerous wavy worm-like lines, or vermiculations, cover its back and dorsal fin. Scattered red spots surrounded by blue halos are seen on its flanks. The belly and lower fins of a spawning male are brilliant red in autumn.

The bull trout, *Salvelninus confluentus*, was previously considered an inland version of the coastal Dolly Varden, *Salvelinus malma*. Bull trout caught in all Idaho waters must be released. It has no worm-like markings like the brook trout, and white edges on lower fins are less distinct.

The lake trout, *Salvelinus namaychush*, was introduced into the West in the late-1880s. Also called Mackinaw, it inhabits large, deep lakes, but it is occasionally washed through dams into the rivers below. Its overall coloration is gray. It has no colored spots like the brook trout or the bull trout. The lake trout's tale is deeply forked. The tail of both brook trout and bull trout is square.

Brook trout reach sexual maturity in two or three years. Its life span ranges from six to 10 years, although a fish over five is rare. It is a fall spawner and breeds in both streams and lakes. For this reason Henry's Lake tributary creeks open to fishing have a shorter season and their bag limit is two fish, the same as the lake's.

It hybridizes with other trout species. Introduction of the brook trout into the West, habitat loss, and pollution are the main contributors to the demise of the native bull trout throughout much of its former range.

There is at least one record in California of brook trout naturally cross-breeding with the fall-spawning brown trout, an introduced European species. The two are crossbred in hatcheries. The hybrids are called "tiger trout" due to their yellowish coloration marked with dark, wavy stripes. Some states also cross brook trout with lake trout in hatcheries for introduction into a few lakes. These hybrids are called "splake."

Brook trout populations in Idaho are largely a product of former hatchery distribution programs. Today only a few small lakes are stocked. Wild fish populations are concentrated in upper-elevation stretches of streams feeding down from the Continental Divide in eastern Idaho, in alpine lakes of the central highlands and Sawtooth National Recreation Area, and in numerous small streams and lakes of the northern Panhandle.

Southeastern Idaho waters rated as significant wild fish streams include upper Beaver and Medicine Lodge Creeks and the upper Big Lost and Pahsimeroi Rivers. Significant wild brookie streams in the northern Panhandle include Cocolalla, Hoodo, and Round Prairie Creeks.

The brook trout is the classic coldwater fish. Anglers who like to fish small waters can do well seeking it out in the churning pocket waters and small pools of Idaho's cascading mountain streams. In quieter waters, it can be found lurking under overhanging stream banks and under log jams. Beaver pond and lake haunts include the edges of weed beds near deep pools and long bushy banks. As the summer heats up, they often hang out in the cooler water at the mouths of tributary streams or spring inflows.

Rarely found in waters with prolonged temperatures above 65 degrees Fahrenheit, it is most active in waters ranging from 45 to 65 degrees. Activity peaks at 58 degrees.

Its primary food base is aquatic insects and other small aquatic invertebrates, but brookies will also attack terrestrial insects with abandon. Larger brook trout eat small fish, including their own kind.

In fast waters, high-floating buggy patterns, like the Goddard caddis or humpy, and easily seen attractor patterns like the Royal Wulff or Royal Trude work best. Standard nymphs can include the gold-ribbed hare's ear and caddis emergers. The new beadhead patterns eliminate the bother of dealing with split shot. Streamers also can be effective in streams and lakes. Leech and freshwater shrimp patterns, dragonfly nymphs, and woolly buggers are good producers in lakes and ponds.

Some consider the brook trout only slightly less gullible than the cutthroat. On small streams or alpine lakes where populations are profuse, brookies offer a good chance for young anglers to practice their fly fishing skills.

Brook trout can be overexploited like the cutthroat, particularly by hotspotting anglers going after big fish in a lake or pond. Most often, though, larger fish are more cautious, usually active only in the early morning or evening hours or on heavily overcast days. On quiet waters, such as smooth flowing streams and beaver ponds, they should be approached slowly and quietly, taking advantage of available cover.

Many fly fishers like to pursue brook trout with light tackle, like a 2-weight rod or one of the smaller backpacking models. A substantial brookie taken on one of these is a true challenge.

Large or small, a brook trout in the hand is a portrait of beauty taken in a picture-postcard setting.

BROOK TROUT IDENTIFICATION

Brook trout (*Salvelinus fortinalis*)

The most distinctive markings on a brook trout are the white and black edges on the front of the lower fins, the wavy or worm-like markings on the back, and scattered red spots surrounded by a blue halo on the flanks. Brook trout are dark green or blue-black on the back to white on the belly. The belly and lower fins turn brilliant red on spawning males in the fall. The tail is square.

Brook trout were introduced in the West in the 1880s.

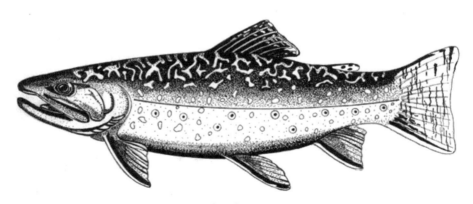

brook trout

Other Species

BLUEBACK TROUT / SUNAPEE TROUT

(Salvelinus alpinus oquassa)

An exotic char that may be listed as a threatened species in its native range in New England is unique to Idaho as an introduced non-native fish. The blueback trout, *Salvelinus alpinus oquassa* (formerly the Sunapee trout which was synonymized with the blueback trout by taxonomists) was introduced into high mountain lakes of central Idaho's Sawtooth Mountain Range in 1925.

Seemingly forgotten for decades, the blueback trout was recently officially recorded again by biologists. But because it is not a native fish, it will not be listed as a species of special concern. However, protection of blueback trout and its habitat is a high priority.

Idaho Fish and Game is protecting this species by suppressing publicity, carefully monitoring populations to determine status, and by not stocking species that would adversely affect blueback trout in waters where they occur.

It was listed in 1989 by the American Fisheries Society as threatened.

A deep water fish, the blueback trout has a pronouncedly forked tail like the lake trout. It has a dark back, and spotting on its body is very pale, with yellow, pink or orange spots. Fins are orange with white outer edge. Spawning males assume a golden coloration.

If you catch one, take a photograph and let it go.

BULL TROUT: PERSECUTED PREDATORS

Once pursued like a coyote with a bounty on its head, even poisoned in attempts to eradicate it, the bull trout has gained new-found respect as a gauge of the aquatic health of the Pacific Northwest's wild forests and mountains. But the bull trout hangs on the brink of extinction.

It is found in only 42 percent of its native streams in Idaho, Montana, Oregon, and Washington. In 1994, the U.S. Fish and Wildlife Service found that bull trout warranted protection under the Endangered Species Act but declined to list it. The decision was repeated in 1995.

There were two reasons given: there are too many other species in danger of extinction; and the states' political and wildlife officials prefer to attempt to save the species without federal intervention. Programs to protect bull trout and encourage their comeback are under way in all four states. Their efforts will be a long, uphill battle if they are to avoid their greatest fear—another northern spotted owl fiasco. But aside from curbing harvest of the fish, Idaho and the others have only limited control over habitat protection on the broad expanses of federal forest lands within their borders.

Bull trout were placed off-limits to anglers in 1993 on Idaho waters, except on one lake and one stream. Legal harvest on Lake Pend Oreille and the Lower Clarks Fork River ended in 1995 when the state declared these bull trout fisheries catch-and-release also. And in 1998 the U.S. Fish and Wildlife Service listed the fish as a threatened species in the Pacific Northwest.

The Rodney Dangerfield of cold water fish, it got no respect from old time fishermen and biologists. Because of its predatory nature, it was persecuted as a cannibal and slaughtered for preying on so-called good trout. Idaho's legal bag limit in the 1920s was 25 pounds of bull trout in addition to the normal trout limit of 15 pounds plus one fish.

But even with modern reconsideration by anglers of bull trout as a trophy fish and by biologists ranking it as an indicator species, respect may have come too late.

In their petition for endangered species listing, environmentalists said bull trout populations and habitat were seriously degraded by logging, forest road-building, cattle grazing, mining, dam construction, irrigation, pesticides and home construction in flood plains. Other threats to the fish have included overfishing—particularly during spawning runs—poaching, and introduction of non-native char species that out-compete and hybridize with bull trout.

Their key importance to the Northwest is their dependence on pristine waters, clean and silt-free, cold and oxygen-rich. This makes bull trout a prime indicator species to monitor the health of forest ecosystems and watersheds. Sharing the same wilderness waters are native salmon, steelhead and cutthroat trout.

Native to inland waters of northwestern North America, the bull trout, *Salvelinus confluentus*, is a char, not a trout. It is long-lived and grows to trophy proportions. An average adult from a large river or lake weighs three to eight pounds. Fish as large as 20 pounds are common.

The U.S. record, 32 pounds, came from Northern Idaho's Lake Pend Oreille in 1949.

Formerly lumped with the Dolly Varden, *S. malma*, it was reclassified as a separate species in the early 1970s. The Dolly Varden is more common to the coastal waters of Canada and Alaska. Arctic char, found in the Northwest Territories and Alaska, and brook trout and lake trout, native to eastern North American waters, are in the same genus.

Bull trout in Idaho have three life histories, fluvial fish which dwell in large rivers or small streams, and adfluvial fish which dwell in lakes. Adfluvial bull trout grow to adulthood in resident lakes and migrate to headwater streams to spawn. Fluvial bull trout are year-round residents of their rivers and streams and also migrate upstream to spawn. Fall spawners, bull trout are known for migrating 50 to 150 miles to their spawning beds. Sexual maturity occurs at four to five years of age and individual fish spawn every two or three years. Siltation covering the redds or water temperatures rising above 41 degrees can be lethal to the eggs.

The species was once common from the headwaters of the Yukon River in Canada to as far south as northern California. Today, it is "essentially extinct" in California and occurs in only the Jarbridge drainage in Nevada. The largest remaining population outside Idaho's Pend Oreille region is in Montana's Flathead Basin. Washington and Oregon also have significant populations. Some bull trout along the West Coast are anadromous and go to sea like salmon and steelhead.

In Idaho, bull trout still reside in the Kootenai, Priest, Pend Oreille, Spokane, Snake, Clearwater, Salmon, Weiser, Boise, and Payette River drainages. Isolated populations are in the Little Lost River and the headwaters of the Jarbridge River, a tributary of the Bruneau River.

Anglers should exercise caution in these waters. Proper identification will prevent unnecessary loss of bull trout.

Chars are distinguished from trout by their light spots on a dark background. Trout have dark spots on a light background.

The spots on a bull trout's olive-green to bronze back and flanks are pale-yellow, orange or red. There are no spots on the dorsal fin and no black line on the ventral fin.

A key feature in identifying brook trout is the white line followed by a black band on the leading edge of its orange-colored ventral fin. It has markings or spots on its dorsal fin. The spotting pattern along its flank includes pale red spots surrounded by blue halos.

The lake trout differs from both with its overall grayish coloration, dull markings and deeply forked tail.

While it's not a spectacular fighter, bull trout resist the hook with dogged tenacity. Downstream flights can be long and strenuous. Terminal tackle, which consists mostly of large streamers that include saltwater patterns, is tied onto 10-pound leader tippets because of the fish's great strength and toothy mouth.

Bull trout are most active at dawn and dusk. During the day, they hide out in the deep pools of streams, among the roots of undercut banks or in large logjams. They are vulnerable to bank casters on lakes because they prowl shallow waters and the mouths of tributaries looking for prey fish.

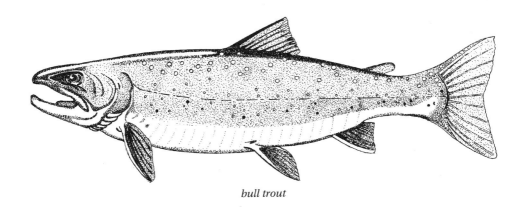

bull trout

BULL TROUT IDENTIFICATION

Bull trout (Salvelinus confluentus)

Bull trout are olive green to brown above and on the sides with shading to white on the belly. They lack the worm-like marking seen on brook trout, and the white border on the fins is less distinct. There are no spots on the dorsal fin. There are yellow spots on the upper body and red or orange spots on the flanks, but no blue halos around spots like in brook trout. The tail is square.

Bull trout are a native species.

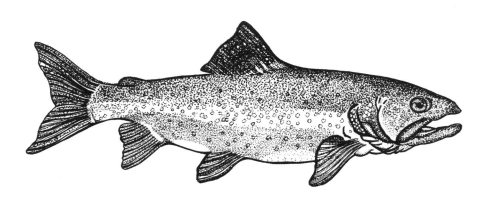

lake trout

LAKE TROUT IDENTIFICATION

Lake trout (Salvelinus namaychush)

Lake trout are dark gray or gray-green on the head and upper flanks. The belly is slightly gray to white. They have irregularly shaped gray spots on the back, sides, dorsal fin, and tail. No pink or blue spots. The white border on the fins is less distinct than in brook trout. The tail is deeply forked.

Lake trout are an introduced species.

Mountain Whitefish: Unheralded Game Fish

One of the most abundant game fish in Idaho, the whitefish gets little respect from fly fishers on trout-rich waters.

There is almost a social stigma against taking whitefish in eastern Idaho. They are viewed with more favor on the state's western and northern waters. Fishing for whitefish is most popular in winter when they are more active than trout. There are winter whitefish seasons on most drainages, which often become defacto catch-and-release seasons for trout.

Some anglers scorn the whitefish because they presume it competes with trout; however, the two species evolved to occupy separate niches in a shared habitat. There is no biological evidence that high whitefish numbers harm trout populations.

While it is in the same family as trout, salmon, and chars, *Salmonidae*, the whitefish's silvery body is slender and almost round in cross-section. It has a small head and tiny mouth, with a slightly overhanging snout. Its scales are large and coarse. Like its cousins it has an adipose fin.

The most common species in the Northern Rockies, the mountain whitefish, *Prosopium williamsoni*, prefers clear, cool streams. It is also found in some lakes. The species was first recorded for science by the Lewis and Clark Expedition. Other species that occur in Idaho are the lake whitefish, Bear Lake whitefish, Bonneville whitefish and pygmy whitefish.

A similar species is the rare arctic grayling, *Thymallus arcticus*, whose trademark is its huge, colorful sail-like dorsal fin.

Mountain whitefish average 10 to 12 inches, but on nutrient-rich streams 18- to 20-inch fish are relatively common. The Idaho record, 5 pounds, 4 ounces, was taken from the South Fork of the Payette River in 1941.

Whitefish hang out in deep pools and shallow, slow-water runs. They feed actively in riffles on mayfly nymphs and caddis larvae. Surface feeding on adult insects occurs most often toward evening.

Among the best wet flies for whitefish are small green-colored nymphs, caddis larvae and emergers. Beadhead patterns are very effective. Perhaps because of their small mouths, many whitefish fail to take a dry fly when they strike. These misses can be frustrating, but they are also a sign that actively rising fish aren't trout.

Whitefish spawn in late fall and remain active through the winter. Midge patterns can be productive at this time.

WHITEFISH IDENTIFICATION

Mountain Whitefish *(Prosopium williamsoni)*

Light grayish blue on back, silvery on sides, dull white belly. Scales large. Small mouth without teeth. Body almost round in cross-section. (Similar species, Arctic grayling, *Thymallus arcticus*: Dorsal fin large, sail-like and colorful. Dark spots on front half of silvery body.)

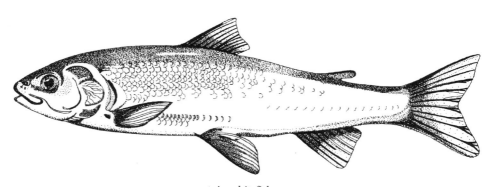

mountain whitefish

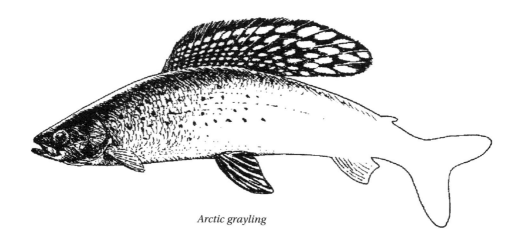

Arctic grayling

Other Game Fish

BASS: PUGNACIOUS ACROBATS

Acrobatic leaps and a line-sizzling skirmish are guaranteed when tying into a smallmouth bass, considered by many to be the most dynamic fighter among freshwater game fish. Largemouth bass are husky brawlers that rocket into the air, too, before ripping off line in a run for cover.

Bass were first transplanted to Idaho in the late 1880s. By the 1990s most of the suitable waters of the state had received bass introductions, and management strategies switched to improving warmwater fisheries. Stricter regulations and trophy fish management policies are in place on a number of low-land impoundments.

Unlike trout, bass have no adipose fin. The dorsal fin is long with two distinct parts, stiff spines in front and softer rays in back; scales are large and obvious. The key difference between the two black bass species is the size of the mouth. The jaw of the largemouth extends behind the eye; the jaw of a smallmouth ends in front of the eye.

Largemouth bass, *Micropterus salmodies*, and smallmouth bass, *M. dolomieui*, are members of the sunfish family, *Centrachidae*. It includes the sunfishes, crappies and other basses. Native to North America, only one member of the family, the Sacramento perch, was originally found west of the Rocky Mountains. Many species have been introduced successfully all over the world.

The native range of largemouth and smallmouth bass overlapped from southeastern Canada south to Georgia and throughout the Great Lakes and Mississippi drainages.

The Florida strain of largemouth grow much larger than their northern cousins, and even in some Western waters may exceed 20 pounds. Most transplants to the West belong to the northern strain. Size can range from 1 to 12 pounds, although a 5-pounder is considered a good largemouth anywhere. The Idaho record, 10 pounds 15 ounces, came from Anderson Lake in the Panhandle. Date wasn't recorded.

Largemouths live in warmwater lakes and ponds, and quiet backwaters and sloughs of streams. They prefer clear water with good cover like weed beds, reeds, lily pads or flooded snags, but also do well in somewhat barren irrigation reservoirs with radically fluctuating water levels.

Smallmouth bass inhabit cool, clear lakes and streams with rocky and gravel bottoms and shoals. Size averages 1 to 3 pounds. A 5-pounder is considered a trophy; an 8-pounder, a monster. The Idaho record was set in October 1995 with an 8-pound, 1/2-ounce bronzeback from Dworshak Reservoir. The previous record, 7 pounds, 5.6 ounces, came from Dworshak in 1982

Both species are photosensitive and retreat to shadowy lays or deeper waters on bright days. They are more active at dawn and dusk, and in water temperatures above 50 degrees. Optimum water temperatures are 60 to 70 degrees.

The males of both species jealously guard egg nests and newly hatched young in spring. The determined defense of their progeny against predators makes them very vulnerable to anglers at this time. Most of the quality bass lakes and reservoirs in Idaho are restricted to catch-and-release fishing until July 1. Many have size limits, none between 12 and 16 inches, to protect spawners, or none under 20 inches to produce trophy fish.

Lakes and reservoirs that hold both bass and trout are called two-story fisheries. In summer, bass typically stick to the warmer waters closer to shore and trout retreat to the cooler depths. In streams, smallmouths orient toward the banks or along cliff walls, and prefer slower and warmer holding areas than trout.

Black bass are voracious fish eaters, and can be instrumental in curbing population explosions of pan fish and nongame species. They take both aquatic and terrestrial insects and other invertebrates. Smallmouths display a strong preference for crayfish. Largemouths are known to take frogs and mice—and other "things that go bump in the night."

Intrepid bass hunters pound reed lines and shoreline shallows after dark or before dawn with noisy popping bugs, hair-mice, diving bugs like the Dahlberg Diver, and large streamers, muddler minnows and woolly buggers, No. 3/0 to 6 The same techniques are employed throughout the day, usually with slightly smaller flies.

Most fly fishers favor spun-hair or cork-bodied popping bugs with bushy tails and rubber legs. The theory is that the bass will hang on to soft-bodied patterns longer that plastic lures. Be wary of patterns with extra-stiff weed guards. They may push the fly away from the fish's mouth.

Because of the size and wind-resistance of the fly patterns, a rod in the 8-weight 9-foot range is more effective for largemouth bass fishing. Light-weight rods and smaller flies and streamers offer lots of fun on panfish, especially for children.

Generally, dry fly action on lakes is better with largemouths and panfish, than smallmouths. Bronzebacks tend to hold deeper in lakes, around bottom structure and boulders.

Effective smallmouth flies in streams are weighted nymphs, woolly worms, crayfish imitations, white marabou muddlers and black marabou streamers for pools and riffles. Cork or elk hair popping bugs and hair-wing dry flies produce when surface action occurs.

A 5- to 7-weight rod works for bronzebacks. Presentation can be less delicate than for trout and leaders can be stouter, 4-pound or heavier.

The state's best largemouth bass enclaves are trophy management waters in the southeastern reservoirs, C.J. Strike Reservoir on the middle Snake, Lake Lowell south of Nampa, C. Ben Ross Reservoir on the Payette, and the lowland lakes of northcentral Idaho and the Panhandle.

Prime smallmouth bass waters are Anderson Ranch Reservoir on the Boise, the Snake River in the Hagerman area, C.J. Strike, Brownlee and Oxbow Reservoirs, and downstream from Hell's Canyon Dam, the lower Salmon River, and Dworshak Reservoir on the North Fork of the Clearwater.

BASS IDENTIFICATION

Largemouth bass *(Micropterus salmoides)*

Dark green on back and flanks, belly white. Dark, irregular horizontal band along flanks. Upper jaw extends behind eye. Deep notch in dorsal fin.

Smallmouth bass *(Micropterus dolomieui)*

Dark olive to brown on back, flanks bronze, belly white. Dark ventricle bands on flanks. Eyes reddish. Upper jaw ends in front of eye. Shallow notch in dorsal fin.
Introduced to Idaho; native east of Continental Divide.

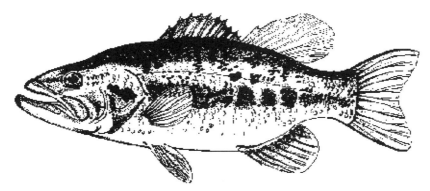

largemouth bass

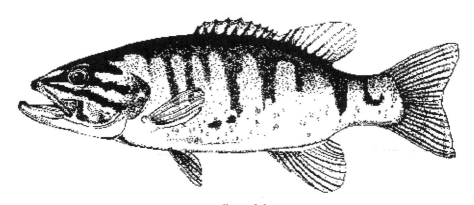

smallmouth bass

Food for Thought

Aquatic insect prey of trout

I was standing on the boardwalk of a little western resort town a few years ago when I overheard two women behind me discussing the slogan on the back of my T-shirt. Its words of wisdom circled a large colorful drawing of a royal Wulff.

"The way to a man's heart is through his fly," the first woman read aloud.

Her companion laughed. "Isn't that the truth."

They laughed again and one of them tapped me on the shoulder. "I like your T-shirt," she declared.

The double entendré is intended to draw a chuckle. Some also might assert the message is that the many colorful fur, feather, chenille and wool imitations tied in newer and better patterns each year, catch more fly fishers than trout. But the record is clear. The way to a trout's heart is through a well-presented fly.

The dry fly fisher's task is determining what's the Blue Plate Special of the day. Most know, though, that 90 percent of a trout's daily grub is consumed underwater. A working knowledge of the life histories and habitats of aquatic insects can add significantly to bringing more fish to the net.

Aquatic insect forms are available to trout in two basic groups, depending on how they metamorphose after their eggs hatch. Caddisflies and midges, which have a complete metamorphosis, are food sources for trout as larvae, pupae and adult flying insects. Mayflies, stoneflies, and dragonflies have an incomplete metamorphosis and are eaten by trout as nymphs and adults.

Each type of insect is in a biological classification known as an order. An order is divided into families, genera and species. Aquatic insects of most interest to Idaho and Northern Rocky Mountains fly fishers include:

EPHEMEROPTERA / MAYFLIES

Adult mayflies rest with their large wings in an upright position and their long, slender bodies curved in a graceful arc, front to back. When floating on water they look like miniature sailboats. They usually are quiet and docile on the water, rarely fluttering except for emergers that failed to shuck their nymphal casings. Mating swarms can be very busy and thick. The adults are literally ephemeral. Few species live longer than a day.

The newly emerged adult is known as a subimago, or dun. Large mayfly duns are called drakes. Body color is dull, non-reflective, and the wings are dark or grayish. After molting into the imago, or reproductive form, body color is bright and wings are clear or transparent. Spent females that complete egg laying fall to the water with out-spread wings and are called spinners.

Nymphs can live one to three years underwater, although a few species have two or three generations in a single season. The nymphs go through growth stages, called instars, where they shuck their exoskeleton each time they outgrow it. As they approach the emerger stage, the dark wing pad on the back of the thorax becomes more prominent.

The four categories of nymphs—swimmers, crawlers, clingers and burrowers—reflect their habitats and habits. When it is time to emerge into adults, the nymphs of most species float or swim to the surface as they shuck their exoskeleton and unfold their wings. Most fly off immediately. On cold or rainy days their float on the water can be more prolonged. The nymphs of a few species crawl ashore or up the stems of aquatic vegetation to emerge.

Trout will grub for nymphs in their hiding places, move up into riffles to snatch nymphs or emergers, or wait in their feeding lanes to snare dislodged nymphs. Emergers and floating adults are taken as they pass down a feeding lane, flow over the lip of a riffle, or are swirled together in the backwaters of an eddy. When a multiple hatch occurs, trout will often key on a single species—and not always the larger one.

Characteristics of mayfly species are reflected by the colors and other descriptive terms assigned to their common names and popular dry fly patterns.

Major mayfly hatches in Idaho include:

Siphlonuridae

This family has only one major genus in Idaho, and most of the West. A large fly, the gray drake is somewhat rare but very important on streams where it occurs. Key hatches are in late-summer into fall.

Siphlonurus/gray drake

Habitat: Swimming nymphs prefer quiet pools and slack waters in streams, the edges and shallow waters of lakes and ponds. Nymphs find food and shelter in weed beds and around stems of aquatic vegetation. Emerge by crawling up stems of plants or onto logs.

Nymphs: gray drake, black drake, No. 10 to 14.

Hatch/dry fly: *Siphlonurus occidentals*—gray drake dun, gray drake spinner, gray Wulff, Adams, No. 10 to 12; mid-August to mid-October.

Baetidae

One of the most abundant and hardiest families in the West, its many important species guarantee blue-ribbon action. Carpet hatches of blue-winged olive (BWO) are common. Baetis hatches overlap through the season from early spring into late fall.

Baetis/blue-winged olives

Habitat: Swimming nymphs prefer flowing waters. Mostly found in shallow riffles but also in rapids and eddies. Feed and find shelter in crevices and rock cobble of stream bed, sometimes in weed beds. Emerge by floating or swimming to surface to shed nymphal casing. Present adults downstream and across.

Nymphs: Soft-hackle and emerger patterns tied sparsely in olive, brown-olive or tan, No. 14 to 24.

Hatches/dry flies: *Baetis tricaudatus*—blue-winged olive, iron blue quill and Adams; late-March through mid-May, No. 16 or 18, and October through November, No. 18 to 22.

Baetis bicaudatus—tiny blue-winged olive, No. 22 or 24; July through August.

Baetis parvus—tiny brown dun and tiny blue quill, No. 20 or 22; mid-July through October.

Pseudocloeon edmundsi—tiny blue-winged olive, No. 22 or 24; mid-July through October.

Callibaetis/speckle-wing dun

Habitat: Very important species on lakes, ponds and reservoirs; also found in slow, quiet waters of some mountain streams and spring creeks. Sporadic hatches occur throughout season, spring to autumn, but emergers and spinners offer most action. Swimming nymphs find food and shelter in weed beds, stands of aquatic vegetation and debris of stream and lake beds. Nymphs very active prior to emergence and rise swiftly to surface.

Nymphs: Callibaetis nymph, Sheep Creek Special and gold-ribbed hare's ear, No. 12 to 18. Sizes become smaller as season progresses; usually weighted and fished as rising emergers.

Hatches/dry flies: *Callibaetis coloradensis*—speckled dun, speckled spinner, speckled biot spinner, No. 14 or 16, also light Cahill, compara-dun or parachute Adams; mid-July to mid-August.

Callibaetis nigritus—speckled spinner, No. 14 or 16; July through September.

Ephemerellidae

This family offers perhaps the two most productive patterns on western streams. Tiny pale morning duns (PMD) are a class act throughout the summer and giant green drakes elicit exciting early season action.

Drunella/green drakes

Habitat: This genus marks the beginning of the season on key streams like the Henry's Fork for anglers who seek big fish on big flies. Crawling nymphs are poor swimmers, prefer to find food and hide in haunts of streams with weedy, silty bottoms. Emergers very vulnerable as they crawl to quiet waters or haphazardly rise slowly to surface. Adults equally vulnerable because of long floats after emerging.

Nymphs: Charles Brooks' Ida May, western green drake nymph, lead-wing olive nymph, Zug bug, No. 8 to 10.

Hatches/dry flies: *Drunella grandis*—Western green drake, green drake paradrake, green drake Wulff, green drake compara-dun, great red spinner, No. 8 to 12; late-June to first week of July.

Drunella flavilinea—Flavs, small western drake, slate-winged olive, parachute olive hare's ear, No. 14 to 16; July.

Drunella coloradensis—Slate-winged olive, parachute olive hare's ear, No. 14 to 16; August.

Ephemerella/pale morning dun

Habitat: Crawling nymphs are poor swimmers, prefer to find food and hide in haunts of streams with weedy, silty bottoms. Emergers very vulnerable as they crawl to quiet waters or haphazardly rise slowly to surface. Small size of adults requires downstream or down and across presentations.

Nymphs: pale morning dun nymph, hare's ear, yellow soft-hackle partridge, No. 16 to 20.

Hatches/dry flies: *Ephemerella infrequens*—pale morning dun, hair wing dun, compara-dun PMD, parachute PMD, rusty spinner, No. 14 to 18; June and early July.

Ephemerella inermis—pale morning dun, hair wing dun, compara-dun PMD, parachute PMD, No. 16 to 20; July through September.

Ephemeridae

Principal fly in this family is the brown drake, a large slow-water species which may overlap with the green drake hatch on some streams. Usually hatches in early summer.

Ephemera/brown drake

Habitat: Nymphs burrow into silty sand bottoms of streams and lakes and feed at night. Hatch occurs at twilight or at night, with emergers rapidly rising to the surface.

Nymphs: brown drake nymph, No. 10 to 12.

Hatch/dry flies: *Ephemera simulans*—brown drake, brown drake parachute, brown drake spinner, No. 10 to 12; mid-June to early July.

Leptophlebiidae

Principal fly in this family is the mahogany dun, a tiny fast-water species with a relatively long season. Late-summer hatches common.

Paraleptophlebia/mahogany dun

Habitat: Crawling nymphs prefer flowing waters, like fast riffles; hide and feed in debris and gravel of stream bed. Poor swimmers, they move to quieter waters prior to emerging.

Nymphs: Charles Brooks' floating natant nylon nymph, hare's ear nymph, No. 14 to 18.

Hatch/dry flies: *Paraleptophlebia bicornuta*—mahogany dun, mahogany spinner, No. 16 or 18; late-August through September.

Tricorythodidae

The very tiny flies of this family are a major feeding source for selective trout, mostly on streams but also on some lakes. Tricos are especially important on the Henry's Fork and Silver Creek. Late summer hatches common.

Tricorythodes/white-wing black

Habitat: Nymphs prefer slow waters of streams; hide in bottom debris. Floating emerger and dun patterns work, but the spent female spinners are most vulnerable to slurping trout.

Nymphs: white-black nymphs, black or olive midge pupa, pheasant tail nymph, No. 20 to 24.

Hatch/dry flies: *Tricorythodes minutus*—white-wing black, parachute Trico, black or olive midges, Griffith's gnat, Trico spinner, No. 20 to 24; August into September.

Heptageniidae

Common to fast mountain streams, species of this family prefer clear, cold water. Mid-summer hatch continues into fall.

Eperous/Pink Albert

Habitat: Nymphs cling to substrate of tumbling riffles and fast runs. Emergers and floating duns most vulnerable to quick-acting trout.

Nymphs: Soft-hackle patterns and hare's ear nymph, No. 10 to 16

Hatch/dry flies: *Eperous albertea*—pink Albert, pink lady, pink Cahill, cream dun, No. 14 to 16; July to September.

TRICHOPTERA / CADDISFLIES

Few anglers bother to learn the Latin names of caddisflies. Almost none have common names although on many streams they are more prolific than mayflies.

Popular caddis patterns are impressionistic but take tons of trout. Larval patterns are effective year-round because caddis are so common. Emerger patterns generally are more productive during a hatch than dry flies. A dry fly plays best when females return to deposit their eggs, but a dry fly is a good attractor pattern in spring and summer because caddis are on the water throughout their adult stage.

When resting the two pairs of wings of the caddisfly slant back over the body in a tent-like position. In the air, caddis have an erratic, bouncing flight pattern. On the water, they often continue fluttering or swimming about. Their wings are not transparent and coloration tends toward earth tones in shades of tan, brown, gray, or black. Body color can match the wings or be in shades of green or yellow. Adult caddisflies may live one to two weeks.

In the larval stage most caddis live in cases built from small grains of sand, sticks, strands of vegetation, or a combination of materials. Some live in a free-swimming form or construct a silken retreat with a web.

Caddis hibernate a week or more during pupation, like caterpillars, as they change into winged adults in their cases. When the transformation is complete, the pupae shuck their casings as they soar to the surface in a dash to freedom. Most adults fly off as soon as they hit the air.

Trout chasing caddis emergers often rocket fully out of the water in their pursuit. Their next best shot at caddis is when the females return to deposit their eggs. It is a busy affair, with lots of buzzing wings and swimming about, although a few dive straight to the bottom. With all that activity, trout hit caddis hard. Fishing strategies should follow suit.

Two most common families in Idaho are *Brachycentridae*, dark-gray and dark-brown caddis with wood-case larvae, and *Rhyacophilidae*, green caddis with free swimming larvae.

The most effective dry fly to cover the bases is the elk hair caddis in No. 12 to 20 with green, tan, brown, or gray bodies. Other popular patterns include Colorado king, Goddard caddis, humpies, Henryville Special, Hemingway caddis, bucktail caddis, and stimulators.

Larval and pupa patterns in No. 10 to 18 can include the peacock herl caddis, latex caddis, or soft-hackle patterns like the green partridge, Charles Brooks' little green caddis and little gray caddis and Moss' caddis emerger.

PLECOPTERA / STONEFLIES

These prehistoric monsters of the aquatic insect world incite slashing, explosive rises by trophy trout during early season hatches. But for wet fly fishers, the 2- to 3-inch nymphs of the largest species, *Pteronarcys californica*, are a standard pattern year-round.

The incredible "salmonfly" feeding frenzy can extend from mid-May through late July in eastern Idaho's golden circle of trout streams. But nature doesn't always make it easy. Local weather or spring runoff conditions can speed up or slow a hatch dramatically. Elsewhere in the state, hatches can be very sporadic and nymph patterns often perform better than dry flies.

Stone flies look a lot like giant caddisflies, although their two pairs of heavily veined wings lie flat over their backs. Their flight is helicopter-like, with the long body hanging below the whirling wings. Nymphs follow the same life history as mayflies and live underwater one to four years. All species are found in swift, rocky waters, rich in oxygen.

Members of the *P. californica* species were dubbed salmonflies because of the bright-orange highlights on dark-brown bodies of nymphs and adult flying insect. A smaller species, the golden stonefly, *Acroneuria pacifica*, is highlighted by golden-yellow markings on its light-brown body. Golden stones hatch toward the end of a salmonfly hatch. They also come in a wider variety of sizes and can be an effective dry fly pattern for a longer duration.

Stone flies do not emerge in mid-stream. The nymphs crawl across the stream bed to water's edge, climb a rock or bush and shuck their shells as they metamorphose into short-lived, flying insects.

Key to fishing salmonflies is staying at the front of the hatch as it moves upstream, usually about five miles a day. A hatch's head is determined by the point where only a few flying insects or nymph casings can be found. The best bet here is to cast nymphs toward the shoreline from a boat or parallel to it when wading.

Behind the vanguard of the emerging nymphs, dry flies come into play. Late afternoon flights of salmonflies occur when egg-laying females ride the up-swells of hot air flowing up the canyons cut by the rivers. The large, black egg sacs are deposited like bombs in rocky, fast-water stretches of the stream to begin the cycle anew. Many females fall exhausted onto the water and the bugs are often blown off stream side bushes by high winds.

There are hundreds of patterns, ranging from super realistic to plain buggy-looking impressions, and new ones are being created annually. Check with local fly tackle shops on what's hot.

A variety of salmonflies, No. 2 to 8, is highly recommended. Golden stone patterns range from No. 8 to 14. Popular dry flies include the sofa pillow, Bird's stonefly, golden stonefly, large yellow or orange stimulators and double humpies. One of the latest inventions is the Rainy's salmonfly, tied with a Rainy float foam body. Traditional nymph patterns include the Charles Brooks Montana stone, Box Canyon stone, Montana stone, Bitch Creek Special, orange or black girdle bug, black rubber-legs, super renegade, and woolly bugger.

Small caddis-like insects on the water with wings resting flat over orange or yellow bodies are small species of brown or golden stoneflies. These are often called willowflies or yellow Sallies, after the *Isogenus* species. Smaller yellow or orange stimulators and yellow Sally or willowfly patterns are very effective, along with humpies, bucktail caddis and yellow elk hair caddis, No. 10 to 14.

Willow fly hatches may overlap salmonfly and golden stone hatches, and typically last through July into August.

DIPTERA / TRUE FLIES

Midges and mosquitoes are the two families in this order of most interest to fly fishers.

Chironomidae/midges

Midges can be a dry fly fishers' best friend in winter and early spring on streams open year-round. Float-tubers often count on Chironomid emergers to ensure a good day on lakes and ponds.

Midge larva and pupa patterns are tied very sparsely with green, olive, light-olive, tan, brown or black dubbing on No. 18 to 28 hooks. Peacock or ostrich herl are used on the thorax of pupa patterns.

Flying midge patterns are tied very sparsely in colors to match a variety of hatches with only two or three turns of same-colored hackle for wings, No. 14 to 26. The Griffith's gnat, tied with a grizzly hackle palmered over a peacock herl body, No. 18 to 28, represents a clump of midges on the water.

Culicidae/mosquitoes

This is the one fly every one can identify.

Both larva and pupa patterns are tied to float in the surface film. Stripped hackle stems or peacock herls are used for the thin body, in No. 14 to 18. The mosquito dry fly and Adams also work in No. 14 to 18.

Odonata/dragonflies

Dragonfly and damselfly hatches on lakes and ponds can rival the excitement of stonefly hatches on mountain streams. But even without a hatch, damsel nymphs, Charles Brooks' Assom dragon, woolly worms, crystal buggers, and Carey Special, No. 4 to 12, should be part of a stillwater fly fisher's arsenal year-round.

Green damsel nymphs, No. 8 to 12, and woolly buggers and crystal buggers, No. 8 to 10, are popular patterns on Henry's Lake during the damselfly hatch from late-June to mid-July.

Long-bodied dry flies also are available at some fly tackle shops.

Favorite Idaho Fly Fish Patterns

by Rocky Barker

Every fall, fly fishers from around the world gather in Jackson Hole, Wyoming to compete in an event called the One-Fly that is more about fun and conservation than competition.

Started by guide Jack Dennis, this event highlights some of the best flyfishing in both Wyoming and Idaho. Ken and I have covered it in the past as journalists and it has prompted our own debates about what flies are best.

The idea behind it is simple. Fly fishers get one fly to fish all day on the Snake River in Wyoming and one fly for one day on the South Fork of the Snake River in eastern Idaho.

For these anglers durability is as important as the pattern and since it all happens on one day, anglers cannot adjust to other flies that are working.

But what if you could only have one fly in your box?

For an Idaho fisherman that one fly likely would be an elk hair caddis. The fly is easy to tie and durable. It is extremely effective early and late in the seasons on finicky rainbows in places like the Henry's Fork and the South Fork of the Boise. Caddisflies are around much of the season from March to November in many rivers. The elk hair also can fool aggressive cutthroats when caddis species are missing. The elk hair caddis floats like a battleship, and for us older anglers with declining eyesight the elk hair caddis is visible in all but the smallest sizes.

Idaho is a big state with big and small waters, lakes and ponds; rainbows, browns and cutthroats, and even salmon and steelhead. An angler who only could fish with a elk hair caddis would inevitably find himself in tough luck on those days and waters where precision is a must.

Alas, we are not limited to one fly. But one can get by in all but the most difficult water with a few patterns.

Here is a quick look at my fly box and the workhorses I go back to over and over:

Hare's ear nymph

This pattern, often with a beadhead, is my go-to fly under the water in virtually every river in the state. Like the elk hair it resembles a caddis and dozens of other nymphs in swifter water.

Adams

This general mayfly imitation works in many places and is popular here as a parachute pattern.

I actually use a high-riding offshoot touted by the late nymph fishing legend Charlie Brooks called the Wilma Jean. I use a bear hair tail with a peacock hurl body anchored by copper wire. I palmer the brown and grizzly hackle around the body and top it off with white poly wings. This fly is good for rainbows and is a knockout for cutthroats.

Super Renegade

This fly on a #10 or #8 hook is the long-time standard for anglers on the South Fork of the Snake River. They tie off a brown hackle on the back, then a black chenille halfway up the hook to another hackle of their choice, white, brown or even grizzly. Then they tie another chenille either, orange, white, green yellow, whatever they like. They finish with a final hackle. This fly is best fished right on the bank just below the surface, usually from a boat. The best pattern for me is the orange and black that appears like a salmonfly.

Grasshopper

From late July until September grasshoppers are everywhere.

Blue-wing olive

The blue dun fly is the first and last mayfly to hatch on many rivers in Idaho. I seem to depend on them more than other patterns.

Renegade

This pattern is Ken's workhorse for cutthroats.

Sofa pillow

This dry fly salmonfly match works from May through July in many Idaho waters.

Pale morning dun

This mayfly pattern is a morning standby on many waters through much of the summer, and a rusty spinner at sunset tops off the day.

Royal Wulff

On lakes and streams through thick and thin this pattern produces when all else fails.

Muddler minnow

This streamer works both dry and wet because it can be either an insect or a minnow to a trout.

Stayner ducktail

No list of Idaho flies would be complete without this unique pattern developed by the late Twin Falls fly shop owner Ruel Stayner. This is a great pattern for lakes. I start by wrapping the hook shank with threat and tying in a red hackle tail the length of the hook. Tie in silver round tinsel and three peacock hurls and wind the hurls three-quarters of the way up the shaft and tie. Wind the tinsel the opposite direction up to the hurl and tie off. Tie in hackle for the beard. On the top of the shaft, tie in wood duck fibers so they lay flat over the body and the tail. Cut the wing flat and whip finish.

As you will see there are countless others from the Pink Albert on the South Fork of the Boise to the Yellow Sally on the South Fork of the Snake that are important seasonally. Other anglers may favor woolly worms or other standard pattern over my list.

But an angler with these flies will get by most places most of the year in Idaho.

Author Rocky Barker with chinook salmon from the
Little Salmon River. Rocky Barker photo.

Recommended Flies

1. Hemingway Caddis

Low-profile dry fly by Mike Lawson

2. Spent Partridge Caddis

Low-profile dry fly by Mike Lawson

3. Last Chance Cripple

Mayfly emerger pattern by Rene Harrop

4. Elden's Golden Stonefly

Foam dry fly by Elden Berrett

5. Pat's Rubber Legs

Stonefly nymph by Pat Pennett

6. JB Stone

Stonefly dry fly by James Bowen

7. Sheep Creek Special

Wet fly attractor pattern by George Biggs

8. Renegade

Dry fly attractor by Taylor "Beartracks" Williams

Recipes on pages 390-398

9. Fifi
Steelhead egg pattern by Scott Schnebly

10. Philo Betto
Sculpin streamer by Scott Schnebly

11. Stayner Ducktail
Streamer attractor by Ruel Stayner

12. Pinky Maroon
Steelhead fly by John Stenersen

13. Bing's Green Drake
Extended body mayfly by Bing Lempke

14. Gem State Nymph
Green drake nymph by Bruce Staples

15. Beadhead Peacock Leech
Sparse leech pattern by Bruce Staples

16. Phil's Hopper
Low-profile grasshopper by Philip Blomquist

Recipes on pages 390-398

Lords of the Fly

Idaho represents vanguard of Western fly tying heritage

by Ken Retallic

The beauty of flyfishing is that trout live in picturesque environs. Yet, nothing captivates a fly fisher more than a progression of rise forms dimpling a stream like the sprinkling of a gentle rain. For, it's in the "ring of the rise" that fulfillment occurs for the fly fisher.

Many people think fishing is passive, but it's not.

Flyfishing, especially, is an art and a science as much as it's a sport. To do it well, you have to understand the habits and habitats of the fish and their prey. One also must be a student of the teachings and traditions imparted by flyfishing's forebears and today's innovators. An enduring aspect of flyfishing's traditions is the ever-present urge of its practitioners to improve techniques and equipment, and dream up and concoct better fly patterns.

The hatch masters who created the tried-and-true fly patterns we still cast today—and today's burgeoning crop of increasingly creative fly tiers—are the true artists of fly-fishing.

Many of the more innovative ones developed their craft through the past 100 years or more fishing Western waters. Early Idaho fly tiers were in the vanguard of this heritage and their successors continue the tradition in solving the mysteries of the Gem State's myriad of premiere trout streams, lakes, reservoirs and high mountain tarns.

The selection of fly patterns presented here is a mini history of Idaho's "lords of the Fly."

Reducing the selection to a mere 16 was the hard part. Acquiring them was the fun part. Three-fourths of the flies came to me from the Eastern Idaho Fly Tying Expo that's continually grown over the past two decades in Idaho Falls, and from interviews I have conducted over the past 30 years at newspapers and magazines in Idaho Falls and Ketchum/Sun Valley.

Further assistance in making a selection of newer fly tiers came through the advice and contributions of Jimmy Gabettas Jr. at Jimmy's All Seasons Anglers Fly Shop in Idaho Falls. Also. I relied on two primary sources in fleshing out the histories of some of the fly patterns or biographies of their tiers: Bruce Staples' "Trout Country Flies: Greater Yellowstone Area Masters" and Greg Thomas' "Best Flies for Idaho."

Enjoy:

1. Hemingway Caddis
by Mike Lawson

HOOK: TMC 100, sizes 12-18

THREAD: Olive

BODY: olive superfine dubbing. Palmer with medium dun hackle. Tie hackle fairly long, extending below the hook point.

UNDERWING: wood duck-dyed mallard flank fibers

WING: mallard quill extended back over body. A third of its length should extend beyond the hook bend.

THORAX: peacock herl

HACKLE: medium dun; palmer through thorax.

HEAD: olive thread

Note: This fly was named for former Idaho Fish and Game commissioner Jack Hemingway, the son of author Ernest Hemingway, but more notably, Jack is remembered in Idaho as the savior of Silver Creek. After nearly 50 years it is still one of the best dry fly patterns to fool a picky trout, especially in spring on the Henry's Fork.

Mike Lawson

Mike Lawson, of St. Anthony, has fished the trout streams of eastern Idaho all of his life, especially the Henry's Fork. He was a shop teacher in St. Anthony for six years and worked as a fly-fishing guide during the summer months. Mike and his wife, Sheralee, also tied flies commercially for many years. In 1977 they opened Henry's Fork Anglers fly shop at Last Chance, Idaho. The shop continues as a full service fly fishing specialty shop and guiding service for the Greater Yellowstone Area. Mike remains as general manager after selling the business to Mark Rockefeller in 1999. He is the author of numerous magazine articles and several books on fly fishing spring creeks and his beloved Henry's Fork. He travels extensively as a featured speaker at seminars on fly fishing, fly tying and cold water fisheries conservation. He is a co-founder of the Henry's Fork Foundation.

2. Spent Partridge Caddis
by Mike Lawson

HOOK: TMC 100 #12-20

THREAD: 8/0 Black

ABDOMEN: olive Superfine dubbing

WINGS: matched Hungarian partridge body feathers

HACKLE: brown and grizzly rooster neck

THORAX: peacock herl

Note: This pattern imitates a spent caddis after it has laid its eggs and is dying, as well as a healthy adult. Wait to trim the hackle until you observe your fishing options, since the fully hackled version is effective as a skittering adult. Trim the hackle off the bottom when you want a lower floating profile.

3. Last Chance Cripple
by Rene Harrop

HOOK: TMC 100BL

THREAD: 8/0 Uni-thread

TAIL: Sparse tuft of TroutHunter C.E.N. "sparkle" dubbing over three wood duck fibers

ABDOMEN: Stripped goose biot or turkey biot tied to appear with segmented ridges.

THORAX: TroutHunter Professional Dry Fly Dubbing

WINGS: Paired CDC feathers set at a forward angle over the eye.

HACKLE: Whiting Hackle

Note: The colors and sizes of the Last Chance Cripple can be adjusted to effectively match any mayfly that emerges in streams or lakes. The fly shown in the color photo is a callibaetis pattern. Don't think of this as only a spring creek or slow water pattern. It is very effective on the tumbling, crystal clear mountain streams of Idaho and throughout the Northern Rockies, especially when tied as a Flav or Pink Albert.

René Harrop

René Harrop, of St. Anthony, Idaho, has fly fished for almost five decades and has been a professional fly tier for more than 30 years. He has made his living as a fly tier, painter, writer, and guide. He is a pioneer in the use of CDC plumes and primary feather biots, and has developed a complete series of CDC/biot patterns replicating the life cycles of mayflies. House of Harrop was born on the banks of the Henry's Fork in 1968. Formed as a small fly tying business by René and Bonnie Harrop, the company still operates from their home. René is a founding partner of TroutHunter lodge, fly shop and guiding services located at Last Chance, Idaho.

For more information on TroutHunter fly tying materials, contact: House of Harrop, 33 W 4th N, St. Anthony, Idaho 83445 Tel: 20-624-3537; Fax: 208-624-3455; www.houseofharrop.com

4. Elden's Golden Stonefly
by Elden Berrett

HOOK: Dai-Riki 270 #4-10

THREAD: Tan 6/0

UNDERBODY: white open cell foam, 1/16-inch thick and 1/8-inch wide.

BODY: dubbed, Hairline #43 Ginger

HACKLE: brown

OVER BODY: tan or brown closed cell foam, 1/8-inch thick by 3/16- to 1/4-inch wide

LEGS: medium round rubber, brown

POSTS: closed cell foam 1/16-inch thick, 1/8-inch wide, 1/4-inch long: orange and yellow

Note: Use a normal drag free float for most presentations, although an occasional little jiggle of the fly is a good idea. Even in faster water, jiggle the fly occasionally to attract attention.

Elden Berrett

Elden Berrett was born and raised in Idaho Falls, Idaho, and currently lives in Blackfoot. He started guiding on the South Fork of the Snake River for Heise Expeditions in Heise in 1998 and went to work for South Fork Outfitters In Swan Valley in 2001. Elden is an extremely innovative fly tier. Several of his patterns are among the most popular on the South Fork and are carried home to other great streams of the Northern Rockies as well as to Canada. He used one of his fly patterns to win top scoring guide honors in the Jackson Hole One Fly contest in 1998. Elden works as a security guard for the Department of Energy and guides for South Fork Outfitters during his days off.

5.Pat's Rubber Legs
by Pat Bennett

HOOK: Dai-Riki 710, sizes 2–10

THREAD: black 6/0 Uni Thread

BODY: weighted with .25 non-lead (non-toxic) wire; dark brown or brown variegated medium chenille

LEGS, TAIL, ANTENNA: amber or brown Angler's Choice super floss (also known as flexi-floss)

Note: The use of super floss for legs, tail and antenna is the key ingredient contributing to the success of this fly. Its proper name as a "rubber legs" is a misnomer–so, word to the wise, don't substitute rubber legs. Chenille colors may include dark brown or brown variegated for big salmon flies, but also consider a variegated brown/yellow or orange for golden stones, and a variegated green/yellow for skwalas.

Pat Bennett

Pat Bennett, of Rexburg, Idaho, has been fly fishing the Henry's Fork area since 1970 when his grandfather built a cabin in Island Park. After 22 years as an infantry officer, Pat retired from the Army and began doing what he truly loves, fly fishing. He began guiding on the Henry's Fork for Hyde Outfitters, a subsidiary of Hyde Boats in Idaho Falls, in 1997. Pat was a member of the Hyde team that placed third in the ESPN Team Fly Fishing Challenge in 2002. He is a representative for Solitude Fly Company during the off season.

6. JB Stone
by James Bowen

HOOK: Dai-Richi 1730, sizes 8 to 4

THREAD: dark brown 6/0 and florescent orange A+

BODY: dark brown deer body hair; tied as a tight, extended round body, ribbed by orange thread

RIB: florescent orange A+ thread
WING: bleached elk hair; tied flat without excessive flare
HEAD: bullet head style with dark drown deer hair
LEGS: brown medium or large rubber legs; tied in Madam X style with orange thread securing bullet head
Note: This is a beautiful design of a low-profile stonefly pattern. Drift it against the banks with an occasional twitch. Don't overlook chances to swing it past midstream boulders and other structure.

James Bowen

James Bowen, of Idaho Falls, Idaho, has been tying flies for more than 30 years. He has tied for many big regional shows and conclaves, including the internationally renowned East Idaho Fly Tying Expo in Idaho Falls. He's custom tied flies for some of the bigger fly suppliers, such as Idylwilde Flies. He has produced several fly tying videos and fishing videos, and has guided on the Henry's Fork and South Fork of the Snake River.

For more information: James Bowen Flies, 1480 Mound, Idaho Falls, Idaho 83402, 208 542-9998

7. Sheep Creek Special
by George Biggs

HOOK: TMC 5262, sizes 10-16
THREAD: dark olive
TAIL: Bbown hackle wound on the shank as for a dry fly; tie in thread ball or tag first to keep hackle from sliding off bend of hook.
BODY: dark olive chenille
WING: 5-7 mallard flank fibers
Note: Lighter colors of variegated chenille also may be used for the body. A fine gold ribbing may be used within the original pattern. The fly suggests many different aquatic organisms, including leeches (in larger sizes), midges (in small sizes), and damselfly or dragonfly nymphs. Use an intermediate line and a countdown-and-retrieve or slow retrieve presentation.

George Biggs

A pioneer Idaho float-tuber, George Biggs, of Jerome, dreamed up this minimal though excellent still water attractor pattern in the 1930s for Sheep Creek Reservoir, which is on the Duck Valley Indian Reservation on the Nevada-Idaho border, south of Mountain Home. Biggs and two other early Idaho float tubers and lake fishing experts, Ruell Stayner, of Twin Falls, and Marv Taylor, of Boise, produced many still water patterns that are still quite popular today in the Northern Rockies. All three are fondly remembered for being very outgoing in assisting other fly fishers.

8. Renegade
by Taylor "Beartracks" Williams

HOOK: TMC 100, sizes 8-18

THREAD: black

REAR END TAG: gold mylar (the tag, which may also be just a built up hump of thread at the bend keeps the rear hackle from sliding off the back of the hook.)

REAR HACKLE: brown or ginger

BODY: peacock herl, tied full in "egg-shape"

FRONT HACKLE: white or cream

Note: This is mostly used as a fast water, pocket water attractor pattern, but in very small sizes it is an effective midge pattern, even on spring creeks like Silver Creek. The Renegade also can be fished wet with a small split shot placed ahead of it on the leader tippet.

Taylor "Beartracks" Williams

The Renegade was conceived by Taylor "Beartracks" Williams, the first guide at the Sun Valley Lodge, established in 1936 at Ketchum, Idaho, as the nation's first destination ski resort. Williams tied the Renegade in 1928 at his Sawtooth Shack fly shop in Gooding, Idaho. A hunting and fishing companion of Ernest Hemingway, Williams also took Papa's son Jack under his wing. But Jack's first trip to Silver Creek in 1940 was not his most auspicious outing on a spring creek. "I believe (Williams) also mentioned the Renegade as a possibility, which I rejected out of hand, though I probably shouldn't have as it does a fair job of giving an impression of an egg-laying caddis," Hemingway later related.

"The Renegade has probably caught more fish in Idaho than any other dry fly pattern," says Marv Taylor, a Boise author, columnist and fly tying innovator.

9. Fifi
by Scott Schnebly

HOOK: Mustard AC92553R (offset) or Mustard 36890 Salmon Fly Hook, sizes 2-10

THREAD: burnt orange, B or A+, wrapped full length of hook shank

TAIL: short, sparse mix of red Krystal Flash and pearl Flashabou

BODY: one-third to one-half strand of orange egg yarn tied so that it lies perpendicular to hook; gather together both sides of yard strand, pull straight up and cut straight across at 3/8 to 1/2 inch. Yarn will "poof" out in shape of segmented egg when cut ends are rolled down over shank of hook. Can also be tied with red or lime egg yarn.

HEAD: one-eighth inch chrome eyes (aka "dumbbells"), tied and cemented to hook

Note: A modified egg pattern, this fly was designed in 1992 for spring steelhead fishing in the shallow waters of the Upper Salmon River and other thin water situations. Fish it with a floating line, dead-drifting it like a nymph with a strike indicator. Scott calls it the "Fifi" because it reminds him of a poodle fresh from a grooming session.

Scott Schnebly

Scott Schnebly is the owner of Lost River Outfitters and Fly Shop in Ketchum, Idaho, which has been serving fly fishers on the waters of the Sun Valley/Ketchum area since 1984, including world famous Silver Creek and the Big Wood and Big Lost rivers. Scott also has been guiding spring steelhead anglers on the Upper Salmon River out of his lodge in Stanley since guiding this run of fish was allowed in the 1980s. Salmon River steelhead swim 900 miles upstream from the Pacific Ocean to spawn in the Stanley Basin, making this the longest run of any anadromous fish in the world.

10. Philo Betto
by Scott Schnebly

HOOK: Mustard 9672, sizes 4-8

THREAD: olive or black

TAIL: Ten or 12 strands of silver Krystal Flash, the length of a pheasant rump body feather (dyed olive, with the lower after-shaft feather removed) tied flat and extending beyond bend of hook.

BODY: Palmer olive-dyed pheasant rump "filoplume" feather(s) to the head. The filoplume (aka philoplume) are the compact feathery/downy underbody feather on a skin beneath the body feather.

HEAD: olive or black thread.

Note: This is another great thin water fly that was tied in the winter of 1988 to represent sculpin found in high mountain streams. Do not weight this fly with non-toxic wire or a bead head. Fish with a floating line with split shot attached to leader about a foot above the fly. Make it dart with short strips of the fly line. It's named after Philo Betto, the character Clint Eastwood played in "Every Which Way But Loose."

11. Stayner Ducktail
by Ruel Stayner

HOOK: Mustad 9672, or 3X long equivalent. Sizes 6 - 14.

THREAD: Black, 6/0 pre-waxed.

TAIL: 10 or 15 orange saddle hackle fibers, ½ body length.

BODY: Dark-olive chenille, sizes medium or small.

RIBBING: Gold 16/18 mylar tinsel, 4 or 5 wraps.

BEARD: 10 or 15 orange saddle hackle fibers, reaching to hook point.

WING: Natural mallard flank feather, tied flat, reaching to end of tail.

HEAD: Black thread.

Note: While it's known primarily as a still water pattern, the ducktail also is a very effective streamer fly in small streams. The fly shown in the photo was tied by Marv Taylor, of Boise, and included in his book, "Marv's Favorites." "Since I am a bit of a nervous fly fisher, I enjoy fishing ducktails. I fish a quick retrieve a lot of the time. In presenting ducktails to hungry fish, the angler should work his line to make his fly dart like wounded prey," states Taylor.

Ruel Stayner

A still water fly-fishing expert, Ruel Stayner of Twin Falls, Idaho, is most noted for his Stayner Ducktail fly pattern, which helped garner him a national reputation, but his influence on Idaho fly fishing played a much larger role for more than 50 years. "Two men—Ruel Stayner and Dick Alfs—were responsible for keeping fly fishing alive during the late 1940s when fly fishing had become an orphan to the (spin casting) industry. Ruel Stayner opened Stayner's Sporting Goods in Twin Falls in 1946 and according to Don Anderson, the retired head of Sun Valley's Sports Center, 'Anyone who fished in southern Idaho hung out at Stayner's.' Dick Alfs of Ketchum was a fixture, learning about resources and retailing with an eye to eventually open his own store," states a remembrance by Silver Creek Outfitters, of Ketchum, Idaho.

12. Pinky Maroon
by John Stenersen

HOOK: Gamakatsu T10-6H Salmon Tapered Loop Up-Eye, sizes 4-6, red
THREAD: UTC 70 black
TAIL: golden pheasant tippet dyed red
TAG: pearl tensile
BODY: maroon dubbing
RIB: pearl tensile
WING: peacock breast feather, blue
HACKLE: fuchsia lace black hen neck
Note: This is a classically tied western steelhead fly with contrasting bright and somewhat subdued colors. It's a strategy favored by many modern day Idaho steelhead fly tiers and fly fishers who ply the Salmon, Clearwater and lower Snake rivers.

John Stenersen

John Stenersen, based in Idaho Falls, Idaho, is the lead sales representative for ClackaCraft fiberglass drift boats in its principal national sales office outside Oregon. An avid fisherman who grew up on the banks of the Upper Salmon River in Salmon, Idaho, and a renowned fly tier, John instructs the art of tying and fly fishing at Idaho State University and for Jimmy's All Seasons Angler in Idaho Falls. John and his son, Parker, can be found throughout the seasons prowling the anadromous fishery waters of the Northwest, especially on Idaho's two premier steelhead and chinook salmon fishing streams, the Salmon and Clearwater rivers.

13. Bing's Green Drake
by Bing Lempke

HOOK: TMC 9300 or equivalent, size 12
THREAD: black 2/0
WING: Canada goose primary sections with rounded tips
TAIL AND EXTENDED BODY BEAM: three stiff black mono fibers
UNDERBODY: Art Foam strip, 3/8-inch wide

EGG SAC: two peacock herl fibers
RIB: yellow nylon thread, size A
BODY: peacock olive floss
HACKLE: one grizzly dyed yellow, one blue dun
Note: A heirloom fly, Bing tied it in the mid-1980s in the photography studio at the Idaho Falls Post Register.

Cyril "Bing" Lempke

Bing Lempke, of Idaho Falls, Idaho, is the only fly fisher that I've met who was featured in a "Time" magazine profile. So many accolades to him have been written that I'll let a Henry's Fork Foundation tribute sum it all up: "... Bing's first fly-fishing trip to the Henry's Fork of the Snake River was in 1929 with some flies given to him by a kind man in his hometown of Idaho Falls. Lempke caught 26 fish that day and was hooked on fly fishing. His profession was pipefitter, but his avocation was as an artist of extended body flies and a fly fisherman of the first order. His masterpiece was the extended body Green Drake ... He often said that the Green Drake hatch cost him three good jobs as he couldn't elude the whispering call of the Henry's Fork every June. He was chosen as the Fly Fishing Federation 1988 Buszek award winner for his contributions to the sport of fly-fishing and fly tying ..." A memorial to Bing is located in the picnic area at the Last Chance fishing access in Island Park.

14.Gem State Nymph
by Bruce Staples

HOOK: Mustard 3906B, or equivalent, sizes 8-14
THREAD: black 6/0
WEIGHT: nontoxic wire warps under thorax
TAIL: ginger hackle fibers
RIB: fine gold wire
UNDERBELLY: strip of gold or yellow floss
BODY AND THORAX: peacock herl
SHELL BACK: 3 or 4 peacock herl fibers pulled over top of hackle and coated with head cement
HACKLE: ginger neck or saddle
Note: This is a green drake nymph in sizes 8-12 and in size 14 it represents a flav (aka "little western green drake"). Hatches of the two mayflies often overlap and a tandem rig with the flav following the green drake works well on small mountain streams, like the Big Wood River.

Bruce Staples

Bruce Staples, of Idaho Falls, Idaho, has fly-fished the Greater Yellowstone Area since the 1980s. He began tying flies in the 1970s and during the 1980s began writing of his Greater Yellowstone angling adventures in numerous periodicals and magazines and as a columnist for the Idaho Falls Post Register. Among his special interests is preserving the fly-fishing heritage of the Greater Yellowstone region. His books on the region include "Snake River Country: Flies and Waters," "The Yellowstone Park: A

River Journal " and "Trout Country Flies: Greater Yellowstone Area Masters." In 1990 Bruce was awarded the Fly Fishing Federation Western Rocky Mountain Council's Fly Tyer of the Year award for outstanding contributions to fly tying and the teaching of fly tying. In 1998 he received FFF's Charles Brooks Memorial Life Award. In 2001 he was awarded FFF's Buz Buszek Memorial Fly Tying Award.

15. Beadhead Peacock Leech
by Bruce Staples
HOOK: Mustard 9672, or equivalent, sizes 4-10
THREAD: black 6/0
BEAD: 3/17- inch brass
TAIL: dark ginger marabou with a few fibers of pearlescent Flashabou
RIB: copper wire counterwapped around hackle and body
HACKLE: ginger saddle palmered length of body
BODY: peacock herl
Note: From his long list of innovations, Bruce declares this "the most effective fly I have created."

16. Phil's Hopper
by Philip Blomquist
HOOK: Mustard 94831, or equivalent, sizes 8-14
THREAD: yellow 6/0
ANTENNAE: Monofilament, 5-10 lb. test
BODY: yellow yarn, extended on monofilament beam
UNDERWING: multi-colored Krystal Flash
WING: Ringneck pheasant church window feather
LEGS: medium yellow, orange or red rubber legs, tied Madam-X style
HEAD: deer or elk tied bullet-head style
POST: (optional) tuff of red yarn
Note: This is a great low-silhouette fly for picky trout on slow meadow streams and spring creeks. Use of a Ringneck pheasant church window feather for the wing is an artistic and effective innovation.

Philip "Phil" Blomquist
Philip Blomquist, 55, of Irwin, Idaho, died tragically in a boating accident on the South Fork of the Snake River in 2010. A custom fly tier, Phil was a river guide who loved fishing and a hunter and hiker who continually explored the mountains, lakes and streams of eastern Idaho and western Wyoming. A free-lance writer, he wrote fishing articles for the Idaho Falls Post and a number of other periodicals and magazines. A great favorite was his annual holidays newsletters advertising his Christmas Fly Boxes featuring his tying inspirations for the mayflies, caddis and terrestrials that encompass the seasons of the Henry's Fork and South Fork. They made excellent presents for friends and family planning to visit this epicenter of fly fishing.

Guided Trips
Learn all you can about your outfitter first
by Idaho Outfitters and Guides Association

Idaho's outfitters are friendly, helpful, knowledgeable people. They also are as varied as the state's landscapes. One may be a master storyteller, another a person of action and few words. One may specialize in high-adventure, physically challenging trips. Another may concentrate on relaxing excursions for all ages. One may provide a luxury, everything-included trip. Another may supply you with equipment and instructions to do your own trip. So take the time to browse the list provided and to talk to individual outfitters on the phone. Find the one who best matches your interests and needs.

OUTFITTERS AND GUIDES

Licensed outfitters and guides are available to lead sightseeing, fishing and hunting trips. A number of lodges and guest ranches offer accommodations. For more information contact the Idaho Outfitters and Guides Association, P.O. Box 95, Boise, ID 83701, or call 1-800-49-IDAHO. The IOGA website includes a search engine which will help you locate outfitters by type of activity and by area at http://www.ioga.org

A list of licensed outfitters and guides also may be obtained from the Outfitters and Guides Licensing Board, 1365 N. Orchard, Room 172, Boise, ID 83705, or call 327-7380. The OGLB website includes a search engine which will help you locate outfitters by type of activity and by area at:
    www.state.id.us/oglb/oglbhome.htm

EARLY PLANNING QUESTIONS

Before you book a trip, take a few minutes with family, friends or group to talk over what each member wants from the trip. Ask yourselves:

- What are your priorities for this trip? Do you want to relax, get away from it all, spend time with your family, have an adventure, take risks, test your limits?

- How long do you want to be away? A day, a weekend, a week, two weeks, or longer?

- When do you want to go? How flexible are the dates and times?

- Where do you want to go? What kind of terrain/scenery are you looking for? Mountains, meadows, lakes, canyonlands?

- How much can you spend? Be sure to include travel, meals, and the trip itself.

- Where do you want to stay? Tent camp, wilderness lodge, remote log cabin, motel at the edge of town, deluxe guest ranch?

- How many people? Do you want to travel only with your private group? Or would you enjoy meeting others?

FOR FAMILIES/MIXED GROUPS

Idaho outfitters can recommend trips and activities suited to many different ages and abilities. Some trips are specially designed for families or youth groups with or without experience in the outdoors. Others are designed for older, skilled groups looking for challenge and adventure.

FOOD

Idaho outfitters take pride in their cuisine. Ask about their cooking styles and specialties. Let your outfitter know in advance if you have any special dietary requirements.

SPECIAL NEEDS

Idaho outfitters often can meet the special needs of guests. Ask about accessibility and special accommodations ahead of time. Inquire about adaptive trips. If you have a medical condition, be sure to notify the outfitter when inquiring about the trip.

WHAT'S INCLUDED (WHAT'S NOT)

Make sure you understand what the price includes and what it doesn't. How much gear will the outfitter provide? How much will you need to bring? What meals are included? Does the outfitter provide transportation from the airport or is that additional? Be specific about which supplies and services you want to have included.

RESERVATIONS/CANCELLATIONS

Find out how much lead time you need to reserve a trip? Some Idaho trips and guest ranches are in such demand that it is best to reserve a year in advance. Others may require a three- to nine-month lead time. Very short trips, such as an afternoon rafting trip or family horseback outing, can wait until the day or week before. Remember to ask about deposits and cancellation policies. Many outfitters recommend trip cancellation insurance in case of an emergency.

RISKS/RELEASES

Although Idaho outfitters emphasize safety first, risks can never be totally eliminated. You may be asked to sign an acknowledgment of risk or to agree to accept the inherent risk of an activity.

STAY IN TOUCH

Stay in touch with your outfitter. He or she will provide you with complete trip information. It may include travel arrangements, packing lists, reading lists, pre-trip fitness suggestions, and where to stay before and after your trip. If you have questions, call your outfitter and ask. With an Idaho Outfitters and Guides Association member, you can expect ready answers — and a great trip!

(EDITOR'S NOTE) Ask your chosen outfitter or guest ranch for references and call them before signing a contract.

Catch and Release Tips

All anglers can help make future fishing better by releasing wild trout.

Because the cutthroat, Idaho's state fish, is so easily overfished, special regulations are imposed to protect them. On some waters anglers can only harvest certain sizes. Some streams are strictly catch-and-release. Waters designated wild trout streams for rainbows and browns fall under the same rules.

The set-free, no-harvest rule also applies to endangered stocks of Snake River salmon, wild steelhead, bull trout, and sturgeon.

Artificial flies or lures with only one barbless hook are required on catch-and-release waters to make release of fish easier.

Catch and release procedures:

1. Use the strongest terminal tackle conditions permit to make the landing battle as short as possible.

2. Land fish with a net.

3. Wet your hands if you must touch the fish. Do not squeeze it.

4. Do not touch the gills or hold fish by gill covers.

5. If possible, leave the fish in the water while removing the hook. Use of needle-nose pliers or medical forceps is recommended. Work quickly but gently.

6. If the hook cannot be easily removed, cut the leader. The hook will rust out rapidly.

7. If the fish is exhausted, hold it in an upstream swimming position in the water and move gently back and forth until it pulls itself out of your hands and swims off on its own.

Avoid excessive and unnecessary handling of the fish.

Fishing Fees, Special Rules and Seasons

IDAHO FISH AND GAME OFFICES

Administrative Regions

Administratively, the Idaho Department of Fish and Game is divided into regions with offices in Coeur d'Alene, Lewiston, Nampa, Jerome, Pocatello, Idaho Falls and Salmon. In addition, a subregional office in McCall operates in conjunction with the Nampa office. All offices are open Monday through Friday, except state holidays, 8:00a.m. to 5:00p.m. Offices in the Panhandle and Clearwater regions are in the Pacific time zone; all others are in the Mountain time zone.

The headquarters office, located in Boise, is organized into bureaus representing department functions: Administration, Fisheries, Wildlife, Law Enforcement, Communications, Natural Resources, Information Technology and Engineering. Each bureau is responsible for direction and consistency for programs implemented by regional staff.

Headquarters Office

Mailing Address: P.O. Box 25, Boise, ID 83707
Street / Walk-in Address: 600 S. Walnut, Boise, ID 83712
Phone: 208-334-3700 / Fax: 208-334-2114 or 208-334-2148
Director's Office: 208-334-3772
Wildlife Bureau: 208-334-2920
Enforcement Bureau: 208-334-3736
Administration Bureau: 208-334-3781
Web site: http://fishandgame.idaho.gov

Regional Offices

Panhandle Region

2885 W. Kathleen Ave., Coeur d'Alene, ID 83815
Phone: 208-769-1414, Fax: 208-769-1418
The northernmost area of the state consists of Boundary, Bonner, Kootenai and portions of Benewah, Latah, Clearwater and Shoshone counties.

Hunters, anglers and outdoor enthusiasts will find dense forests and the greatest concentration of lakes in the western states. The St. Joe, the world's highest navigable river, provides premier cutthroat trout fishing.

Elevations in the Panhandle range from 2,100 at Priest River to 8,643 at Needle Peak. Idaho record fish including rainbow trout, bull trout, chinook, kokanee, northern pike and tiger muskie were all taken from Panhandle waters.

Southwest Region

3101 S. Powerline Road, Nampa, ID 83686
Phone: 208-465-8465, Fax: 208-465-8467
McCall Subregion
555 Deinhard Lane, McCall, ID 83638
Phone: 208-634-8137, Fax: 208-634-4320

The southwestern corner of the state consists of Adams, Valley, Washington, Payette, Gem, Boise, Canyon, Ada, and part of Valley, Owyhee, Elmore and Idaho counties. The regional office is located in Nampa and Fish and Game Headquarters is located in Boise.

Diverse in terrain, the Southwest Region offers a wide range of outdoor sports and activities. From high mountain streams and lakes to lowland desert reservoirs, this areas rainbow trout fishing is unsurpassed.

Elevations range from 1,688 at Hells Canyon dam to 10,582 at Elk Peak.

Magic Valley Region

319 South 417 East, Jerome, ID 83338
Phone: 208-324-4359, Fax: 208-324-1160

The southernmost central portion of the state consists of Camas, Blaine, Gooding, Lincoln, Jerome, Minidoka, Twin Falls, Cassia, and part of Elmore, Owyhee, Power and Oneida counties.

Home to such natural marvels as the mighty Snake River, Thousand Springs and Shoshone Falls, this area brings the vast desert to life with ample hunting, angling and outdoor opportunities. Anglers will find a wide variety of game fish in the miles of the beautiful Snake River.

Elevations range from 2,797 at the Snake River to 10,339 at Cache Peak.

Southeast Region

1345 Barton Road, Pocatello, ID 83204
Phone: 208-232-4703, Fax: 208-233-6430

The far southeast corner of the state consists of Bingham, Power, Caribou, Bear Lake, Franklin, Bannock, Oneida and part of Bonneville counties.

With Utah and Wyoming on its borders, this region has abundant wildlife and scenery. Anglers may choose to partake in the tradition of ice fishing at Bear Lake for the Bonneville cisco, a species found nowhere else on earth.

Elevations in the southeast range from 4,354 at American Falls Reservoir to 9,957 at Meade Peak. Idaho record fish harvested in this region include the number one cutthroat trout, Idaho's state fish, taken at Bear Lake.

Upper Snake Region

4279 Commerce Circle, Idaho Falls, ID 83401

Phone: 208-525-7290, Fax: 208-523-7604

The eastern part of the state consists of Butte, Jefferson, Madison, Teton, Fremont, Clark, Bonneville and part of Lemhi, Custer, and Bingham counties.

Adventures abound, the gateway to the Continental Divide brings the best of what nature intended. Known to anglers everywhere for the best flyfishing in the world, enjoy locations from the Henrys Fork of the Snake River to Henrys Lake for Idaho's famous cutthroat trout.

Elevations range from 4,735 at Idaho Falls to 10,740 at Tyler Peak.

Salmon Region

99 Hwy. 93 North, (Mailing Address): P.O. Box 1336, Salmon, ID 83467

Phone: 208-756-2271, Fax: 208-756-6274

Directly north of the Magic Valley, the Salmon Region consists of Lemhi and Custer and portions of Blaine, and Valley counties.

Home to the "River of No Return," the Salmon river is one of the few undammed waterways left in America. The river and its forks serve as the only pathways into the River of No Return Wilderness Area, the largest single wilderness in the lower 48. Anglers can enjoy high mountain lake trout fishing.

Elevations reach up to 12,662 at Borah Peak, the highest peak in Idaho.

FISHING LICENSES AND PERMITS

Idaho resident

Adult licenses required if 18 years or older

Fishing.	$25.75
Fishing - three year	$73.75
Daily (first day)	$11.50
Each consecutive day at initial time of purchase add	$5.00
Combination hunting and fishing	$33.50
Disabled combination: SSI, SSDI, DAV	$5.00
Disabled fishing	$5.00
Military furlough combination	$17.50
Military furlough fishing	$17.50
Sportsman's package	$124.25

Senior license: 65 years and older (five years residency prior to license purchase required)

Combination hunting and fishing	$11.75
Combination hunting and fishing - three year	$31.75

Youth licenses: 10 to 17 years

Junior combination (14 to 17)	$17.50
Junior fishing (14 to 17)	$13.75
Sportsman's package	$117.25

Permits and Validations

Salmon permit	$12.75
Steelhead permit	$12.75
Two-pole permit	$13.75

Nonresident

Season fishing	$98.25
Fishing - three year	$291.25
Daily fishing (first day)	$12.75
Each consecutive day at initial time of purchase add	$6.00
Three-day salmon/steelhead (includes three-day general fishing license)	$37.50
Combination hunting and fishing	$240.00

Junior Mentored & Youth Licenses

Junior fishing (under 18)	$21.75
Junior - three year	$61.75

Permits and Validations

Salmon permit	$25.75
Steelhead permit	$25.75
Two-pole permit	$15.50

Note: In 2013, diehard anglers and hunters were given the option of purchasing a three-year hunting or fishing license. The cost of the license is three times the cost of an annual pass. There is no real savings, except people pay one vendor service fee, which saves them $3.50 compared to the cost of buying a pass every year.

INVASIVE SPECIES FUND BOAT STICKERS REQUIRED

A new state law requires the owner of any boat and any non-motorized vessel (sailboat, canoe, kayak, raft, drift boat, etc.) to buy and display the Idaho Invasive Species Fund sticker on the vessel to legally launch and operate the boat in Idaho.

Only inflatable, non-motorized vessels less than 10 feet long are exempt.

The sticker fee is in addition to any annual boat registration fee requirements. Therefore, the sticker cost is as an additional $10 for a motorized vessel registered in Idaho. Each motorized boat owner only gets a boating registration sticker but it proves he has paid for the invasive species prevention program.

New, however, is a $22 fee for an out-of-state motorized vessel and $7 fee for all non-motorized vessels, including both Idaho and out-of-state boaters.

Discounts for non-motorized commercial fleets are available.

The fees generated from the sale of stickers will fund vessel inspections, washing stations and informational materials that will help Idaho prevent the introduction of aquatic invasive species, such as quagga mussels.

Warning: Out-of-state boaters may be stopped at key border crossing locations with wash stations and be required to clean their boats before use in Idaho waters.

IISF stickers may be purchased online at:

http://parksandrecreation.idaho.gov/stickerpurchase.aspx

A list of state parks, regional Idaho Parks and Recreation regional centers, and local vendors where IISF stickers may be purchased also is available at this web site. Also check with local fly shops and sporting goods stores if they can sell the permit or for help in finding a vendor permitted to sell one.

The IISF sticker is included with registration of motorized Idaho boats.

The Idaho Fish and Game, Idaho Department of Parks and Recreation and Idaho Department of Agriculture web sites have links to provide boaters with a list of vendors and their locations where IISF stickers may be obtained. Sales of the permits will primarily be run through the Fish and Game vendors system, and the permits will no longer be available at state parks offices.

Safeguard your boats

To prevent the spread of invasive species all boaters should:
- Inspect all exposed surfaces: small mussels feel like sandpaper.
- Wash the boat thoroughly with high pressure or hot water.
- Remove all plant and animal material.
- Drain all water and dry all areas.
- Dispose of all bait in appropriate on-land location.
- Wait five days and keep boat dry between launches.

LICENSES AND TAGS—WHERE TO BUY THEM

All licenses, permits, general season tags and applications for controlled hunt drawings may be purchased at IDFG offices, on the Internet, over the telephone via credit card (1-800-554-8685), or at any of the more than 400 license vendors statewide. You may add a tag for another species as long as the quota on the tag you want has not been reached. Licenses and tags for the following year go on sale each December 1. Another person may make this purchase for you. When you apply for licenses, be sure to include your name, mailing address, social security number, height, weight, date of birth and telephone number. If you take advantage of the convenience of ordering by Internet or by telephone with a credit card, there is an additional processing charge for that service which will be explained at the time of purchase.

SEASONS AND RULES BROCHURES

IDFG prints brochures explaining hunting and fishing seasons and rules. If you buy over the telephone, be sure to ask the operator to put you on the mailing list for the type of brochure you will need. You can also download these from the IDFG website. This is the fastest way to get information. Scheduled availability for brochures is as follows: wild turkey: Jan. 1; moose, goat, sheep: March 7 (available now); deer, elk, antelope, black bear and mountain lion: April 15; upland game birds, rabbits, doves furbearers, sandhill cranes: July 15; waterfowl: Sept. 15; fishing: Dec. 17.

FISHING INFORMATION

The general stream fishing season opens the Saturday before Memorial Day and runs through November. Most large lakes, larger rivers and reservoirs are open to fishing year round, but variations exist and rules should be consulted before fishing.

Idaho is famous for its fishing. The most sought-after species are trout, including sea-run steelhead, rainbow, cutthroat, brown, brook, Mackinaw (lake trout) and salmon, including kokanee and chinook (see salmon information, below). Largemouth and smallmouth bass, perch, crappie, bluegill, northern pike, bullhead and channel catfish are also available in Idaho. Angler guides to lakes and reservoirs and regional fishing reports can be found in the fisheries menu of the IDFG website.

Idaho has approximately 25,000 miles of fishing streams, 225,000 acres of lakes and 239,000 acres of reservoirs. Much of the state is public domain and most waters are open to public fishing. Many large lakes and reservoirs have facilities for boats and other accommodations. Idaho's mountain lakes offer good fishing and splendid scenery. Fishing pressure is light because most of the lakes are accessible only to hikers and by horseback. Many mountain lakes have no established or maintained trail access.

Salmon and Steelhead

Salmon and steelhead migrate from Idaho to the Pacific Ocean. Their main routes to Idaho spawning beds are the Snake, Clearwater and Salmon rivers. Wild salmon and steelhead runs in Idaho are all listed as endangered species, due primarily to development of hydropower dams within the historical migration routes of the Columbia and Snake rivers. Fishing is still supported by hatcheries for steelhead. Depending on run size, localized fisheries for hatchery salmon may be possible. Anglers had a great season on hatchery salmon in 1997 and 1998.

The best fishing for steelhead is usually in October, November, March and April. Anglers must buy salmon and steelhead permits. Steelhead regulations, which are printed in the fishing rules brochure, should be checked closely because they differ substantially from general fishing rules. Anglers younger than 14 can purchase the required steelhead permit without a license.

Sockeye salmon and three groups of chinook salmon enter Idaho-spring-run, summer-run and fall-run. Sockeye and wild (not hatchery-produced) chinook are protected under state law and the federal Endangered Species Act.

Some lakes and reservoirs have landlocked forms of chinook, coho, Atlantic or kokanee (blueback) salmon. In general, these fall under the daily trout limit, but some waters have special regulations printed in the fishing seasons brochure.

Sturgeon

Catch-and-release fishing for sturgeon is available in several segments of the Snake River in southern and central Idaho. Heavy tackle is recommended for sturgeon fishing because sturgeon exceeding six feet in length and weighing more than 100 pounds are common. They must be released immediately without being removed from the water.

Bull Trout

Bull trout are protected under state law and the federal Endangered Species Act. No harvest is allowed. Any bull trout caught while fishing for other species must be released unharmed immediately.

Equipment Checklist / Travel Tips

When setting off on an Idaho fishing trip, make your travel list and check it twice. Nothing ruins a vacation more than forgetting to bring a key piece of equipment. Be paranoid, check off your rods, reels and fishing vest a third time.

Come prepared for inclement weather and be physically fit to handle high-elevation trekking.

A RECOMMENDED SUMMER FISHING EQUIPMENT CHECKLIST

1. Selection of rods and reels, such as a 6-weight, 8½- or 9-foot graphite rod and a 4- or 5-weight, 8½- or 9-foot graphite rod. Optional: Extra reel spool(s) equipped with shooting-head floating line or sinking line.
2. Fishing vest or fanny pack to hold tackle.
3. Forceps to remove hooks from fish; line nippers or fingernail clippers to trim leader tippets, trim flies.
4. Selection of tapered leaders and tippet material, 2X to 6X; selection of sinking tips.
5. Selection of standard aquatic insect fly patterns, wet and dry, like pale morning dun, blue-winged olive, elk hair caddis, parachute Adams; beadhead hare's ear, pheasant tail and prince nymphs; PMD and caddis emergers; muddler minnows, Zonkers, woolly worms. Attractor patterns can include renegades, humpies, stimulators, royal Wulffs. Terrestrial patterns should include grasshoppers, beetles, ants. Inquire locally for specialized patterns or seasonally appropriate dry flies, emergers and nymphs.
6. Fly floatant.
7. Nontoxic split shot.
8. Fishing net.
9. Stocking foot chest waders and wading shoes.
10. Wading staff if you plan to wade rocky or swift waters.
11. Polarized sunglasses.
12. Stout fishing hat to protect neck and ears.
13. Light-weight rain jacket.
14. Wool or fleece sweater, wind-breaker jacket, fingerless gloves for cool mornings and evenings.
15. Water bottle or canteen.
16. Sunscreen.
17. Insect repellent.
18. Camera, extra film and batteries; wet bag to protect camera and equipment.

FALL AND WINTER ADDITIONS

19. Neoprene chest waders and wading shoes.
20. Extra warm clothing to wear in layers.
21. Warm hat or wool ski cap that covers ears.
22. Neoprene gloves.
23. Heavy wool socks and polypropylene foot liners.
24. Cigarette lighter in waterproof pouch.
25. High-energy snacks.
26. Full change of clothing in vehicle in case you get wet.
27. All-purpose tool (Leatherman).

STEELHEADER'S CHECKLIST

1. Stout graphite rod(s), 7- or 8-weight, 9- or 9½- foot.
2. Heavy reel(s) with disc-type drag, able to handle 150 to 200 yards of backing, and fly line.
3. Floating or weight-forward lines; sinking tips.
4. Heavy tapered leaders, 2X and 1X, 7- to 9-foot.
5. Good selection of Western steelhead flies, No. 6 to 2, such as skunks, purple perils, sunrise series, polar shrimp, egg patterns and skating water-walkers.
6. Neoprene chest waders and wading shoes.
7. Polypropylene underwear and foot liners, heavy wool or neoprene socks.
8. Rain gear, windbreaker jacket, warm hat or wool ski cap, gloves and layering-type warm clothing.
9. Water bottle, canteen or thermos bottle.
10. High-energy snacks.
12. Cigarette lighter in waterproof pouch to start fire.
12. Full change of clothing in waterproof pack or bag in case you get wet.
13. Parka and down vest for camp wear, gloves or mittens, warm hat.

TRAVEL TIPS

Fly fishers embarking for Idaho via commercial airlines should plan on transfers at one or more service hubs, some with layovers. Plan accordingly and protect your equipment.

Pack rods in aluminum or plastic rod holders or a rod-holder caddy, securely sealed and clearly labeled with name and home address. Make sure flight destination tags are firmly attached.

Better yet, carry onto the plane all the rods and reels you can. A good option is to have a travel rod that breaks down into three or four pieces. It may be more difficult to carry on a two-piece rod but some airlines permit it. Stuff your basic equipment and bare essentials into a duffel bag for the second carry-on piece of luggage.

Never ship cameras or telephoto lens as cargo in recognizable photography equipment containers. If you don't plan to take them as carry-on luggage, stuff them into your suitcases.

Only pack essential clothing. Your fishing equipment is most important.

Be in shape: Idaho is high, wide and handsome, its rivers big and powerful. Be prepared for their physical challenges.

Coastal visitors should remember that as soon as the plane lands you're already almost a mile above sea level in southeastern and central Idaho. Your next destination is often higher. This is less of a problem in the southwest corner of the state and in northern Idaho. But even in these locations, there is a lot of up and down to the terrain.

Don't overextend yourself wading or boating. Appreciate the volume of the bigger rivers. One cubic foot per second of water, the standard measurement of flow, is roughly equivalent to one foot of water continually flooding a football field. A football field is flat and rock-free. Idaho rivers are not—their waters are almost always frigid. Below some dams flows can change radically without advance notice.

Information Links and Sources

NOTE: The area code for the entire state of Idaho is 208.

IDAHO TRAVEL DEPARTMENT

Idaho Travel Department
700 W. State Street, 2nd Floor
Boise, ID 83720
1-208-334-2470
1-800-VISIT ID
http://www2.state.id.us/HOME/tourism.htm

GENERAL INFO PHONE NUMBERS

Idaho Dept. of Commerce BBS...1-208-334-3646

Idaho Relay Service for hearing impaired (TTY)...................1-800-377-3529

Idaho Relay Service for hearing impaired (Voice)................1-800-377-1363

Coeur d'Alene Indian Tribe Fish and Wildlife........................1-208-686-6503

Idaho hunting/fishing info, regulations,
nonresident applications, map orders 1-800-635-7820

Nonresident license and tag sales by
Visa, MasterCard, American Express, Discover 1-800-554-8685

Report a Poacher (Idaho)..1-800-632-5999

CONDITIONS AND REPORTS

Ask Fish (fishing reports).. 1-800-ASK-FISH

Hell's Canyon - Brownlee Water
Conditions and Campground Reservations 1-800-422-3143

Idaho River Flow Information (Mar. - Oct.) 1-208-327-7865

U.S. Bureau of Reclamation
Reservoir and Stream Conditions............................ 1-208-334-9134

USGS Stream Flows Information
http://wwwidaho.wr.usgs.gov./rt-cgi/gen_tbl_pg"

Idaho Road Conditions
http://www2.state.id.us/itd/ida-road/index.html

Idaho Weather Conditions
http://www.state.id.us/fishgame/weather.htm

National Interagency Fire CenteR
http://www.nifc.gov./information.html

STATE AND FEDERAL AGENCIES

U.S. Fish and Game State Agencies
http//www.state.id.us/fishgame/agencies.htm

Idaho Outfitters and Guides
http://www.state.id.us/oglb/oglbhome.htm

Idaho Dept. of Commerce
http://www.IDOC.state.id.us

Idaho Dept. of Parks and Recreation
http://www.IDOC.state.id.us/StateParks/spdir.html

U.S. Forest Service
http://www.fs.fed.us

Bureau of Land Management (Idaho)
http://www.id.blm.gov

Bureau of Land Management (U.S.)
http://www.blm.gov

US Fish and Wildlife
http://www.fws.gov

US Fish and Wildlife - Pacific Region
http://www.r1.fws.gov

SPORTSMAN ORGANIZATIONS

Idaho Fish and Wildlife Foundation
   http://www.idfishnhunt.com/~IFWF

Idaho Wildlife Federation
   http://www.idahowildlife.org

Trout Unlimited (Idaho State Council)
   http://www.idfishnhunt.com/tutedt.htm

Idaho Bass Anglers Sportsman Society
   http://www.idfishnhunt.com/idahobass.html

Idaho Steelhead and Salmon United
   http://www.idfishnhunt.com/issu.html

Idaho Rivers United
   http://www.desktop.org/iru

River Shuttle Services
All area codes are 208

South Fork of the Snake
Barnee's Amoco, Ririe 538-5038
Laurie's Lift's; Idaho Falls.. 528-1572
Drifters of the South Fork; Swan Valley 483-2722
Julie's Shuttle Service, Swan Valley 483-2903
Sandy Mite Fly Shop and Cafe, Irwin............................ 483-2609
South Fork Lodge, Conant Valley 483-2112

South Fork of the Boise
Conny Carrico, Parrie... 868-3255

Middle Fork of the Salmon
River Rat Express, Stanley 1-800-831-8942; 774-2265
D & D Shuttle, Grangeville 983-2062

Main Salmon
River Rat Express, Stanley 1-800-831-8942; 774-2265
D & D Shuttle, Grangeville 983-2062
Lloyd Chadwick, Grangeville 983-0887

Lower Salmon
Lloyd Chadwick, Grangeville 983-0887

South Fork of the Salmon/Payette
Jim Cook call 634-3522
    or e-mail chwhite@cyberhighway.net

Hell's Canyon
Hell's Canyon Adventures 1-800-422-3568
    for an exciting Jet Boat ride back to the top.
Hell's Canyon Shuttle, Dianna Jensen 1-800-785-3358
D & D Shuttle, Grangeville 983-2062

Selway River
Marilyn Johnson, Conner, MT 406-821-4421
Marvin Smith, P.O. Box 1011, Darby, MT 59829.......406-821-3167
    Fax 406-821-4117
D & D Shuttle, Grangeville 983-2062

Owhyee River
Eva Matteri... 1-541-586-2352
    (no tow available across reservoir, will leave you a motor)
Ken Haylett 459-1292
    Yheervr1@ix.netcom.com (tow available across reservoir)
Rome and Leslie Gulch 459-4808
    e-mail: marmotstar@aol.com

Bruneau River
Jumbo's Auto Service, Bruneau 845-2150
Ken Erwin, Brunea.. 845-2756

The Murtaugh
Idaho Guide Service, Twin Falls 734-4998

Four Rivers Lottery System

PERMITS REQUIRED TO FLOAT WILDERNESS RIVERS

The Forest Service has turned over its non-commercial boating lottery and reservation process for four Wild and Scenic rivers in central Idaho and eastern Oregon to an entirely online process hosted by the National Recreation Reservation System (www.recreation.gov). The rivers are the wild sections of the main Salmon, Selway and Hells Canyon of the Snake, and the Middle Fork of the Salmon.

Paper applications are no longer accepted. Forest Service Ranger Offices in charge of each of the four rivers will still take phone calls, e-mails and written requests for information to assist boaters planning floats. However, Forest Service personnel can no longer accept payment for trip fees. All financial transactions and reservations must be conducted through the www.recreation.gov website.

A key benefit of the new system is that now each river will have a separate lottery to assign launch reservations. They will no longer be combined into one drawing system.

In the past, you could enter applications for several people at one time. But because the new system will be used for processing cancellations (and payments on the Middle Fork and wild main Salmon rivers), each applicant will need to be registered under a unique e-mail address with a password to access his profile.

Also, before, a potential river floater could file only one application with four possible launch dates spread across all four rivers. But with the new system, applicants can

Flyfishermen on the Middle Fork. Rocky Barker photo.

file as many as four applications, one for each river, and list four possible launch dates on each application. The fee is still $6 for each application.

Officials feel the new system will save time, paper and money, and make the lottery run faster since confirmations will be handled by e-mail.

Overview:

Starting in December 2009, the Forest Service switched to managing all float reservations for the wild section of the main Salmon, Selway, Hells Canyon of the Snake, and Middle Fork of the Salmon entirely online. The new system replaces an obsolete, paper-based lottery. It also replaces technology and database management functions that we are losing the capability and expertise to support and provide a more secure environment for the privacy information that our clients need to provide.

The lottery runs annually from December 1 to January 31. Those dates won't change under the new system. The lottery allocates permits for each river's most popular floating seasons, called "control seasons". Control seasons occur between May and September; specific dates vary from river to river.

Under the old system, people were limited to one application per season. An application could contain four launch date choices on any of the four rivers -- four possible trips. The application fee was $6.

Under the new system, people may apply for up to four dates on each of the four rivers. However, they will have to submit an application for each of the four rivers, each costing $6. Applicants will now find out in a matter of days, instead of weeks, if they got their permits.

In addition to moving the permit lottery to an entirely online process, these four rivers will use this new system to allocate all reservations, including reassigning cancellations.

The Middle Fork and wild section of the main Salmon Rivers will also use this online system to assign pre- or post-season reservations which occur outside their control season. This new system will also be used to process the payment of recreation fees for the Middle Fork and the main Salmon Rivers.

Changes apply to the lottery (allocation) method; neither the number of permits nor the available launches will change. Any future fee changes will be implemented under the Federal Lands Recreation Enhancement Act.

Key Points:

The Forest Service has used online cabin and campground reservations for many years. The Boundary Waters Canoe Area Wilderness in Minnesota currently uses an online lottery system that works well.

The web address is www.recreation.gov.

The new system allows applicants to list as many as 16 launch date choices, four dates for each of the four rivers in just one visit to recreation.gov.

The Forest Service's river managers will post safety alerts on the latest river conditions on the recreation.gov website.

The information entered online is secure and private.

The lottery will run faster, smoother, and more reliably. By eliminating the workload of handling thousands of paper permit applications, Forest Service staff will be free to answer questions and address river issues instead of doing paperwork.

For more info, go to www.fs.fed.us/r4/sc/recreation/4rivers/index.shtml and follow its links to detailed information for trip requirements provided by each of the state's four wild rivers' management offices.

To learn more about the reservation system and to create your unique e-mail profile visit www.recreation.gov

Additional contacts: Sheri Hughes (Recreation Planner) 208-879-4107; Kent Fuellenbach (PAO) 208-756-5145.

FYI: Invasive species boat sticker required

An Idaho State Boating Law, also initiated in 2009, requires that all vessels (motorized and non-motorized) display the Idaho Invasive Species Fund sticker to legally launch and operate on Idaho waters. Inflatable, non-motorized vessels less than 10 feet long are exempt. Go to http://parksandrecreation.idaho.gov or call 1-800-247-6332 for more information and purchase options.

Indian Reservations in Idaho

Fort Hall Indian Reservation

The Shoshone-Bannock Tribes of the Fort Hall Indian Reservation issue permits to hunt and fish on their lands, south of the Blackfoot and Snake Rivers, west of Blackfoot and north of Pocatello. Hunting permits issued by the Shoshone-Bannock Tribes include waterfowl and ring-necked pheasant. The tribes also require a refundable deposit against possible damages.

Fees and regulations change annually. Rates in 2010 ranged from $175 annual pass (175 limit) to $35 per day or $50 for two-days (6 rod daily limit). Annual passes go on sale first week of April and often sell out first day. Permits are sold only during business hours, 8:00a.m. to 4:00p.m., at the Fish and Game Department office at the Fort Hall town site. However, daily permits will be post-dated for next day or the weekend.

The season for the Fort Hall Bottoms opens third Saturday in May and ends October 31.

For more information, call the Fort Hall Hunting and Fishing Department at 1-208-478-3956.

For general Fort Hall Indian Reservation information, call 238-3700.

Tribal hunting and fishing permits include information on where non-resi¬dents are permitted on the reservation. Study it carefully to avoid trespass.

Duck Valley Indian Reservation

The Shoshone-Paiute Tribes of the Duck Valley Indian Reservation, based at Owyhee, Nev., permit fishing on three reservoirs: Sheep Creek, Mountain View and Lake Billie Shaw. Sheep Creek and Mountain View are managed for catch-and-keep fishing. Billie Shaw is a trophy lake where anglers are limited to keeping one fish per day. A 10-mile stretch of the Owyhee River also is open to fishing.

The reservation straddles the Idaho-Nevada border, about 95 miles south of Mountain Home, Idaho, and 100 miles north of Elko, Nev.

In 2010, Mountain View and Sheep Creek fees ranged from Adult Daily Fishing Permit, $7.50, to Season Individual camping and fishing, $50. Lake Billie Shaw fees range from Daily Individual permit, $25, to Season Individual permit, $275. Campgrounds are located at all three reservoirs.

Limited upland bird hunting is also permitted on the Duck Creek Indian Reservation, which straddles the Idaho-Nevada border south of Mountain Home.

To check on current conditions, visit with Boise or Twin Falls fly shops, or call the tribal fish and game office in Nevada at 775-757-2921.

Call 208-759-3100 ext. 410 for automated fishing report.

Website: http://duckvalleyonline.com/Fishing_Information.htm

Nez Perce Indian Reservation

The Nez Perce Tribe of northern Idaho issues a permit to fish for sea-running steelhead trout in the Clearwater River, which is the northern border of the Nez Perce Indian Reservation, east of Lewiston. Anglers may fish for steelhead in the Clearwater with either a tribal permit, which is available at local fishing tackle shops, or an IDFG permit.

For information on where to buy a license and steelhead permit to fish the Clearwater River, contact Idaho Fish and Game at 208-334-3717 or the Nez Perce Tribe at 208-843-2383.

Coeur d'Alene Indian Reservation

The Coeur d'Alene Indian Reservation is located southwest of the resort town of Coeur d'Alene. Tribal headquarters are at Plummer.

The tribe manages the southern portion of Coeur d'Alene Lake. Anglers who are not members of the Coeur d'Alene Tribe are required to obtain a tribal fishing permit, in addition to a state license, to fish reservation waters, including the southern end of Lake Coeur d'Alene: Youths, 14 to 17, $10 annual license; Adults, 18 to 55, $25 annual license; Seniors, 55 or older, $5 annual license.

Licenses are available at the Coeur d'Alene Tribal Fish & Wildlife Office at Plummer and a number of regional commercial vendors. For more information, call the Fish, Water, Wildlife, Lake Management Office at 208-686-5302.

Other Tribes in Idaho

The Kootenai Tribe of northern Idaho does not permit hunting or fishing on its lands.

Federal Public Lands in Idaho

Approximately 30 million acres of Idaho are administered as national forests and federal range lands open to the public for hunting, fishing and other recreational pursuits.

The U.S. Forest Service administers more than 17.2 million acres of mountainous forest lands. They include five wilderness areas and a national recreation area. The forest service also manages a national grasslands. Idaho's 3.4 million acres of wilderness and 9 million acres of roadless areas make up the largest combined tract of roadless forests in the Lower 48 States.

The U.S. Bureau of Land Management administers more than 12 million acres of public range lands in the high desert plains of eastern, southcentral and southwest Idaho. It also administers small pockets of land in north Idaho.

Two additional large expanses of federal lands in eastern Idaho are closed to hunting; Craters of the Moon National Monument, south of Arco, is a major tourism attraction and worth a side trip. However, the Idaho National Engineering and Envi¬ron¬mental Laboratory, west of Idaho Falls, is a U.S. Department of Energy research facility entirely closed to public access, except during guided tours.

U.S. FOREST SERVICE AND NATIONAL FORESTS

There are 10 national forests in Idaho, including the Panhandle National Forest that is composed of the Coeur d'Alene, Kaniksu and St. Joe national forests. All are open to hunting under the rules and regulations of the Idaho Department of Fish and Game.

Vehicles are not permitted in wilderness areas, although landing strips are maintained for fly-ins by outfitters and owners of private land in-holdings. Also, many national forest roads are closed in fall to reduce hunting pressure on big game animals. Study travel maps for individual forests before hunting.

Travel maps and forest information, including wilderness areas, are available from each forest's supervisor office and their respective district ranger offices.

Panhandle National Forest

More than 2.5 million acres north and south of Sandpoint, and east and south of Coeur d'Alene. Includes part of the Mallard-Larkin Pioneer Area. District ranger offices are located at Wallace, Avery, Fernan, St. Maries, Sandpoint, Bonners Ferry, and Priest Lake.

Supervisor
Idaho Panhandle National Forest
3815 Schreiber Way
Coeur d'Alene, ID 83814
208-765-7223

Clearwater National Forest

Nearly 1 million acres north and east of Orofino. Includes part of the Selway-Bitterroot Wilderness and the Mallard-Larkin Pioneer Area. District ranger offices are located at Orofino, Kamiah, Kooskia and Potlatch, Idaho. An office is also located in Lolo, Montana.

Supervisor
Clearwater National Forest
12730 Highway 12
Orofino, ID 83544
208-476-4541

Nez Perce National Forest

More than 2.2. million acres east and south of Grangeville. Includes portions of five wilderness areas: Selway-Bitterroot, Frank Church-River of No Return, Gospel Hump, and Hells Canyon. District ranger offices are located at Grangeville, Elk City, Red River, White Bird and Kooskia.

Supervisor
Nez Perce National Forest
1005. Highway 13
Route 2, P.O. Box 475
Grangeville, ID 83530
208-983-1950

Payette National Forest

More than 2.5 million acres north and east of McCall and northwest and southeast of Council. Includes portions of Frank Church-River of No Return and Hells Canyon wilderness areas. District ranger offices are located at McCall, Council, Weiser and New Meadows.

Supervisor
Payette National Forest
800 West Lakeside Ave.
P.O. Box 1026
McCall, ID 83638
208-634-0700

Boise National Forest

More than 2.6 million acres north and east of Boise and east of Cascade. Includes portions of Frank Church-River of No Return Wilderness. District ranger offices are located at Boise, Emmett, Cascade, Lowman, Idaho City and Mountain Home.

Supervisor
Boise National Forest
1249 S. Vinnell Way
Boise, ID 83709
208-364-4100

Sawtooth National Forest

More than 2.1 million acres; majority of the forest is north of Ketchum-Sun Valley, scattered portions are located southeast of Twin Falls. Includes the Sawtooth National Recreation Area and Sawtooth Wilderness. District offices are located at Fairfield, Ketchum, Stanley, and Burley.

Supervisor
Sawtooth National Forest
2647 Kimberly Road East
Twin Falls, ID 83301
208-737-3200
also:
Supervisor
Sawtooth National Recreation Area
Highway 75 & North Fork Canyon Road
Ketchum, ID 83340
1-208-727-5000

Challis National Forest

More than 2.5 million acres west and south of Challis; under joint supervision of Salmon National Forest. Includes one-third of Frank Church-River of No Return Wilderness. District ranger offices located at Challis, Clayton, and Mackay.

Supervisor
Salmon-Challis National Forest
1206 S. Challis Street
Salmon, ID 83467
208-756-5100

Salmon National Forest

More than 1.8 million acres east and southeast of Salmon; also administers Challis National Forest. Includes portion of Frank Church-River of No Return Wilderness. District ranger offices located at Salmon, North Fork, Cobalt, and Leadore.

Supervisor
Salmon-Challis National Forest
1206 S. Challis Street
Salmon, ID 83467
208-756-5100

Targhee National Forest

More than 1.8 million acres north, east and south of St. Anthony; it also administers Caribou National Forest. Large parts of Targhee in Wyoming include the Jedidiah Smith Wilderness and Winegar Hole Wilderness. District ranger offices located at Ashton, Island Park, Driggs, Dubois, and Idaho Falls.

Caribou-Targhee National Forest
Headquarters Office
1405 Hollipark Drive
Idaho Falls, Idaho 83401
1-208-524-7500

Caribou National Forest

About 1 million acres east, south and southeast of Pocatello, under joint administration with Targhee National Forest; also administers Curlew National Grasslands. District ranger offices located at Pocatello, Soda Springs, Malad, and Montpelier.

Caribou-Targhee National Forest
Headquarters Office
1405 Hollipark Drive
Idaho Falls, Idaho 83401
1-208-524-7500

Waterfall in the Caribou National Forest. Art Today photo.

U.S. BUREAU OF LAND MANAGEMENT PUBLIC RANGELANDS

There are approximately 12 million acres of public rangelands administered by the Bureau of Land Management and they include many key waterways that lace southern Idaho's high plains deserts, sagebrush plateaus and lava flows. These riparian zones are critical gamebird and wildlife habitat in the semi-arid region. Also of importance to upland gamebird and big game hunters are Idaho BLM lands in dry mountain foothills adjacent to the state's 10 forests.

Idaho's BLM headquarters are located in Boise. District administrative offices are located at Boise, Idaho Falls, Burley, Shoshone, Salmon and Coeur d' Alene. The BLM maintains a system of remote public campgrounds. Recreation and travel maps are available from Idaho BLM headquarters and each of the district offices:

Idaho BLM State Office
1387 South Vinnell Way
Boise, ID 83709-1657
208-373-4000

Boise BLM District

Areas of interest include the Boise Front mountain foothills and remote Owyhee desert and mountains, and lower Snake River, Owyhee River and Jarbridge River drainages. District also administers the Snake River Birds of Prey National Conservation Area and the Owyhee Scenic Byway. Field offices in Boise (Four Rivers), Bruneau (Owyhee) and Marshing.

Boise BLM District Office
3948 Development Avenue
Boise, ID 83705-5389
208-384-3300

Twin Falls BLM District

Areas of interest include middle Snake River, and the Bruneau River, Bruneau sand dunes, Salmon Falls Creek, Raft River and Lower Goose Creek drainages. Field offices in Burley, Jarbridge and Shoshone.

Twin Falls BLM District Office
2536 Kimberly Road
Twin Falls, ID 83301
208-735-2060

Idaho Falls BLM District

Areas of interest include the Big Butte Desert, St. Anthony Sand Dunes, Centennial and Bitterroot mountain foothills, and Big Lost River, Little Lost River, Birch Creek, Camas Creek, Blackfoot River and Bear Lake drainages. District also cooperatively manages South Fork of Snake River and the St. Anthony Sand Dunes - Sand Creek wildlife wintering area. Field offices in Pocatello, Challis and Salmon:

Idaho Falls BLM District Office
1405 Hollipark
Idaho Falls, ID 83401-2196
208-524-7500
also:
Idaho Falls Visitor Center
(USFS, BLM, Idaho Falls Chamber of Commerce)
630 West Broadway
208-523-1010

Coeur d' Alene BLM District

District has scattered pockets of federal land in north-central Idaho. It cooperatively manages lower Salmon River. Field offices in Coeur d'Alene, and Cottonwood:

Coeur d' Alene BLM District Office
3815 Schreiber Way
Coeur d'Alene, ID 83815
208-769-5000

NATIONAL WILDLIFE REFUGES

Four of Idaho's NWRs and a USFWS waterfowl production areas are located in eastern Idaho and administered by its Pocatello office. The state's two other national wildlife refuges are west of Boise and north of Sandpoint, almost on the Canadian border.

Southeast Idaho NWR Complex

The Southeast Idaho NWR Complex office in Pocatello administers Bear Lake NWR, Camas NWR, Gray's Lake NWR, Minidoka NWR, and the Oxford Slough Waterfowl Production Area. For more information, call or write:

U.S. Fish and Wildlife Service
4425 Burley Drive, Suite A
Chubbuck, ID 83201-4372
1-208-237-6615

Minidoka National Wildlife Refuge

Minidoka National Wildlife Refuge
Rt 4, Box 290
Rupert, ID 83350
1-208-436-3589

Directions: From Rupert, which is 75 miles west of Pocatello on Interstate 84, drive 6 miles northeast on State Highway 24 via Acequia, then 6 miles east on County Road 400 North.

Habitat: 20,721 acres, including 11,000 surface acres of Lake Walcott on the Snake River. Surrounding uplands are typical high desert sagebrush and grassland.

Gray's Lake National Wildlife Refuge

Gray's Lake National Wildlife Refuge
HC 70, Box 4090/74 Gray's Lake Road
Wayan, ID 83285
1-208-574-2755

Directions: Drive south from Pocatello on Interstate 15 and take U.S. Highway 30 to Soda Springs (about 60 miles). From Soda Springs, go north on State Highway 34 about 35 miles, turn at refuge sign 2 miles west of Wayan. (Alternate Route: From Idaho Falls drive 65 miles east on U.S. Highway 26 to Alpine, Wyo., turn south on U.S. 89 and drive 10 miles to Freedom. From Freedom, drive 20 miles west to Wayan and turn north to refuge.)

Habitat: 18,330 acres of high mountain marsh in basin below Caribou Mountains; water levels often depleted by irrigation diversions.

Bear Lake National Wildlife Refuge

Bear Lake National Wildlife Refuge
Box 9, 370 Webster Street
Montpelier, ID 83254
1-208-847-1757

Directions: Drive south from Pocatello on I-15 to turn off on U.S. 30. From Soda Springs, drive 30 miles south on U.S. 30 to Montpelier. Refuge located 7 miles southwest of Montpelier. From town, drive 3 miles southwest on U.S. 89, turn east onto Bear Lake County Airport Road and drive 5 miles to north entrance of refuge.

Habitat: 17,600 acres of marsh, open water, and grasslands at elevation of 5,900 feet in Bear Lake/Bear River valley. Marsh often severely depleted of water due to irrigation diversions in late summer.

Camas National Wildlife Refuge

Camas National Wildlife Refuge
2150 East 2350 North
Hamer, ID 83425
1-208-662-5423

Directions: Located 35 miles north of Idaho Falls. Drive north on Interstate 15 and turn east at Hamer; go north on frontage road 3 miles and turn west over I-15 overpass at sign, continue west 1.5 miles to refuge.

Habitat: 10,578 acres of marshes, ponds, meadows and sagebrush uplands. No Fishing

Deer Flat National Wildlife Refuge

Deer Flat National Wildlife Refuge
13751 Upper Embankment Road
Nampa, ID 83686
1-208-467-9278

Directions: Located 5 miles southwest of Nampa, which is 12 miles west of Boise on Interstate 84. From Nampa, turn off 12th Street and drive west on Lake Lowell Road to Upper Embankment Road; refuge headquarters are 1 mile west of upper embankment.

Habitat: The Lake Lowell sector—10,587 acres—includes a Bureau of Reclamation reservoir. Annual irrigation drawdown exposes mud flats.

Snake River Islands: This sector of the refuge complex includes 107 islands on the Snake River, extending for 113 miles from Ada-Canyon county line to Brownlee Reservoir.

Kootenai National Wildlife Refuge

Kootenai National Wildlife Refuge
HCR 60, Box 283
Bonners Ferry, ID 83805
1-208-267-3888

Directions: Located west of Bonners Ferry, 18 miles south of Canadian border in the Kootenai River Valley. Bonners Ferry is 35 miles north of Sandpoint on U.S. Highway 95. From Bonners Ferry go west on dike road along south bank of Kootenai River for 5 miles to the refuge; refuge headquarters another 1.5 miles. Watch for logging trucks.

Habitat: 2,775 acres of ponds, grasslands, cultivated croplands, shrubs and timbered western edge on foothills of Selkirk Mountains.

Whirling Disease

Status of Whirling Disease Uncertain in Idaho

Just like the old saying goes, there's good news and bad news when it comes to whirling disease in Idaho and, particularly, the Upper Snake Region. The bad news is that the presence of myxozoan parasites has been found in many waters throughout the region. The good news is that not all of these parasites are the dreaded *Myxobolus cerebralis* and in most waters where *Myxobolus cerebralis* has been confirmed, clinical symptoms have yet to be observed.

"We felt it was important to let anglers know what has been happening with whirling disease in the region," Region 6 Fishery Manager Mark Gamblin said in a 1998 report.

"The only waters in the region where we are really seeing adverse impacts are on the Teton and Big Lost Rivers, where we are seeing a breakdown in the younger age class of fish."

Whirling disease hits younger fish hardest because their skeletons are made of soft cartilage that has not yet hardened into bone and is open to attack by the *Myxobolus cerebralis* parasite. The parasite itself may not kill the fish but renders them unable to feed normally so they starve to death. Whirling disease causes fish to swim around in a whirling pattern also leaving them vulnerable to predators.

The spores of *Myxobolus cerebralis*, released when infected fish die, are ingested by Tubifex worms, which live in mud. Inside the worm, the parasite takes on a new form called a "TAM," which are then released into the water where they can infect members of the salmonid family.

Researchers are still working to find out exactly how *Myxobolus cerebralis* operates. "There are still a lot of unknowns in the field of *Myxobolus cerebralis* study," said Region 6 Fishery Biologist Jeff Dillon. "In order for *Myxobolus cerebralis* to take hold it needs a specific Tubifex worm to serve as an intermediate host."

Tubifex worms have been located in some, but not all the waters in the Upper Snake Region. Fortunately, of those worms identified, not all are the host required to sustain the whirling disease chain.

"One area of specific concern has been regarding infected fish found during a population survey being done in the fall of 1997 in the Stone Bridge section of the Henry's Fork. Last fall, about a half dozen trout were collected that exhibited clinical symptoms of whirling disease," Gamblin said. "Even though we found these infected trout lower downriver, fishing has still been great in the Box Canyon section through to Riverside Campground. In fact, we have not even find the Myxobolus cerebralis parasite in samples collected from these areas."

However, a 1999 report indicates the threat is more widespread.

The Henry's Fork Foundation hired Daniel Gustafson, a Montana State University biologist, to conduct a study in the Henry's Fork basin.

"Based on the observed presence of Tubifex, there are eight distinct high-risk areas for whirling disease in the Henry's Fork River drainage", Gustafson stated. "Based on the observed absence of Tubifex and the intact, highly diverse communities, there is also a large area of the Henry's Fork River drainage that seems safe from whirling disease."

According to Gustafson's report:

- The first high-risk area is the low-lying area from Henry's Lake to Island Park Reservoir. Some fish with the whirling disease parasite have already been reported from Henry's Lake, so it now seems safe to assume that the entire area has been exposed. The apparent lack of a whirling disease problem in this area may be due to the low recruitment value of the streams with the most Tubifex or to any number of unusual conditions here.

- The second high-risk area is the Sheridan Creek area west of Island Park Reservoir. I have neither seen nor have I heard of any reports of the whirling disease parasite here. There are currently very few salmonids in much of these stream. This severely degraded stream is now being restored. Ironically, it could develop a whirling disease problem at some state of partial restoration. The poor condition of the upper stream makes the prospect for eliminating Tubifex seem unlikely.

- The third high-risk area is the tailwater of Island Park Dam. This area has repeatedly tested negative for the whirling diseases parasite. The best Tubifex area is between the power plant and the Buffalo River. This is not a large area, but it is a potentially dangerous one as it is above the important Box Canyon area.

- Osborne Springs are the fourth high-risk area. This appears to be a small and isolated area for Tubifex. I do not know the importance of this area to trout recruitment. If it is important, the whirling disease danger might also be important.

- The fifth high-risk area is the lower Warm River. Tubifex extends from the mouth upstream to beyond the Warm River Spring. I detected parasites that are probably the whirling disease parasite at the Warm River campground. Fish that were infected with the whirling disease parasite have been reported in the mainstem of the Henry's Fork River near the Warm River mouth. As this part of the Henry's Fork appears to be free of Tubifex and it seems mostly unsuitable for spawning, the most likely source of the parasite is the Warm River. The severity of the infection here is unknown and difficult to predict.

- The sixth area that was identified at high-risk is a section of Porcupine Creek in the Robinson Creek drainage. A few other streams in this area seem at risk for Tubifex. The relative high position of this population of Tubifex make it all the more threatening.

- The lower Fall River is the seventh high-risk area in the drainage. This area probably starts just blow Conant Creek it may include the lower reaches of Conant and Squirrel Creeks. The lower parts of the main river may not be that important to trout spawning and early rearing.

- The eighth and final, high-risk area for whirling disease in the Henry's Fork drainage is the entire Teton River Basin, except for the most headwater areas. Whirling disease is already widespread here and it is probably responsible for the recent declines in rainbows and brook trout populations.

Whirling disease has been found in at least 21 states, including Idaho. Concern over the disease has led to large-scale research studies in several places including Montana State University and University of California-Davis.

Steve Elle, Senior Resident Fish Biologist for Idaho Fish and Game, said in a 1997 report many Idaho streams carry the parasite but the effects of many factors including drought and stream gradient are not clear yet.

One example of the puzzles: streams with steep gradients had been thought to be safer for trout than low-gradient, slow-flowing streams. Yet, Silver Creek, a classic meadow creek, appears to have almost no detectable whirling disease problem. Another example: the Wood River is much like Montana's Madison in habitat and fish populations but rainbows are thriving in the Wood River.

A former Region 6 Fisheries Manager, Elle was the first to report the Big Lost River has distinct trout populations problems. He said trout numbers are down and samples show no first- or second-year fish and no rainbow fry. Trout kept there in live boxes in 1996 were "pretty sick." Those trout showed the effects of whirling disease but Elle suspects other factors as well.

Elle said it is clear that the Tubifex worm does carry the parasite but he needs more research to learn whether other hosts might be involved as well.

One little-known fact Elle has discovered in his research is that Idaho whitefish carry the parasite. Published articles have dealt only with trout up to now. "Where we looked (in Idaho), we found infected whitefish," Elle said.

(EDITOR'S NOTE) This report was compiled from published studies by the Idaho Fish and Game and the Henry's Fork Foundation.

IDAHO FLY SHOPS-SPORTING GOODS STORES & OUTFITTERS-GUIDES

Area code for the entire state of Idaho is 208

EASTERN IDAHO

Ashton

Premier Fly Fishing, 1051 N Highway 20 / 652-7349 / www.premierflyfishing.net
Idaho Irresistibles Fly and Tackle, 286 N Hwy 20 / 652-3669 /
   www.henryslakeanglers.com
Three Rivers Ranch, 1662 Hwy 47 / 652-3750 / www.threeriversranch.com

Driggs

Teton Valley Lodge, 379 Adams Road / 354-2386 / www.tetonvalleylodge.com
Robson Outfitters, 781 N Hwy 32, Tetonia, ID / 456-2805 /
   www.robsonoutfitters.com
Three Rivers Ranch Orvis Fly Shop, 30 East Little Avenue / 354-1200 /
   www.threeriversranch.com

Idaho Falls

Jimmy's All Season Angler, 275 A Street / 524-7160 / www.jimmysflyshop.com
Hyde Outfitters Fly Shop, 1520 Pancheri / 529-4343 / 800 444-4933 /
   www.hydeboats.com
Sportsmans Warehouse, 2909 S 25th E / 542-1900 /
   www.sportsmanswarehouse.com
Rio Products, 5050 S. Yellowstone Highway / 524-7760 / www.rioproducts.com
B&B Drug Center, 2425 Channing Way / 523-2277
Fred Meyer, 1765 N Yellowstone / 524-1440 / www.fredmeyer.com
Gateway Chevron Service, 291 S US HWY 26, Ririe / 538-7771
Kilgore General Store, 1595 Kilgore Road, Dubois / 778-5334
Little Lost Store, 3503 N LLR Hwy, Howe / 767-3132
Heise Expeditions, 5116 Heise Rd, Ririe / 538-7453 / www.heiseexpeditions.com
Cabela's, 3693 S. 25th E., Ammon / 208-932-2900 / www.cabelas.com

Island Park

Henry's Fork Anglers, 3340 Hwy 20 / 558-7525 / www.henrysforkanglers.com
Trouthunter, 3327 N. Hwy 20 / 558-9900 / www.trouthunt.com
Three Rivers Ranch, PO Box 856, Ashton, ID 83420 / 652-3750 /
   www.threeriversranch.com
Wild Rose Ranch, 3778 Highway 87 / 558-7021 / www.wildroseranch.com
Elk Creek Station, Highway 20 / 558-7871

SHUTTLE SERVICES
Idaho Irresistibles Fly and Tackle, 286 N Hwy 20 / 652-3669 /
www.henryslakeanglers.com
Linda B's Shuttle Service / 558-9600

Jackson, Wyoming

Orvis of Jackson, 485 West Broadway Street / 307-733-5407 / www.orvis.com
High Country Flies, 185 North Center Street / 307-733-7210 /
www.highcountryflies.com
Jack Dennis Outdoor Shop, 50 East Broadway / 307-733-3270 /
www.jackdennis.com
West Bank Anglers, 3670 North Moose-Wilson Road / 307-733-6483 /
www.westbank.com
Rendezvous River Sports, 945 West Broadway / 307-733-2471 /
www.jacksonholekayak.com
Snake River Angler, 10 Moose St. Moose WY / 307-733-3699 /
www.snakeriverangler.com
Reel Women Fly Fishing Adventures, PO Box 24, Wilson, WY / 307-413-6671 /
http://reel-women.com

Montpelier
Sidekick Sporting Goods & Auto, 410 North 4th Street, Montpelier / 847-1150

Pocatello
Ace Hardware, 222 S. 5th Avenue / 232-8722 / www.acehardware.com
Bill's Sport Shop, 273 West Pacific Street, Blackfoot / 785-2290
K-Mart Sporting Goods, 3945 Pole Line Rd / 237-4330 / www.kmart.com
Portneuf River Outfitters, 257 North Main Street / 232-4776
Sportsman's Warehouse, 760 Yellowstone Ave / 208-232-3100 /
www.sportsmanswarehouse.com

Rexburg
Fur-Feather & Fly, 2955 W 5200 S / 352-9522

Soda Springs
Dave's Tackle Shop, 190 S Second E / 547-3023

St. Anthony
House of Harrop Flies, Box 491 / 624-3537

Swan Valley
The Dam Store, 3846 Swan Valley Hwy, Palisades / 483-2531
South Fork Anglers & Lodge, P.O. Box 22 / 483-2112 / 877-347-4735 /
www.southforklodge.com
The Lodge at Palisades Creek, 3720 Hwy. 26, Irwin / 483-2222 / 866-393-1613 /
www.tlapc.com
Old Irwin Lodge, 1591 Old Irwin Road, Irwin / 483-5634

SHUTTLE SERVICES

Julie's Shuttle Service, Swan Valley / 483-2903
South Fork Lodge, Conant Valley / 483-2112 / www.southforklodge.com

Victor

Victor Emporium, 45 Main / 787-2221

West Yellowstone, MT

Arrick's Fly Shop, 37 N Canyon St / 406-646-7290 / www.arricks.com
Blue Ribbon Flies, 315 Canyon / 406-646-7642 / www.blueribbonflies.com
Bud Lilly's Trout Shop, 39 Madison Ave. 406-646-7801 / www.budlillys.com
Jacklin's Fly Shop, 105 Yellowstone / 406-646-7336 / www.jacklinsflyshop.com
Madison River Outfitters, 117 Canyon St / 406-646-9644 /
    www.flyfishingyellowstone.com
Eagles Tackle Shop, 11 Canyon Street / 406-646-7521

CENTRAL IDAHO

Challis

River 1, 651 7th St / 208-879-5300 / www.river1.com
Bent Rod Outdoors, Highway 93 / 879-2500 / 866-0451 / www.thebentrod.com
The Valley Junction, Junction of Hwys 75 & 93 / 879-2448
Horse Creek Outfitters, PO Box 950 / 879-4477 / www.hcoutfiters.com
Salmon River Scenic Run, P.O. Box 935 / 940-2257 / www.scenicriver.com
White Cloud Outfitters, P.O. Box 217 / 879-4574 / www.whitecloudoutfitters.com
Mile High Outfitters, 172 Stephens Lane / 879-4567
Idaho Wilderness Company, 505 River Run Road / 879-4700

Ketchum/Sun Valley

Silver Creek Outfitters, 500 North Main Street / 800-732-5687 /
    www.silver-creek.com
Sturtevants Hailey Fly Shop, Main St & Carbonate, Hailey / 788-7847 /
    www.sturtos.com
Sturtevants Hailey Fly Shop, 340 N Main Street / 726-4501 / www.sturtos.com
Chateau Drug, 451 Leadville Avenue / 726-5696
High Desert Sports, 201 N River St, Hailey, / 788-3804
The River Company, P.O. Box 2329, Sun Valley / 788-5775 / 800-398-0346 /
    www.therivercompany.com
Ketchum on the Fly, 680 Sun Valley Road / 726-7572 / www.ketchumonthefly.com
Sun Valley Outfitters, P.O. Box 5860 / 622-3400 / www.sunvalleyoutfitters.com
Sun Valley Rivers Co., P.O. Box 1776 / 726-7404 / www.sunvalleyriver.com
Lost River Outfitter, 171 N. Main / 726-1706 / www.lostriveroutfitters.com
Idaho Angling Services, 208 David Street, Picabo / 788-9709 /
    www.anglingservices.com
Far & Away Adventures, Middle Fork River Company, P.O. Box 54 / Sun Valley / 726-8888 / 800-232-8588 / www.far-away.com

Mackay

The Western Store, P.O. Box 25 / 109 S Main / Mackay, ID 83251 / 588-2671
Wild Horse Creek Ranch, 5536 Old Chilly Road / 588-2575 /
　www.wildhorsecreekranch.com

Salmon

Silver Spur Sports, 403 Main Street / 756-2833
93 Outdoor Sports (Exxon Mobil), 517 South Challis Street / 756-3002
Village at North Fork, 2046 U.S. 93, North Fork / 865-2412
Aggipah River Trips, P.O. Box 425 / 756-4167 / www.aggipah.com
Wilderness River Outfitters, P.O. Box 72, Lemhi / 756-3959 / 800-252-6581 /
　www.wildernessriver.com
Idaho Adventures, P.O. Box 834 / 756-2986 / 1-800-789-WAVE /
　www.idahoadventures.com
Kookaburra, 1115 Highway 93 South / 756-4386, 888 654-4386 / www.raft4fun.com
Rawhide Outfitters, 204 Larson Street / 756-4276 / www.rawhideoutfitters.com
Salmon River Lodge, P.O. Box 927 / 503-519-6670 / www.salmonriverlodge.com
Silver Cloud Expeditions, P.O. Box 1006 / 756-6215 / www.silvercloudexp.com
Twin Peaks Ranch, P.O. Box 774 / 894-2290 / 1-800-659-4899 /
　www.twinpeaksranch.com
Warren River Expeditions, P.O. Box 147, Carmen / 756-6387 / 800-765-0421 / www.
　raftidaho.com
Arctic Creek Lodge, 22 Hammon Drive / 756-1657
Barker-Ewing Idaho, P.O. Box 3032 / Jackson, WY 83001 / 307-733-1000 / 800-448-
　4202 / www.barker-ewing.com

Stanley

McCoy's Tackle Shop, P.O. Box 210, Ace Of Diamonds / 774-3377
Redfish Lake Lodge, Redfish Lake Road off of Hwy 75 / 774-3536 /
　www.redfishlake.com
Triangle C Ranch,One Banner Lane / 774-2266 / www.trianglecranch.net
Adventure Guides, P.O. Box 24 / 774-2200
Torrey's Burnt Creek Inn, Highway 75 Mile Post 210 / 838-2313 /
　www.torreysburntcreekinn.com
Sawtooth Adventure Company, Highway 75, Lower Stanley / 866-774-4644 /
　www.sawtoothadventure.com

SOUTHWEST IDAHO

Boise

Anglers (Orvis), 7097 Overland Road / 323-6768
Fly Logic, 511 Melba / 495-2090 / www.flylogic.com
Idaho Angler, 1682 S. Vista Ave / 800-787-9957 / 389-9957 / www.idahoangler.com
Angler's Habitat, 716 Blaine St, Caldwell / 454-8188 / www.anglershabitat.com
Bear Valley River Co., 7864 Highway 55, Horseshoe Bend / 793-2272 /
　www.bearvalleyrafting.com

B T's Fly Fishing Products, 11965 Reutzel Dr. / 362-2663 / www.btsflyfishing.com
Cabela's, 8109 W Franklin Rd / 672-7900 / www.cabelas.com
Cascade Outfitters, 604 East 45th Street / 322-4411 / www.cascadeoutfitters.com
Idaho City Grocery, 3868 Hwy 21, Idaho City / 392-4426
The Riverkeeper Fly Shop, 1224 Broadway Ave / 344-3838 / www.troutlie.com
Custom River Tours, Box 7071 / 939-4324 / 800-432-4611 / www.selway.net
Middle Fork Rapid Transit, 12410 N. Humphrey's Way / 888-IDFLOAT /
    www.idahoraftadventure.com
Northwest River Company, P.O. Box 1101, Driggs / 709-8033 /
    www.northwestriver.com
Mackay Wilderness River Trips, 1602 W. Hays Street, Suite 306 / 800-635-5336 /
    www.mackayriver.com
Sawtooth Wilderness Outfitters, P.O. Box 81 / Garden Valley, ID 83622 / 462-3416 /
    Fax: 462-3813 / Email: swo@micron.net / www.sawtoothadventures.com

Jerome
Thirsty Fish Outfitters, 204 North 100 East / 324-6475
Pioneer Outfitters LLC, 441 North Road / 774-3737 / www.pioneermountain.com

McCall
Salmon River Outfitters, PO Box 1006, McCall / www.salmonriveroutfitters.com
Outdoor Solutions, 204 Mission St / 634-5340 / www.shopoutdoorsolutions.com
McCall Anglers, 307 E Park Street / 634-4004 / www.mccallanglers.com
Medley Sports, 809 N 3rd St / 634-2216 / www.medleysports.com
Tackle Toms, 304 N Main, Cascade / 382-4367
Canyons Incorporated, P.O. Box 823 / 634-4303 / 1-888 634-2600 /
    www.canyonsinc.com
Cascade Adventures, P.O. Box 1385 / 634-4909 / 800-786-9953 /
    www.cascadeadventures.com
Whitewater Expeditions, HC 83 Five Mile Bar, Cascade / 382-4336 /
    www.whitewaterexpeditions.com
Wapiti Meadow Lodge, 1667 Johnson Creek Road, Cascade / 633-3217 /
    www.wapitimeadowranch.com
Hughes River Expeditions, P.O. Box 217 Cambridge / 257-3477 / 1-800-262-1882 /
    www.hughesriver.com
Mud Creek Outdoor Gear, 1000 North 3rd Street / 634-1968 /
    www.mudcreekoutdoorgear.com

Meridian
Sportsman's Warehouse, 3797 E Fairview Ave / 884-3000 /
    www.sportsmanswarehouse.com

Nampa
Sportsman's Warehouse, 16865 N. Market Place Blvd / 208-468-7600 /
    www.sportsmanswarehouse.com
Howard's Tackle Shoppe, 1707 Garrity Blvd. / 465-0946 /
    www.howardstackleshoppe.com

Dream Drifter Adventures LLC, 650 Dooley Lane / 880-2994 /
www.dreamdrifteradventures.com
Larry's Sporting Goods, 704 2nd Street So. / 467-9201 / www.larryssg.com

Twin Falls

Reds Trading Post, 203 5th Ave South / 733-3546 / www.redstradingpost.com
Sportsman's Warehouse, 1940 Bridgeview Blvd. / 737-9900 /
www.sportsmanswarehouse.com
West Addison Sportsman, 101 W Addison BX 181 / 733-0340
K-Mart Sporting Goods, 2258 Addison Ave E / 734-5400 / www.kmart.com
Mountain Sports & Pawn Brokers, 1410 West 6th South, Mountain Home / 587-8858
Clear Lake Country Club, 403 Clear Lake Lane, Wendell / 543-4849
Idaho Guide Service, 563 Trotter Drive / 734-4998 / 888-73IDAHO /
www.idahoguideservice.com
High Adventure River Tours, 1211 East 2350 South, Hagerman / 800-286-4123 /
www.highadventurerivertours.net
Washington Street Pawn & Coin, 321 Washington Street / 735-0012

Wendell

Simerleys, 280 S Idaho / 536-6651

NORTHCENTRAL IDAHO

Grangeville

Rae Bros Sporting Goods, 247 E. Main / 983-2877 /
www.raebrossportinggoods.com
Idaho Afloat, N D Street / 983-2414 / 800-700-2414 / www.idahoafloat.com
South Fork Outfitters, HC 67 / 983-1957
York Outfitters, 1726 Long Haul Rd / 983-3453
Sobriety Adventures, RR 1 Box 144 / 983-2414

Lewiston

The Traditional Sportsman, 814 Main St / 746-6688
Black Sheep Sports, E 1701 Main / 746-8948
Lochsa Lodge, Box 578, Powell Ranger Station, Lolo / 942-3405 /
www.lochsalodge.com
Tri-State Outfitters, 120 Thain, Lewiston, ID 83501 / 746-5307
Beamer's Landing, P.O. Box 1243 / 509-758-4800 / 1-800-522-6966 /
www.hellscanyontours.com
OARS-Dories, P.O. Box 67, Angels Camp, CA 95222 / 800-346-6277 / 800-346-6277 /
www.oars.com
Sportsmans Warehouse, 2002 Thain Grade / 208-743-2000 /
www.sportsmanswarehouse.com
American River Touring Association, 24000 Casa Loma Rd., Groveland, CA / 209-
962-7873 / 800-323-2782 / www.arta.org
River Quest Excursions, 4203 Snake River Avenue / 746-8060 /
www.riverquestexcursions.com

Missoula, MT

Bob Wards, 3015 Paxson Drive / 800-800-3550 / 406-728-3220 / www.bobwards.com

Wholesale Sports, 2323 North Reserve Street / 406-523-9000 / www.wholesalesports.com

Missoulian Angler, 520 N. Higgins Ave. / 406-728-7766 / 800-824-2450 / www.missoulianangler.com

Grizzly Hackle, 215 W. Front / 800-297-8996 / 406-721-8996 / www.grizzlyhackle.com

The Kingfisher, 926 E Broadway / 406-721-6141 / www.kingfisherflyshop.com

Kesel's Four Rivers Fly Shop, 501 S Higgins Ave / 406-721-4796 / www.fourrivers.net

Brady's Sportman's Surplus, 2315 Brooks St / 406-721-5500 / 800-473-GUNS

Lewis & Clark Trail Adventures, 912 E. Broadway / 406-728-7609 / 800-366-6246 / www.trailadventures.com

World Class Outfitting Adventures, P.O. Box 351, Arlee, MT / 406-726-3829 / 800-203-3246 / www.packin.com

Five Valleys Fishing Company, 2140 S 13th Street West / 877-783-0218 / www.fivevalleysfishing.com

Blackfoot River Outfitters, 1522 South Reserve Street / 406-542-7411 / www.blackfootriver.com

Renegade Flyfishing Outfitters, 1815 S 10th Street West / 406-880-7221 / www.flyfishmissoula.com

Clear Creek Outfitters, 5400 Arnica Road / 406-370-7039 / www.clearcreekoutfittersmt.com

Montana Troutaholic Outfitters, 6166 Larch Canyon Road / 406-370-0074 / www.montanatroutaholics.com

Double Up Outfitters, 1522 South Reserve Street / 406-240-9498 / www.doubleupoutfitters.com

Moscow

Moscow Fly Shop, 210 S. Main / 882-2868 / www.moscowflyshop.com/

Northwest River Supplies, 2009 South Main Street / 882-2383 / www.nrsweb.com

Tri-State Outfitters, 1104 West Pullman Rd / 882-4555 / www.t-state.com

Orofino

Riverside Sport Shop, 11320 Highway 12 / 476-5418

Tom Cat & Frank's Sporting Goods, P.O. Box 326, 618 Business 12, Kooskia / 926-4359

Three Rivers Motel and Rafting, Highway 12 & Lowell, Kooskia / 926-4430

The Guide Shop / Clearwater Drifters, 14012 Hwy 12 / 476-3531 / www.theguideshop.com

Clearwater Outfitters, 4088-A Canyon Creek Road / 476-5971 / 800-826-7370 / www.clearwateroutfitters.net

Cayuse Outfitting, 1831 Glenwood Road, Kamiah / 935-0859 / www.cayuseoutfitting.com

Flying B Ranch, 2900 Lawyer Creek Road, Kamiah / 935-0755 / www.flyingbranch.com

Lochsa River Outfitters, 9133 US 12, Kooskia / 926-4149 / www.jacksidaho.com

Three Rivers Resort/Rafting, 115 Selway Road, Kooskia / 926-4430 / 888-926-4430 / www.threeriversrafting.com

Red Shed Fly Shop, 20652 Big Canyon Rd, Peck / 486-6098 / www.redshedflyshop.com

River Dance Lodge, 7743 Highway 12, Kooskia / 800-451-6034 / www.riverdancelodge.com

Riggins

Riggins Tackle Shop, 112 N Main / 628-3578

Epleys Whitewater Adventures, 1512 N. Main Street / 634-5173 / 800-233-1813 / www.epleys.com

Salmon River Challenge, 201 Time Bridge Road / 628-3264 / 800-732-8574 / www.salmonriverchallenge.com

River Adventures Limited, 101 N. Main / 628-3952 / 1-800-524-9710 / www.riveradventuresltd.com

Exodus Wilderness Adventures, P.O. Box 1231 / 628-3484 / 800-992-3484 / www.riverescape.com

Shepp Ranch, P.O. Box 5446 / Boise, ID 83705 / 343-7729 / www.sheppranch.com

Tightlines, 47611 McKenzie Hwy., Vida, OR / 541-896-3219 / www.tightlinesfishing.com

NORTH IDAHO LAKE COUNTRY

Bayview

Boileau's, Box 66 / 34152 Lakeside Avenue / 683-2213

Bonners Ferry

Far-North Outfitters, 6791 Main Street / 267-5547

Clark Fork

The Hut Conoco, 218 E. 4th / 266-1751

Coeur d'Alene

Castaway Fly Fishing Shop, 1114 N 4th St / 765-3133 / 800-410-3133 / www.castawayflyfishingshop.com

Fins & Feathers Tackle Shop & Guide Service, 1816 Sherman Ave / 667-9304 / www.fins1.com

Black Sheep, 308 W. Seale Ave. / 667-7831 / www.blacksheepidaho.com

Cast & Blast, 9521 N Government, Hayden / 772-3748

Wholesale Sports, 3534 N Government Way / 664-7900 / www.wholesalesports.com

Northwest Outfitters (Orvis), 2171 N Main St / 667-2707 / www.nwoutfitters.com

Blue Goose Sports, 621 Main, St. Maries, ID 83861 / 245-4015

Avery Trading Post, 71 Old River Road, Avery / 245-3996

R.O.W. (River Odysseys West), 202 Sherman Ave. / 765-0841 / 800-451-6034 / www.
rowadventures.com

Tri-State Outfitters, 6275 Sunshine Street / 772-0613 / www.t-state.com

Western Waters, PO Box 397, Superior, MT / 877-822-8282 /
www.westernwaters.com

Panhandle Outfitters, 12601 S. Thunder Mountain, Valleyford, WA / 509-922-8289 /
www.panhandle-outfitters.com

Harrison

Red Horse Mountain Ranch, 11077 East Blue Lake Road, Harrison / 888-689-9680 /
www.redhorsemountainranch.com

Hope

Hope Marine Services, 47392 Hwy. 200, Hope / 264-5105 / www.hopemarine.com

Ponderay

Sandpoint Outfitters, 400 Schewitzer Plaza Dr. / 263-9119 /
www.sandpointoutfitters.com

Post Falls

Cabela's, 101 N Cabela Way / 777-6300 / www.cabelas.com

Westside Resort, N 6905A Hauser Lake Rd. / 773-4968

Priest Lake

Priest Lake Guide Service, c/o Priest Lake Marina, 6515 Lakeshore Rd / 610-3535 /
www.fishpriestlake.com

Anglers Pursuits, 4777 W Lakeshore Road / 771-2483 / www.anglerspursuits.com

Priest River

Hill's Resort, 4777 W. Lakeshore Road / 443-2551 / www.hillsresort.com

Sandpoint

Outdoor Experience, 314 N 1st Ave / 263-6028 / www.outdoorexperience.us

Selkirk Powder Company, 10000 Schweitzer Mountain Road / 263-6959

Sports Plus, 819 U.S. 2 / 263-5174

St. Maries

Baldy Mountain Outdoors, 1840 West College Avenue / 245-3605 /
www.baldymountainoutdoors.com

Blue Goose Sporting Goods, 621 Main St / 245-4015

St. Joe Outfitters & Guides, 8311 Windfall Pass Road / 245-4002 /
www.stjoeoutfitters.com

St. Joes Sport Shop, 402 West College Avenue / 245-4417

Curt Gowdy, renowned outdoorsman and broadcaster, enjoys a day on the South Fork of the Snake River.

Index